The New Life

The New Life

JEWISH STUDENTS OF POSTWAR GERMANY

Jeremy Varon

WAYNE STATE UNIVERSITY PRESS DETROIT

18 17 16 15 14   5 4 3 2 1

Library of Congress Cataloging Number: 2014936560
978-0-8143-3961-9 (paperback); 978-0-8143-3962-6 (ebook)

Designed by Keata Brewer
Typeset by E. T. Lowe Publishing Company
Composed in Adobe Garamond Pro and Walbaum

To my father, Bension Varon

Contents

Acknowledgments

This project originated in the double take I did when I first learned of the Jewish university students of postwar Germany years ago. What? Holocaust survivors from Eastern Europe studying in German universities, immediately after the war? The questions multiplied as my curiosity swelled: Who were these young Jews, and what were they doing in Germany? How, after all they endured, could they think to study at university and focus on their academic work? And how could they bear to have Germans as professors and fellow students? My colleagues, even when expert in Jewish, German, or Holocaust history, were likewise puzzled when I told them of the Jewish students.

Subsequent research revealed my initial surprise to be a consequence of my naïveté, which at least had good cause. For decades, the period from the spring of 1945 to 1948 represented the lost years of European history, largely passed over by scholars as an interregnum between the end of a calamitous shooting war, the start of the Cold War, and the emergence of a new Europe. Meanwhile, the great majority of Holocaust scholars had little inkling of what happened to survivors after liberation, save that most eventually made it to the United States or Israel.

Finally, there existed in the popular mind a massive gap in understanding, reflected in the common imagery of survival. Broadly familiar are images of skeletal figures, freshly liberated from concentration camps, staring blankly, as if emissaries of the living dead. One next typically "meets" the Holocaust survivor—whether in videotaped testimony or in a synagogue, church, or school—bearing the traces of trauma but also clearly returned to life. My early hope was to use the study of the postwar students to fill the spaces in between, even while having little frame of reference to situate the students' experiences and temper my surprise.

Over the course of the project, that landscape dramatically changed. Intrepid researchers began reconstructing the dizzyingly complex world of Jewish refugees and the larger postwar scene, while institutions dedicated to the Holocaust began opening up spaces for serious consideration of its aftermath. An entire historiography and memorial culture focused on Jewish and other displaced persons after the war came into being. The struggles, perceptions, and decisions of the students, as I came to know them through interviews and other research, grew stepwise less mysterious. Germany, as historians documented and the alumni explained, was not quite Germany any longer, but instead a subdued nation under occupation. Jews from Eastern Europe, among them tens of thousands who had fled or been deported to the Soviet interior during the war, flocked to the American-occupied zone of Germany. While in limbo, and largely in the displaced persons camps, Jewish refugees created a thriving culture that both sustained prewar traditions and pointed to a future beyond Europe. A minority of Jews lived outside the displaced persons camps and, like the students, pursued private passions that had long defined them.

Placing the students in the postwar world, while also adding to our understanding of it, the entire project has an aura of making sense of what at first appeared uncanny to me. A grand thanks, beyond typical collegial gratitude, therefore goes to the many scholars whose own research made that process of making sense possible. My hope is that the reader shares in this drama of discovery and accumulating comprehension.

At the same time, I have never quite shed my awe that the events and the people I have studied are fully real. My essential question persists: How could young people—as was the case for many of the students—be terrorized, interned, enslaved, starved, and nearly murdered; have most everything they had ever known and loved violently taken from them; and, as orphans in the land of their persecutors, find the wherewithal to enter university and earn degrees in such demanding fields as medicine and engineering? No amount of historical context and inquiry into personal motivations has fully solved this riddle for me. I therefore hope that the reader also shares in a sense of enduring mystery and the radical otherness of a past that can be described but likely never definitively explained.

The project, put otherwise, is about unlikely human destinies in extraordinary circumstances, for which the alumni are both the essential subjects and sources. My greatest gratitude therefore goes to them for enabling my research by bringing to life a world both sensible and remote. Several dozen consented to lengthy interviews, inviting me into their homes, their biographies, and their often difficult emotional worlds. Their families deserve thanks as well for bearing with a process that entailed revisiting the pain of the past.

Each interview was both historically valuable and special to me as a human encounter. Some testimonies, however, proved more useful for my purposes than others. And though I tried to interview as many alumni as I reasonably could—and weave as many interviews into the book as feasible—many alumni are not included in this study, or receive comparatively slight mention. This is in no way a reflection of their place within the student cohort, the significance of their lives, or the quality of their testimony. This book, in a real sense, belongs in part to all of the alumni, whether alive or dead, and regardless of my research access to them.

Some of the alumni played especially strong roles in facilitating my research. The idea for the entire project came from Sabina Zimering, who first inquired if a professional historian might take interest in the group. Frederick Reiter, an officer in their alumni organization, brokered contacts with many of the former students and invited me to reunions and other alumni meetings. Arnold Kerr, the last president of the students' association in Germany, was particularly helpful in navigating their archives and, with his stunning memory, filling in historical detail about the Student Union. Simon Schochet, himself an accomplished author, took special interest in the project, conveying early in the research the texture of the times and the existential state of survivors. Roman Ohrenstein, a passionate advocate of the students when in Germany and a conscious bearer of their historical legacy, gave the most persistent counsel. He did multiple interviews, answered repeated questions of historical fact, and, not long before he died, provided invaluable encouragement when it was so welcome. He is also the source, along with Sabina Zimering, of the wonderful documents and photographs displayed in this volume. I would like to thank, finally, Brian Bergman. Though I did not conduct an extensive interview with him, we shared an instant personal connection, livened by his audacity, sense of the absurd, and hint of mischief, which mirrored qualities of the larger, otherwise serious student group.

The book has had another indispensible partner, Professor Bella Brodzki. Indeed, it was Bella who suggested that her aunt, Sabina Zimering, reach out to a historian. Joining the project in its early phases, Bella—herself the daughter of survivors—introduced me to the world of the alumni. Together with me, she explored that world, helped set up and was present at most interviews, and diligently reviewed early parts of the text as I generated them. Feeling like historical detectives with a near-sacred sense of mission, we literally toured the globe in search of this special past, forming a bond I continue to treasure. This book, in its guiding spirit and many of its insights, belongs as well to her. Her own writing on the legacy of the Holocaust within its second generation is among the most poignant, arresting, and insightful work ever produced on the subject.

Special thanks goes as well to the late professor Stephen Feinstein, whom I knew while he was director of the Center for Holocaust and Genocide Studies at the University of Minnesota and who gave me the opportunity to work on this project. Other scholars shared their perspectives and research tips as they engaged the work in its many phases. Atina Grossmann, a luminary in post-Holocaust history, did so much to help shape and improve this study. Anna Holian, author of a superb book on the postwar period, likewise enriched the project. David Kohn at Drew University, Dominick LaCapra and Michael Steinberg at Cornell University, and my colleague Federico Finchelstein at the New School also lent their professional wisdom.

The proverbial village that raised this book includes many others: Ramiza Koyla, who transcribed most of the interviews, crunched survey numbers, and flagged key parts of the alumni's testimony; Sifrah Hollander, Rivka Schiller, Sandy Fox, and Peretz Blum, who translated the Hebrew and Yiddish texts of the student group; and the archivists at YIVO (Institute for Jewish Research), where the students' archives are housed. The project benefited also from institutional support. Drew University and Sarah Lawrence College awarded me and Bella Brodzki research grants, while the Lucius N. Littauer Foundation extended generous support for the research.

The team at Wayne State University Press has been terrific, taking interest in the project and expertly guiding it through every phase. I am immensely grateful to the editor-in-chief, Kathryn Wildfong, as well as her staff of Kristin Harpster and Maya Whelan. So too, I benefited immensely from the two anonymous reviews by experts the press secured. Mindy Brown has been a copy-editor extraordinaire, meticulously training her attention on the language, form, and content of the study, making it immeasurably better.

The village, in its closest circle, comprises family. My late (non-Jewish) German mother, Barbara Frass Varon, born in 1940 in Berlin, had the innate decency—guided by her mother—to feel ashamed of the Germany of her age. She lived a politics of reconciliation and atonement by emigrating, embracing the best of American democracy (while opposing the society's many flaws), and marrying my father, Bension Varon, a Sephardic Jew from Istanbul. She surely would appreciate the scrutiny of German crimes and guilt, as well as reportage of moments of genuine German contrition, the book contains. Her titanic intellect and gifts with language, equally much as her moral sense, ground the entire text. My father, as he always insists, had the good sense to marry her, whatever their vast differences in heritage. His own study of and writing on Sephardic history was an inspiration to my research, and his own strong commitment to his Jewish heritage enriched my sense of the importance of the piece of Jewish history my study explores. I have the good luck to have a sister, Elizabeth Varon, and a brother-in-law, William Hitchcock, who are accomplished authors and university professors. Both contributed their historical acumen, editorial guidance, and good cheer as we discussed the challenges, rewards, and occasional misadventures of historical research.

Finally, I extend my vast appreciation to my wife, Alice Varon. She never questioned for a minute my years-long obsession with the subject of this book, nor ever complained as my work on it took me for spells away from her and our son. Together we share a sense that the intellectual and ethical commitments such as this book entails are always to be supported, no matter the sacrifice. Without this freedom to be captive to an obligation, I never would have created this book, so thank you, Alice.

Introduction

The war had finally ended, and Germany was in ruins. More than two million of its soldiers and one million civilians had died. Years of battle had sapped its once mighty resources and left whole cities in rubble. But if Germany was hollowed out by the war, it was also filled anew: by the armies of four occupying powers; by the military and civilian authorities administering life in the American, British, Soviet, and French "zones" into which Germany was now divided; by the relief agencies aiding the war's many victims; and, most of all, by refugees.

Germany had become a land of displaced peoples. Nearly two million were German—those uprooted by battle, as well as ethnic Germans who had fled or been forced from their homes in occupied Poland, Czechoslovakia, and Lithuania. But a great many more—eight to nine million—were non-Germans: Poles, Ukrainians, Hungarians, Yugoslavs, Russians, French, Scandinavians, and Baltic peoples from territories Germany had occupied; Soviet, British, and other soldiers taken as prisoners of war; and Europeans of every variety who had spilled out of the vast system of Nazi camps. And then there were the Jewish survivors of the genocide. More than 50,000 had been liberated within German and Austrian territory, often found—starved and broken—in places like Dachau and its satellite camps.[1]

These foreign refugees made up the massive ranks of the "displaced persons," or "DPs," as the Allies designated them.[2] Some nine hundred assembly centers, mostly in the American Zone, cared for the DPs as they waited to be resettled.[3] By September 1945 an astonishing six million had been repatriated.[4] But as some DPs left Germany, new ones entered. This was true most of all of Jews.

1

Even as the war was ending, word spread among Jews in Eastern Europe that they could find food, freedom, and safety in the parts of Germany occupied by Western powers, and by the Americans especially. Repelled by anti-Semitic threats in their native lands, tens of thousands among the *She'erith Hapleitah*—a term drawn from the Hebrew Bible and used by Jews to designate the "surviving remnant" of European Jewry—migrated into Germany.[5] The Bricha, a semi-legal Zionist network intent on bringing Jews to Western Europe and then to Palestine, aided in the migration.[6] By July 1946 the American, British, and French zones of Germany held, in the approximate reporting of occupation authorities, more than 105,000 Jews. That number swelled to more than 170,000 by November and reached its likely peak, in the summer of 1947, at 182,000.[7] Of these, the majority were wartime refugees in the Soviet Union, and therefore not necessarily survivors of direct German assault.[8]

In the midst of the loss, dislocation, and deprivation, something remarkable happened: hundreds of Jews, starting in the fall of 1945, entered universities in the American Zone of occupied Germany. These were not, by and large, German Jews intent on reclaiming their place in German society. The great majority came from Poland. Others had grown up in Lithuania, Hungary, Czechoslovakia, Romania, and the Soviet Union. Mostly strangers in a forbidding land, the students faced the challenge of building new lives in the country that had just recently sought their annihilation.

Many of the students had been in concentration and death camps. Others had survived in hiding or under false papers, and a few had been partisans. Some had fled or been forced to the Soviet interior, though in greatly lower percentages than among Jewish DPs as a whole. Likely the majority now had no parents. Those from Poland had no homeland, since repatriating was all but impossible. Most were between the ages of twenty and twenty-five when the war ended, and therefore just teenagers when it had broken out. A great number had not completed *gymnasium* (secondary school), and thus had to make up for years of missed schooling before entering, or while attending, university. Deprived of the attachments of family, place, and community, the students were also weighed down by the psychological and emotional burdens of their wartime suffering and loss.

Despite this tragic profile, shared by tens of thousands of other Jewish DPs, the students took to university life with striking determination. The large majority studied in the Bavarian city of Munich, the birthplace of Nazism and official *Hauptstadt der Bewegung* (Capital of the Movement). After the war Munich and its surrounding areas were home to the greatest concentration of displaced persons in the American Zone and to an array of international aid organizations. With three nearby DP camps designated specifically for Jews, Munich also became a magnet for displaced Jews and home to prominent Jewish DP organizations. Munich's Deutsches Museum served as both an important transit point for DPs and the site of a short-lived university for refugees run by the United Nations Relief and Rehabilitation Administration (UNRRA). A core group of survivors first attended the UNRRA school before matriculating into established universities, chiefly Munich's Ludwig-Maximilians-Universität (LMU) and Technische Hochschule (TH).

In December 1945 they formed an organization called the Jewish Students' Union in Munich (*Vereinigung Jüdischer Studenten in München*), adding to the great variety of DP organizations. The Union was indispensable to the students, as it both addressed practical challenges and served as the catalyst for their close-knit community. Led by elected officers and boasting a staffed office, it secured food, clothing, and academic supplies for its members; lobbied German university and government officials for greater enrollments, tuition aid, and stipends; administered certification exams for aspiring students recognized by occupation authorities and the Bavarian state; and served as an institutional base for the students, giving them a certain prestige on the occupation scene. It also helped secure housing for its members, virtually all of whom lived in Munich proper and not, like most other Jews, in the DP camps. Conceiving the student existence as a comprehensive identity integral to Jewish community life and the national future, the Union sought to secure a valued place within the Jewish DP world and prevailing conceptions of Zionist struggle. Finally, the Union organized numerous social activities, which both drew the students closer to one another and signified their reengagement of life.

As word of the Union quickly spread through the DP camps and beyond, dozens and then hundreds of Jews entered Munich schools. By the fall of 1947, 460 students belonged to the Munich group.[9] Jews also attended universities in Berlin, Darmstadt, Erlangen, Frankfurt, Heidelberg, Marburg, Regensburg, and Stuttgart, where they established student unions of their own that performed, if on a lesser scale, functions similar to that in Munich. These banded together to form an umbrella organization, anchored in Munich, to represent the interests of Jewish university students throughout the American Zone. Its peak membership neared 800.[10] In absolute terms, this figure is small. But given that in Poland and other Eastern European countries before the war the number of Jews pursuing higher education was extremely small—and given that the Holocaust claimed so many of them—the postwar student cohort was substantial.

The students pursued courses of study in such demanding fields as medicine, engineering, and the law. The young Jews were closely bonded, studying and socializing largely among themselves and generally avoiding contact with their German peers. Acutely aware of the Nazi assault on the intelligentsia, they assumed the burden of rebuilding Jewish student and intellectual life, with the Union leadership framing the students' collective endeavor in precisely these terms. They also experienced together the restorative joy of living, evident in group excursions to mountains and lakes, trips to the opera, and dances hosted by the Union. Most completed their degrees by the early 1950s and then immigrated to the United States or Israel, where they raised families and built careers, typically in the fields in which they had been trained after the war.

Reflecting on their time in postwar Germany, the alumni describe an exhilaration defined not only by intellectual engagement and professional ambition but also by sheer vitality, the rush of autonomy, camaraderie, and an almost reckless defiance of the adversities of history, circumstance, and setting. Since leaving Germany many of the Jewish alumni have remained intensely close, holding reunions in the United States and Israel, and, for decades, meeting in small groups in their adoptive cities and towns. The former classmates regard one another with an appreciation approaching reverence—as if they owe one another not quite their actual lives but essential parts of their return to life. Decades after leaving Germany Bernard Stone recalled: "I found an established group of Jewish students upon my arrival in Munich in 1946, and this was a wonderful day, a day of revival. Here, in this prototypical German city, one of the capitals of Nazism, we were to find a new family that sustained us for several memorable years, memorable not only for [our] achievement[s], but also for the lifelong relationships we have discovered and maintained."[11] In a collective voice, the alumni proclaimed at a 1997 reunion in Florida:

> A half century ago, forlorn, frustrated, bereaved of friends, family, and loved ones, we survivors of Hitler's tyranny and German bestiality . . . arose from the ghettos, concentration camps, partisan forests, and Siberian territories to face a world of uncertainties and hopeless days. . . . Determined not to hand over posthumous victory to Hitler, we found in our hearts the physical and spiritual strength to seek a future in the lands of a hating Europe. . . . A mysterious power from those we loved and lost provided us with the courage we needed to face, and sit alongside [at university], those who only a short while ago might have been the murderers who

wore SS or German military uniforms. . . . In the free lands of the Western world, especially in North America and Israel, we achieved great things: success in professions, business, science, government, and culture.[12]

Decades before, when in Germany, the students had given their newspaper the Yiddish title *Wiedergeburt*, titling it also in English "The New Life."[13]

"How Come These People Were, or at Least Looked, Happy?"

The rarified world of the postwar Jewish students has been virtually unknown outside the alumni and their families. Scholarship on Jewish DPs pays the students very limited attention, and the young academics occupy only a small place in efforts to pay tribute to DPs' lives and accomplishments.[14] This book seeks to tell the students' story, both in its distinct qualities and as it illuminates the larger historical narratives of which the students were a part. The choice to enter university was certainly atypical among Jewish DPs, and the students had a sense of standing at the edge of the main currents of the Jewish DP world. They felt, moreover, poorly supported by Jewish organizations, some of whom saw their decision to study in German institutions as a betrayal of Jewish suffering and, as it took them away from Zionist struggle, of Zionist duty. They therefore represent a fascinating exception to dominant DP narratives, further revealing the variety of DP experiences.

At the same time, the students faced similar challenges—material, psychological, and emotional—as those experienced by other DPs. Neither were the alacrity and vigor with which they rebuilt their lives unique among DPs and survivors. Thus I present their lives as, in part, exemplary of DP experiences more broadly. Finally, the students were embedded in the institutional life of occupied Bavaria and the Jewish DP community there, interacting extensively with major aid organizations, layers of Allied and German government, Germans in both public and private settings, Jewish DP organizations, and some of the leading figures of the postwar scene. They therefore provide a special vantage point from which to reconstruct the shifting constellation of authorities, geopolitical forces, organizations, ideologies, subjectivities, and desires that defined postwar Germany.

The project is distinguished as well by the research access I had to the students. That research entailed interviews with several dozen alumni, use of the voluminous records the Union left and papers students donated to me, and interactions with the alumni over many years at reunions and other gatherings. From these I seek not only to recover the voice of DPs, as so much recent scholarship has done, but to provide a rare level of granular detail about the public and private struggles of a distinct DP cohort. The project thus takes the form of at once a collective biography, individual profiles, an institutional history, a description of the postwar milieu, and a loose ethnography of a group persisting in time. The narration runs from the students' childhoods, through the war years, and then their time in postwar Germany, with periodic engagement with their postmigration lives and the perspectives of their distant hindsight.

Most fundamentally this book is about survival, conceived as a protracted process in which liberation is only one moment. More specifically it explores the drama of existential restoration: how victims of severe trauma and radical displacement may again gain a sense of purpose and power and a vision of the future—indeed, how they may make the transition from victims to survivors. For decades little attention was paid to the means by which survivors rebuilt their lives in the war's immediate wake. This process was overshadowed by the monumental nature of the Holocaust itself, long represented as a bounded event receiving closure with "liberation." The notion of survival, moreover, was conceived either in limited temporal terms—as if once physical survival is assured, everything else is a postscript—or in strongly psychologized terms, as a highly individual process of coping with trauma that takes place within the survivor's psyche and in small social units such as the family. A disciplinary cordon thus separated various modes and objects of inquiry, such that research on the Holocaust, a clinical literature on survivors, historical accounts of survivors' postwar experiences, and theoretical discourses on trauma rarely connected.

In more recent years attention to immediate postwar experience has grown dramatically, marking the transition from the haunting images of Jewish victims and witnesses to more diffused representations, often crossing disciplinary lines, of people building new lives in diverse contexts. As early evidence of this shift, the United States Holocaust Memorial Museum in 2000 held a major conference, "Life Reborn: Jewish Displaced Persons, 1945–51." In addition to scholars, the event drew people who had lived, worked, or been born in DP camps, and featured presentations on their administration, politics, and internal culture, as well as other aspects of DP life. In a telling scene, a reception reconfigured the symbolic landscape of the Holocaust to highlight its aftermath and a different network of identifications: former DPs grouped themselves under signs bearing not the familiar titles of concentration camps but instead the names of the DP camps in which they had been.[15]

In the conference's keynote address, Elie Wiesel marveled with respect to survivors' postwar lives, "How did these men and women, who had seen the absurdity of what we call culture, education—how did they get, where did they get the courage, the imagination, the need, to believe in them [again]? And how come these people were, or at least looked, happy? Were they really happy? How did they manage to overcome the despair that they must have carried in themselves through ghettos, hiding places, and death camps?"[16] These enduringly elemental questions regarding Jewish DPs in general have great relevance to the university students in particular. The students not only sustained their faith in the value of culture and education but almost immediately rededicated themselves to their pursuit, even at German institutions. Just as clearly, they found a way at least to contain their despair, and they often confessed a genuine, if complicated, happiness in occupied Germany.

This curious apparent "happiness" may serve as a starting point for elaborating the main themes of this study. The first relates to psychology, broadly defined. According to Eva Fogelman, the core challenge for survivors was to "integrate [the] fragmented self [by] reconnecting to their core identity [and] pre-Holocaust selves."[17] This certainly describes the students' situation. Many recount the decision to enter school as a near-automatic response to a pressing, inner need to learn. Alumnus Mark Fintel recalled, "We had our minds [and] knew that we want[ed] an education. And there is an opportunity. So there is no question, we took it."[18] Sabina Zimering reports, "After the long horrible interlude," which included time in a ghetto and the murder of her mother, "I finally had returned to what I loved most and had waited for for so long—the classrooms, lectures, professors, and students."[19] The key to building "the new life" was asserting continuity with the old.

The students' experience has bearing as well on more conceptual understandings of trauma. In the last two decades or so, analyses of witness and survivor testimony especially have done a great deal to combat suspect representations of survival and the Holocaust. These range from sentimental tributes to survivors' "resilience," to over-attention to acts of rescue by non-Jews, to the attribution of redemptive meaning to the genocide. Yet the Holocaust's grim essence as death and destruction undermines not only these externally imposed, distorting frames but also survivors' own efforts to make cognitive and moral sense of their own narratives. Trauma, by extension, becomes the unbreachable horizon of survivors' lives, defined by an eternal haunting. The Holocaust, in a broader extrapolation, exemplifies the catastrophic nature of the modern condition.[20]

But this understanding of trauma and its afterlife may yield its own distortion: one that denies survivors the possibility for recovery and casts them as perpetual victims. To be sure, many of the alumni suffer enduring pain and even "damage," as well as difficulty in comprehending their own ordeals. There is also, however, the reality of their highly functional lives, rich with affective commitments, and oftentimes studied perspectives on their pasts. The challenge with respect to survival, then, is to understand the coexistence of ruin *and* restoration, life destroyed *and* life reborn. Further, the achievements of DPs had a social and political character, valuable for appreciating how, as a collective endeavor, the effects of catastrophe can be mitigated.

This project is also deeply historical, generating additional themes. It seeks to build upon, enrich, and at times unsettle the recent historiography on Jewish DPs by situating the students in relation to the narrative lines and analytic categories that dominate within that research. Sketching this new work in DPs' history helps in framing my intervention.

A first generation of DP scholarship focused on Allied policies and their geopolitical roots, as well as on aid agencies such as UNRRA. The DPs themselves were represented largely through the lens of Allied administrative records and as a population acted upon by external forces. More recent research has restored to DPs both agency and voice.[21] Zeev Mankowitz, in a landmark work, reconstructed the institutional infrastructure Jewish DPs created in the American Zone, arguing the contribution of groups such as the Central Committee of Liberated Jews to Zionist goals. In his telling the disparate individuals making up the *She'erith Hapleitah* banded together to form a collective subject to assert itself and the Jewish cause on the world stage.[22] Avinoam Patt, in a more differentiated description of that project, demonstrates the importance of DP youth to postwar Zionism.[23] More variegated portraits of DP life qualify these Zionist-oriented representations. Atina Grossmann presents individual decisions in personal as well as political terms. DPs participating in the Jewish baby boom, for example, commonly experienced childbirth less as a way to regenerate the Jewish people than as an assertion of their vitality, and Zionism had as well therapeutic value in the camaraderie it offered.[24] Margarete Myers Feinstein, in her own broad-ranging work, locates Jewish agency in, at once, Zionism, sex, fertility, family life, and Jewish ritual, religion, and culture among DPs.[25] All these studies draw substantially on Jewish sources, whether the records of Jewish institutions or the testimony of DPs.

A second, related focus is the efforts of Jewish DPs to assert continuity with the past while responding to new circumstances. DP Zionism had its roots in Zionist activism before and during the war, with direct links between partisan and DP leadership. Postwar religious life reanimated Jewish tradition, incorporating recognition of the recent catastrophe. The DP

Yiddish press and theater, as well as numerous "self-help" initiatives, represented the rekindling of prewar culture, and private acts such as building a family could be an affirmation of prewar identities. One historian concludes, "While waiting for their resettlement status to change, the [Jewish] refugees recreated in Germany a version of Jewish Eastern Europe."[26]

A third theme in recent historiography is the great range of DP backgrounds and trajectories. Patt and Michael Berkowitz assert, "Far from constituting a monolithic whole as might seem to derive from a shared identity implied in the term 'She'erit Hepletah,' the DPs were composed of diverse groups with diverse wartime experiences."[27] In the first instance DPs were divided among those who had spent the war in Soviet exile and "direct" survivors of the Nazis' assault. Some DPs overtly sought to contribute to the collective Jewish future, while others focused on more ostensibly personal goals. Most Jews lived within the relative security of DP camps, but others resided in German cities and towns. And though the great majority of DPs viewed Germany as a waiting room for futures elsewhere, emigrating by 1948–49, others worked to reestablish a permanent Jewish presence in Germany.

Recent scholarship has explored, in addition, the relationship of Jewish DPs to the wartime period. That engagement ranged from historical projects undertaken by DPs to document the genocide, to reference to the Holocaust in their religious language and practices, to the Zionist emphasis on resistance to the Nazis and the newly urgent need for a Jewish state. By these means Jews asserted a sense of shared suffering and collective identity, linking past and future. Finally, newer scholarship pays great attention to the relationship between Jewish DPs and Germans. Grossmann, in paradigm-shifting research, demonstrates that the world of Jewish DPs was hardly so self-contained as suggested by studies focusing on the DP camps and by Jewish DPs' own, dominant memories of their isolation from Germans. Jewish DPs were in near-constant contact with Allied authorities, and the boundaries separating them from the Germans were quite porous. As a result there were innumerable "close encounters" between Jews and Germans in various contact zones. Grossmann, followed by Myers Feinstein and others, discloses the patterns of hostility, resentment, and occasionally connection that characterized the interactions between Jews and Germans, as well as the "existential revenge" commonly felt by survivors on German soil.

The postwar students participated in many of the dominant patterns of DP life. Given this, I draw on existing scholarship to elaborate the contexts and experiential frames shaping the students' existence. As young adults they were part of the dominant DP demography, relevant to research on the ideological construction of DP youth. Theirs is certainly a tale of Jewish revival, fitting within a broader picture of DPs' reclaiming individual and collective identities. Especially germane within that picture are the comparable efforts of groups such as Jewish writers to organize on professional lines after the war.[28] Moreover, the Student Union in Munich became a fixture (albeit small) on the occupation scene, with the students circulating within the city's institutions and culture. The students therefore contribute to portraits of postwar Munich as, simultaneously, a ruined Nazi capital, the seat of Allied power, a DP city, and a thriving multicultural center.

The students are fascinating also in their interactions with Germans. In occupied Germany a moral economy often underwrote the allocation of resources and conditioned modes of interaction. The students, as one interest group among many, mainly sought coveted university slots and material support. Toward these ends, they made claims against both German universities and the state government, arguing that the Germans were duty-bound to invest in their education given Nazi assaults on Jewish academics. The students played, in short, to German consciousness of their crimes and fear of the Allies, lending a subtext of shaming and even threat to superficially cordial relationships.

Like many others living outside the DP camps, they boarded with Germans, including former Nazis. And as students they participated on a daily basis in German institutions and had Germans as their peers. Frequent interaction with Germans was therefore unavoidable. Such moments, as well as their interpretations of these encounters, provide especially rich insight into the mutual suspicion that dominated among victims and victimizers; the often subtle means by which anti-Semitism now expressed itself; the sense of triumph Jews could feel in postwar Germany; and the possibilities for genuine dialogue between sharply contrasting groups. By extension, their experiences add perspective on the question that has defined much of the historiography of postwar Germany: the degree to which Germans clung to, denied, repressed, evaded, or confronted their criminal past.

And yet much about the students represents the exception to various rules, and they were often distinctive among the exceptions. The students tended to disdain the DP camps as places of constraint and had little interest in revitalizing Jewish culture in them. Neither did they participate in the baby boom among Jewish DPs nor, by and large, work to rebuild religious life. Overwhelmingly, they were committed to secular learning as a prelude to professional lives. And whatever their Zionist sympathies, most resisted Zionist urgings to leave for Palestine before completing their degrees. My goal is not simply to mark these differences as additional evidence of DP "diversity" but to see in them important tensions within Jewish DP culture as well as potential areas for expanding existing research.

A major area of difference between the students and other Jewish DPs was their relationship to the recent past. Virtually without exception the students never discussed with one another their wartime trials, explaining that dwelling on the past would have made facing the challenges of the present impossible. Their experience represents both a rebuke to the contemporary therapeutic assumption holding that the best way to deal with trauma is to confront it through dialogue and introspection and a challenge to the now-common picture of postwar survivors obsessed with the recent past. That silence, I argue, complicates portraits of the place of the Holocaust in the emotional, relational, and expressive lives of survivors, and suggests different pathways for coping with trauma.

The students' existence also raised in pointed ways a question deeply dividing Jews in occupied Germany: whether it was appropriate to participate in German culture and the Enlightenment heritage of which it was a part. Some argued that the European Enlightenment had failed Jews and therefore must be rejected. Universities were emblems of that heritage, where Enlightenment values (and German culture) were embraced. Courting controversy, the students insisted on their rightful claim to the Enlightenment and the validity of their endeavor.

This tension points to a final, major domain of my study: the relationship of the students to other Jews and the Zionism dominating Jewish DP politics. The students' presence at university was grudgingly accepted by Germans. Overt resistance came from Jewish authorities, chiefly the Central Committee, which insisted that Zionism needed "pioneers," not scholars, and for a time withheld aid from the students. Angered and even hurt by this regard, the students defended their academic pursuits as vital extensions of Jewish culture and assets for the Jewish future. Much of the drama of their entire narrative rests in their struggle to win legitimacy in the eyes of other Jews, revealing fissures within conceptions of Jewish heritage, identity, and destiny.

The Research Journey

Circumstance and both professional and personal fascination brought me into the world of the Jewish students. The project's earliest inspiration came from Bella Brodzki, a professor of comparative literature in the United States expert in autobiography and translation.[29] The daughter of survivors from

Poland, Professor Brodzki was born in Munich in 1951, and has close relatives among the alumni. One of them, at her suggestion, in 1998 approached the Center for Holocaust and Genocide Studies at the University of Minnesota to see if the students' experiences might attract the interest of professional historians. As I was working there at the time, I began pursuing the subject.[30]

I had studied the Holocaust in graduate school, focusing on its relation-ship to modernity.[31] I was most fascinated by survivors and their collision with vast systems of power and violence. My interest was tinged as well by my background. Born in the United States, I bear the unusual parentage of a Sephardic Jewish father raised in Istanbul, Turkey (with no personal connec-tion to the Holocaust), and a nominally Protestant German mother (with both a war criminal and a heroic opponent of the Nazis among her uncles).[32] I have therefore had a longstanding fascination with the postwar relation-ship between Jews and Germans, both in terms of conflict and possibilities for connection.

I quickly drew Professor Brodkzi—initially hesitant to become immersed in a project tied to her own roots in such immediate and complex ways—into the research. Thus began a years-long research collaboration with Pro-fessor Brodzki and research journey with the alumni. Briefly narrating that journey serves to elaborate the project's sources and methods, and how these shaped—and were shaped by—its emerging themes.

The research was greatly enabled by the students' alumni association. Its officers facilitated contact with individual alumni and helped in navigating the group's internal culture. Most active in the New York City area but with members worldwide, it was thriving when Bella and I began the project, as were the alumni as a whole. Many had retired (or were nearing retirement) from successful careers, chiefly in the United States and Israel, and remained in good health. Their children were grown, often enjoying, as is common among the "second generation," high levels of academic and professional achievement. And they had the resources for travel or second homes, as well as time to reflect with new focus on their lives, doubtless informed by their advanced age and accompanying thoughts of their mortality.[33]

They appeared as well to rally around each other with a special enthusi-asm, as if to affirm simultaneously the satisfaction of having made it through the common challenges of career and family, their survival of the Nazi assault decades before, and the origins of their new lives *with each other*, under cir-cumstances nearly lost to history. Conscious of their potential legacy, they were open to having their past put in historical perspective. With many ac-ademics among them, they understood the demands of scholarship and the need that the researcher have total autonomy of judgment. Their enduring request was simply that their history be represented with rigor, intelligence, and sensitivity to the extraordinary qualities of their moment.

The research began with a sixty-two-question survey sent to 225 or so of the living alumni worldwide in late 1999. It inquired into such subjects as their families' socioeconomic status, prewar education, religiosity and exposure to Zionism, wartime experiences, university tenure, and interaction with Germans. Answered by more than a fifth of the alumni, the survey yielded valuable information for situating the students demographically and discerning common patterns, as well as differences, among them. By the same token the rather impersonal format and the short answers the questions summoned were a poor means for capturing complexities, whether of the precise nature of their prewar schooling, their wartime trials, or their lives as students.

The far richer source was the nearly forty oral histories I conducted with the alumni between 2000 and 2006.[34] The alumni leadership brokered many of the contacts, who were commonly part of preexisting networks of former students. By means of the snowball effect, wherein one interviewee suggests another, who then suggests a third, Bella and I were able to move quickly through clusters of interviews in various locales. These included the New York City area, Minneapolis-St. Paul (where a group of alumni, among them Bella's relatives, settled), the Florida coast (drawing alumni from throughout the United States), and, in Israel, Tel Aviv, Jerusalem, and Haifa. The interviews were typically conducted in the alumni's homes and lasted between one-and-a-half and four hours. Nearly all the testimony was given in English, sometimes aided by German or Hebrew.

Familiar with the survivor milieu and the sensibility of Eastern European Jews of a certain generation, Bella was invaluable in establishing an initial sense of connection with the alumni and quickly winning their trust. (My partial German parentage was a potential liability; even while aware of ubiquitous interest in the Holocaust, some alumni initially wondered why a putative outsider would have such curiosity about their pasts.) I conducted the interviews, though Bella was usually present for them, after which we parsed together their meaning and points of special interest. Most interviews were then transcribed by a research associate, Ramiza Koyla. Though Bella helped in the development of certain frames and formulations, I did nearly all the archival work and authored the text.

In terms of whom to interview, the main goal was diversity with respect to gender, educational background, wartime experience, field of study, degree of involvement in the Student Union, and so on. Especially important was to interview both alumni who had migrated to the United States and those who settled in Israel. I came to appreciate that these paths represented very different trajectories, and provided the source of enduring tensions between some of the alumni.

Certain kinds of diversity, however, proved inaccessible, reflecting distinctions among the students going back to their time in Germany. Reflected as well in the networks they maintained, the divisions condition the scope of my study. Jews from Poland made up the great majority of the students, with small numbers from Hungary, Romania, and elsewhere. In Germany the students tended to socialize, partly for linguistic reasons, on lines of national origin. The students from Poland dominate even more strongly the alumni networks and comprise nearly all those whom I met. As a consequence this project is oriented toward Jewish DPs from Poland. Similarly, the Munich Student Union was by far the largest and most active, with its former members at the helm of the alumni organization. Given this, as well as the documentary record left by the Munich Union, I focus mostly on one city and community but make reference to the experience of students elsewhere in Germany. Though a very small number of Jews studied at universities in the British Zone, I deal almost exclusively with the American Zone (which dominates DP research). Finally, a small number of the alumni settled in Australia, with whom I had no meaningful contact.

My approach to the interviews evolved, influencing the substance of the project. In the earliest sessions, I engaged prewar and wartime experience very selectively, focusing on the students' time at university. I quickly realized the inadequacy of this approach. The alumni made it clear that their decisions to study after the war were deeply rooted in talents and inclinations stretching to their childhoods and the values both of their families and their broader milieu. To understand the continuity they embodied, I soon adopted a more conventionally chronological approach and explored with them at length the prewar education of Jews in Poland—a topic, to my surprise, about which relatively little scholarship exists. As I integrated their recollections with existing sources, the project took on the feel of working backward from a DP cohort to recover an important dimension of the history of Eastern European Jews.

Among the most difficult decisions was how much interview time to spend on the war years, given that my main concern was the alumni's lives as DPs and given that the broad contours of survival are well known. The increased time I devoted to the war proved well spent. It provided a window into additional under-researched topics—chiefly how Soviet occupation (until June 1941) affected the education of Jews and what (for those experiencing this fate) deportation to the Soviet interior was like in general and with respect to schooling. This material also helps to give the project its distinctive character. Much of the literature on the Holocaust ends with liberation and says little, if anything, about its aftermath. An opposite emphasis characterizes so much literature on DPs: it begins with liberation and says little about DPs' prewar and wartime experiences. As a consequence the relationships among the prewar, wartime, and postwar selves and the complex process, at the individual level, of survivors' restoration remain somewhat opaque, even as the postwar period is seriously engaged. To understand that process I try to connect, based on specific knowledge, multiple phases of their lives.

In the interviews I certainly sought key facts of the alumni's biographies—documentary material whose richness and reliability depend on the strength of their memories. But more than that I sought a record of their states of mind and feelings through all they experienced. Throughout I was attuned to the textual quality of both testimony and memory—the way in which self, world, and past are constructed in language. Many students suffered severe persecution; theirs is necessarily a traumatized discourse in which the capacity of experience to evocatively shape language is pronounced. I recognize, in addition, that the biography created in testimony is not a definitive account of the life of the teller; it represents one memory act, executed at a particular time, in a specific setting, and for specific ends. Testimony, finally, is influenced by the personality and technique of the interviewer, who serves as a collaborator in the narratives he or she elicits. To convey the relational quality of the interviews and the research more broadly, I occasionally make reference to the interactions Bella and I had with the alumni.

The project is also the history of an organization, the Jewish Students' Union, and the environment it inhabited. While fulfilling his duties as the last president of the Munich chapter, Arnold Kerr sensed that the materials in the group's office had historical value. So he filled three large crates containing its papers and sent them in 1954 to New York City's YIVO (Institute for Jewish Research), the great center for Jewish learning founded in Vilna, whose original location was nearly sacked by the Nazis and then exiled to a permanent, American home.[35] The materials, from both the Munich chapter and the zone-wide federation, include membership rosters, reports on union initiatives, minutes of meetings, and extensive correspondence with occupation authorities, German institutions, relief agencies, and Jewish organizations. Other documents, chiefly memoirs, university registration cards, diplomas, and photographs, come from the alumni themselves.

The study benefited, finally, from interaction with the alumni at group events. These included two global reunions in Florida, regional gatherings in the New York City area and the Catskills, and a trip in 2005 to Munich in conjunction with an exhibit on Jewish DPs in Bavaria at the Bavarian state capitol. The alumni, very few of whom made the Munich trip for reasons I later explain, were invited by Ruth Snopkowksi, the wife of the late Bavarian state senator and Jewish alumnus Simon Snopkowski. At these gatherings I gained a palpable sense of the importance the alumni hold for each other, how they approach their shared past, and the combination of confidence and vulnerability they project.

Indeed, when together the group often exuded a sense of its specialness. Born of the satisfactions referenced above, that sense is rooted as well in the alumni's enduring self-image—approaching a collective mythology—of their positive difference from many other DPs: that they "hit the books" and worked hard at being independent while others were content with the relative comforts of the DP camps. In truth most Jewish DPs struggled to meet significant challenges (which the alumni, on reflection, readily acknowledge). My role as researcher has been to maintain analytic distance from and contextualize their self-regard, yielding perhaps my key, speculative insight about the mindset of the alumni. For them surviving the Holocaust does not register as a personal achievement or point of pride. Their survival was too arbitrary, and surrounded by too much death and destruction, to permit that perspective. What they accomplished afterward with each other, however, is intensely meaningful to them, partly as an expression of the renewal of the very autonomy and capacity for self-fashioning the Nazis had nearly annihilated.

Even with rich source material, reconstructing the Union's life and the broader occupation scene proved an enormous challenge. My initial naïve hope was that the testimonial material would neatly line up with or fill gaps in the documentary record, and vice versa. But the recollections of how things worked in practice often had little bearing on how they worked according to the relevant administrative rule. So too, various procedures quickly gave way to new ones, as conditions on the ground changed. This dissonance and dynamism, while frustrating for research, ultimately helped to reveal defining traits of the occupation world: its extreme instability, opacity, and improvised quality. It teemed with the undocumented and the transient, many of whom misrepresented their identities. The German population, fearful of Allied reprisals, was cautious in what it revealed. Sorting through masses of refugees, multiple authorities struggled to impose administrative, legal, political, and semiotic order on chaos. And despite the largely efficient distribution of aid to diverse populations, suspicion and mistrust suffused the relationships among various groups. Occupied Germany, in short, existed in shades of gray, whose nature can be distorted by drawing bright lines and certain shapes in the slowly lifting fog of occupation, displacement, and catastrophe.

Giving voice to the dual reality of recuperation and loss in the students' lives proved the greatest challenge. In chronicling the students' substantial winning back of self and world, this study encompasses multiple, edifying tributes: to the adaptability and resilience of the young; to the persistence of core values through war and oppression; to the importance of survivors of trauma having something to live for; to the therapeutic value of education, ambition, and routine; to the rewards of initiative and the miracle of second chances. All these have a universal resonance and, in an era of continued displacements through war, genocide, ethnic cleansing, famine, and other disasters, continued relevance. Though identified with specific historical circumstances, the students may therefore serve as examples for others facing the sorrows of dislocation and persecution.

And yet the reality of irredeemable loss pervades many of their lives, balancing and even, in moments, eclipsing the radiance of their revival.

CHAPTER 1

"I Knew One Thing—
I Have to Study"

Early Education and Dreams of the Future

In 1998 leaders of the "Jewish University Alumni in Germany" wrote to its members worldwide, asking for reflections on their backgrounds, their time in postwar Germany, and their lives since. Rita Schorr, a native of Poland and student in Munich, responded: "January 1945 I was liberated in Oswiecim [Auschwitz] facing a present full of uncertainties, a past too painful to face and deal with, and a future with no roadmap or parachute to land. . . . August 1945—World War ended yet for me the effects of the War and the Shoah were an abyss to face. Survived for what I asked myself. I was still defined by others. I had no records, no documents, no homeland and slowly it was becoming clear my parents and my sister were dead, my extended family annihilated. I felt—ex-nihilo—<u>Lost</u>."[1]

Schorr's words, while reflecting her own especially harrowing ordeal, describe in broad terms the experiences of both so many young survivors and those among her student cohort. (Schorr's body had completely given out in Auschwitz, and she defiantly refused to go on a death march. Left for dead in the camp, she was liberated by the Soviet army.) The Holocaust left many of them not only orphans but radically dispossessed—exiled from their homelands, shorn of existential markers like birth certificates and school records, and robbed of much of their young lives. "I did not have an adolescenthood," Schorr laments. "[The] Shoah destroyed it as well as my happy childhood."[2] Schorr speaks also to the dread that could accompany survival—the condition of being "liberated but not free"—which brought the challenge of building, virtually from nothing, new lives.

Schorr's narrative then shifts: "1945–1951 I lived in Munich and basically my core decisions about my life were formed there. My goals: to get an

19

education so I can be self-reliant. A desire to have my own life with a voice and a vote. To have <u>choice</u> was my obsession."[3] Postwar Germany became for her the catalytic setting for that new life, defined by the reemergence of choice and suggesting the leap from one world and self to another. Schorr says outright, "I was born twice."[4]

This image of rupture is, however, deceptive. Schorr reports that she had always excelled in school, that her family was "very education-minded, with a commitment to integrity, professional standards, and excellence," and that higher education had always been the goal for her.[5] In Munich she began to fulfill that destiny, first attending a Jewish school and then a German *gymnasium*, followed by a year at the Technische Hochschule, and then immigrating to the United States and gaining a scholarship at a prestigious American university. Her core decisions about life were in fact shaped long before she came to Munich; her postwar self remained an extension of who she had been and what she had wanted to become before the war.

Schorr's commentary points to a defining tension in the lives of the student survivors: the coexistence of both rupture and continuity, the recreation of the self from ruin but also its partial repossession through the pursuit of longstanding talents and ambitions. The side of oblivion is the more obvious and has dominated portraits of survivors. Yet the continuity could be potent too, and it is conspicuous in the case of the students. So many of them, when explaining their motivation to resume their education immediately after the war, insist that it seemed the utterly natural thing to do, no matter what they had suffered. Attending university, in short, was a bridge to both their pasts and their futures.

Understanding this bridge as leading both backward and forward, and thus as the deepest source of their decision to study, demands focus on key aspects of their pre-Holocaust lives: the opportunities for and barriers to achievement for Jews in their native lands; the education level, social status, and ethos of their families; the extent of their own education and religiosity; and their early proclivities, desires, and senses of their futures. Their early lives also help explain the ardor with which they defended their decisions to study after the war.

The continuity the students asserted is illuminating beyond their particular biographies and trajectories. At one level it opens a window into under-researched aspects of the prewar world—specifically, the place of education in the lives of Poland's Jews, as well as how education helped determine Jews' place in Polish society. On another, the students' experiences give cause to qualify recent understandings of Jewish DPs. Avinoam Patt, in his impressive study of DP youths in *kibbutzim* in postwar Germany, concludes,

"While prewar and wartime experiences could be significant in influencing the decisions of [Jewish survivors], ultimately the choice of what to do next would be dictated by postwar reality."[6] He adds that survivors typically had "few remaining attachments" and "no roots to return to."[7] To be sure, the roots of family and homeland had been torn up for so many DPs. The choices of all DPs were conditioned by circumstances, and the fulfillment of any decision depended on opportunities for its realization. Patt's conclusion, moreover, is reasonably suggested by his focus on *kibbutzim*. The members' involvement, he found, little depended on their having any prior inclination toward Zionism. The sight of a familiar face could be enough to cause a young person to join, and the family feeling—acutely appreciated by those orphaned—was perhaps the main factor in staying on.[8]

The example of the students indicates, however, that "prewar experiences" could be the primary drivers of postwar choices. Through individual determination and the advocacy of their student unions, they often created opportunities for university study in postwar Germany that had not existed, illustrating the power (albeit circumscribed) of will over circumstance. In so many cases they returned to roots defined intangibly in terms of personal desires and what they perceived as essential Jewish values. The very idea of roots and the continuity of Jewish experience may therefore expand to include connections to broadly cultural legacies and habits of the mind, beyond the practices, traditions, community institutions, and shared memories that most clearly defined the Jews of Eastern Europe.

The Jewish Students

While in Germany the Jewish students enjoyed a close bond predicated on their mutual choice to enter university. Attesting decades later to that affinity, one alumnus remarked that "my soul" is with the Jewish students.[9] Yet the students were bonded, in a sense, long before they met. A principle of self-selection drew them after the war to the student life and to each other. The most common denominator among them was a passion, talent, and discipline for learning that stretched deep into their childhoods. These capacities served them well at university, enabling them to overcome their foreignness, the limitations of their often tender ages, and the inherent challenges of their task.

Throughout their existence the Jewish Students' Union in Munich and unions in other cities compiled thorough documentation of their members, whether for internal records or to present to occupation and German authorities, university administrators, aid agencies, and Jewish organizations.

Various rosters record some combination of the years and places of their births, the cities and schools in Germany in which they enrolled, their academic fields, and their residences. From these, their basic biographical profile as a group can be established. That profile puts the student cohort squarely within the broad demographic patterns of Jewish DPs as a whole, while also pointing to the challenges they faced at university and to their place within the DP community.

Union membership was highly dynamic. New students entered university, existing students joined the unions, individuals switched between universities, and others dropped (or failed) their studies, emigrated, or moved elsewhere in occupied Germany. Occasional ambiguity as to who was officially enrolled further caused the figures to fluctuate. At the beginning of the winter term in October 1946, the Munich Union reports having 254 members, which likely comprised nearly all Jewish DPs at local universities. The number rose to 408 by the end of January 1947.[10] By July membership stood at 402, reaching its recorded peak in October 1947 at between 413 and 460.[11] Students at Frankfurt (94), Erlangen (57), Stuttgart (34), Marburg (34), Heidelberg (27), and Darmstadt (7) brought American Zone–wide membership to 655 in the summer of 1947.[12]

Of the 402 students in Munich in July 1947, 307 came from Poland, with 31, 22, and 15 from Germany, Hungary, and Lithuania, respectively.[13] The others were from Romania (8), Czechoslovakia (7), Austria (7), or Russia, France, and the United States (one each). Those from Poland—76.3 percent of the total—clearly dominated, followed by small percentages from Germany (7.7%), Hungary (5.4%), and Lithuania (3.7%), and tiny numbers from all other places (.24%–2%). Further skewing the de facto distribution, those born in Germany sometimes came from substantially Polish areas, like the Silesian town of Gleiwitz or the Prussian city of Kalisch, and were raised within an essentially Polish-Jewish milieu. Likewise, students from Austria might be from Polish-Ukrainian areas of Galicia, part of which was incorporated into Poland following World War I.

The origins of students elsewhere in Germany were also strongly Polish. Of the 83 students in Erlangen in October 1947, 69 came from Poland, 10 from Hungary, just 2 from Germany, and one each from Czechoslovakia and Austria.[14] A Marburg Union list records 24 of 27 students as coming from Poland.[15] Of 27 students in Heidelberg, 15 came from Poland, with 7 others from Hungary (the rest were from Lithuania, Czechoslovakia, and Romania, with two from Germany).[16] Adding these figures to those for Munich, 415 of 539 students—77 percent—came from Poland, with the numbers from Hungary rising to 39 (7%). As to gender, 115 of the 402 (28.6%) Munich students in July 1946 were women, with the percentage slightly higher by October 1947 (29.1%).[17] Zone-wide, women comprised nearly a quarter of the Jewish students.

These figures closely conform to the Jewish DP population in the American Zone. Starting in October 1945, surveys by US authorities and aid agencies put Jews from Poland at around 75 percent of all Jewish DPs, with Hungarians and Romanians at 6 and 3 percent, respectively.[18] Among Jews officially registered with UNRRA in November 1946, 71 percent were from Poland, 6 percent from Hungary, 4 percent from Czechoslovakia, 2.5 percent each from Germany and Romania, and 2 percent from Austria (with 10% declaring themselves "stateless").[19] In a statistical survey of Jews at the Landsberg DP camp, females older than age 14 comprised 30 percent of the population, males made up 65 percent, and the remainder were children.[20]

As the students were more or less of school-going age, the university cohort was by definition comprised of youth, and in that sense also mirrored the Jewish DP demographic. As Patt summarizes, "Young adults composed the vast majority of . . . Jewish DPs, with surveys pointing to individuals between the ages of eighteen and forty-four comprising 85.8 percent of DPs in November 1945 and 80.1 percent in February 1946." At the later date 61 percent were between nineteen and thirty-four, and more than 40 percent were fifteen to twenty-four.[21] In the fall of 1946, the great majority of students in Munich—212 out of 254 (83%)—were listed as between ages eighteen to twenty-six, with steeply declining numbers for ages twenty-seven or older (just thirteen were ages thirty or older, with the oldest aged fifty-four). Amalgamated, roughly contemporaneous figures from the Munich, Erlangen, Heidelberg, and Darmstadt unions show 77 percent as twenty-six or younger, with another 9 percent ages twenty-seven to twenty-nine. The students, in sum, were a subset of Jewish DP youth.

For the Jewish DPs university study in postwar Germany was an imposing challenge, beginning with language. The great majority of the students were not native German speakers. Of forty-six survey respondents, only two—both from Germany—indicated German as their native language, and twelve others listed it as a language of secondary fluency.[22] A small number of those from Poland had learned German from parents who had German backgrounds or had grown up in the German or Austrian parts of pre–World War I Poland, where German had been the official language. (In areas of western Poland, German remained the dominant language, used even by the Jewish press; many Polish cities, moreover, had large German populations.) Others had German instruction in school and grew quite proficient, if short of fluent. Many others spoke or were exposed at home to Yiddish, a language close to German, and some even learned basic German in Nazi camps or when "passing" as non-Jews by using Aryan papers. Finally, most had been raised in the trilingual culture of Polish Jewry (Yiddish, Hebrew, Polish), wherein language acquisition was somewhat routine. Even so, acquiring the German language was for the majority an initial barrier; scrambling to learn grammar and vocabulary is a frequent theme in the alumni's memories of their early studies at university.

The women in the group faced added adversity. Especially in the hard sciences, they might have numbered among a tiny handful of female students, Jewish or not. Given the rather strict segregation of students by field in Germany at the time, this isolation could be very extreme. But above all the students' ages presented the greatest difficulties. The 1946 list of 254 Munich students records 65 born in the years 1920 and 1921.[23] They were ages seventeen to nineteen when the war broke out in 1939, at which point their formal education may have stopped entirely.[24] Many but not all in this group had completed the first phase of secondary school and were thus well enough poised for university study. Called *gymnasium* in the Polish system (as elsewhere in Europe), secondary school typically concluded at age sixteen or seventeen. Some from this age group, moreover, had continued with two-year lyceum study (typically at the same school) in preparation for university and passed the qualification exams earning them a *Matura*. The Polish equivalent of the German *Abitur*, the *Matura* was recognized throughout Europe and certified one for admission to university.

Forty-three alumni from the list of 254 were born in 1923, and so in 1939, at ages sixteen or fifteen, were at a less certain threshold. Some of these, especially if they had lived under Soviet occupation until 1941, could plausibly have completed *gymnasium* prior to 1945 (though the Soviet system required two additional years of secondary school). And anyone deported to Soviet Central Asia had additional time for schooling. Others born in 1923, based on when they first began school, their birth month, and other circumstances, may have only just started *gymnasium* when the war broke out. This leaves 77 of the students—nearly a third—fifteen or younger in 1939, and 20 percent had been fourteen or younger. Figures from unions elsewhere in Germany generally align with those from Munich, showing a student population that is slightly younger.[25] Many of the Jewish students, then, were decidedly on the young side for university, with some dramatically so. And an indeterminate portion of the data is skewed to show union members older than they actually were.[26] Determined to be admitted to German universities, which often set age requirements just after the war, some reported false dates of birth.

Given this age distribution, the education level of the students upon entering universities in Germany spanned a great spectrum. Some had already begun university, whether before the war, in the Soviet Union during the war, or in Eastern Europe between liberation and their departure for Germany. Others had received their *Matura* and were therefore eligible for university. But a great many others had not completed secondary school, and some had finished only primary school. To enter university, as I will later detail, these young Jews might lie about their credentials, first attend *gymnasia* in Germany, or engage in feverish, private study to pass qualifying exams.

The students' age introduced a final, if very different, form of pressure, insofar as "youth" in Jewish discourse was not just a demographic but also an ideological category. Even prior to the war, Jewish leaders in Poland and elsewhere portrayed youths as representing the political future of the Jewish people. After the war the overwhelmingly Zionist, Jewish DP leadership charged the surviving Jewish youths—the capacious category of the *jidisze jungt*, which might refer to anyone ages fifteen to thirty—with contributing to the creation of the state of Israel.[27] DP youths were ideally to join Zionist youth groups, *kibbutzim*, and agricultural collectives, and otherwise engage in Zionist education and productive labor, in preparation for being pioneers in Palestine. As Patt observes, "DP society [as a whole] accorded an esteemed position for those who made the choice to affiliate as youths and thus as part of the Zionist future."[28] The students, as youths making different choices, had to navigate their potentially competing commitments to their studies, to certain conceptions of the Jewish future, and to the expectations of their community.

"I Shall Die if I Shall Not Study"

The students enrolled in some of Germany's—if not Europe's—most elite universities, with notoriously rigorous curricula. Food and clothing were scarce, and basic academic items like textbooks in short supply. Their classmates, whether Germans, Poles, or Baltic displaced persons, were from countries hostile to Jews. The majority had not been in a proper school in years (though this was true for many non-Jews as well). And they had to cope with a more fundamental if less perceptible challenge: the massive injury of the war and the Holocaust.

In sum, in order to survive and even thrive in German universities, the students had to have been high achievers with great aptitude and motivation. With a mix of humility and self-assuredness, the alumni confess just that, typically describing themselves as having been curious and diligent children and adolescents, at the tops of their classes. (A small minority confessed that they were only average students.) Elaborating, many attribute their early academic achievement in large part to their seemingly instinctive makeup—to the way they simply were as young people.

Munich alumnus Philip Balaban, born in 1928 in a small town in eastern Poland, readily admits a precocious nature. "I was always a bookworm. I finished the whole school library by the age of eight or nine. So I used to take from my mother, from her library. Some of the books [whether in Polish, Russian, or Hebrew], I shouldn't have read. She didn't know about it." Balaban's talents carried over into the schools he attended under Russian occupation and then in exile in Siberia. "Always the smartest kid," he earned from his classmates the nickname "the Professor."[29]

Alexander White, raised in an Orthodox family in the small Polish city of Krosno, was a true wunderkind. His father worked in the family's glass business and owned, with his cousin, the largest building in town. By the time he was four, White admits, "I could recite the prayers . . . of the Bible by heart after just one or two readings" and read the Torah, inspiring his grandmother to praise him for his "iron brain" and hope that he would become the greatest "super Rabbi" in Poland.[30] Though barely speaking Polish—the family spoke Yiddish at home—he entered grade school one year early, and he could soon repeat verbatim the teachers' lectures.[31]

Alumna Sabina Zimering, raised in the substantially Jewish city of Piotrkow, also had an intellectual bent, highlighted by the contrast with her younger sister's abilities. Their father, largely self-educated, had a small business selling coal, which was hit hard by the depression of the early 1930s.[32] On Saturdays he would take the two girls to the town's nicest café, order them pastries and himself tea, and for hours read the café's free Yiddish and Polish newspapers. Sabina first attended a public Polish primary school. As a Jew, she was exempt from the lessons about Catholicism, and her teacher permitted her to go home or stay on the playground. Quickly finding these alternatives "boring," she happily stayed for the religious instruction. (Knowledge of the catechism and her excellent Polish proved invaluable during the last years of the war, which she survived by passing as a Polish Catholic laborer in Germany.) Sabina next went to a private Jewish *gymnasium*, graduating at age sixteen just before the 1939 German invasion.

Her sister Helen's talents ran in another direction. Helen "was a born businesswoman. She didn't care about education" (though she did finish primary school). Instructed to mind the coal shop, Sabina was once so absorbed reading *Anna Karenina* that customers walked off with the coal without paying, earning her the scolding of her father. Helen, on the other hand, would at her own initiative go to the homes of customers who were late in paying for coal purchased on credit and demand that they settle their debts. The two sisters survived the war together, but responded to different callings after it ended.

Mark Fintel, who studied with his brother Nat in postwar Munich, recalled of his upbringing in Rovno, Poland, that "school was very important, we took it very seriously. And obviously, we were good, good in school." His father, educated in "the traditional Jewish way," earned a living as a medium-scale merchant. His mother was a graduate of a Russian secondary school in pre–World War I Rovno, which was then still part of Russia. By their parents' design the boys first attended a Polish public school and then a private Jewish *gymnasium* with instruction in Polish. Together they dreamed of university study abroad, or at least in the capital city of Warsaw.[33]

Native inclinations or character, however, go only so far in explaining the students' early academic proclivities. Their own recollections stress also the importance accorded education by their families and, in their young perceptions, by Jewish culture. Mark Fintel remarked that academic achievement was "seemingly in the nature of the Jewish upbringing" and promoted by "the general atmosphere in the social class that we belonged to." In his Polish primary school, which had just a handful of Jews, "the teachers gladly admitted that their Jewish pupils are the best in school." Balaban's grandfather, himself permitted only limited schooling in pre–World War I Russia, was "obsessed" with education, impressing its importance on the entire family.[34] Education was also the greatest value of Alex White's father, who had been essentially raised by a famous scholarly minded rabbi in Dabrowa. A voracious reader of literature, philosophy, and periodicals (buying bundles of old newspapers to read the editorials), he harassed his children by reading Goethe and Schiller, Aristotle and Spinoza to them in idle moments.[35] Fulfilling his father's wish that he receive both a religious and secular education, Alex attended yeshiva for religiously oriented schooling at 6 AM and then a full day of Polish public school.[36] Sabina Zimering's father, also deprived of a full modern education, modeled a commitment to the life of the mind for his daughters. Their mother, an independent-minded, *gymnasium*-educated woman (rare for her day) from a well-to-do family in Russia, did the same, reciting Russian and Polish poetry for her daughters and insisting that the family make great sacrifices to pay Sabina's *gymnasium* tuition.

In these four cases, as in so many among the Jewish students, the passion for learning at the root of their eventual decisions to study in Germany was greatly overdetermined: instilled and nurtured by the family, supported by Jewish values, promoted by their social milieu, and enabled by the opportunities afforded by their class position. These factors were not in themselves sufficient to breed intellectual and professional ambition; other young Jews in equivalent circumstances pursued different interests. But they do appear all but necessary conditions for the emergence of the students' defining drives in life, including after the war. Alumnus Frederick Reiter, asked why education was so important, conceded, "I can't really explain [it]. I knew one thing—I have to study. And always study."[37] Mark Hupert, just fourteen when the war broke out, related: "[It] was a given in our house that we are going to go to school. Then, right after the war, there was no doubt in my mind, that's what I'm going to do. . . . I guess education was always part of the Jewish life."[38]

Georg Majewski, a founder of the Jewish Students' Union in Berlin in 1947, gave perhaps the ultimate expression of how this inner need to learn, sealed early in life, propelled his decisions as a DP. A *gymnasium* graduate prior to the war, he secured a university degree during his chaotic wartime exile in the Soviet Union. After the war he abandoned an extremely lucrative black market trade—first in sausages, then in diamonds, gold, and currency—to continue university study at a German school. Explaining the shift, he recalls feeling that "I shall die if I shall not study."[39]

Commonwealth of Many Nations?

The place of education in the lives of Poland's Jews was also powerfully a function of where Jews fit into the new Polish society. This context was critical in shaping the students' ambitions, as well as their understanding of their collective pursuits in postwar Germany, as efforts to resurrect a near-vanquished Jewish intelligentsia. In 1918, after more than a century of partition, Poland again became an autonomous state. Through additional wars, plebiscites, and international treaties, the Second Republic of Poland was soon consolidated, passing a constitution in 1921. The new state comprised territories from the former Austro-Hungarian empire (Galicia and Austrian Silesia, in the south), from Germany (chiefly Eastern Prussia, in the west), and from Russia (in the center and east). While the majority of the population was Polish, nearly 30 percent was made up of minorities, chiefly Ukrainians, Germans, Byelorussians, Lithuanians, Romanians, and Jews. Ukrainians were the largest minority, comprising up to 15 percent, and Jews too were great in number, making up between 8 and 10 percent of Poland's population.[40] Poland was thus a highly pluralistic society facing the challenge, in an era of intense and often destructive nationalisms, of achieving meaningful national unity while formally protecting the rights of minorities. In parts of the country, ethnic Poles were only a bare majority or even outnumbered, and could themselves feel "embattled and marginal."[41] One's class standing, moreover, could be more important than ethnicity in determining one's social position and relative empowerment. Polish politics proved a struggle between a progressive conception of the country as a "commonwealth of many nations" and an aggressive vision of "Poland for the Poles."[42]

Among minority groups nationalism took a variety of forms. Some sought integration within their "homelands," such as ethnic Germans desiring incorporation into a "greater Germany" or Lithuanians hoping for inclusion in the newly created Lithuanian state. (Vilna, the traditional Lithuanian capital, was incorporated into Poland in 1922, before becoming part of the Lithuanian Soviet Republic in 1940.) Others, like many Ukrainians, agitated for the creation of an autonomous state, while others still simply sought greater powers of self-rule within Poland. Whatever their ultimate ambitions, and aside from strongly assimilationist elements, all sought to retain their languages, religions, and other aspects of their heritage.

Jews were in many respects unlike their Polish neighbors and distinctive among minority groups. As of 1921, according to a national census, there were 2.8 million Jews in Poland, nearly 10 percent of the total population; by 1931, they numbered 3.1 million.[43] The Jewish population was markedly urban. Though nearly 80 percent of non-Jews lived in rural areas, more than three-quarters of Jews lived in cities, with a quarter residing in Warsaw, Lodz, Krakow, Vilna, and Lwow, where they made up 30 percent of the population.[44] More than 200,000 Jews lived in Warsaw and Lodz alone, with 100,000 in Lwow and in Vilna, the latter dubbed the "Jerusalem of Lithuania." [45] Such intense urbanization was, however, something of a recent development, and by no means complete. As of 1921 most Jews still lived in small towns, with many moving to the cities in the subsequent decade. More than 60 percent of urban Jews, moreover, lived in cities with fewer than 20,000 people.[46]

Jews were distinguished as well by their economic activities. In a country of farmers, just 4 percent of Jews were employed in agriculture. Almost eight in ten were involved in industry and commerce.[47] Jews were strongly represented at the top of the commercial ladder, having substantial interests in nearly 30 percent of Poland's largest enterprises.[48] Especially in the cities, there was a sizable and prosperous Jewish business class. Yet for most Jews, particularly in the countryside, commerce meant a modest or even poor living as a small-scale shopkeeper, merchant, or peddler. Industrializing late and haphazardly, Poland remained very poor relative to much of Europe, with fairly stark lines separating the haves and have-nots among Jews and non-Jews alike.[49]

Despite restrictions on Jewish employment in administration, the civil service, the military, and academia, Jews had a strong presence in the professions, especially teaching, medicine, and law.[50] The numbers of Jews studying in universities was also high. Professionals and university graduates, along with writers, artists, clerics, community leaders, and politicians, made up the intelligentsia—a term designating educational level and social status more than wealth. By one estimate members of the Jewish intelligentsia and large-scale entrepreneurs, along with their families, numbered 400,000–500,000 people.[51] These constituted, for reasons both of class and caste, a prewar Jewish elite.

Jewish distinctiveness—a mix of religion, language, dress, traditions, and economic functions—was more complex than that of other minorities. Jews were also subject to greater Polish prejudice and nationalist hostility.[52] Jews were set apart, finally, by the special difficulties of the national question as it pertained to them. The Bund, a socialistic party in Poland (with affiliates elsewhere in Eastern Europe), favored a Yiddish-based cultural nationalism within the framework of a socialist internationalism. Much of the Orthodox community wanted to retain traditional practices and governance structures with minimal state intrusion. It largely opposed secular nationalist aspirations.[53] Zionists, across the political spectrum and of varying degrees of religiosity, agitated for a state in Palestine, while preparing Jews, through the cultivation of a Hebrew language–based nationalism, for emigration. All of these passionately defended options—each opposed by elements in Polish society—gave Jewish politics a highly dynamic, fraught, and even desperate quality.

Class, Religion, Zionism, and the Future

So much in the students' backgrounds favored their pursuit of (secular) education. They tended to be urban in even greater proportion than other Jews in Poland. A large number were from the Jewish centers of Warsaw, Lodz, Vilna, Lwow, and Krakow. Many others were native to smaller cities with large Jewish populations such as Radom, Rovno, Kovno (in Lithuania), Bielsko, Bedzin, Stanislawow, Piotrkow, and Kielce.[54] In the cities, the schools were more numerous and diverse, economic and professional opportunities greater, and the outlook more modern than in the countryside. Very few of the future university students came from shtetls—the small towns often described in nostalgic and even mythic terms as the heart of Jewish life in Poland, tranquil places of intimacy and traditionalism. Those from the shtetl tended to be part of the small-town elite of wealthy, educated, or otherwise prominent families; these generally made up no more than 1 to 5 percent of the local population.[55] The extended Balaban family, by way of small example, lived on a street lined with linden trees that the townsfolk called "Balaban Street," and they summered in a beautiful Polish mountain town.[56]

A small minority of the students were born to the professional class and essentially followed in their parents' footsteps. The great majority of their parents, however, were businesspeople, educated to varying degrees—in some cases frustrated intellectuals—for whom the education of their children was a priority. Some were enormously wealthy, providing opportunities for their families inaccessible to nearly everyone in Poland. Most, however, were merely well off, and upwardly mobile in the sense that they did not want their children to work so hard—or so hard in the same way—simply to earn a living. Their children should be free to explore their intellectual talents and pursue a proper profession, as opposed to a life in business or a trade, in ways that they were not.

Indeed, fully thirty-one of forty-six alumni reported in the survey that their fathers were businessmen. Their activities ranged from the management or ownership of construction companies, factories, and mills; to import-export enterprises; to leather and jewelry production and trade; to, at the lower echelons, the running of small shops and work as traveling merchants. Significantly, only nine of the students' fathers were professionals proper, in such fields as law, accounting, and engineering, and one each was in politics and the military. Entrepreneurship clearly dominated over professional life, with only some of the alumni's families having sufficient wealth or community standing to qualify as members of a Jewish sociocultural elite.

Equally significant, only one alumnus responding to the survey had parents who were farmers, and three had fathers who worked in skilled trades such as watchmaking, tailoring, and woodworking (though the owners of businesses might also know the trade of their companies). The students, in sum, almost without exception came neither from low-income sectors of the economy nor arenas, like the military, from which Jews were traditionally excluded. (Among the exceptions, Georg Majewski reports that his father was a small trader who "scarcely made a living.")[57] Few alumni recorded in the survey any profession for their mothers, suggesting that the women cared for their families and perhaps helped out with the family business. Three of their mothers, nonetheless, worked in pharmacies, two were professional teachers, and another an office manager. One respondent made a point of conveying that his mother was a well-educated, extremely bright woman and a leader in her community.[58]

The alumni's recollections of their life goals when growing up confirm a collective trajectory—at least in terms of aspiration—from business to professional life. Many of the alumni were quite young when the war broke out, and some had not yet developed a sense of what they "wanted to be" when they grew up. Thirty-four of forty-seven survey respondents did, however, record the vocation they desired early in life. Not a single person listed business, no matter how likely a future in business may have remained. Instead, they preferred to be professionals. Medicine (11) and engineering (7) dominated. Some answered very specifically, listing such specialties as law (2), dentistry (1), pharmacy (1), physics (2), biological science (1), accounting (1), mathematics (1), and building (1). Broadly humanistic and artistic pursuits such as education, politics, journalism, and music (one each) were in the minority. Two alumni answered somewhat whimsically, listing careers in astronomy and philosophy as their childhood dreams. Virtually all of the desired professions required university education and formal professional credentialing. Higher education was therefore an assumed part of their hopes for their futures.

The female alumni, equally as much as the men, report having had professional aspirations when growing up. Sabina Zimering parsed varying attitudes toward the education of girls. She explained that some Jewish families, especially those with few resources, did not think it worthwhile to invest in their daughters' education, encouraging instead marriage and starting a family. Other families favored education for their daughters by reasoning that "the chances for a good marriage will be improved."[59] Others still, like Zimering's parents, believed in the intrinsic value of education irrespective of gender, and wished for their girls the full range of opportunities it afforded. Whatever specific messages they received growing up, the female alumni were a determined group, pursuing university study after the war with the same sense of belonging as the men.

In explaining the importance of their rearing, some alumni invoked a hierarchy foreign to our era of mass, public education in the developed world.[60] Simon Schochet came from a highly cultured and acculturated family in Poland. Close relatives of his were officers in the Polish military, which was historically connected at its high echelons to the nobility, and Simon imagined a military career for himself. Accounting for how confidently the Jewish students took to university life in Germany, he explained, "We had a prewar caste system. Very, very pronounced . . . like in England."[61] So many of the German students also came from what he termed "the upper class"; whatever the immense differences between the two groups, they shared the structural affinity of being members of an educated European elite.

Frederick Reiter's lineage and rearing exemplify the connection between education and a sense of caste. He was raised in a tiny, mostly Christian town in Galicia. While his father's side of the family was made up of businesspeople, his mothers' relatives were "intellectuals." They included a senator and an uncle who, though deaf from a childhood accident, was sent to school in Vienna and spoke fluent German. [62] Intent that Fred focus on schooling, his parents "would not let [him] close to the business." And though he attended a Polish school, he had a live-in tutor to teach him Hebrew and special prayers. Proud of what all of his Jewish university cohort accomplished, Reiter was especially admiring of those who reached high levels of professional achievement without "background," by which he meant a mixture of economic resources and elevated cultural standing. [63]

Lydia Eichenholz, who studied medicine in Munich, came from a "very wealthy" family strongly identified with a pan-European elite. She exemplifies how strongly social class and educational aspiration were linked. Her father and his brothers, given the absence of quality schools in their hometown of Dubno, were sent to Belgium for their schooling so that they could "speak French without accent." When World War I broke out, her father, along with nearly his entire class, enlisted in the military to battle the Germans. He fought with the Belgian underground and was later brought to England, where he completed his education. Trained there as a mechanical engineer, he found that his area of expertise—the combustion engine—was little in demand in the Poland of his day, so he pursued a lucrative business in textiles on his return. Lydia Eichenholz attended an excellent private Jewish school in Rovno which had instruction in Polish and enrolled some gentile students (Czech in origin); the school offered the study of Hebrew, German, and English as foreign languages. Fifteen at the outbreak of the war—which she alone among her family survived, by passing as a Polish maid—she would likely have attended university in Belgium or France. [64]

The students generally came of age in the 1930s and thus were part of a modernizing generation of Jews in Poland. The kind of elite pedigrees sketched above—which themselves showed a growing investment in opportunities in Poland—were less and less requisite for the path toward university. Among the alumni whose parents might be termed "upwardly mobile," their grandparents, perhaps from the shtetl or smaller cities and speaking Yiddish, were typically more observant than their parents. The parents, in turn, wished that their children retain a strong sense of Jewishness but also be thoroughly exposed to secular culture. As a result the children were more strongly "Polonized," as typified by the use of Polish as their primary language and attendance (in many cases) at Polish schools. Born in 1925 in the town of Sosnowiec in southwest Poland, Henry Krystal began attending university in Frankfurt after the war. His parents, though raised with Yiddish, made a point of speaking Polish to their children so that they "could go as far as [they] could" with their education. The broad goal for the children was greater integration into Polish society.[65] Some alumni confess even limited indoctrination into Polish nationalism, despite its accompanying anti-Semitism. In one tragicomic example, Mark Hupert recalls as a teenager in Lodz feeling sanguine at the prospect of a German invasion, as the attitude among his classmates was that the Polish army was "going to knock out" the mighty German army "in a day!"[66]

A minority of the alumni describe their families as having been very religious. In the sample of the survey, roughly a fifth of the students characterized their upbringing this way, which likely meant some version of Orthodox Judaism. In cases such as that of Alex White, even Orthodox parents encouraged secular education and pursuits for their children. In others, such pursuits amounted to a rebellion within the family. At the other extreme, a near-equal portion of alumni reported that they and their families were not religious. A plurality of the students, around 40 percent, describe their background in terms that can be characterized as "somewhat" or "not very" religious. This might meant that they kept kosher only irregularly, observed and celebrated the High Holidays but did not strictly observe the weekly Sabbath, and related to Judaism primarily in cultural, ethnic, and national—not religious—terms. Reflecting a middling, if still substantial, religiosity, one alumnus reported, "We observed all major holidays, the house was kosher but I and my mother were not observant outside the house." (The father presumably was; oftentimes one parent was more observant than the other.) He "had Bar Mitzvah, some private Jewish education, [and] Hebrew lessons."[67] Toward the other end of the scale, Sabina Zimering's family went to synagogue and celebrated holidays but did not keep kosher at home, eating Polish sausages made of smoked ham—a "big sin" in Zimering's jocular description. (The sausages first entered the household at a Jewish doctor's winking suggestion, to put some weight on Sabina following a health scare, but were then enjoyed by the entire family.)[68] Joseph Taler, in another variation, reports that he affiliated with a congregation but "tried to escape from Shul on High Holidays." "[I] prefer[ed] to have," he allowed, a "personal relationship with 'Supreme Being.'"[69]

Finally, some of the alumni convey a process of secularization taking place within their own families. This might sustain a trend begun by their parents or even grandparents. Philip Balaban's maternal grandfather had been removed from a Russian secondary school by his father because the boys were not permitted to wear head coverings in class. The grandfather's dedication to the education of his own children and grandchildren stemmed, in part, from this denial. Sabina Zimering reports that her parents' paltry observance caused "big problems" with her Orthodox grandparents, who "wouldn't touch a thing" in her non-kosher household.[70] Henry Krystal's grandfather was a follower of a Hassidic rebbe from Ostrowiec. But Henry's father had already largely broken with that tradition, evident in his decisions about his son's education.[71] More than 10 percent of the alumni in the survey state that their parents were substantially more religious than they were, and roughly equal numbers indicate that they themselves became less religious over time, likely as they moved into adolescence. (One alumnus, for example, reported that he was "very" religious until the age of thirteen but "then turned agnostic.")[72] Only one student reported growing more religious over the course of his youth.

Strong skill in Hebrew, which was hardly a common spoken language among Jews in interwar Poland, was rare among the alumni. Just five of forty-seven alumni listed it as a fluent language in their youths, and for none was it primary. Most often the students had learned it in written form and for prayers in the context of religious instruction. Some, however, had extensive Hebrew instruction in school, especially if they attended Zionist-affiliated private schools. But some of them, like many other Jewish DPs, had little or no exposure to Hebrew before the war.

These data, which interviews with additional alumni reinforce, reveal that the students were not, in the main, strongly religious when growing up. Instead, most practiced Judaism in ways more common to Jews in Western European countries like Germany and rather like many modern American Jews. This quality, itself a sign of changing times, doubtless reflected their modern outlook and cosmopolitan bent, and inclined them toward their pursuit of secular higher education.

Regardless of their religiosity, all the alumni were very conscious of being Jewish. Anti-Semitism, prevalent and growing in Poland, itself reinforced Jewish identity. The students typically recollect experiencing slurs and sometimes even physical violence, sensing a climate of general—if intermittent— hostility, and at least intuiting that the future for Jews in Poland would be fraught. Affluence certainly limited one's exposure to anti-Semitism. At one extreme Lydia Eichenholz described anti-Semitism as something "esoteric" that had "nothing to do with me."[73] (Her father, hedging on the future, had set up a massive trust fund for her; nonetheless, she described her family as living "in the valley of the blind," especially with respect to the escalating German threat.) So too could the Jewish world erect protective boundaries, especially for the youngest among the alumni. Growing up largely unaware of whether they had it worse or better than Jews in other places, many describe their childhoods with basic affection, their worlds as highly local and essentially benign. For Fred Reiter, childhood was dominated by "family, family, family."[74] This seemed to him the happy essence of Judaism, which the encircling anti-Semitism could not overwhelm.

The alumni's early exposure to and involvement in Zionism varied greatly. Gaining strength as a modern political movement in the late nineteenth century, Zionism had by the 1920s and 1930s a strong presence in Jewish life in Poland. Only a minority of the alumni report negligible exposure to Zionism. For others Zionism was integral to their prewar, postwar, and even wartime identities. The founder of the Jewish Students' Union in Munich, Josef Silberman, had been a Zionist youth organizer on the political left. He, along with other student union leaders, were thoroughly grounded in Zionist politics and impressed upon both the student membership and the Jewish DP authorities the group's purported value to the Zionist cause. Alumnus Albert Genis was first raised in the small town of Plissa, Poland, before being taken by his father to Vilna to enroll in a Zionist-Hebrew "Tarbut" *gymnasium*. During the war he was a partisan in a Betar cell that fought the German occupiers. (Betar was a strongly Zionist party among the so-called Revisionist movement, which backed an educational program known as "Tarbut.") In the description of his wife and fellow medical student, Alice Genis, it was "the spirit of Tarbut that influenced him later to becoming a Partisan."[75] Mark Fintel stressed how prevalent Zionism was in cities in eastern Poland like his hometown of Rovno, as opposed to the more religious western regions. Zionism was "very strong" in his family and broader community. Most families in his circle were affiliated with Zionist organizations or parties, with the children belonging to Zionist youth groups.[76]

It is still important to remember that many of the alumni were barely teenagers when the war broke out. Even if raised in Zionist environments, they might be only nominally aware of or interested in what differentiated various Zionist ideologies and parties and how contemporary geopolitics influenced prospects for emigration and actual statehood. Henry Krystal, whose father was a local leader of a Revisionist religious Zionist organization, likened the Zionist youth group to which he belonged early in *gymnasium* to a "scout organization," suggesting a bond that was more social than political.[77] Philip Balaban's family, also in eastern Poland, was likewise "very Zionistic." His grandfather was the head of the town's main Zionist organization, and two of his uncles and aunts had left already for Palestine in the 1920s. At his "totally Israeli-Zionistic" secular Hebrew school, he learned the geography and history of Palestine (or at least a Zionist version of it). Polish felt "almost like a foreign language." Even so he confesses developing only a vague sense growing up that Palestine "is the land of the Jews and that's where we'll all end up, and everything will be like paradise."[78] Mark Fintel reports that the Zionism of his region, however passionate, had not yet evolved beyond a political and cultural orientation into an organized effort to settle in Palestine.[79]

Some families, finally, had divided loyalties, leaving their children ambivalent. Sabina Zimering's father was an avowed socialist and her mother "more Zionist." Her father would argue, in the fashion of the Bund, that "the Jews don't need to go anywhere. All we have to do is change the Polish system and we'll be fine." Her mother answered, in a typical Zionist retort, that "you are very naïve, this is easily said but the Jews are Jews, and we know how they [Poles and other gentiles] treat us, and Israel is the answer."[80] Just the power of competing arguments existing outside the family might leave one torn. Rubin Zimering (Sabina's eventual husband, whom she met at university in Munich) attended a Zionist primary school in Dubno and then a Polish *gymnasium*. In the tempest of Jewish interwar politics, he recalls, the Zionists and socialists intensely competed for "the allegiance of the younger people." Given the strengths and weaknesses of all positions, choosing among them seemed to him like "guessing blindly. . . . One day I believed one [view], the next day another."[81]

The students, in sum, grew up in a new phase of both hope and struggle for Jews. Poland was modernizing, opening up opportunities for all groups in the society. The Bund offered the promise, however faint, of a peaceable future predicated on a social revolution. Zionism kindled dreams of resettlement and renewal in Palestine. Other developments were less encouraging. The depression of 1930–35 hurt Jews as well, forcing many into manual, wage labor and exacerbating "economic anti-Semitism"—the perception that, as Jews held unfair economic advantages, political remedy was required.[82] And in 1935 the hero of Polish independence, Józef Pilsudski, died. Coming to power through a coup in 1926, he had ruled until his death as something of a benevolent despot. He was mourned by Jews, many of whom saw his rule as "the only restraint against Poland's deeply ingrained anti-Semitism."[83] After his death Polish nationalism developed a more sharply anti-Semitic edge. Among the most aggressive campaigns was one that severely limited the presence of Jews in the universities.[84] The resulting irony was that precisely as the impetus among Jews for university education was growing, opportunities for such study were narrowing. For young Jews especially, Poland on the eve of war was an unsettled and unsettling place, casting shadows on the future.

Jewish Education in Prewar Poland

The educational opportunities for Jews in interwar Poland—and hence the specific experiences of the future university students—were intimately tied up with the legal and political status of Jews. The Polish republic was created as an experiment in multinationalism. The international community, alert to the vulnerability of subnational groups, was intent that minorities have a secure and equitable place within the new society. Toward this end, it drafted under the broad auspices of the League of Nations the Minority Rights Treaty, which Poland ratified in 1919 and whose principles it codified in its 1921 constitution.[85] Centrally concerned with protecting Jews, the treaty held that "no citizen may be restricted in the rights granted to all citizens because of his faith or religious views."[86]

Polish commitment to the treaty's principles was, however, far from total. One question was just who would be made a Polish citizen. Ethnic Poles were easily granted citizenship. Others had to prove "habitual residence" in newly Polish territories. This was especially difficult for Jews in formerly Russian areas, where records were scant.[87] Another question was how to create a uniform, equitable system of law, given that large parts of Poland had previously been under Austro-Hungarian or Russian jurisdiction, where anti-Jewish laws had prevailed. In Austrian territories Hebrew and Yiddish had been banned as public languages; discrimination in Russia affected everything from land ownership, to mining rights, to taxation.[88] For years the Polish legislature and judiciary debated whether the constitution automatically annulled all prior discriminatory laws or whether new laws had to be passed repealing them. Only in 1930 was a law passed voiding such measures. The spirit of equality proved short-lived. In 1934 Poland formally renounced the Minority Rights Treaty, while legislative efforts—if mostly unsuccessful—sought to restrict the rights of Jews through such measures as a ban on kosher slaughter (couched in humanitarian terms) and means for the revocation of citizenship, similar to Germany's Nuremberg Laws.[89]

Education was crucial to the ability of Jews and other groups to retain an autonomous identity—indeed a major crucible for determining the basic character of Polish society and Jewish life within it. Through control over schools Jews could promote the Jewish languages, religion, and heritage, as well as a Jewish national consciousness. Education was also an arena for conflict within the Jewish community—a means by which to encourage secular or religious values, greater integration or Jewish particularism, and partisan politics. Finally, in its relationship to Jewish education, Poland faced a virtual litmus test for its commitment to minority rights.

The promise of autonomy with respect to education greatly exceeded the reality. The Minority Rights Treaty required that minorities "be assured their rightful part in benefits and allocations from [state] funds [for] educational, religious, or charitable purposes."[90] A separate article directed the allocation of "public funds for the benefit of Jewish schools [run by] the Jewish community."[91] The constitution declared the right of minorities to "maintain at their own expense charitable, religious, social, and educational institutions and freely use them in their language as well as practice the rules of their religion."[92] It remained unclear, however, whether the state must devote *public* funds to such institutions.

The Polish state ultimately chose not to fund a system of Jewish education, deeming Jews a religious but not a national minority.[93] Accordingly, it restricted the *Kehillah*—the centuries-old, Orthodox-dominated system of community governance—to dominion over religious affairs and very limited social services.[94] The state did establish a system of compulsory, free primary school public education in the Polish language open to all citizens, with mandatory instruction beginning at age seven and lasting six or seven years.[95] (Different schools completed varying numbers of "grades," each of which might span more than one year.) The major accommodation for Jews was the setting up of public "Sabbath schools" (*szabasówka*). The language of instruction at such schools remained Polish, and religion was studied as a secular subject, with Jews, as in the regular public schools, learning about the Jewish religion. They met, however, on Sundays, not Saturdays, to complete the six-day school week; they observed Jewish holidays and had mostly Jewish teachers.[96] Even though the education in such schools was essentially Polish, conservative nationalists still opposed them.[97]

In the interwar period some 80 percent of Jewish primary school children attended free Polish public schools (Sabbath or not), where they made up nearly 8 percent of all students.[98] The other 20 percent attended private secular schools under Jewish auspices, in which Jewish languages and themes were prominent. Conceived as a bulwark against the Polonizing effects of the state system, these schools formed a parallel world of Jewish education. They presented an array of options: Zionist and Hebrew revivalist Tarbut schools based in Hebrew; Yiddish-based schools (named collectively as "Tzisho") with ideological roots in socialism, the Yiddish cultural movement, and the "autonomist" movement promoting a Yiddish-based nationalism; [99] Jewish schools offering the full Polish curriculum, with limited Hebrew used for prayers; and, most prominently by the late 1930s, bilingual schools in which Polish was the main language but Hebrew or Yiddish were used for Jewish subjects. Finally, there were unaffiliated private Jewish schools, and *heder* and Talmud Torah schools run by the Orthodox, which in time satisfied the state's compulsory education requirement.[100]

The educational challenges for Jews were even greater at the secondary level. There was an enormous dropoff in numbers of students between primary and secondary schools; the latter were academically rigorous *gymnasia* accessible largely to children from educated and prosperous families. (In 1934–35 nearly 500,000 Jews were enrolled in primary school, but only 30,000 in secondary school.)[101] The state ran highly competitive secondary schools, which complemented the private, often prohibitively expensive, Polish *gymnasia*. In both, Jewish enrollment was functionally restricted, though nearly half of Jewish secondary school students attended these institutions. The Jewish networks also ran secondary schools, which could be attractive for financial, cultural, or ideological reasons. There were, for example, a small number of both Tzisho and Tarbut secondary schools, with the latter administering a separate "Hebrew *Matura*" that tested in Jewish history and religion. The majority of those in Jewish schools, however, attended fully private Jewish *gymnasia*.[102] These might have primary instruction in Polish, teach Hebrew along with other languages, and focus on Jewish history and religion as secular subjects. Total Jewish attendance in secondary schools— as much as one-fifth of all students—was higher than that of the Christian population.[103] In 1927–28 more than 17 percent of Jewish boys and nearly 30 percent of Jewish girls attended secondary schools.[104] (The attendance of Orthodox boys in religious *yeshivot* accounts for the skewed numbers.)

Jewish secondary schools battled for state recognition, resulting in a tiered system regulating how and where state matriculation exams could be administered.[105] Jewish secondary education was hurt by the depression of the early 1930s, which prompted a shift to vocational training, and by deepening anti-Semitism. Between 1922 and 1938 Jewish enrollment fell by 40 percent.[106]

Problems were worst at the university level, where enrollments dropped by half over the same time period.[107] In the early 1920s Jews were prominent in Poland's handful of universities, making up more than 40 percent of students in some institutions. Jewish numbers were especially large in law and medicine, which could be practiced privately, irrespective of restrictions on state employment.[108] In Warsaw, Krakow, Lwow, and Vilna, Jewish students had their own organizations.[109]

The gravitation of Jews toward university was doubtless a result of Jewish determination and the investment in learning the alumni felt when growing up. Yet the conservative National Democratic movement and its student organizations saw things very differently. Charging that Jews stole the places of Poles in professional life, they agitated in parliament for a statewide *numerus clausus*, by which Jewish numbers in the universities could not exceed the percentage of Jews in the general population. (Similar measures were pursued with respect to Ukrainians.) Though a national law failed, the movement managed to exclude Jews from various student and pre-professional associations and to authorize individual faculties to limit Jewish enrollments. Thus by the mid-1920s, a de facto *numerus clauses* was in place in some institutions. In the last years of the depression, the shrillest demands were for a *numerus nullus* for Jews. "A Day without Jews" in the universities, marked by the intimidation of Jewish students, became a popular nationalist campaign.[110] Referencing both anti-Semitism and the effects of a poor economy, one historian reports that "the deep crisis affecting Jewish youth and the intelligentsia resulted in a massive decline in the numbers pursuing an academic career and [higher] education in general."[111]

Starting in 1935–36 the "ghetto bench" system was instituted in some universities, by which Jews were confined to special seats in lecture halls. Many Jews and some of their sympathizers stood in protest throughout the classes. For their actions they were harassed and even badly beaten. One rabble-rousing leaflet asserted, "Progress, Learning, Democracy—they all sound wonderful. But what is hidden under this façade? The repulsive Jewish spirit. And this disgusting use of clubs which makes you recoil, is in fact a glorious struggle to free the nation from its Jewish fetters."[112] Supported by reactionary clergy and politicians, the campaign was largely successful. Whereas Jews represented 20 percent of students enrolled in universities in 1928–29, their numbers decreased to 11.7 percent by 1936–37. As a result of the anti-Semitic campaign, Jews numbered only 4 percent in Warsaw universities, and in Poznan none were left.[113]

"There Was Not a Big Future for Jewish Boys in Poland"

The early education of the postwar students was dictated by geography, class, custom, predilection, and their families' particular values. Academic excellence was common nearly to all. Their precise schooling, however, ranged from a strictly Polish education, to a Polish primary school followed by a Jewish one, to Polish school supplemented by instruction in Jewish languages and religion, with many possible variations within each framework. Sampling several trajectories underscores both how enduringly vital education was to the students' sense of identity and how particular opportunities, constraints, and pressures created diversity within their ranks.

Alumnus Elias Epstein, born in Radomsko in 1925, embodied the mix-and-match quality of Jewish schooling, fashioned for him by parents holding education as a supreme value. He first attended a Hebrew kindergarten, followed by Polish "Sabbath school," added lessons at a private Hebrew school, and then enrollment in a Jewish *gymnasium*.[114] For some the educational

41

path was fluid; for others it had the quality of a struggle, whether against the prejudices of Polish society or Jewish resistance to the secular world.

Roman Ohrenstein, raised in a Hasidic family in the small town of Slomniki, near Krakow, exemplifies both kinds of struggle. His father had a leather business. Neither rich nor poor, the family was nonetheless better off than so many of the area's Jews. "A Jew in Poland could not even become a [municipal] janitor. . . . But we were like worms in a bag of radishes. When the worm gets into the radishes, it's [in] paradise. Because we didn't know anything else . . . that was our life."[115]

Yet the young Ohrenstein in fact dreamed of a life very different from what his family imagined for him or which Polish society would easily permit. Though "a secular book was not allowed" in his household, he secretly read Nietzsche, Darwin, and Dostoevsky "like a thirsty person." Secular education, as we have seen, was encouraged by many Jews as a path to professional success, at least partial assimilation, and acceptance by the non-Jewish world, as anti-Semitism was least strong among the Polish intelligentsia. But religious education was a way to keep Jews "in the fold" of tradition. Torn between his defiant passions and his father's expectations, Roman got heavy doses of each: as a boy he attended public school until 1 PM and then a *heder* until 8 PM.

The choice he one day faced between two town libraries epitomized Roman's predicament. He was fearful of going to the Jewish library lest he be harassed by Poles; he was also fearful of going to the municipal library lest he be seen by Hasidim. Observed with secular books under his "Hasidic coat," he was reprimanded in his religious school. The teenaged Ohrenstein commuted at dawn to a private Jewish trade school in Krakow with a general studies curriculum, changed his clothes before going home, and then attended yeshiva. (His father would not permit him to wear the secular school uniform in the house.) Above all, he wanted to become a lawyer, the pinnacle of professions in the Jewish perceptions of his day, and even took some university courses. But here the Polish system proved the greater barrier. A teacher who affectionately called him "Spinoza" lamented, "It's too bad that you won't be able to study" in a proper Polish *gymnasium*, to which access for him was effectively barred. Before he could navigate a life course through this terrain, the war broke out.

After the war Ohrenstein's competing loyalties persisted. Although he earned an economics degree in postwar Munich, he first became a rabbi when he immigrated to the United States. Later returning to academia, he published a book on the salience of the Talmud for modern economic theory.

At the other end of the spectrum was Sophie Schorr, who had been poised to be the quintessential European professional woman. Born in 1927, she grew up in a small town outside Lwow, where her father was a beloved physician.[116] Her mother had attended a year of medical school in Kiev. The family, which spoke only Polish at home, owned a car—terribly rare for 1930s Poland—and was friendly with the local intelligentsia, which included Ukrainian clergy. To teach young Sophie the piano, the French language, and other refinements, the family employed a governess. Growing up Sophie "felt Polish," though "of the Jewish religion." It was only during the war, when she witnessed Poles "denouncing Jews for a cup of sugar [or] just out of hatred," that she "realized anti-Semitism exists" among her countrymen.

Sophie's father had hoped for a son to follow in his footsteps. An only child, she was determined to do so. "I dreamt of medicine all my life. . . . [His] office was in the same part [of town] where we lived and [when] children would cry, my mother would say to me, 'Don't you feel sorry for them?' and I would say, 'No, my daddy is helping them.'" Barring the Nazis' ascent, she would likely have gone to France, Czechoslovakia, or Austria to receive a medical education. After attending medical school in postwar Munich, she maintained both her father's professional legacy and, though married, his name. For decades known as "Dr. Schorr," she worked as an obstetrician in a small town in New York state, where she claims to have delivered nearly 10 percent of the babies.

Most of the postwar students fell somewhere between Ohrenstein's and Schorr's experiences: neither so religious nor assimilated, neither so conflicted about nor secure in their world. Felix Korn, born in 1921, represented the promise of the new Poland and the precarious place of Jews within it. His father had left the small, "very observant" Jewish town of his own youth for the "big city" of Lodz.[117] Korn's family was "traditional, not Orthodox." The father, in his son's admiring description, was a "technical genius" who became wealthy for a time from fashioning improvements in the gaslights used throughout Lodz. When the age of electricity came to Poland, he embraced it.

Felix attended an excellent private Jewish *gymnasium*, where he excelled in math and science. But it was his eldest brother, who "fix[ed] radios when nobody knew what a radio is," who most clearly inherited their father's talents. Along with a third brother, they would devour technical magazines from Germany and even, from America, *Popular Mechanics*. The image of the siblings—a far cry from the stereotypes of Polish backwardness and Jewish provincialism—is one of curious and gifted teenaged boys bonding over the latest technology like boys might do anywhere.

Yet Korn sensed that "there was not a big future for Jewish boys in Poland." To convey the anti-Semitism of his youth, he described the danger when Polish and Jewish soccer teams played. "If the Jews were close to winning, you better get out at the end, otherwise stones started flying." Asked if he had in any way felt like a Pole, Korn responded, "No way, I'm a Jew!" In his household, a "Zionist spirit" prevailed, and relatives of his had already left for Palestine. But the Zionist talk seemed to him more "a dream about the Jewish state" than anything concrete. With university study increasingly limited for Jews, the gifted Korn brothers seemed destined to work in their father's business. Ironically, postwar Germany provided Korn and other Jews opportunities for higher education that barely existed in their native land. After he earned an engineering degree in Germany, his own inventive nature blossomed in the United States, where he devised innovative packaging for major American corporations.

Isaac Minzberg, born in Oswiecim in 1921 to a deeply Zionist family, was certain that his future lay elsewhere. Having been beaten up in a Polish grammar school, he transferred for refuge to a private Jewish school, and eventually graduated from a Jewish *gymnasium* in Kielce that sent many of its graduates to Palestine. Desperate to emigrate as well, Minzberg was accepted in 1939 to Haifa's Technion University, where he was set to study engineering. The intention and even just the dream of emigrating, he conceded, were very much determined by class. Most Jews in Poland had no means to leave; Minzberg had the option by way of his grandfather, who had become wealthy selling industrial paint. (By the same token, wealth could disincline emigration, as families could reason that they had a good life in Poland.) Asked if he had intended to return, he was adamant, "There was no idea to come back to Poland. . . . And if Israel was not independent, if the British made it difficult, we would try to go somewhere else."[118] The outbreak of the war scuttled Minzberg's plan to study in Haifa and his family's hopes to emigrate.

Henry Miller, one of a small number of alumni to have attended a Polish university before the war, knew firsthand the anti-Jewish hostility in the universities. Though fluent in Hebrew from an early age, and raised by a strongly Zionist mother, Miller had his deepest roots in Yiddish culture. His father was an impresario of the Yiddish theater, owning a famous playhouse in Lublin; his household was a hub for the Jewish arts through which international performers and playwrights passed. Henry's knowledge of literature growing up was prodigious, ranging from Tolstoy to Chekhov, Goethe to Schiller. (During our interview Miller, at age eighty-two, offered to recite lines from *Faust* in the original German; his house was decorated with extremely accomplished paintings he had done in retirement.) After receiving his *Matura* in 1937 from a private Jewish *gymnasium*, he entered the law program at Warsaw University, renamed in 1935 after the late Józef Pilsudski (whose regime had, at least rhetorically, opposed the *numerus clausus*).

Decades later Miller fulminated: "[In] a population of twenty-eight million people there were four [Jewish] professors at the university [level]. Four professors, would you believe it? One had to convert to Christianity. And, in Warsaw there was no Jewish professor. No Jewish professor!"[119] Indeed, the Warsaw University community was a seedbed of the radical-nationalist organization Mlodziez Wszechpolska (All Polish Youth; MW) and especially hostile to Jews. In 1926 the school's anatomy director required that, to gain admittance to lectures and lab tutorials, Jewish students were to provide their own corpses, in violation of the Orthodox ban on dissection. In 1931 MW members severely beat Jewish students in the law faculty, prompting the university's temporary shutdown and censure from members of the university senate.[120] In Lwow, a Jewish university student was killed by nationalists. Miller personally experienced the indignity of the ghetto benches, which the university administration effectively supported. Despite this adversity, Miller completed four semesters of law in Warsaw. Just days after the German occupation, and at his father's insistence, he fled east to Soviet-occupied Poland with four of his Jewish classmates.

"What You Learn, No One Can Take It Away from You"

From the early educational odysseys of a sample of the Jewish university alumni, as well from the historical context of those journeys, several themes emerge, with implications for broad understandings of Jewish survivors and DPs. First and foremost the alumni's eventual choice to enter university in occupied Germany was clearly a function of their prewar backgrounds. After the war and the Holocaust, the students asserted deeply personal and very specific continuities with their prewar selves. Though their postwar decisions were conditioned by circumstance, their narratives are striking in the degree to which, by attending university, they resumed trajectories and achieved desires established early in life.

Second, as the students' stressed when in Germany, education in prewar Poland was a demonstrably Jewish value (though not exclusive to Jews or held by all Jews). This is borne out by the high Jewish rates of enrollment in all levels of education, as well as by strong Jewish representation in the professions. It is also supported by the alumni's recollections of the importance accorded education by their families, communities, and larger culture. That value was embedded in Jewish history and tradition but also conditioned by class, with more affluent families greatly more capable of developing and realizing educational goals. Increasingly, education was also a means for Jewish social mobility and greater empowerment within Polish society, even as Jewish schools might also reinforce Jewish identity. By a fateful irony, just as the demand for advanced education was increasing among Jews, a poor economy and rising anti-Semitism limited opportunities.

Third, attending university in prewar Poland, as elsewhere in Europe, signified far more than simply "going to college" in the contemporary sense in the Western world (whether for pre-professional credentialing or existential growth). A highly restricted—though not wholly elite—enterprise, university study often reflected and certainly conferred economic opportunity and high degrees of social and cultural distinction. Some of the alumni were already part of the intelligentsia by virtue of their families' status. Others in essence aspired to enter the intelligentsia—a functional class that would have grown less exclusive had modernizing processes continued and opportunities for Jews remained open.

There appears, in sum, a great kernel of truth to the claim of the students—made with the same vehemence by student union representatives to occupation authorities, German authorities, and the Jewish DP leadership in appeals for aid—that they represented the remnant of a historic Jewish intelligentsia seeking to renew itself and evolve. In this way they asserted a continuity that was also collective and cultural, not simply personal and psychological. A view of the postwar university students emerges as a statistically meaningful, if proportionally incalculable, subset of Eastern European Jews escaping murder who had already begun, had been destined for, or strongly desired university study. Insofar as they embodied a variation within diverse DP experiences, they reflected differentiations within prewar Jewish life.

Offering ballast in a world of great contingency, education had final value in prewar Europe, relevant to the calamity to come. Alumna Lucy Fink, just twelve when the war broke out and having survived as a hidden child, said of her motivation to study: "I grew up in uncertainty. Nobody knows what the world brings. So this is why I decided I better have some profession to lean on."[121] Raised in Russia, Sabina Zimering's mother knew well the ravages of revolution and war. "Remember," she would tell her daughter, "you can never tell what life will bring. But what you learn, no one can take it away from you."[122] These words rang true to Sabina Zimering's own experience of war and dislocation, influencing her to resume her studies as soon as she could, even if in occupied Germany.

CHAPTER 2

"You Survive Because You Survive"

Occupation, Exile, and the Holocaust

When asked to start our interview where and when he was born, Felix Korn joked, "It's so long ago that I don't remember."[1] Later struggling to recall the details of his childhood and its place in the nearly vanished world of Jewry in Poland, he broke away from his narration to say, "It's like a dream." Korn's responses evoke more than how the mists of time may cloud the memory and seem different from the kind of quip any seventy-five-year-old might make about a distant youth. Instead, they signal the overwhelming rubbing out of his origins by extreme events. Rita Schorr, the Auschwitz survivor profiled at the start of chapter 1, gave her date of birth with the month and day but three possible years, explaining that she truly could not remember, nor did she have any document to settle the question.[2]

Their comments serve as stark reminders of the extent of survivors' losses—the loss not only of a past but of future possibilities implied by that past. In broad historical terms there were a variety of alternate scenarios: In the absence of a German invasion, would Poland have come undone through competing nationalisms and reactionary chauvinism or achieved a lasting internal peace? Would its Jews have been driven farther to society's margins, or made a large-scale exit to Palestine, or attained sufficient voice to make life in Poland more bearable, even fulfilling? The students experienced the question of "what if" with respect to vastly smaller outcomes, which nonetheless help to put the monumental loss in perspective by making it more personal and tangible. Would they have fulfilled their dreams to go to university, or have a profession, or settle in Palestine? These possibilities, in their original forms, were also destroyed, no matter that some accomplished these goals after the war.

There is no way to capture the full range of the students' wartime experiences or to do justice to the suffering many endured. It is, however, valuable to describe certain qualities, as well as the broad paradigms, of their survival. Above all attention to wartime experience enables greater understanding of processes of restoration while filling out the portraits of many of the characters populating this study. The majority of the students are what can be termed "direct survivors" of the Holocaust, having endured German occupation. What stands out in their stories, as in so much testimony, is their incomprehension and fear at the ferocity of the German assault; their anguish and shock at the loss of family; their physical and psychological torment in perilous settings such as ghettos and camps; and, at an extreme, the grinding away, hollowing out, and hardening of the self. (Often woven into these stories are also moments of life-saving solidarity and compassion.) The students' postwar rehumanization, in short, existed against the backdrop of what had been for some a radical dehumanization. Sketching a sample of the students' trials during the war serves to underscore the achievement of their postwar "rebirth."

In addition, the seeds of the students' postwar unity and even their individual accomplishments are already detectable in their wartime profiles. What the students shared most crucially was their youth, meaning that they were perfectly poised between childhood and adulthood. While Jewish children were the most vulnerable—only 11 percent of those under age sixteen survived the Holocaust—the postwar students had the developmental advantages of having achieved a relative sense of personal and social identity and acquired a certain skill set (including knowledge of languages and psychological and physical resilience).[3] Increasing their chances of survival in practical terms, being young—but not too young—meant that a special vitality or Eros was on their side, enhancing their resolve and, in some cases, their resistance to a potentially fatal resignation. By their own admissions this stubborn or even naïve attachment to life and a primal faith in the future helped see them through the war and the challenges they faced thereafter.

Finally, focus on the war years illustrates how strongly education, for so many of the students, functioned as a motivator or through-line in their lives, sustained even through the monumental adversities of occupation, war, and genocide. Many were able to continue their formal education in trying circumstances such as ghettoization or deportation. For others, deprived of schooling by the German assault, the longing to resume their education was a crucial dimension of their desire to survive. The academic impulses with which they would eventually reconnect helped spur them on to live.

A large number of the students were first subject in 1939 to Soviet occupation, whether as a prelude to the German assault in 1941 or to effective salvation for the remainder of the war as evacuees or deportees in the Soviet Union. Their experiences are especially illuminating with respect to how Soviet rule affected education for Jews. The narratives of the students surviving the war in the Soviet Union both help to fill in, at an impressionistic level at least, the very incomplete picture of wartime exile and are particularly pertinent to the study of DPs. Images of Jewish survival, just after the war and among DPs, focused overwhelmingly on those who had endured German occupation. Yet the great majority of Eastern European Jews surviving the war did so in the Soviet Union. Migrating west in large numbers in 1946, they made up as many as two-thirds of all Jewish DPs, and 85 percent of those from Poland; this created an experiential divide, with resulting tensions, within the DP community.[4] The student group, as it functioned collectively after the war, illustrates how DPs negotiated the reality of dramatically different narratives within their ranks.

For the Jews of Central and Eastern Europe, the ravages of the Holocaust were slow or sudden, merely destructive or fully devastating, depending on where one lived, the will of great and impersonal powers, the choices available, the decisions one made, the cruelty or kindness of strangers, and the pains or rewards of caprice. Painfully aware of German anti-Semitism (if often also underestimating it), Jews in Germany were the first to recognize the need to escape. By the start of the war on September 1, 1939, nearly half had left Germany, and German Jews survived the Holocaust in much greater percentages than those in Eastern Europe under German occupation. With the invasion the Jews in Poland experienced a divided fate. German forces sped east, quickly taking the capital of Warsaw, systematically killing Polish elements who might organize resistance, and brutalizing Jews. On September 17, the Soviets invaded, with the two countries soon splitting Poland by prior secret agreement. The Soviets claimed territories in the east, holding more than one million of Poland's Jews.[5] The Germans annexed the northern and western territories and created the "General Government" in the south and center, over which they held control.

The division of Poland was chaotic and somewhat improvised. In the first weeks German forces advanced east and then withdrew west; the Russians did the same from the opposite direction. As a result some populations at the boundary of the two armies, such as in the eastern province of Lwow, were briefly under German occupation and then under Soviet authority. Adding to the chaos, 350,000 to 400,000 Jews fled east, preferring Soviet to German occupation, or were forced there by German efforts to clear the border areas.

Lesser numbers, more fearful of communism and the Russians, fled west.[6] And in June 1940, the Soviets took the Baltic states of Latvia, Estonia, and Lithuania, creating Lithuania as a Soviet republic in August. The division lasted until the German invasion of Soviet-occupied Poland, the Baltic regions, and western Ukraine on June 22, 1941, when the systematic killing of Jews in Eastern Europe and the Holocaust began in earnest.

The alumni's wartime experiences varied greatly based on where they fit into these patterns of war and occupation. One group was under German occupation from September 1939 until their liberation. A second was first under Soviet occupation and then German rule. Together, these "direct survivors" make up as much as two-thirds of the students. A third group was first under Soviet occupation and then moved or were exiled to the Soviet interior. A final group survived in the Soviet Union, while having first experienced the German invasions of 1939 or 1941. Some lost their parents to the Germans, and they typically lived in the Soviet Union as more or less "free agents" rather than as deportees controlled by Soviet policy. Hard to classify, this last group both suffered the losses common to "direct survivors" and enjoyed effective refuge in the Soviet Union.[7]

I begin by describing the alumni's experiences of Soviet occupation, focusing on the treatment of their families, its impact on their education, and their impressions of Soviet rule. I next discuss those surviving as deportees and exiles in the Soviet Union, highlighting the tangle of hardship and opportunity it entailed. I conclude by profiling alumni who were subjected to the full horror of the Holocaust.

War and Soviet Occupation

The Soviet occupation of eastern Poland and the Baltic states between 1939 and 1941 has a muted place in accounts of the war and the Holocaust, overshadowed by attention to the German occupation and its catastrophic consequences for Jews and others. [8] Yet the occupation has its own complex dynamic that greatly shaped the destiny of those in its maw, including many of the students.

The occupation was driven by a broad policy of Sovietization. It entailed the liquidation or takeover of governmental structures and political parties; the suppression of various churches; the collectivization of agricultural lands, expropriation of businesses, and effective takeover of cultural institutions; the mass arrests of Poles, Ukrainians, and other nationals as political and class enemies; and the deportation, often ending in death, of hundreds of thousands of these "enemies" and forced laborers into the Soviet interior.

The endgame was more or less total Soviet domination, which grew more urgent as fears of a German invasion mounted. At the end of their brief reign, the Soviets carried out mass evacuations as part of a broad military strategy to survive the German attack. Though everywhere feeling its effects, the populations experiencing Sovietization seemed hardly aware of its overall design and implications.

For Jews the consequences of the occupation were mixed. The great majority received, at the very least, a reprieve from mortal persecution. Many Jews actively cheered the Soviet army as it swept in, especially in places like the eastern provinces of Poland where the German military had been. Many others, on the left and among the working class especially, embraced the Soviets not just as their protectors but as ideological and political allies. In new administrative structures Jews were strongly represented, prompting long-standing charges of Jewish "collaboration" with the Soviets.[9] Most important, Soviet occupation for hundreds of thousands of Jews meant escape from the Germans throughout the war. Some were conscripted into the Soviet army or the Soviet-sponsored Polish army.[10] Many more—up to 100,000 just among the Jewish refugees from western and central Poland—were deported as "class aliens" into distant areas in Siberia and Soviet Central Asia.[11] Others were evacuated or themselves fled east. The resettlements, which came in stages, were driven by ideology, the fierce pressures of war, and complex ethnopolitics, not the desire to provide sanctuary for Jews. (One historian remarked that he could find "no evidence that in 1941 the Soviets had any policy which was based on the special peril created for the Jews by the Nazi invasion.")[12] Nonetheless, for most of these Jews they proved lifesaving.

By the same token Jews were subject to wide-ranging repression based on politics, ideology, religion, and, importantly, class. The leftist Bund was branded intolerably "revisionist," Zionism a form of bourgeois colonialism, and Orthodox politics anathema to atheistic communism. Though linguistic policy varied, Yiddish was generally accepted as a secular "socialist" language, while Hebrew, considered a language both of religion and of Zionism, was essentially forbidden. Jews in industry and large-scale trade were commonly deemed "class aliens," subject to expropriation, arrest, deportation to gulags, and, death. The evacuations of "laborers" could be swift and callous. In evacuations undertaken just before or after the German invasion, by which point many Jews *wanted* to go, priority was given to "comrades." In transit and when resettled, exiles suffered the often mortal hardships of disease, hunger, and the cold. Perhaps most damagingly, the Soviets decimated Jewish leadership structures, political organizations, institutions, media, and social networks, as it had done with the non-Jewish populations. Without these, some scholars have argued, Jews could neither stay adequately informed about the looming German threat nor, when the Germans invaded, organize a mass escape.[13]

Education policy embodied the good and ill of the occupation. Schooling quickly became universal, public, and free through the secondary level, if partly as a means of indoctrination. Eager to incur loyalty, and fulfilling the Soviet constitution's mandate for the instruction of ethnic groups in their "mother tongue," the Soviets set up a system of Ukrainian schools for the Ukrainians, Byelorussian schools for the Byelorussians, and so on.[14] Jews were provided, at least in principle, instruction in Yiddish where a locality's parents requested it.[15] Yet the schools met on the Sabbath, and the curriculum was manipulated to praise communism and suppress Jewish history and culture deemed ideologically suspect.[16] The existing Jewish school system was largely dismantled, with many schools—especially those based in Hebrew—simply shutting down. Many Jewish parents, by 1941 especially, wanted their children to attend Russian-language schools so they would have some chance of social advancement within the Soviet system taking root. All the changes, finally, were so rapid as to often make real education difficult or even impossible. A number of the alumni recount that their school was one day in Hebrew, shifted to Yiddish, and just as suddenly switched to Ukrainian or Russian.[17]

The diverse fates of the alumni under occupation reflect the complexity of its design and consequences. One's experience depended greatly on where—and who—one was. Marion Glaser, born as Marion Landau in Berlin to a German-Jewish father and a Protestant mother, was among those who fled east before the war started. In 1938, with the situation deteriorating even for "mixed" families, Marion's left Berlin and resettled in the Lithuanian town near Kovno where her father had been raised. From the age of twelve, she had wanted to be a doctor, and she pursued her studies with zeal, including during the occupation. She repeated her twelfth grade in a Lithuanian *gymnasium*, with the promise from her parents that she could then complete her matriculation in a superior school in cosmopolitan Kovno. The move to Kovno proved lifesaving, as her father's hometown was soon overrun by the Germans and its Jews wiped out. In Kovno she completed her last exams on June 20, 1941, two days before the German attack, and just before the Soviets completed the deportation of many of Kovno's Jews. Yet her parents, as Germans especially fearful of Soviet exile, thought it better to be under German occupation and declined the chance to leave. The family was soon placed in the Kovno ghetto.[18]

The wealth, social standing, and expertise of many of the students' families made them both vulnerable to Soviet punishment as "class aliens" and useful to their occupiers. Sophie Schorr's father, the doctor in provincial Lwow, was friendly with clergy, doctors, and attorneys within the local Ukrainian intelligentsia. The Germans briefly occupied Sophie's town in late September 1939, arresting and killing members of the intelligentsia, including family friends. Likely part of the notorious *Intelligenzaktion*, the assault sought to decimate potential kernels of local resistance by attacking the intelligentsia and other elites. The Germans also began terrorizing Jews, and she and her mother narrowly escaped the SS.

Soon the Germans withdrew and the Soviets came. The Soviets, in Schorr's telling, "treated us poorly because they thought my father was a very rich man," perhaps based on his ownership of a car.[19] The family's home was seized, and they were pushed to the edge of town. Nonetheless, there was a great need for physicians, and her father was employed to organize a hospital. On the whole, the occupation was a period of relative calm for the family. Sophie, age twelve when the war started, continued to attend school, and even skipped a grade.

The cultured nature of the alumni's families—and especially their ingrained view of Germany as representing the pinnacle of European cultural achievement and refinement—caused some to badly misapprehend the nature of the German threat. Just prior to the second German invasion, the Soviets offered to allow Sophie's family to leave. The father, raised in Lwow under Austrian rule and fluent in German (as well as Ukrainian, Polish, and Hebrew, and well-trained in Latin and Greek), still thought the Germans "too cultured [to] commit atrocities," no matter what he had seen during the first invasion. He, like Marion Glaser's father, refused the offer. Though strongest among elite families, the view of the Germans as civilized was widespread among Eastern European Jews, including those in the Soviet Union.[20]

Genuinely wealthy families might fare both better and worse under the Soviets. After the invasion the lucrative textile business of Lydia Eichenholz's father was seized, and prominent Jews were arrested. But the father, trained as an engineer in England, was conscripted to help build a road, with Polish POW labor, eastward from Rovno. Other engineers were quartered in the family home. The language in Lydia's school in Rovno immediately switched to Russian, which she had fortunately learned from the family's Russian maid. She and her classmates "did not take seriously" the heavily ideological instruction, focusing instead on the well-taught subjects of math and science.[21] She soon switched to a public school in nearby Dubno, where there was no instruction in Hebrew or in religion. A savvy teacher, however, wove Jewish history into lessons on the Roman empire. Merely a decent student in the much bigger Rovno school, Lydia "became a celebrity" in her new, more provincial one. Frankly, she confessed, she was "more interested in boys" than in studying, conveying how adolescent preoccupations could survive the new circumstances. Sick with malaria, her father was not able to bring the family east ahead of the German invasion. He was soon executed by Ukrainian guards, with Lydia taking eventual refuge as a Polish maid.

Robert Nenner, from the city of Lwow proper, spoke ruefully about the Soviet occupation. His father was extraordinarily wealthy from the leather trade, directing four hundred employees and dealing extensively with European companies. He owned a six-story home, two cars, and a horse-drawn carriage, which brought him to work each day. He also was a philanthropist, helping to build a synagogue and fund a hospital in Lwow; he later paid vast sums in efforts to appease the Soviets and to aid other Jews. In some respects highly assimilated, Robert first attended a private Catholic school, whose instructors were nuns, and learned fluent Polish, Ukrainian, and German. He was also tutored three times a week in Hebrew and Torah study.

Just a teenager when war broke out, Robert initially greeted it as an exciting spectacle. Yet soon after the Soviet takeover, he saw the family's tailor "riding on a horse with the Soviet Army" and looking coldly at him.[22] His mother explained that the tailor "is now the commandant in the area." Hitherto a secret communist, the tailor, like others among the Jewish "working class," was elevated to a local potentate. Betrayed to the Soviets by the tailor, Robert's father was arrested, and an uncle killed, with no explanation. Freed after two months by means of a bribe, the father "was very down. . . . [His] whole demeanor changed completely. I would say everything changed in the house." At first Robert clung to a boyish enthusiasm. He loved, for instance, wearing "the [Soviet] red star on my jacket, like any American kid wants to wear the American flag." When he saw "the look on [his] father's face" upon seeing the star, Robert removed and hid it.

The climate of intimidation affected the whole community. "I still went to school, quote unquote. Because I had to go to school. But even the teachers were frightened. They were not sure what to teach. How to teach. And suddenly, we got a class in Leninism and Stalinism . . . total, total propaganda. . . . There was a fear in the street, there was a fear in the stores, there was a fear in school." Routine pleasures soon disappeared, as a local football field became a military installation. "At home everybody talked in a whisper. And there was no smile, nobody smiled anymore."

The Soviet control of news deepened the sense of isolation. "We didn't know too much about the west. You must understand, when the Soviets came in, everything died. No information, no newspaper, no nothing. The only thing you knew is the glory of the country, the glory of the communists, the glory of the proletariat." Soviet communism, Robert concluded, offered "the people" mostly petty power and the license to be ruthless. Workers "still had to go to work, they didn't get better clothing, they didn't get better food, but they were in charge." Even so he wishes in retrospect that the Soviets had "taken [him] to the reeducation [camps]" in Siberia and far away from the Germans. His father, in his description, "paid his way into the grave" (though the family ultimately survived), likely meaning that he bribed the Soviets *not* to be deported east.

Philip Balaban's family offers an example of how one might be both persecuted and then saved by the Soviets. The military commander of the region was quartered in the Balaban house, leaving the family one room and half of the kitchen. His father's business partner urged the family to leave for Romania and then go to Palestine, as some Jews were doing. But the father, the eldest in his family and not wanting to abandon his parents, declined. He was arrested on March 10, 1940, ostensibly as a "class alien," given the family's affluence. The family "never heard from him again."[23] The Soviets, in Balaban's telling, were "not very astute" in terms of whom to arrest, and likely apprehended his father simply to fulfill an arrest quota. Uncles of his, no less "guilty" by the terms of Soviet ideology, had fled to a neighboring city and were left alone (only to be later killed by the Germans). Three days after his father was taken away, the family was deported to Kazakhstan, where they spent the remainder of the war.

Deportation and Exile

If the Soviet occupation of Eastern Europe has a muted place in histories of the Holocaust and the war, the mass transfer of Jews from these territories into the Soviet interior speaks still more quietly. For decades the picture of internal Soviet policy was dominated by official state histories, which stressed Soviet sacrifice and beneficence. Equally important, Jewish DPs themselves marginalized the experience of Soviet exile in accounts of Jewish survival.

Only recently has a full-length treatment been published, Rebecca Manley's *To the Tashkent Station: Evacuation and Survival in the Soviet Union at War*, on the Soviet Union's wartime movement of population. Though primarily concerned with the resettlement of Soviet citizens in the summer and fall of 1941—and not, therefore, with the prior deportation of many Jews and others as putative state enemies—the work describes the logic and patterns to great swaths of resettlement policy. It thus provides valuable context for understanding the eastward flight of Jews and the odysseys of individual alumni.

In Manley's telling the resettlements were part of an earnestly conceived yet horribly managed policy of nonpunitive evacuation in the face of German invasion. The overarching goal of the program, taking shape just before the June 1941 attack, was not to save population per se. Rather it was to protect productive, military, and administrative capacities, as well as to relieve the pressure of feeding large populations in cities such as Moscow.[24] The plan was to evacuate managers and skilled workers, the party leaders, cadres, and intellectuals thought vital to state administration, men of military age, and, as possible, women and children. Yet those tasked with organizing the evacuations themselves often fled, as did countless people not designated as potential evacuees. Party privilege often determined who evacuated.

Amid the chaos, and given the existing policy of punitive deportations, it was difficult for individuals and families to know quite where they were being sent, under whose orders, and for what reason. Manley asserts a "slippage between evacuation and deportation [in the] official mind" of the Soviet state and in practice. The resettlement zones overlapped, and both tactics were used as means of population redistribution and for the maintenance of "social order" and "security."[25] In deciding what to do, potential evacuees might agonize over whether to view resettlement as expulsion or refuge; a sign of defeatism and even disloyalty or a prudent retreat to save the nation; a greater or lesser risk than German bombardment or occupation.[26] As to the Jews, Manley asserts that they, "although evacuated in substantial numbers as party members, workers, writers, and the like[,] were not evacuated as Jews," and that no special attention was given to the threat posed to them by the Germans.[27] For all its problems of design and execution, the policy brought to relative safety and with remarkable speed millions of people at a time when the German military was routing the Red Army.[28]

The dearth, until recently, of Jewish accounts of survival in the Soviet Union is its own complex story. In an illuminating article, Laura Jockusch and Tamar Lewinsky attempt to explain the relative silence among DPs about this history.[29] The first Jewish DPs, they note, had been liberated in German and Austrian territory, having survived camps like Dachau and the death marches. This kind of survival dominated their own understanding of the recent Jewish experience, and quickly exerted dominance over other narratives. Moreover, the early DP leadership, especially the heavily Zionist Central Committee, was largely composed of "direct survivors" such as these. They sought to honor Jewish sacrifice and, importantly, to present to the international community images of both Jewish vulnerability and defiance in hopes of winning sympathy for the Zionist cause.

The exiles themselves recognized that their hardship generally paled in comparison to what those under German occupation had endured, and were reticent to proclaim their suffering. Perhaps above all, politics were at play. In postwar Poland, prior to their transit to occupied Germany, exiles were loath to describe experiences that might include criticism of Soviet communism (as Poland itself was falling under its sway). And exiles eager to immigrate to the United States concealed having spent time in the Soviet Union so as not to arouse suspicion of communist affinities. Only somewhat recently, with the collapse of the Soviet Union and the broadening of Holocaust research, has Jewish survival in the Soviet Union come into sharper focus, partly through a proliferation of memoirs about time in the Soviet Union.[30]

The Jewish students, at the time and in the years since, participated in limiting recognition of Soviet exile. As we will later see, in Germany the student group was almost totally silent about the recent past. Some lied to US occupation authorities, claiming that they were in German camps, and not in the Soviet Union, during the war. They may have also lied, at the height of the Cold War, to US immigration authorities suspicious of any interaction with Soviet communism. Still anxious decades later about possible repercussions, some alumni declined in interviews to talk at all about the war years.

Most alumni who spent time in the Soviet Union spoke, however, with candor about their exile. They found in it both salvation and adversity, new opportunities for community, friendship, and learning, but also the suppression of their religion, the loss of basic freedoms, and the dramatic rerouting of their lives. To a striking degree the pursuit of education served as a guiding thread through their experiences and memories of exile. And though critical of the Soviets, whose occupation claimed countless lives, they also express gratitude for their safety and Soviet resistance to the Germans.

"I Went to School, I Had Some Friends"

The Balaban family, we have learned, was deported in March 1940, presumably as "alien enemies." Though Philip Balaban was just twelve at the time, his memories of exile remained vivid sixty years later. The family was first placed on cattle trains, fifty to a car of the so-called echelons, which took three weeks to reach the destination of Kazakhstan. They were then taken by truck to survey the houses of locals in which they could board, likely at the order of the government. With resourcefulness and grit, the deportees found that eking out a decent existence was possible. Up to the German invasion in 1941, the family was permitted to send letters home to Poland and to receive care packages twice weekly with up to eight kilograms of food, clothing, and other goods, which the Balabans then bartered. Among the items was clothing belonging to Balaban's father, with whom the family vainly hoped to reunite. Given a plot of land, they planted potatoes, whose harvest yielded a year's supply.

Philip's mother, trained as a pharmacist, also provided for the family by trading vodka—an essential currency at a time when money was "meaningless"—lifted from a nearby training base for Soviet pilots. In the summers Philip worked for a shoemaker, crafting soles from old rubber tires. Paid in bread and perpetually hungry, he recalls running home more than two miles so as not to eat the valuable commodity on the way. He earned, in addition, a liter of milk by tutoring his classmates in algebra.

Throughout, the children's education was a priority for his mother. "Wherever you were during the war, no matter what happened, how bad it was, hunger and disease and whatever, I had to go to school. No matter where. She always found a school for me to go." He described the education—notwithstanding the mandatory lectures on Stalin and Lenin— as "very good. . . . Very science oriented. Much better than it was in Europe at the time." "It was cold and hungry," Balaban concluded. "But, it wasn't bad for me. I went to school, I had some friends."[31] Isolated from news, Balaban, like many other Jewish exiles, had no idea for the entirety of the war that the extermination of Jews was taking place.

Frida Karp, born in 1925 and raised in a Polish town near the Lithuanian and Russian borders, had a similar experience. The town was first occupied by the Soviets, who seized her father's building material and agricultural supply business, arrested him as an "undesirable element," and soon shipped the remaining family by train to Krasnoyarsk Krai in central Siberia. The father never returned. In Siberia she worked on a collective farm and attended school, recalling that the local population was friendly to the family, despite knowing its official status as state enemies.[32]

For others finding refuge in the Soviet Union, the German threat had been more imminent and the quest for education no less strong. Academically gifted, Rubin Zimering earned the reputation of being one of the "top students of all the schools" in the region of his hometown of Dubno.[33] When his father, a hops-processing expert, was unemployed for a spell, Rubin supported the entire family with money he earned as a tutor. Initially falling under the period of Soviet occupation, during which he finished *gymnasium*, Zimering gave great credit to the Soviets for offering free, universal education and liberally providing scholarships for university study, which was his goal. When the Germans invaded, his family fled to a nearby river with others engaged in what Soviet officials referred to as "spontaneous self-evacuation [under conditions of] panic." A rumor briefly held that the Soviets would provide arms for the men to fight the Germans as an untrained militia. Rubin continued east into the Ukraine, but his parents stayed behind, and were later killed by *Einsatzgruppen*. Their reasoning had been that young males were especially endangered but "women, children, older people like my parents" wouldn't be mistreated by the Germans.

Amid this dislocation and uncertainty, Rubin felt his "greatest hope [lay in] not interrupting my studies," earning a degree, and preparing for a career after what he and others optimistically assumed would be the Germans' relatively swift defeat. He made it to Stalingrad and entered a technical university to study physics, winning a scholarship based on his good grades and the Soviets' need for young talent to serve the state. At the university he became a "big hero" for his academic prowess, completing his program with lightning speed.

Conscripted into the Soviet military in 1942, Zimering put his engineering knowledge to use in building defensive fortifications and later designing bridges. He fought the Germans as an opposing army, not as his genocidal persecutors, but later learned through the contemporaneous stories of "the best writers" in the Soviet press of German atrocities against Jews. He wound up stationed with the Soviet army in the town of Auschwitz just after the nearby camp was liberated and cleared of its inmates.[34] So vivid were the press accounts that he was hardly shocked when he saw the camp for himself. Throughout his ordeal, he remarked, "My salvation was in school." Accepting his duty to help defeat the Germans, Zimering nonetheless considered his service in the army "on a personal basis . . . a big loss for me because I interrupted my studies for three years."

For Georg Majewski the war, as conveyed in his memoir, was likewise bookended by German invasion and military conscription, but his journey in between was significantly different. The Majewski family initially fled their hometown of Ciechanow, Poland, but soon returned to face German rule. "We still believed in the Germans. We saw in them the people of Goethe and Schiller, the people that we knew."[35] The family was later murdered by *Einsatzgruppen*. Majewski pushed east not long after the initial German occupation in 1939, and eventually helped to liberate Berlin with a contingent of the Polish army consolidated in the Soviet Union.

Majewski's wartime existence was peripatetic, coursing through areas of Soviet control and the Soviet interior. Whatever his initial thoughts of the Germans, Majewski had quickly decided that he "could not live under th[eir] cruel tyranny" when he fled.[36] (On a work detail, a German had put a gun to his head, threatening to shoot.) Settling briefly in Vilna, he stayed with underground cells of the leftist Zionist group Hanoar Hatzioni, soon landing in the tranquil setting of Zosle, Poland. He left six months later, reasoning that there was little chance, if he remained in Zosle, that he would attain his goals of emigrating to Palestine, meeting "single girls," or, most of all, continuing his studies. (He recalls also that "Jewish communists" were "betraying" the Zionists to communist officials.) Returning to Vilna, he attended university full time, despite not being able to prove, as per the requirement of the Soviet state, that his parents were "proletarian."[37] Majewski remained in Vilna until July 1940, working at the YIVO Institute—the center that later relocated to New York City and to which the Jewish students in Germany eventually sent their records. At YIVO Majewski catalogued works of Yiddish folklore in preparation for their shipment abroad. Devoted to preserving the memory of Eastern European Jewry, the center soon fell under the control of the Yiddish section of the communist party (*yevsektziya*), "whose aim," it seemed to him, "was to destroy Yiddish culture."[38] Majewski's university diploma, written in Russian and Lithuanian, had the status of an official document and came with the injunction (which he ignored) that he was not to live in cities of greater than 100,000 people.

The day after the German invasion of Vilna, Majewski left for the USSR. Thus began an odyssey that would take him from Minsk to Borisov, Smolensk, and Moscow, to the "ethnic" areas of Tashkent, Kuibyshev, Semyonov, Astrakhan, Alma-Ata, Ashgabat, Yolotan, and finally to a prison in Altaiski Krei in central Siberia. Throughout he saw refugees of all descriptions (including many Jews) who made the Soviet Union a land of displaced peoples long before the crisis faced in postwar Germany. He traveled mostly by train, adopting the intricate Soviet system of bribes (in which vodka was the premium currency), observing how people at each layer of state control attempted to evade the watchful eye of the higher authorities, and learning how to avoid the notorious NKVD. Spending time with Tatars, Tajiks, Kyrgyz, Kazakhs, and Uzbekis, he also learned their long history of ethnic persecution, deportation, and the gulags.

He came closest to leaving the Soviet Union when he tried to cross into Afghanistan with the aid of Bukharan Jews, only to be captured by the NKVD. (The paid smugglers had sold the group out.) Sentenced to three years of labor in Siberia, Majewski served his time with enemies of the Soviet state from Russia and elsewhere in the Soviet Union before being released to fight with the Polish army as an artillery specialist. He arrived in the

Majdanek concentration camp one month after its liberation, having until then heard nothing of the extermination of Jews. Majewski's memoir pulses with incessant motion but with little inflection of emotion—especially about his murdered parents—as if the force of rapidly moving events overcame his ability to absorb their meaning.

A final group of the students survived nearly the entire war, with their families intact, in Soviet exile. Born in 1927, Guti Kanner was among the many Sephardic Jews (rare elsewhere in Poland) in the renaissance-era city of Zamosc.[39] Her father, who had died before the war, had practiced law, although without a diploma, and her mother was an enterprising seamstress. As a young girl Guti felt great sympathy for those less well-off and briefly fell in with a small communist youth group. The Germans occupied Zamosc for only a few weeks, after which the family crossed into the nearby Soviet Union.

In the summer of 1940, they were taken in the middle of the night for deportation to Siberia. There Guti attended a proper Russian school outside the work collective into which the family was placed; "day and night" she read classics by Dostoevsky, Tolstoy, and Pushkin. Her teachers, from Moscow and Leningrad, were "excellent." Having brought her sewing machine and bags of zippers from Poland, Kanner's mother earned valuable income, keeping the family well fed. After the German invasion in 1941, they were released from the Soviet work collective and free to travel. (The Soviet Union at that point restored diplomatic relations with Poland, whose government was in exile in England, and released many Polish nationals.) The family settled in Fergana in Uzbekistan, where a Polish army-in-exile was assembling. There Guti lived with more than a dozen other relatives. She stayed in Fergana until the end of the war, thereafter going to university in Tashkent, "not because I wanted to study medicine [but] because I wanted to be without [my] family." On the whole, Kanner reports, "we didn't suffer much."

Soviet exile, as some alumni testify and scholars have documented, could entail significant hardship, from the shortage of food, medical care, and proper housing to disease, physically demanding labor, the stigma of classification as a state enemy, the resentment of the local population, and political persecution.[40] Jockusch and Lewinsky conclude that "many thousands [of Jews] died as exiles or evacuees." They also report that exiled Jews, when not functionally censored, typically express ambivalence about their experience, given the Soviet Union's "dichotomous role as both savior and victimizer."[41] The alumni's reflections have this quality.

As we have seen, the Soviet occupation, during which repression was direct and systematic, could be more trying than evacuation and even deportation as a class alien. Some alumni judged the Soviet Union primarily within the overall context of the war. Among those fleeing, Rubin Zimering likened his regard for the Soviets to that of the Allied powers in the West: the sense of being united against a common German enemy, and grateful for the immense wartime effort. He stressed the Soviet commitment to education. And, describing literary Russian as the most beautiful among the nearly dozen languages he acquired, he seemed able to separate Russia's richly poetic culture from the capricious Soviet system.[42]

For others this contrast came as a disturbing revelation. In his travels Georg Majewski met a highly educated Kazakh woman whose husband, a communist party intellectual, had fallen victim to the purges. She and other Kazakhs described things "that did not fit in at all with what I had read of Russia in the works of Sholokhov and Pasternak. They taught me about everyday life under the Soviet regime, about exiles, the pattern of morals, murders, the burning of villages, the shooting of peasants and the annihilation of almost the entire Russian intelligentsia."[43] Majewski, in sum, was acutely aware that the Soviet Union was not a monolith but instead a tapestry of diverse peoples and interlocking legacies of persecution.

Henry Miller, a student in postwar Munich, lost both his parents in the initial German invasion but himself made it to Lwow, where he attended a Russian university until the second German attack in 1941. He wound up thereafter in Kazakhstan, where he met his wife and led a decent life. He concluded that the Russians were "good people" under a "horrible" system.[44] Frida Karp described "the average Russian people" as "really good souls." Having seen Russian evacuees from Leningrad arriving in Siberia "dead and dying," she observed that the war was "terrible" for "the Soviets [and] not for us." Guti Kanner had what she considered a more or less "normal childhood" thanks to the Soviets. She and others understood well the immense sacrifices they made in fighting the Germans and confessed no bitterness. "We laughed at Stalin, but we didn't hate him," she explained. An experience in Israel, where she settled after leaving Munich, underscores that regard. In Jerusalem in the 1980s she attended a performance of the famous Red Army Choir—representatives of the officially "anti-Zionist" Soviet Union. By its end, those in the audience of her generation, so many of whom had been saved by the Soviets, were in tears.[45]

"You Have Strength Because You['re] Young"

Most of the alumni did not escape German persecution. Those in central and western Poland, under German occupation from the start, typically experienced the squalor and dangers of ghetto life and worked as forced laborers until June 1941. Some lived in hiding or "passed" as Christians by using false papers, while a small handful joined partisan groups. With the June 1941 attack, the deportation of Jews in these territories to concentration and death camps began. Those in Soviet areas were forced into the desperate task of avoiding liquidation, whether at the hands of the *Einsatzgruppen* or through the process of ghettoization, deportation, and mass extermination now begun in the east.

In many respects mirroring the broader DP demographic, the alumni deviate significantly in their wartime experiences. Whereas up to two-thirds of Jewish DPs had survived in the Soviet Union, only a third of the alumni did so. So important is this datum for understanding the group and its place in the DP community that a brief account of my estimate is in order. One data set is drawn from the survey I circulated. Sixteen of forty-six respondents (35 percent) report that they survived the war not under German occupation. This did not mean, however, that they escaped entirely the German onslaught. Three of these (Mark Fintel, Rubin Zimering, and Georg Majewski), as I learned in interviews, first lived under German occupation and lost their parents in the genocide. Ten of the sixteen report the deaths of "all" (2), "most" (4), or "some" (4) of their family members at German hands, and several indicate having been in ghettos or in hiding prior to Soviet exile. I know as well—from interviews I conducted, personal conversations, and other definitive sources (such as memoirs)—the wartime experiences of another twenty-seven of the alumni. Of these, eight survived in the Soviet Union. Combining these figures with the survey results, twenty-four out of seventy-three alumni—almost exactly one-third—lasted the war outside of German occupation.

Two-thirds of the alumni were therefore "direct survivors," even by narrow definitions, of the Holocaust. Their narratives span the myriad ways—broadly familiar to the world through countless memoirs, testimonies, histories, and other representations of the Holocaust—by which Jews survived. Amid the range of their experiences, recurrent themes emerge that are the focus of my treatment of a handful of their survival stories.

Youth played a central role in their survival, though exactly *how* youth figured into that survival, their experience of it, and their outlook on life varied enormously. Important as well is their sense of coming from somewhere and belonging to something. Being part of a family is at the center of their stories and defines the tension between continuity and rupture, even when the family was lost.

At one extreme, Fred Reiter remained in the protective bubble of his family throughout the war. His hometown of Zurawno was under Soviet occupation until June 1941. Though viewed by the Soviets as an "enemy of the people," Reiter's father was judged too important to the small community to be either arrested or deported. When the Germans invaded, the family was saved from a liquidation operation by a friend in the Ukrainian clergy. For the next two years they hid in a tiny ditch in a farmer's stable, over which cows spewed their filth, and they subsisted for long stretches on a single potato a day.

Fred rebelled against this demoralizing isolation: "I felt after a month, my God, my few friends are still [aboveground] and I'm under a cow, that's crazy. Daddy, please, I want to go out."[46] His father, who made periodic forays aboveground, relented, and the two were soon captured and taken to a mountain slope to be shot. But the Jewish town butcher, who had also been captured, ran down the hill, drawing the Germans' attention and permitting the escape of Fred and his father and their return to their hiding spot. Warding off hopelessness and his parents' protectiveness during his time in hiding was a constant challenge. "My mother, [like a] typical mother, wanted to prepare me that we are going to die. . . . I didn't want to hear that. I said, 'I think about living.'. . . Plus, funny thing, I was so curious to know how the world will look after the war." In Reiter's own account it was only after liberation, as a student in Krakow and then in Munich, that he really saw the world and grew into an autonomous adolescent.

The role of the family also loomed large in the survival of Sophie Schorr. In 1939 the Germans briefly occupied her town near Lwow, during which she was witness to her mother's courage. The two sought refuge with a Ukrainian priest, but an SS man entered the priest's house and confronted the mother: " 'Do you know who I am?' and she said 'No,' and then he pointed to his collar [with the SS pin] and said 'Don't you know what that is? . . . We are SS, and we kill the Jews.' So she said, 'Well, go ahead, I'm a Jew.' "[47] The SS man, so taken aback at the mother's audacity, spared her life and instructed her to keep her family hidden.

The German reoccupation provided Sophie another defining image, this time fully terrifying. "My father had a friend who went to medical school with him, who lived in a neighboring town. . . . [He] had a six-year-old child, I believe a girl. . . . The Germans came to look for the Jews, they took the child by her legs and tore her in half in front of her parents." With the family now ghettoized in Lwow's "old city," the fate of the little girl loomed large in Sophie's sense of her own future. "It was probably 1942 when we knew that we are all going to die. And my parents were very anxious to send me away to a safe place. . . . I was a very obedient daughter. And I thought if I go away at least my parents won't see me die the way they did the friend's child." Here family roles reversed, as the child—acutely aware of her elders' near-powerlessness—struggled to emotionally shield the parents.

The entire family survived, mostly hiding separately and, for great spells, unaware of each other's safety. During her ordeal Sophie was exposed to the worst and the best in people. In a town outside Lwow, her parents had paid a Polish peasant to hide her two cousins. But the peasant betrayed the boys to German authorities. The local German policemen refused to execute the boys, known to them as "Dr. Schorr's nephews"; during the town's early occupation, the Germans had themselves been treated by the Jewish doctor. To resolve the matter, a policeman was called in from out of town, and he killed the boys the following day. Years later the Schorr family returned to Poland, exhumed the boys' bones, and gave them a proper burial.

By contrast Sophie was saved by a Catholic woman named Roma, who took her into hiding out of a sense of Christian duty. Roma's anti-Semitic mother did not know Sophie was Jewish, saying in her presence, "What a wonderful thing the Germans are doing, getting rid of the Jews so we don't have to dirty our hands." After the war, Schorr attempted to have Roma declared a Righteous Gentile at Israel's Yad Vashem, but with her mother now dead, she lacked the necessary second witness to Roma's compassion. In Munich Schorr dedicated her doctoral dissertation both to her birth parents and to her "war parents" (as child survivors often dubbed their adult saviors), which included Roma and one other savior.

Rochelle Eisenberg, born in 1929 in a small Polish town, provides an unusual example of the redemptive bonds of family and of the Holocaust as an oddly sheltering experience. Her father owned a grain mill that "employed half the city."[48] With the German occupation in 1939, her formal learning ended, but instruction still continued in her house, which became a makeshift school. At the house the neighborhood children were divided by age and subject matter, and lookouts stood at the windows, as the Germans forbade even private study. By paying bribes the family survived several liquidation operations and went to work in an ammunition factory. They later escaped a nighttime selection near the factory, as the father had paid to have his wife, son, and daughters work the nightshift. Accompanying her father during a subsequent selection, Rochelle survived by sneaking into the group chosen for work. Asked how she had such savvy at such a young age, she replied, "I don't know, I probably didn't have any philosophy, I just had the instinct of survival. And we were very devoted to one another and the family, everybody did everything for everybody."

In August 1944 the family was sent to Auschwitz. As they completed the journey partly on foot, Rochelle's youngest sister "gave up" and was "practically carried" by her mother and sisters. The father and brother did not survive the cattle cars. Learning of their deaths from other inmates, the sisters concealed the news from their mother, lest she be crushed. In Auschwitz the sisters and their mother slept side-by-side and shared what little food they had. As a true family they complemented the numerous "camp families" formed by female inmates in which strangers united for physical and emotional support. Rochelle's mother and youngest sister, in her telling, failed Auschwitz's last selection in November 1944, just before an order was delivered to evacuate and dismantle the gas chambers. Rochelle was put into what she described as a "starvation camp" within the complex and later made to carry away the bricks from the crematoria, which she took as a hopeful sign of the Soviets' advance. Rochelle and her surviving sisters were among the very small number of children and young teenaged survivors of Auschwitz.[49]

Looking back, Eisenberg sees that when under German capture her identity was totally subsumed within the collective. "You were not your own person, no . . . you were a family, you were a group." Not until several years after the war did she even want "to have my own identity and be by myself and independent." She took a remarkably gracious attitude toward the brutality she suffered: "I never felt after the war [that] I would like to avenge myself. I just vowed that I would never be like that."

For Reiter, Schorr, Eisenberg, and a whole group among the alumni, the Holocaust was an experience of radical dependence on the family and other adult protectors. For them the war years entailed their arrested growth; the drama of individuation and autonomy commenced to a great degree only afterward, when they were students, giving their new lives the quality of first awakenings. And for those whose parents survived, continuing their education was typically the fulfillment of an active familial wish. These students thus embodied continuity not only with their prewar lives but also with living legacies.

Many of the alumni, however, were older—late adolescents or young adults, though as yet unmarried and without children. Their survival was conditioned by a separate dynamic, their youth an asset in other ways. They, by contrast, were thrust into a garishly isolating maturity. What they most sought after liberation was a sense again of human connection and solidarity, much in the fashion of the orphans drawn to postwar *kibbutzim* that Avinoam Patt describes. Their postwar education was often the extension of a different kind of legacy—one based in the memory of deceased family.

For Jews facing the German onslaught, family ties could be a liability. Grandparents and younger siblings were most vulnerable to starvation and disease; they were more likely to be deemed unfit for labor and "selected" for death. Yet parents were also vulnerable as the caretakers of the very old and very young or by virtue of social, economic, and emotional attachments to home, both of which limited possibilities for fleeing to safety. Young adults were not, beyond a certain point, dependent on their parents for survival (though the parents were often instrumental in their initial escape or hiding). Conversely, no one was dependent on the young adults, save, in select cases, much younger siblings. Although against great odds and even in places of hideous confinement like Nazi camps, they could make it on their own as free agents whose autonomy gave them options others lacked.

Indeed, a pivotal moment in so many of the alumni narratives is when this qualified autonomy became fully realized through their separation from their parents or by learning of their parents' deaths. Always traumatic, such moments were typically followed not by conventional grief—circumstances would hardly permit it—but by a stunned, instinctive resolve to go on. Mark Fintel, age seventeen when the war broke out, lost both parents in a liquidation operation in Rovno. He explained, "Obviously the first shock, finding out that my parents were dead, was a very difficult shock. And it probably took several months to get through that idea. But then we had to fight. . . . I think the strength of being, of wanting to live and being alive and having to do something . . . is an overwhelming, overwhelming force."[50]

Mark Langer and his family, residents of Stanislawow, Poland, were forced into its ghetto in 1941. In the first month the Germans shot and killed 12,000 Jews at the city's Jewish cemetery. A week later Langer, suspecting that his parents were among the dead, went to the site. There he saw two mass graves and a pile of documents taken from the victims. The first item he pulled at random from the top of the pile was the identity card of his father.

Langer kept the card in the ghetto until the Germans took it from him. He did, however, manage to keep throughout the war other pictures of his parents, his birth certificate, and his *Matura*, earned in 1939. Surviving as well was his stubborn hope that he "will someday need it."[51] This was indeed the case in postwar Munich, where having proof of his matriculation allowed him to enter university with relative ease. Langer's narrative and its symbolism are striking. He suffers first the murder of his parents, who had hoped he would pursue higher education, and then the loss of an emblem of his father's identity. But other documents, secreted through years of persecution, helped him to keep an image of his parents alive and to realize, through his university career, their wish for him. He thus experienced a deeply personal continuity with a shattered past that so many of the parentless Jewish students shared: with their postwar studies, they honored their parents' values and memories, remaining dutiful sons and daughters even when cast into an unsettling independence.

For Alex White, of Krosno, Poland, the intellectually precocious son of an Orthodox father, the separation from family was still more wrenching and the sense of legacy more directly communicated. In the last phase before his liberation, White survived by working in the "factory" of Oskar Schindler.[52] Of thirty-four immediate family members, only he and two other males survived.

The family's glass business had been seized in 1940, with its wares sent to Germany. In May 1941, as Germany's preparations for its attack on the Soviets were in full swing, the business was ordered to help build a ghetto in Krosno. The family survived a "resettlement action" in August, soon learning that close relatives were among the 3,500 Krosno Jews gassed in Belzec or shot. The massacre prompted Alex's older sister to suggest that the family obtain cyanide from a local druggist and take the pills if they were separated. "No, Mania," Alex objected, "even if only *one* of us survives to tell the story to the world, it is worth it." He privately wondered if "selfishness" and a simple "fear of dying" were behind his protest.[53]

Alex's mother and sister were rounded up when they were lured out of their hiding place in the Krosno ghetto by the Gestapo's false promise that they would issue them work permits. They were later killed. His eleven-year-old brother, Heniek, sobbing and begging, was taken away from him and his father during the December 4, 1942, liquidation of the ghetto. After working in a Luftwaffe labor camp for a year, Alex and his father were next shipped to the notorious Krakow-Plaszow camp. In May 1944 his father failed a selection and was soon taken to Auschwitz.[54] Alex's father, "in complete clarity about his fate," gave him a gold coin and the final injunction to "be a *mensch*, a good human being. 'Don't be stubborn, be considerate of others, and be honest.' "[55] To "be a *mensch*" served as White's guiding aspiration in his life thereafter. He made good use of his mental gifts, earning a medical degree in Munich and building a career in internal medicine in the United States.

Maintaining a sense of connection to the past, harboring hopes for the future, and retaining a consistent sense of self were not, however, always possible. Isaac Minzberg's education and intelligence quite literally spared his life in Auschwitz, and in that sense his survival was an extension of his prewar self. Yet his experience was also so devastating that it shook the foundations of his identity, which he, like many of the alumni, had to dramatically reclaim.

With the German invasion, Minzberg was sent to the Kielce ghetto, whose liquidation in 1941 claimed his family. Decades later, the horror of this event is inscribed in Minzberg's elusive telling of it: "All the people went to Treblinka. You heard of Treblinka? So you know the story. And Treblinka was, I was left alone. . . . Left my parents. My grandparents. My sister. My cousins."[56] Minzberg uses a shorthand both to convey information quickly and to mute—with a descriptive minimalism in which place (Treblinka) stands for death—his jarring memories. Ambivalent about his survival, he frames the annihilation of his family both as their abandonment of him ("I was left alone") and his abandonment of them ("Left my parents").

In 1942 he was sent to Auschwitz, where he was told by a German-Jewish pharmacist that he had to have a trade, prompting him to claim he was a locksmith. As for so many other intellectually minded Jews, it was the false claim of some *practical* skill that extended his chances of survival. Yet when Minzberg began work under the supervision of an actual German locksmith, the situation reversed. The locksmith was a poorly educated family man who quickly saw through Minzberg's ploy. As the German military situation deteriorated, he approached the clearly educated Minzberg with a German newspaper and asked him to report on what it said. Minzberg recounted its tales of German valor and victory, when the locksmith interrupted, " 'What the paper says I understand. I don't need you to tell me. What do *you* think?' . . . So I told him . . . 'the Germans have lost the war.' " Until the camp's evacuation, Minzberg served as the locksmith's confidant, reading between the lines of German propaganda and advising him about how to keep his family safe as the Soviets advanced. In return the locksmith gave him bread, kept Minzberg's secret, and tried to shield him from death.

Yet Minzberg was hardly spared the camp's cruelties. Interned in a section for young males, he recalls,

> Every day, they killed one or two or three boys. And they shot them, it was horrible. It's unbelievable. If I, sometimes I wake up at night, I don't believe that I could stand it. But so what, I was young. . . . [The] future belongs to the young people. I lost a whole family. And, I, I was thinking sometimes about suicide but I had no means to kill myself. So I got up, and I got a piece of bread and the soup, and that's all, and then when you walk to the factory. . . . On the way they were shooting and killing inmates. . . . You expect any day that you may die or you may be killed. . . . But you live, you young. You have strength because you['re] young.

His disjointed words express a dual disbelief: first, that what he was experiencing was actually happening, and second, in the shock of broken sleep, that he could endure it. In fact he could not so resolutely stand it, as

69

evidenced by another "doubled" memory. Minzberg confesses intermittent thoughts of suicide; but he also implies, with an abrupt shift in temporality ("So I got up"), that there was a literal *moment* of suicidal reckoning, uneventfully ended by his reentry into the camp's stream of living death.

His explanation of why he "got up" contains a final ambiguity, which reinforces an uncomfortable sense of the enigma of survival under such conditions. Minzberg offers two plausible, partial accounts for his resisting suicide: that he simply lacked the means, and that, as a young person, some elemental life force rebelled against the thought. But he over-reaches with the bromide that "the future belongs to the young." His own testimony suggests that, beyond a certain point, there was no "reason" for his going on, save as an inert response to a world of routinized horrors.

Asked if anything like hope existed, his answer ended in outright contradiction: "I don't know if you have hope. . . . [W]e knew that there's the Jewish people in Palestine [and] in other parts of Europe. There were Jewish people in Asia and Africa, so on. So you thought if you survived, if your parents are not more here, that you go, you emigrate somewhere. But you didn't think that way, nobody was thinking for the future. [It] was a question of survival, every day was a question of survival." Here an image of continuity shifts to one of oblivion. Prior to the war, he had dearly sought to go to Palestine or some other haven. Even in Auschwitz, he first claims that this was a sustaining hope. Yet in the next stroke, he concedes that the whole idea of the future had vanished.

Minzberg never quite gave up, but he did at last give out. On a death march from Auschwitz, he refused orders to push on while at a Nazi sub-camp in Blechhammer, Germany. Asleep on a straw mat, finally indifferent to his survival, he woke to find the SS gone and himself free. But the damage done was severe, leaving his identity in crisis. Though he had attended Sabbath services every Friday and Saturday growing up, Minzberg emerged a nonbeliever. "The war convinced me this is all the imagination. I don't believe God exists, I'm sorry to tell you." His doubt extended not only to his faith but to his very Jewishness. By the time he returned to Poland, he was convinced that he no longer wanted to be Jewish or marry a Jewish woman. He explained this to a friend of his grandfather's, who counseled, "You got to change your accent. You have to change your belief, everything." Minzberg then realized, "I cannot run away from the Jewish people."

Minzberg's recovery of his roots was rapid, modeling how the self can be rebuilt from extreme ruin. In 1945 in Poland, he married a Jewish woman he had known before the war. He also recommitted to the Zionist cause, helping to organize a kibbutz in Kielce that prepared Jews for migration to

Palestine. The Kielce pogrom of July 1946, in which a female cousin of his was among the massacred Jews, convinced him to leave Poland. Studying medicine at the time in Breslau (a German city taken over by Poland after the war), he sought the aid of the Bricha to bring him to the American Zone in Germany, where he continued his university career. He finally settled as a doctor in Chicago, after first going to Israel. As to his faith, he came to feel that "men need God" for ethical guidance, and he takes great pride in his commitment to ethics and the relative absence of vengeance among Holocaust survivors.

"You Survive Because You Survive"

Robert Nenner, also a medical student in postwar Munich, provides a final profile of the Holocaust's destructiveness, additional perspective on the relationship between ruin and restoration, and an indication of how, for the students, education was integral to their renewal. As was the case for Minzberg and others, liberation saved Nenner from the absolute brink. Unlike Minzberg, however, he had no inclination to retroactively see or posit continuity with prewar ambitions, even as he experienced that connection. Indeed, what is perhaps most instructive in Nenner's testimony is how little reconciled he is to his wartime experience. His brutal honesty may thus serve as a reminder of just how young the student survivors were—apt to feel disdainful of their persecutors, cheated by life, and failed or even betrayed by their parents and other Jews. He neither accepts evil nor feels it mitigated by intermittent goodness, nor does he derive any contrasting ethic from it that might balance his anger and shame. Not necessarily a truer rendition of survival, his testimony nonetheless articulates feelings and perceptions that others in his survivor cohort surely felt and struggled to repress, rationalize, and even overcome. It therefore frames the challenge of existential restoration, of a postwar rehumanization, with special power.

In 2002 Bella Brodzki and I met Robert Nenner, a tall, imposing man in his late seventies. Retired from his cardiology practice, he lived in a spectacular seaside condominium in Florida. Greeting us there, he remarked, "It's a waiting room," threw his arms open, and added with a warm smile, "but at least it's a nice waiting room."[57]

His greeting set the tone for his early testimony, which stressed the caprice of warring powers and had the cast of the tragic-absurd. Asked where he was born, he explained that the city had no proper name: it was Lemberg when part of the Austro-Hungarian empire, Lwow when part of Poland, Lviv as a Ukrainian city, and L'vov when under Soviet occupation. He admitted to being "a spoiled brat" in his childhood, as evidenced by family trips to Paris and vacations on the Caspian Sea. Members of the Polish intelligentsia, frequent visitors to his household, would bring him gifts. Cocooned in privilege, Robert had grown up with little inkling of the anti-Semitism around him.

A theme throughout his narrative was the futility of his parents' efforts to protect him with their love and money, and the rage this caused. "You must understand the Jewish psyche. Everything was spoken, but always exclude the youngsters. . . . The famous statement [was], 'It doesn't affect you.' But it did." From the Russian occupation on, fear, incomprehension, and a boyish rebellion against circumstance dominated his existence. With the German occupation of Lwow in the summer of 1941, things grew far worse. Stripped of its fortune, the family was placed in the Janovska ghetto, where the poorer inhabitants soon began dying on the streets from hunger. Asked if he pitied his parents for their powerlessness, he confessed, "From a kid's point of view, you were not sorry. You were overwhelmed. . . . You blame your parents, if you want to [know]."

Breaching the ghetto's barbed wire, the young Nenner was caught by Polish sentries and "beaten up to hell." Inside the ghetto violence also came from other Jews—those of the *Judenrat*, charged with enforcing the ghetto's laws and filling Nazi work orders. "I was very upset that I am there. Why? No, really, why? I challenged that, and I was beaten up by the guards. By the Jewish guards." His anger turned back to his parents: "You ask why, you ask how come? But there's no answers. Your mother says, 'Take it easy, my dear.' 'What the hell, take it easy? Take it easy for what!' And you're young, and you want to fight back. . . . There was always a group of guys who wanted to fight . . . but the parents used to say, 'Don't do that. Don't do that, they are hooligans.' But they were not hooligans. They were people who wanted to fight."

Nenner was soon captured by the Gestapo, which was making a sweep of the ghetto, and sent to a work camp "with no goodbye to my parents, nothing." A darker descent had begun. The camp was "cold blooded. . . . You were the enemy. I was the enemy. I was a kid and I was [the enemy]." His duties included clearing dead bodies, prompting another punishing refusal: "I just got fed up. So what. They hit me with a [rifle] butt in my face and they knocked out all my teeth." A cruel itinerary took him briefly through Theresienstadt and Auschwitz to Buchenwald, where he lived for fourteen months until his liberation. "When I wind up in Buchenwald, I felt like a hardened criminal."

The brutality of his new setting and his survival within it seemed to pass beyond his comprehension; his testimony now ranged from uninflected descriptions of horrible things to anguished recollections of a moral abyss:

As a youngster you really don't understand it that much. You know you'll die but dying is not an issue. Dying is a condition. And you saw people dying, and you know they're dying from hunger. You saw people being shot. So they were killed. But you never feel . . . that you [will] be killed. . . . And then I worked in Buchenwald, in the infirmary, as they called it ["Another waiting room," he conceded]. . . . It was nothing. I used to steal bread from them. Because I know he'll die. So should you take his portion and eat so I can survive? . . . You felt that somehow, some way life will go on. But you don't know how, you didn't know how, and you didn't know why.

His narration jumps from the second to the first person and then blurs the two. He subtly detaches from his own experience ("you saw people dying"), then claims it ("I worked in Buchenwald"), and then poses a dilemma dreadful in the abstract but which for him was real—"should you take his portion . . . so I can survive?" His tearful, paralytic breakdown soon occurred during the interview, clearly prompted by his confession to others—perhaps for the first time in his life—that he had stolen bread from dying "patients" in Buchenwald's "infirmary." Mentally returned to the "gray zone"—that place described by Auschwitz survivor Primo Levi where all options are self-annihilating or corrupt—he cannot think his way out, only collapse in confusion and remorse, even as he knows his "theft" does not amount to conventional guilt.

He elaborated on the condition in Buchenwald, and on his condition: "You are animal. Numb. Totally numb and totally animalistic. And you live because of the inborn, like animal[s], they live. You put the animal in slaughterhouse, did you ever look at their eyes? I went to look at it. I felt the same way. I found friends. I looked at friends, in the slaughterhouse." Confused by this shifting image, Bella and I quickly learned that in the United States after the war he had actually gone to a slaughterhouse to see perhaps less a metaphor for than a re-creation of what he had experienced, epitomized by his solidarity with the doomed animals. Asked if, as a medical doctor, he had since developed any sense of how he held out physically, he marveled, "I don't know how my bones survived. Because where the hell did I get the calcium . . . the iron for my hemoglobin . . . the proteins to form the matrix of the body?" When researching weightlessness for the US Air Force in the 1960s, he in fact became obsessed with the physiology of extreme deprivation—an obsession he traced to his past.

Pressed to account, in the last instance, for that survival, he broke form to address me directly, as if confiding the answer to a profane mystery:

Jeremy, you have no idea what life can do to you. And it's not the will of living. It's the anatomy of living. It's the physiology of living. You function. You function as a unit of brain cells, eye cells. . . . You don't think, you can't think. Thinking is a luxury. . . . The survival of the human body is not a body, it's the mind. And what keeps you going is there is something within your system that says, "Let me get over that hurdle. Let me see what's down the road." Why, you don't know. How come, you don't know. But I think it's more a physiological function than . . . [a] psychological function. . . . The next step is always, maybe something will change . . . maybe tomorrow I will be able to get his piece of bread. Maybe tomorrow, I'll . . . you don't think like I or you think now. There is, this doesn't exist. . . . If you ask me the definition of a survival, I will not be able to give you. Because there is no such thing. . . . You think about the morsel that you can get. You think about . . . not tomorrow as tomorrow, but tomorrow as later. There is no tomorrow, it's later. That's how I can only explain to you. . . . You don't care [about pain]. . . . You walk practically without shoes, you don't feel the cold. You scoop the snow because it melts in your mouth. Because it's something that will melt in your mouth. You find a grain. You pick it up. Because it's food. . . . You hate everything. You hate everybody. ["Yourself included?" I ask.] Yes. For what you do [to] survive. That you don't help anybody, that you live in a total denial . . . intellectually you never survive. But what you survive is, physiologically, I call it. You survive because you survive.

He offers of course no final answer to the mystery—only the suffering impression that the body propels the mind, through some essentially material mechanism, to fashion the faint hope of change. That hope, in turn, both transcends the body—as pain is now absent—and sustains it. The whole image ends in a starkly poetic solipsism in which survival is its own cause and its own end.

Nenner does provide, however—with the image of "tomorrow" eclipsed by "later"—a potent sense of the Holocaust's worst ruin. By this image the Holocaust is a sin not only against humanity but against nature: the destruction of the fundamental unit or form in which expectation, hope, and the concept of the future exist; but also the negation of the most basic symbol or instance of organic renewal. "Believe me, when the tomorrow came," he added, "you didn't believe it." Against all odds, his parents too had survived, although in other camps. Meeting them by chance in a displaced persons camp, he first embraced them only cautiously for fear that "they're a mirage, that they will disappear."

Nenner's imagery also frames the postwar recovery, linking to a symbol of his fellow students. Beginning in 1946 the Jewish Students' Union in the American Zone published a newspaper. Under the name *The New Life*, the second issue had as its masthead logo an open book over which rises a brilliant sun.[58] The graphic radiates symbolism: learning as the basis of life; the survival of Judaism, rooted in the study of texts; the existence again of tomorrow, of the future, and the students' power to author their own lives; the closing of a chapter of loss and the opening of a new one.

It is that chapter to which I now turn.

CHAPTER 3

"We Create"

The Origins and Evolution
of the Jewish Students' Union

Whether spun as legend or presented as history, stories of social origin are often steeped in personality and place: a charismatic founder seizes the opportunities of a particular setting to create a community that attracts, defines, and empowers many others. In this way a contingent event born partly of chance takes on the aura of destiny.

No contemporary account of the founding of the Jewish Students' Union in Munich exists, and no longer is anyone available to reconstruct with precision the moment from memory. What does exist in the textual record is very much a legend wrapped in the trope of heroic origins. It is conveyed by Munich alumnus and early Union leader Yehuda Knobler in the introduction to a posthumously published collection of essays written for the Yiddish DP press in Munich by his close friend Josef Silberman, the Union's founder. Silberman died of leukemia in Israel in 1951 at age thirty, after having emigrated there and briefly served at the Israeli diplomatic mission in Paris. Written in Hebrew and published in 1952, Knobler's account reads:

> During the winter of 1945–46 rumors passed among the young people in the major [displaced persons] camps in the American Zone of Occupation in Germany that something will happen to improve conditions [there], to prepare young adults for university study. The address was: Munich, the Central Committee for Jewish Survivors. . . . Young men and women continued to arrive at the halls of the Jewish Committee to register in lists designated for the revival of academic careers. . . . Many hopes were initiated by the dry copies of the lists from the earliest registrations. Hundreds of young

people left them in front of a Joint [Distribution Committee] official. . . . One by one they returned without a response, but in their hearts now existed a splinter of hope for "the possible."

And in the corridor stood a young, round-faced man, snowflakes on his dark hair, eyes sparkling with life and intelligence, a kindly smile on his face. . . . "Excuse me please, what is your name?" Supplied by him with a piece of paper, they left the Committee building with a hand-written card in their pocket, and on it was an address and the name of the young man—"Joseph Zilberman."

Joseph Zilberman . . . established and organized the Jewish Students Union in Munich. For hundreds of Jewish students in the displaced persons camps—survivors of concentration and extermination camps, those who revealed themselves as Jews after destroying Aryan ID papers, repatriated exiles from temporary refuges—a home base and independent organization was established, a group to lead and represent them. . . . The organization strengthened the spirits of hundreds of young people, made it possible for them to stand up straight, function with normal industriousness, and achieve great things in the midst of a wandering life.[1]

This chapter tells the story of the origins and early life of the Jewish Students' Union—not as legend, but as history. Part of the task is to reveal what little is known about Silberman, to explain the meaning of the organizations and events referenced in Knobler's narrative, and to fill out the very intricate picture of the circumstances from which the Munich Union emerged. My account continues with how the group was formally established, how word of the Union percolated among survivors, and how it navigated the institutional terrain of postwar Munich.

But more than that, this chapter explores the Union's structural predicates or conditions of possibility—what had to be in place for the Union to take shape. The essential elements were a system of care for DPs; the concentration in Munich of Jewish survivors and a group among them aspiring to study; educational opportunities for them; their identification with their Jewish peers and their desire to form a collective as Jews; leadership and administrative talent on which to draw; and a network of institutions to whom they could appeal for both material and moral support. Behind these conditions exists a whole universe of relations and processes defining the immediate postwar period. The story of this small group's founding, by extension, is a way to engage the grand narrative currents of the war's aftermath, from postwar migrations, to Allied policies, to the building of occupation institutions, to the self-organization of DPs, and to the varied efforts of Jewish survivors to construct a future while in a stateless limbo. In addition, focus on the students reveals the way in which these currents were shaped and experienced by individuals and groups—the meaning "on the ground" and at a human level of various occupation policies and the challenges faced by Jewish and other DPs. Some of what the Munich group experienced was specific to the local milieu; other aspects transcended the setting, and therefore speak to the fate of students elsewhere in Germany and to occupation and displacement more generally.

Several themes run throughout. The broadest is the relationship of liberation, defined by extreme instability and dislocation, with displacement, in which those qualities persisted but in reduced form. For the Jewish students and other DPs, postwar existence was a constant process of negotiation in pursuit of personal and group interests; the raison d'être of the Union, like countless other DPs associations, was to project strength and clear a path for purposeful work and a restored future. Displacement entailed also the destabilization and reconsolidation of identity. For the students this meant both a new experience of Jewish solidarity and the articulation of the place of the students in their sense of Jewish history, collective life, and aspiration. The very construct "the Jewish student" was at once a comprehensive individual identity and the basis both for group cohesion and for a set of claims within the occupation scene. In the group's founding rhetoric and early dealings, however, one can already see the tension between the concrete commitment to university study and the Zionist imperative demanding urgent dedication to nation-building in Palestine. The identity the students embraced, in short, created new dilemmas.

In reconstructing the Union's origins, I emphasize the material, political, and institutional infrastructure of "the new life" and the means by which individuals became part of a group narrative. Yet the students' efforts existed against the backdrop of hardship and loss that were deeply personal. An additional, essential condition for the Union's formation is therefore what one might term the young Jews' "existential readiness" to take on the challenges of their new lives. Understanding that preparation entails focus as well on their mental and emotional states and how these informed the students' collective pursuits.

UNRRA and the UNRRA University

Among organizations helping Europe's displaced persons in the western zones, none initially played a more forceful role than the United Nations

Relief and Rehabilitation Administration. For Jews especially, who were largely rendered stateless by the war, UNRRA was an essential benefactor, along with the American Joint Distribution Committee (commonly referred to in official documents as the JDC and called by the DPs simply the "Joint"), an American-based private Jewish charity that invested vast resources in helping Jewish DPs. UNRRA first made university study possible for the young Jews by creating a university of its own, while the Joint soon provided indispensable advocacy and aid.

The United Nations Relief and Rehabilitation Administration was established by the Allied governments in November 1943 in anticipation of the humanitarian crisis that would surely follow Germany's defeat.[2] UNRRA "teams," made up of civilians from many countries, came in just behind the US and British militaries as they invaded North Africa, France, and then Germany, and began relief operations even before the German surrender. Active also in the Mediterranean and China, UNRRA had its most extensive operations in Western Europe, where the displacement crisis was most severe. More than 6,000 UNRRA personnel worked in western Germany in December 1945, with the number rising to more than 7,000 in June 1946.[3]

UNRRA's work consisted, in the main, of helping to establish and run the "assembly centers" for refugees commonly known as "displaced persons camps." Most urgently, this entailed the provision of medical care, food, and clothing, and efforts to reunite separated family members. The political goal, desired by and possible for some DPs but not others, was their repatriation. By the war's end in May 1945, 500 such camps had already been established in the American and British zones, and more than one million refugees had been returned home.[4] Official responsibility for administering the DP camps in the American Zone was given over to UNRRA on October 1, 1945, though the military continued to be involved in their supply, security, and staffing.[5]

As the camps evolved, UNRRA also made great investments in their internal organization and culture, facilitating work and education programs, recreation, press activities, and the building of family life among DPs. Both to relieve its own administrative burdens and to empower the DPs, UNRRA generally encouraged initiative and self-organization among the camp populations. Displaced persons themselves, sometimes hired by UNRRA or other agencies, had important responsibilities in the camps.

The US Army entered Munich on April 30, 1945. UNRRA immediately played a prominent role in the occupation of Bavaria and its capital, helping to run the many DP camps in the Munich environs. Its base in the city was the German Museum of Technology and Industry, known as the Deutsches Museum. A massive, imperious structure, it had been, like so many buildings in Munich, badly damaged during the war. Just weeks after the German surrender on May 8, the facility was designated by the US Army as a "D.P. Transient and Information Center" and put in the care of UNRRA Team 108—an energetic group that responded with great empathy to the population it served, as evidenced by the surviving record of its activities and the remembrances of one of its principal members. Initially providing basic care to convoys of DPs, the center by midsummer 1945 boasted an array of services, including employment and tracing bureaus, legal advising, a translation office, and child care, with regular excursions to the Munich zoo for the children.[6] The center also served as a hostel and billeting office, providing short-term housing to nearly 700 refugees, among them many Jews, from more than two dozen countries. By September 1945 the center received more than 1,500 people per week from throughout the American Zone and beyond, most of whom were searching for their families, employment, or transfers to different DP camps.[7]

The American welfare officer Susan Pettiss, who later published a book detailing her time with UNRRA, conveyed in a field report the crush of human need in the endless questions that greeted staff: "'How can I get a pass to Coberg?' 'Where do I register to live in the city?' 'I am looking for my mother-' 'Who will feed my horses?' 'How can I get to America?'"[8] Another exasperated team member observed that the center "was flooded with a tremendous influx of Infiltrees [as DPs crossing from Eastern Europe into the American Zone were initially designated] at any time of the day and in any numbers," and fed up to 1,900 people for breakfast.[9] Confusion often reigned over whether "to admit a man or woman who claims to have the right to come in and who throws in the face of [the] billeting D.P. Officer a bunch of certificates . . . adorned by all sorts of pictures, signatures, rubber stamps and fingerprints."[10] In the recollection of one alumnus who was part of the refugee influx, the center seemed "a mess of disorganized, crowded, confused, and homeless humanity."[11] Its achievements, moreover, were relative, and not necessarily apparent at first blush. Visiting the facility in December 1945, the Joint's education official Jacob Jaslow described the Deutsches Museum as a "dismal, badly damaged building . . . where no formal program of any sort is possible."[12]

Yet the center had already become a hive of activity—including educational pursuits—among DPs. By midsummer it featured a barber shop; a cafe with waiter service, beer, and live jazz and classical music (as well as a growing reputation for black market activity); a theater and a chapel; tailoring and leather shops and other cottage industries; a lending library; and the publication of a US military–sanctioned newspaper, the *DP Express*, with

Exterior of a registration booklet for the UNRRA University. (Courtesy of Roman Ohrenstein)

material in six languages. The museum also housed the offices of DP organizations. Among these was the early headquarters of the Central Committee of Liberated Jews in Germany (often shortened to Central Committee, ZK, or CK)—a powerful, strongly Zionist group that formed in the war's immediate wake to quickly become the overarching Jewish authority among Jewish DPs.[13] Pettiss reports that the center's "strength and life blood flows from the Displaced Persons staff"—Poles from Dachau and others who, without pay, "plan and operate" under team supervision "all the Center's activities." Together the UNRRA personnel, the DP staff, and the center visitors transformed the museum from "a place for relics" to one where "life passes through" and where refugees could begin to regain "self-confidence" and "self-respect."[14] As part of this process, students and professors among the DPs lobbied for university classes in the summer of 1945, which gave rise to informal lectures and limited courses being offered in late summer, formal lectures in early September, and a full-fledged university by February 1946.

Interior of the UNRRA University registration booklet of Roman Ohrenstein, first issued for the Winter 1945 semester. (Courtesy of Roman Ohrenstein)

The Deutsches Museum has an iconic status in the memories of many Jewish DPs, for whom it might have been the first place they went on arrival in Munich and the tangible origin of a resurrected life. This is especially true for many of the Jewish students. Perhaps several dozen were among UNRRA's first unofficial "class," taking courses in the fall of 1945 before the university got its formal start.[15] From this core developed the idea of a Jewish Students' Union. As of June 1946, the heyday of the short-lived school, 117 of the Union's members attended the university, making Jews a small but determined part of its student body.[16] For some, it was what first drew them from neighboring DP camps to live in Munich proper, or to Munich from other cities in the American Zone, or even to the zone altogether from Eastern Europe. A number of the alumni saved and prize their UNRRA registrations—handsome booklets with the UNRRA University seal, their photographs, and the lists of courses, examinations, and grades, with their professors' signatures.

UNRRA initially had no intention to found a university. Rather, the school came about through the more or less spontaneous union of students (or people of student age) who wanted to study and professional teachers who wanted to teach again. Munich had long been a center of learning and home to many intellectuals. After the war it had a high number of intellectuals among area DPs, whether by simple virtue of Munich's large DP population or the gravitation of intellectuals to the city. In the summer a group calling itself International Academic Self-Help set about trying to register professors and students. By mid-August approximately 800 DP students and 70 professors had been identified.[17] This process kindled the creation of actual classes, which was realized when the Deutsches Museum staff agreed in August to dedicate two rooms for lectures and help administer enrollments. Central to this effort was the DP staff chief Walter Hnaupek, a Pole who had been interned for four years in Dachau, where he organized cultural activities among the inmates. Hnaupek had an engineering degree, fancied himself part of the intelligentsia, and worked hard to create an academic milieu at the Deutsches Museum.[18]

The subject matters of the first formal classes beginning in September were largely a function of the specialties among available professors and not any grand curricular design. Most courses were in the sciences (experimental physics, thermodynamics, inorganic chemistry, etc.), though there were also humanities courses (French and German literature, ethics, etc.) and language instruction in English, French, and Spanish.[19] Approximating the structure of a proper university, the school was loosely divided into "faculties" (within the European system the term denotes something between departments and separate colleges). As of September 11, it had 986 registered students, of which 471 had registered with specific faculties. Most were Lithuanians, Ukrainians (although of Polish citizenship), Yugoslavs, and Poles—groups comprising a great percentage of DPs as a whole.[20] DPs from these countries may have suffered persecution at the hands of the Nazis, the Soviets, or both, and viewed the American Zone as a refuge from the Soviet-dominated communism descending on their homelands. Some among them, however, had entered Germany voluntarily as laborers or had actively collaborated with the Nazis (potentially in the commission of war crimes), and thus resisted repatriation out of fear of retribution. In a shocking revelation in February 1946, the Ukrainian president of the university's student council was exposed as a former SS member.[21]

Doubtless reflecting its mix of students, the university had both an anti-fascist and anti-communist character, but also an uncomfortable, collaborationist undercurrent given that some of the students had aided the

Nazis during the war. The first registration lists have no designation for Jews, for whom religious/ethnic identity was now more important than national origin, though Jewish students may have nonetheless been grouped by nationality or amalgamated under "stateless." This latter category was generally adopted by Russians wanting to stay in the zone (something neither the Americans nor the Soviets favored) but was also imposed on some Jewish DPs or even embraced by them as a means to separate politically from their co-nationals.[22]

UNRRA's initial student population had diverse purposes in attending. For some the classes represented the continuation of interrupted university careers. Others likely used the lectures as *Abitur* instruction so they could qualify to attend an established university in Germany or elsewhere. Others still perhaps simply craved the intellectual stimulation. Possessing a "real thirst for knowledge," and "seeking to make up as best as possible for what they had missed," the UNRRA students likely shared many of the same basic motivations as the Jewish students.[23] Many non-Jewish DPs—the so-called political persecutees—had also been interned in concentration and forced labor camps, had their youths stolen, and wanted to reconnect with their passions.

By late October plans emerged for a formal university, complete with a rector, codified faculties, and proper degrees.[24] The early, somewhat chaotic lectures had given way to a "winter semester," with different categories of courses to meet students' diverse needs. (European universities typically had a winter term stretching from fall through late winter and a summer term stretching from spring to late summer; the UNRRA University calendar approximated this structure.) Registrations had billowed to 1,500 people, though the numbers registered exceeded those who were accepted by screening committees. This number, in turn, exceeded those actually enrolled in classes. And 570 students were attending what UNRRA officials described as "refresher courses to prepare [them] for more advanced study when a fuller program can be implemented," not college classes per se.[25]

The challenges were many, causing the center to scale back its services, principally the short-term billeting of transients, to transition to longer-term, dormitory-style housing, and to reassign staff. New classrooms, laboratories, equipment, and textbooks were needed. Among registered students, more than 800 lived in DP camps, where they received UNRRA care. But 500 were living privately, as were many faculty, and were due assistance in the forms of clothing, rations, and possibly stipends, even though UNRRA generally did not give aid to so-called free-livers. Moreover, given their long commutes, many students living in the camps wanted to move to Munich, adding to the housing demands in the bombed-out city. To function as a proper university, the school also would need credible entrance requirements. But so many DPs—Jews especially—had no proof of their graduation from *gymnasium*, prior attendance at a university, or academic abilities.

In addition to the raw demand of the students and the dedication of the staff, UNRRA's broad, and conspicuously benevolent, stance on education drove the university's formation. UNRRA came into being amid what is now described as a "human rights revolution," inspired substantially by World War II and producing, most famously, the 1948 United Nations Universal Declaration of Human Rights. Perhaps most impressive in this new ethos was the expansive understanding of basic human entitlements—such as education—and the recognition of the need to develop means for their guarantee.[26] Reflecting this ethos, an UNRRA directive issued shortly before the university's launch held that "it is the policy of UNRRA to provide schools and educational opportunities to all displaced persons under UNRRA care, including those residing outside of Assembly Centers."[27] It further specified that "priority shall be given to those who have been in concentration camps or otherwise have suffered from Nazi action." Very clearly, UNRRA saw education as a right and educating DPs as both an obligation of the highest order and a way to repair some of the damage brought about by persecution.

Postwar Germany, in UNRRA's view, bore some of this obligation, conveyed in UNRRA's pledge to "assist properly qualified displaced students to secure registration as students at higher educational institutions in Germany."[28] Occupation authorities in fact established a policy requiring that 10 percent of university slots be given to DPs.[29] But the directive also made reference to what UNRRA's own modest university could do, welcoming "the initiative of language or nationality groups in establishing faculties or colleges for higher education." Just before the school's opening, an UNRRA leader commented sympathetically, if also with some paternalism, "These DP students who had no opportunity to study for six years are most eager to have a part in this program. Even though the standard of this school may not compare to that of a[n established] University . . . it does afford an opportunity to employ the time of [the] students. . . . It is the first opportunity we have had to initiate the second 'R' in UNRRA, namely 'Rehabilitation.' "[30]

The team member's comment ultimately belies what an achievement the university represented. For the DPs it was not simply a place where they could resist the dangers of idleness and make up for lost time but rather a product of their drive to actively recreate what they had known or hoped to achieve before the war. Further, the university is testament to the emergence of the DP as an existential category or subjectivity unto itself, committed to shaping the future by investing in one's "temporary" circumstance. The university shows, finally, the capacity of the DPs, though organized primarily on national lines, to cooperate in the service of forward-looking ideals. According to historian Anna Holian, the UNRRA school was also to be, in the conception of its most spirited backers, a new kind of cosmopolitan transnational institution, dedicated to advancing the "brotherhood of man" and universal, humanistic values beyond even the traditional, humanistic, and nationally oriented charge of universities.[31] One Jewish alumnus remembers it as the "peace university."[32] Moreover, the school claimed a special authority to advance internationalist ideals by virtue of its being composed to a great degree of Nazism's victims, who had suffered the worst of nationalist aggression.

The UNRRA school exemplifies the success postwar relief efforts could enjoy, despite the mutual suspicion and frustration between relief workers and DPs. The former soon recognized that the resourcefulness that served the DPs during the war also nurtured their ability get what they wanted under trying postwar circumstances—to game any system, including relief efforts. Weary of DPs misrepresenting their situations or identities, UNRRA and other agencies repeatedly tried to shore up screening processes to determine just who was who, and who was entitled to what aid. Aid workers also feared black market activity, which, on any grand scale at least, they saw as morally corrosive and inimical to the DPs' true rehabilitation. Any aid, especially when dispensed outside the more controlled environment of the DP camps, had the potential to be abused by being traded on the black market. Jewish DPs in particular might run up against cynical, and surely dubious, assumptions of just who survivors were. The Joint official Jacob Jaslow remarked, "The fact that they are alive is an indication that they possessed either a cunning or a special ability useful to the Hitler war machine. The intellectual members of the Jewish European race for the most part have been 'exterminated,' leaving as remnants of six million only those who were 'hardened' to the type of treatment they endured."[33]

There was also the perception that the establishment of even temporary institutions for DPs might discourage the refugees' repatriation, and thus work against Allied policies. Intelligence operatives in fact monitored the Deutsches Museum for what they deemed "anti-repatriation activities," apt to be organized by intellectuals with strong political positions and leadership skills.[34] The DPs, for their part, frequently felt that aid agencies did not understand the extent of their past hardships and current needs, the inadequacy or wrongheadedness of certain policies, and what made their group, their cause, or their individual case so special.

Those creating the DP university pushed past these perceptions. The UNRRA University officially opened on February 16, 1946, in a ceremony in Munich's infamous Bürgerbräukeller. Key figures in UNRRA and the US military were in attendance, and the event was broadcast on Armed Forces Radio.[35] The lead story of the day's *DP Express* heralded the school's opening, reporting on its eight faculties, several degree opportunities, numerous university lectures and *Abitur* courses, and by this point nearly 3,000 registrations (up from earlier totals when the school was just forming, and with enrollment to be capped at 2,000).[36] Admission, the newspaper explained in strained English, was to work as follows: "All D.P. students are promitted to study at the UNRRA University. A special commission examines every student of his D.P. status the CIC office of the Milt. Govt. grans the promission for study. The student has then to prove by his certificates that he possessed the necessary qualifications. Students, who were nomore in possession of their certificates had to appear for the text examination."

Ukrainians of Polish citizenship accounted for the largest number of registrants (847), followed by Lithuanians (696), "Stateless" (424), "Lettonians" (Latvians, 202), and Poles (202). Jewish students comprised the next largest group, with 174 hoping to attend the school.[37]

Displacement and the Jewish Students

Several months after the war, Jews were a small but important subset of the DP population, comprising 3.6 percent of the nearly 1.5 million DPs, as classified by UNRRA, in Germany, Austria, and Italy.[38] In Munich, as in the American Zone generally, their presence underwent a dramatic shift, eventually reflected in the enrollment of more than one hundred Jews at the UNRRA University. How young Jews made their way into the school is bound up with the story of Jewish displacement itself.

At the war's end in the spring of 1945, up to 35,000 of the approximately 50,000 Jews liberated in German or Austrian territory were in the American Zone.[39] Many of these had been liberated from concentration camps by the Americans, including 2,700 from Dachau alone.[40] An estimate for July 1945 places 14,000 to 15,000 Jews in Bavaria, 7,000 in Vienna, and 8,000 in Berlin.[41] A more comprehensive tally of September 30, 1945, by which point some population movement had occurred, records roughly 10,000 Jews (who were non-German nationals) in the American Zone of Germany, and almost equal numbers in the American Zone in Austria.[42] In Munich the prewar Jewish population had been decimated, falling from 9,000 in 1933 to 525 in 1944. Few who survived deportation returned after the war.[43] As a result most Jews initially in the Munich area were Eastern Europeans who had been incarcerated in camps in Bavaria.

The population of Jews in the zone dramatically rose with the influx of additional survivors from Eastern Europe. The first wave from Poland arrived in the summer and fall of 1945; these survivors had been liberated from camps by the Soviets, or during the war had passed as non-Jews using false papers, survived in hiding, or fought as partisans. In early 1946 large numbers of Jews from Poland who had been deported into the Soviet interior during the war arrived.[44] Official Soviet policy dictated the repatriation of all displaced persons within its borders or the territory it occupied. Countries like Poland, rapidly falling under Soviet influence after the war, tried to seal its borders (even as it expelled German nationals and the ethnic Germans, or Volksdeutsche), making passage for Jews out of the country largely illegal. Underground Zionist networks, some of which had been active in the resistance during the war, greatly aided the movement of Jews west, exploiting several points of passage into Germany, Italy, and elsewhere. The Bricha, as this movement was known, brought as many as 110,000 Jews west from Poland between 1945 and 1946.[45]

A common experience of Jews from Poland was the trek home in search of relatives, no matter the difficulties in getting into, or back out of, Poland (parts of which the Soviets outright annexed and Ukrainian nationalists tried to claim). The sadly common discovery was that these returning Polish Jews found that many or even all of their family members were dead, their property confiscated, the Jewish community destroyed, and their own safety now imperiled by hostile countrymen. Some Jews, especially families that endured intact and had money, attempted to resettle in Poland. With the help of aid agencies such as the Joint, and often with the assistance of the Polish government and even representatives of the *Yishuv* (Jews already in Palestine, whether as historic residents in the area or European and other Jews who had settled there more recently), Jewish communities were able to reconsolidate, albeit precariously. Synagogues, community institutions, and *kibbutzim* populated by politically differentiated Zionist youth organizations intent on migration to Palestine gained new life.[46] As many as 195,000 Jews from Poland were repatriated between the end of 1944 and 1946.[47]

But violence, or rumors of violence, against such returnees soon drove away many for good. The most notorious incident was the pogrom in Kielce in July 1946, during which Poles killed forty-seven Jews. Lesser attacks, both before and after Kielce, also forced Jews to flee. Some 350 were killed by Poles between November 1944 and December 1945, with more than 1,500 dead by the summer of 1947.[48] In response, 33,000 or so Jews left Poland in the last half of 1945, and another 78,000 had left by October 1946 (with nearly 50,000 leaving in July and August 1946, just after the Kielce pogrom).[49] As these numbers climbed, so too did the numbers of Jews in the American Zone in Germany.

Among the alumni, the great majority of those from Poland made at least a cursory trip "home" to see who and what was left. Many quickly concluded their past was gone and their future prospects in Poland dismal, given the lack of resources, encroaching communism, and enduring anti-Semitism. Some of the alumni, however—fifteen of forty-one survey respondents—made an effort to resettle, at least temporarily, in Poland. Some married there, were active in Zionist organizing, and were even able to enter (or reenter) university. But the environment of anti-Semitism proved overwhelming, forcing them west.

Given the complex postwar circumstances and staggered population movements, one cannot determine a uniform sequence as to when certain categories of Jews settled in the American Zone. Those liberated by the Americans were most likely to remain in the zone. Nonetheless, someone liberated from Dachau may have spent months in Eastern Europe before returning to Munich. A Jew liberated by the Soviets in Poland, or even one exiled to Siberia, may have come west shortly after the German collapse on the Eastern Front, settling in the American Zone earlier than someone liberated there. Indeed, the first "class" of Jewish university students comprises a great range of wartime narratives.

To Jews and other DPs, the attractions of the American Zone were obvious. In the chaos of postwar Europe—marked by military checkpoints, convoys of soldiers and refugees endlessly crisscrossing, shifting areas of safety and danger, the constant smuggling of goods and people—rumors and direct witnessing provided for the main transit of information. By these means word of the quality of care the Americans generally provided quickly spread deep into Eastern Europe. As important, the American Zone represented freedom from Soviet domination. Mark Fintel conveyed the appeal of the American occupation. After the war he embarked on a futile homecoming in Rovno, a part of eastern Poland since annexed by the Soviet Union. Upon hearing from former classmates that Ukrainian terror squads were searching for Jews, he left, with the goal of traveling to Poland and then into western Germany. He accomplished the last legs of the trip by passing as a Volksdeutsch slated for deportation from Poland. Along with thousands of expellees, he marched over the German border into the British Zone, and a transport plane finally brought him to Munich. Throughout the journey, he met fellow Jews who often identified one another with the codeword "amchah" ("of the people" in Hebrew). The insistent message was: "Go to the American Zone, because this is where the freedom is. It was in the air . . . you talked to [others], you knew it immediately."[50]

Emanuel Tanay also heard from returnees in Poland of the "food, freedom, and safety" in the west, and he made it from Hungary to Germany in the summer of 1945. The thought that greeted him on crossing captured the core irony recognized by so many Jewish DPs: "Germany, the land of our oppressors, had become our Promised Land." This was so, of course, because of the US occupation, and what distinguished the Americans was immediately evident to him. Their military uniforms "had little in common with the threatening outfits worn by most militaries of Europe." They were "functional, concerned with the comfort of the soldiers"; the army itself seemed to resist the "sadistic need [to] humiliate [and] the degradation inherent in the militaristic tradition," as well as the "totalitarian mind" he had seen operating among the Germans, the Hungarian fascists, and the Soviets. [51] His affection for America began at that instant.

In another irony, the acute problems stemming from the Americans' initial treatment of Jewish DPs eventually made the zone, and the Munich area in particular, even more appealing to Jews. In July 1945 University of Pennsylvania Law School dean Earl Harrison was sent by President Harry S. Truman as a special envoy to assess the care of refugees in the DP camps. Jewish DPs in particular complained bitterly about their treatment. In his report to the president, Harrison blasted what he described as the deplorable and dispiriting conditions the refugees suffered, chiefly inadequate food, squalor, and military confinement that seemed to him evocative of their internment under the Germans. He also criticized the policy, deeply resented by Jews, of grouping camp residents by nationality so as not to reproduce the religious and racial categorizations of the Nazis. As a consequence Jews were living in close quarters with Poles, Ukrainians, and Baltic peoples who may have collaborated with the Nazis or, even if enemies of the Germans, been prejudiced toward Jews. In the wake of the report, widely publicized in major media in the United States, conditions improved. Jews were now grouped together within camps, and three major DP camps near Munich—Foehrenwald, Landsberg, and Feldafing—were converted into facilities for Jews only. Residents in these camps continued to complain of overcrowding and poor facilities, but they soon set about establishing elaborate work and education programs and a thriving cultural and political life. As a result the camps soon became destinations for Jewish DPs from outside and even within the American Zone.[52]

American policy toward Jewish refugees grew steadily more favorable. In their initial planning prior to the end of the war, the Americans had intended to count as displaced persons and assume care for only those refugees who came from Allied countries and who were in Allied zones at the war's end. As the extent of Nazi brutality grew more apparent, those eligible for aid expanded to include individuals persecuted by the Nazis on racial, religious, or political grounds, regardless of their nationality. For the Allies, the concentration camps dominated their initial understanding of Nazi persecution, and camp survivors were most readily accorded persecutee status.

American awareness of the scope of Jewish suffering during the war increased as well. After the Harrison Report especially, the Americans began to regard Jews as victims of persecution even if they had come from enemy or "ex-enemy" countries like Hungary, and regardless of whether they could verify direct harm by the Nazis. Jews' access to the zone also expanded. Refugees crossing into American-occupied territory just after the war had been labeled "infiltrees"; their presence was technically illegal, and some were brought to "infiltree camps" and potentially slated for deportation. Military commanders, among the British especially, suspected that the migration of Jews west was partly a coordinated effort of Zionists to create refugee pressure in occupied Germany, and thus force Britain to permit Jewish migration to Palestine.[53]

By December 1945, however, American directives permitted even these Jewish "infiltrees" to enter DP camps.[54] As with so much concerning the occupation, practical considerations drove policy fully as much as political ones. A confidential report from a US Army captain who toured DP camps in February 1946 observed that "there is great movement [among Jews] in and out of Europe to bring back relatives and attend to other business. A watch to a Russian Guard or a bottle of liquor is the only passport necessary. . . . There is absolutely no differentiation being made between bona fide Jewish DPs and infiltrees. It was the unanimous comment of all UNRRA camp directors that it is impossible to accord different treatment to DPs and infiltrees once they are in the camp so that infiltrees receive the same amount of food[,] as the DPs are housed together and in every other way are treated equally."[55] By late summer de facto American policy held that all Jews were persecutees entitled to basic aid as DPs, though confusion and conflicts over the status and entitlements of individual Jews persisted.[56]

Whatever their complex motivation, such measures surely drew Jews toward the Americans. By February 1946 the number of Jewish DPs in the American Zone had swelled to more than 40,000, climbing to 140,000 by the year's end.[57] As other DPs repatriated, the percentage of Jewish DPs rose greatly as well. By the end of 1947, the Munich area alone was home to nearly 80,000 Jews, close to nine times its prewar number.[58]

The Jews who made up the earliest student cohort in Munich—those who attended university in the fall of 1945 and the winter of 1946—fall into these broad patterns of migration and temporary settlement. Their narratives underscore the chaos of post-liberation Europe and the idiosyncratic nature of individual destinies. They reveal, moreover, that the mere existence of educational opportunities after the war was typically a necessary but insufficient condition for their actually entering university. That passage, rather, often depended both on social interactions and internal processes shaping their states of body, mind, and feeling.

Liberated from Dachau as a "political" inmate, Simon Schochet was brought into nearby Munich under American care.[59] A pass issued by the Americans authorized him to travel east in search of his parents and to return freely. Nearly all his family, he discovered, was gone. His father had been active in the Polish non-communist resistance, and an uncle had been killed in the Soviet massacre of Polish military officers at Katyn in 1940. Resettling in Poland was therefore out of the question, no matter his nationalist pedigree.

Back in Munich at age eighteen, he first spent time with Polish political persecutees, yet he felt "basically lost" in their company and in the city. Learning of a Jewish DP camp at Feldafing, he went there to recuperate. At the camp he met young men of similar background, including a "cultured Jew" from Poland whose grandfather had played music with Sergei Rachmaninoff. Given Schochet's own knowledge of music and his mother's skill as a pianist, he soon bonded with his new friend. Through his friend Schochet met a Hungarian Jewish musician who was intent on entering a conservatory in Munich. The Hungarian Jews, Schochet stressed, had been able to remain in school until the German invasion in 1944; as a consequence, their path back to student life was generally easier. From them Schochet got the notion that he too could study. He entered the first term of UNRRA University as a history student.

Robert Nenner was liberated from Buchenwald by the Americans. As countless survivors report of their experiences, liberation brought him a sense of "relief," not joy.[60] After several weeks in a "quasi-hospital," he discharged himself. Over the orderlies' objections, he insisted, "I'm looking for my family," and they relented. "Nice Jewish boy . . . you go on about the mother," he said of their attitude toward his plea. The staff directed him to the UNRRA center at the Deutsches Museum in Munich, which maintained a list of surviving Jews; they gave him twenty-five marks and "ill-fitting clothes" for the journey. (The American rabbi Abraham Klausner, working closely with the Central Committee, developed the registry, which quickly expanded to several volumes).[61] "I didn't want to talk to anybody. I didn't want to know anybody. I just wanted München," Nenner said of his trip. The list of survivors, he discovered, was "totally incomplete," and the UNRRA staff peppered him with what seemed absurd questions—"where did you see them last?"—as if he had lost his parents in a crowded market. Given a room at the Deutsches Museum, he declared that he wanted to resume *gymnasium*. UNRAA representatives proudly reported that the center was forming a school, and he started attending when the lectures began.

Yet Nenner soon went to Poland in search of his parents, without any pass permitting his return. In Krakow he met and was taken in by hard-core members of the Zionist military underground. They directed him, as part of their operations, to the Ainring DP camp near Salzburg where, utterly by chance, he found his parents, who had survived Dachau. His time at the camp, however, was brief; having come most recently from the east, he was considered an infiltree and his presence illegal. His associates in the underground then helped smuggle him back into Munich, instructing him to maintain his studies there. Even as he continued clandestinely to work with the underground network, he loved his existence at the UNRRA University, where he had housing, meals, and books. "I was in seventh heaven. I had made it." When the Student Union formed, he was among the first to join.

Emanuel Tanay belongs to the category of survivors who had passed as non-Jews using false papers. After first posing as a monastery student in Poland, he survived in Hungary as a (Christian) Polish refugee. After the Soviet conquest of the Nazis in 1945, he made no fewer than six trips between Budapest and Poland, where he saw evidence of Polish hostility toward Jews, including bestial "train murders"—the killing of Jewish passengers by Poles.[62] Through the aid of the Bricha in Prague, and posing for a time as a Slovakian communist, he entered Bavaria and was directed to the Deutsches Museum. Arriving sick, he was sent to the nearby St. Ottilien hospital—a monastery and then medical facility that became a hospital for Jewish survivors. The site of a now-famous concert of the Kovno ghetto orchestra just weeks after the war, St. Ottilien became a locus of early DP organizing, from which the Central Committee took shape.[63] To be eligible for admittance, Tanay claimed that he had been liberated from a concentration camp by the Americans. After a brief stay at the Landsberg DP camp, he obtained an apartment in Munich through the German housing authority (*Wohnungsamt*).

In the early fall of 1945, Tanay accompanied a Jewish friend on an interview with the UNRRA University's dean of admissions, Georg von Studynsky, a Ukrainian professor of political economy. Tanay's companion was accepted by virtue of her *Matura*. Professor Studynsky, impressed in conversation with Tanay's political knowledge, assumed he too had a *Matura* and admitted him. To provide the necessary proof, Tanay had two Jews "verify" to a German notary that he had attended an academy in Poland. Quickly Professor Studynsky's favorite student, Tanay was chosen to say a few sentences in English on behalf of the school's Jewish students at the ceremony opening the UNRAA University. Barely knowing the language, he memorized the words. In a moment evocative of his tentative repossession of self, he nervously repeated "I am" two or three times before saying his name.[64] He became, at age seventeen, and without having finished even grade school in Poland, the Student Union's youngest member soon after it formed.

A variation on this narrative is presented by Sabina Zimering, who had "passed" as a Christian Pole in Germany during the war. In the Bavarian city of Regensberg, she had worked as a maid in a hotel used largely by the Gestapo. After the war, while countless other survivors were scrambling to secure false papers to travel west, she gleefully turned in her Polish "identification" to the Americans, eager to help the victims of the Nazis, in exchange for certificates of her true identity. Beyond their practical benefit, the papers she obtained allowed her "to be myself again."[65] The Americans, sympathetic to her plight as a Jew, provided her and her sister with an apartment in Regensberg. Her intention ultimately was to return to Poland to gather what family was left and bring them to the German city. With her *Matura* from her old *gymnasium* in hand, she quickly turned her thoughts to studying medicine, about which she had long dreamed. The American Joint Distribution Committee, active already in November 1945 in getting students into German universities, advised her to apply to the medical school at Heidelberg University.[66] She was accepted, but the medical faculty had not yet reopened. Learning of the opening of the UNRRA school, she jumped at the chance to attend, and moved from Regensberg to Munich.[67]

Philip Balaban is among those who survived in Soviet exile; his narrative illustrates the complexities of migrating west. Toward the end of the war, and though still attending secondary school, he was haphazardly "trained" to be an officer in the Soviet military.[68] (He mostly recalls drunken conscripts nearly killing each other while practicing with live ammunition.) Throughout their exile, Balaban and his family had sent letters to their hometown in Galicia. They learned the sad fate of the town's Jews in a letter returned by a "Jewish girl" who worked in the post office. The Balabans then left the Soviet Union illegally to return to their hometown. Balaban's mother was "in a coma for about a month," but snapped out of it to put the children into school. Their great challenge was avoiding the Ukrainian "Green Nationalists," who had cooperated with the Germans in opposing the Soviets. After some months the family, along with other Jews and Poles, were expelled by the Ukrainians; they stayed in Warsaw, where Balaban also attended school, until August 1945. In Warsaw he "pretended not to be Jewish" so as not to attract Polish hostility.

The family then resolved to go to Palestine, and they were brought west by the Bricha by posing as Greek Jews who had been liberated from camps such as Auschwitz. (Greeks were permitted passage from Poland and into both US-occupied Germany and Italy.) Initially captured by Soviet officials as they were attempting to leave from Prague, the family snuck onto a train of Germans being expelled from Czechoslovakia. On this transport a US soldier grew suspicious of the family; sensing, however, that the out-of-place passengers were Jewish, the soldier—himself a Jew—addressed them with "amchah" and sent them safely along in the presence of a Soviet guard. Philip Balaban woke up the next day in Munich. He soon arrived at the Deutsches Museum, where he learned of the nascent UNRRA University and immediately tried to register.

As these summaries suggest, for many of the alumni the immediate aftermath of liberation, their arrival in (or return to) Munich, and their entry into the university are intricate parts of their stories. In some cases the level of instability in their lives after the war exceeded that during wartime, as the Nazis' "system" of persecution had represented a kind of order that dissolved with the conflict's end. This very turbulence, and the role of contingency—specifically in their early postwar lives—help to frame the condition of "displacement" for them and other refugees, defining just what the student life first represented for them.

After the German collapse Jewish DPs' lives typically had a catch-as-catch-can quality, requiring relentless improvisation and frequent duplicity in response to opportunity and threat. In Europe as a whole, there was no seamless and coordinated system to govern refugees. Rather multiple powers, policies, and agendas haphazardly governed the DPs, who had their own diverse interests and ways of negotiating, evading, and deceiving authority. Even within discrete occupation areas, inconsistency seemed the norm. In the American Zone, for example, Jewish DPs of similar profiles might receive greatly different designations, instructions, and dispensations. Individual cities and camps could function as micro-geographies, each with their own administrative norm (albeit unstable) and rapidly evolving customs.

For the authorities the essential work of occupation was the imposition of order on this chaos. From the other side DPs sought stability in their uprooted lives and a qualified return to the "normal"; this was a key aim of so much DP organizing. For the prospective students, to enter university was to bring stability into an individual life. At the collective level the Student

Union sought to make university study viable by erecting a reliable protocol for admission, aid, and so forth. Step by step their lives took on much greater order, as did the occupation as a whole. But disorder persisted too. As we shall see as we track individual trajectories and the organization's activities, it was rare that at any point a given "policy" determined the way things were actually done in all relevant cases. Each rule had many exceptions. In short, the contingency of liberation, so evident in the immediate aftermath of the war, persisted. The life of a displaced person, by extension, was fundamentally defined by the tension between chaos and order, contingency and structure, and between creating a new future and reconnecting with aspects of the past.

"Between Being and Non-Being"

Contingency defined the student survivors in another, more intimate sense. The students' entrance into university may have been, at its deepest roots, a function of their backgrounds, dispositions, and drives. Yet the actual decision to enroll—especially in the cases of the earliest students, who entered without the benefit of the Union's resources and advocacy—often had an instigated, or even accidental, quality. (By extension, other Jewish DPs with similar backgrounds and proclivities but lacking such serendipity may never have found the university path.) For Schochet, Tanay, and others, the prompt came from a temporary ally or friend who made that path seem possible and real. Roman Ohrenstein, also an early UNRRA student, wound up at the Landsberg DP camp. For him the trigger to study occurred at the camp when he encountered two childhood friends, Yehuda Knobler and Rina Sklarczyk, who knew well how he had struggled to obtain a secular education during his childhood in Poland.[69] They brought back for him a world of associations and possibilities that had been voided by the war. A group that entered the UNRRA University in the fall of 1945 had coalesced at Foehrenwald, where relative strangers offered mutual encouragement to cross the boundary to a new life together.[70] That crossing had its own complexities.

The students' postwar choices and lives exhibit a high degree of purposefulness and determination, epitomized by the perfunctory claim some years later that they simply emerged from the war intent on studying, saw the opportunity to do so, and took it. These qualities of initiative and will are generally stressed in recent literature on Jewish DPs, which chronicles survivors' efforts to "redeem the future" by investing in Zionist struggle, the creation of families, and cultural activity.[71] This determination often existed, however, against severely disorienting and damaging wartime experiences, mitigating any sense of DPs' lives as having been spontaneously and instantaneously reborn.

In many cases I have found that the students' return to life entailed that they pass after liberation through one or more negative thresholds, only after which were they ready to engage the world more fully. I posit nothing so formal as a stage of post-traumatic shock and recovery, universally endured by the students or by survivors generally. There was simply too great a variety of experiences, even within a small cohort. Nonetheless, such a process seems common within the group as a whole.

For some of the students, the first threshold was overcoming acute physical distress. Ohrenstein survived eight camps, including Plaszow and Auschwitz. He was liberated among the dead and dying in the forests of Gunskirchen—a diabolical scene, even by Holocaust standards—whose survivors were found inert, starved, and rotting.[72] For three weeks thereafter he wrestled, in his description, with "the angel of death" in a makeshift care center. Other alumni report similar experiences of being at a dire physical limit. For a group so defined by the capacities of their minds, it is important not to lose sight of the pains of their bodies—the extent to which "anatomical" survival, as Nenner might put it, was for many of them the precondition of all else. As many as 20,000 Jews of the 50,000 to 60,000 liberated from the camps could not make it past this threshold, dying shortly after the war from disease and the effects of long-term starvation.[73] The physical distress could persist for months or longer. A photograph of Yehuda Knobler taken in a lakeside setting in the summer of 1946—more than a year after his liberation from Mauthausen—shows his torso still somewhat emaciated; the image resembles the iconic photos of Jewish prisoners at liberation.

The earliest roster of Munich Union members' addresses in its archive, a list of sixty students submitted by the Central Committee to the UNRRA University in early January 1945, shows that six students resided at hospitals (five at St. Ottilien; one in the Landsberg DP camp hospital).[74] Two years into its existence, the Munich Union had twenty or so "invalids" (*Invalides*, in German, according to the official designation) who received special medical dispensations.[75]

The brink could be psychological as well. A number of the alumni report passing through a period of existential incapacity or even nihilistic detachment before embarking on their paths as students. Alumnus Simon Snopkowski survived the Groß-Rosen concentration camp, a death march, and Auschwitz, and lost nearly his entire family. He recalled being "overcome with a deep melancholy" while first in the Landsberg DP camp.[76] Three survivors in his immediate circle committed suicide. Recent research affirms

Students Roman Ohrenstein and Yehuda Knobler by a lake near Munich in the summer of 1946. Knobler still shows the effects of his internment at Mauthausen. (Courtesy of Roman Ohrenstein)

what he reports. Though no reliable figures exist, evidence turned up by Margarete Myers Feinstein suggests that suicide among survivors was not uncommon: a US soldier reported three to six suicides a night in a DP camp; a DP reported one or two a night in a hospital; an article in a Jewish DP newspaper lamented the rash of suicides and the sorrow at their core.[77] Speculating on the motive, she concludes that "the loneliness that beset the survivors after liberation as well as the disappointment that the world had not embraced them with open arms was too much for some to endure."[78] Snopkowski, arriving in Munich, wondered, "What should I do in Bavaria without my studies or a profession? I lived for a time between Being and non-Being. My future was, at the same time, open and closed."[79] His resolve to seize that future emerged on the other side of this liminal state.

Tanay's teenage survival required that he be "preternaturally alert" and in near-constant motion to escape various threats, his existence punctuated by seemingly irrational, lifesaving decisions. (While imprisoned he volunteered at one point for execution, reasoning that his captors would not bother killing inmates already willing to die, and would kill others instead.)[80] After liberation he remained on the move both literally and in spirit. After being discharged from St. Ottilien, he went to the Landsberg DP camp. Finding it demoralizing, he quickly explored another horizon, much as he did when confronted with adversity during the war. "Our second liberation" (this time from the Soviets), he tersely explained in his memoir, "was not a bed of roses. It was time to make another choice."[81] That choice was to live in Munich. There he at last became "depressed and utterly exhausted," and for two weeks lay immobilized in his bed, as if "physically ill," while his mother tended to him. "The years of being pursued [and an] anguished awareness of the enormity" of recent events, he later speculated, "had caught up with me." Concluding that "rest and loving care were of little help," he then snapped back to life and soon entered the UNRRA University.[82] But Tanay's conclusion may be at odds with his description; perhaps the rest and loving care—far from a simple interregnum in his postwar journey—helped him get back up for good.

For others the threshold could have a different quality—not a total numbing to life but a protracted sense of detachment and surreality accompanied by a heightened perception. This seems the condition of Schochet, first in Munich just after the war and then in the Feldafing DP camp, where he spent many months. Schochet is a contemplative man, exuding the refinement of a European intellectual of a bygone era but also a palpable melancholy surely connected to his past. Asked years later to describe his mindset and surroundings after liberation, he often avoided direct response, as if to convey the radical otherness of that time and place. "It's a very, very difficult type of question . . . I cannot give you any one particular answer."[83]

In 1983 Schochet published the short novel *Feldafing*. One of a very few works of fiction set in a DP camp, it is an exception to the vast testimonial literature by survivors about the Holocaust. Above all the author's fictive narrator presents Feldafing as a transitional space of profound convalescence and incongruity, in which the imagery and idioms of the concentration camp universe are reinforced even as they are overcome. Set in the Alpine foothills, the camp had been used as a training facility for Nazi youth. Among the key juxtapositions is the lushness of the setting and the DPs' withered state. Schochet described Feldafing as "one of the most beautiful places in the world."[84]

In an arresting moment of contrast, the survivors' search for gaiety collides with the lingering horror when, in the summer of 1945, the narrator approaches a sex-segregated beach at nearby Starnberger See (lake):

> My eyes were drawn involuntarily to several figures standing at the water's edge. They turned slowly, the lake a tortuous mirror reflecting naked, alien forms. This was the first time they had seen the ravages that six years of war had stretched so indelibly on their forlorn bodies. For the first time I also had the opportunity to calmly and objectively observe my comrades' bodies—unbearably scary, shakily supported by swollen, discolored legs, backs and torsos covered with scars. . . . Some of the men had forced themselves to forgo the mirror's truth and now splashed about in an effort to amuse themselves, but in my eyes that splashing became thrashing, and their feeble cries of delight the strangled gurgles of drowning men. Later I learned that some German youngsters had walked to the lakeside of our camp by chance and had come back babbling incoherently about "ghosts." Their teacher finally had to give up trying to convince them that those specters were fully flesh and blood.[85]

The challenge for those at Feldafing, achieved only incrementally, was both to believe and to trust in the reality of their survival. Schochet, one may presume, used his time at the camp to build that trust, preparing him for the world beyond.

Alumnus Henry Frist survived the war as a deportee in the Soviet Union and came west with the Bricha. He therefore did not suffer the massive disorientation of many of the others. Nonetheless, he confessed years later, "I found myself in Munich by sheer chance, [in] early 1946. I did not plan to stay on German soil any more than logistically needed, nor did I [think] 'to do anything productive with myself.' In fact, I did not think at all. I was still in a state of stupor, at least intellectually. Yet under pressure of events I was compelled to function somehow."[86]

The ambivalent condition of survivors and other Jewish DPs can be conveyed by some remarkable visual symbolism during the period. In March 1946 Jewish DPs at Landsberg celebrated what was surely among the most bizarre and symbolically laden Purim festivals in the history of Judaism. In Margarete Myers Feinstein's words, "Purim festivities involve a carnivalesque turning of the world on its head, mocking authority, and reveling in jokes and satire."[87] On this Purim, the first since liberation, the Jewish DPs at Landsberg costumed themselves to reenact, and figuratively reverse, the crushing power of the Nazis. The celebrants dressed a Hitler figure, who was then captured by the DP police and his putative victims, and then hung in effigy.[88] If less audacious, similar Purim celebrations took place in other DP camps and among Jews elsewhere in 1946 and the years thereafter.

Jewish survivors staging a mock Nazi procession at a Purim celebration in Landsberg am Lech on March 24, 1946. Auschwitz survivor Roman Ohrenstein is on the right, giving the "Sieg Heil" salute. (Courtesy of Roman Ohrenstein)

Roman Ohrenstein saved a stunning photograph from the 1946 Landsberg Purim, picturing a mock Nazi procession in which Jews played the part of an exultant Nazi crowd. Ohrenstein himself brandishes the "Sieg Heil" salute. On the one hand, the photograph perfectly reflects the core symbolic gesture of the postwar Purim performance: surviving Jews, exultant at Hitler's demise, stage a comic rendition of vanquished power to signal both the actual and symbolic defeat of that power. Hitler is now diminished to an object of ridicule, not fear. In Ohrenstein's recollection, moreover, the mock motorcade paraded not only through the Landsberg DP camp but also through the center street of the German town Landsberg am Lech, with US troops guarding the procession against the stupefied German onlookers. The symbolic reversal of power relations was thus accompanied by real-life shifts in military authority.

On the other hand, the photo also depicts real victims of the Holocaust, still wearing their prison uniforms (those in striped clothing, according to Ohrenstein's recollection, are Greek Jews), paying obeisance to their cruel master. By extension, the ritual—precisely in the power and poignancy of its simulacrum—testifies as well to the persistence of Nazi power beyond its formal demise and the survivors' continued possession by a terrible past.

Survivors, one may argue, never fully shed that uniform, that second skin, no matter the number of years since liberation.

A final indication of the young survivors' internal challenges comes from the Munich Students' Union itself. Throughout its life, the Union was generally loath to describe its members' wartime ordeals in any detail or draw attention to what one might term their psychic pain. The draft of a letter by Union officers to Albert Einstein in the United States in early 1946 provides a rare exception. (There is no evidence that Einstein ever received the letter.) Addressing Einstein both as a world-famous intellectual and as a Jew known for his humanitarian concerns, the writers report that "the students still live under the heat of the flames and in the wreckage of the recent years. They have not been able to find their place in the world, in which some people committed murder, others sold out their years-long—nay, centuries-long—fellow citizens, schoolmates and comrades for a piece of bread and some alcohol. . . . Others were complicit as bystanders [*Zuschauer*] . . . remaining mute. . . . You can only imagine how hard it was for those left starved and ragged from the concentration camps to enter university study. We were full of cynicism, and wrapped in the armor of apathy and indifference. Nonetheless, we succeeded, as graduates of the *Abitur* and former college students, to return to our studies."[89] Overtly appealing to Einstein for support, the letter plays up the students' pitiable circumstance and their determination in the face of it. But the letter's purpose should give us no cause to doubt the struggle it references. To the contrary it provides a valuable description of their initial despair as rooted in the shattering of trust, their sense of betrayal by humanity. Further, it portrays their dejection, widely observed by relief workers in Jewish DP camps, not simply as a sign of exhaustion and defeat but as a form of *protection*, which eventually gave way to, and possibly enabled as a transitional state, a more confident engagement with life.[90]

There existed a last condition for the students' forming a union—one easy to assume as a given and thus overlook: the urge to seek out and make common cause with one another as Jews. This social impulse was the foundation for the collective they formed. In many respects it was an organic consequence of the war and liberation. Yet in cases that impulse presupposed a new internalization of Jewish identity in response to postwar circumstances, and thus had a highly personal dimension. Not always automatic, it too could be the product of struggle.

Jews in prewar Europe shared a broad affinity, whether based in religion, history, tradition, language, custom, or outlook. That affinity was reinforced during the war. Whatever Jews' nationality, social standing, degree of assimilation, and politics, they were, to a great extent, thrown together and victimized as a group. As a result many survivors emerged from the war with a deepened sense of Jewish solidarity. That solidarity was evident amid the chaos that followed liberation. Countless survivors report that the first thing they would do when entering a city or town in their postwar journeys was to find fellow Jews, cull as much information as possible, and form some plan together in small or large groups. Only other Jews could be counted on any longer as allies.

After the war Zionists explicitly used the comprehensive experience of Jewish persecution as both a practical and ideological argument for building a Jewish state.[91] The embrace of Zionism by so many DPs, though greatly overdetermined, confirms the salience of that argument. And for the Jews from Poland especially, the postwar encounter with anti-Semitism further sealed their identities as Jews. Alumnus Felix Korn from Lodz recalls that a condition for his leaving Poland after the war was that he turn over his Polish identification papers to border guards and renounce his citizenship.[92] Even when this stripping of nationality was not explicit, Eastern European Jews, in the main, were rendered functionally stateless. This reality became a new source of common status, group cohesion, and, in the form of Zionism, shared political belief.

But if the war helped to codify Jewish identity among survivors, it could also be deeply destabilizing and present new choices. Survivors, after all, paid a horrible price for being Jewish. Isaac Minzberg, as we have seen, was tempted to run away from Judaism after the war. In addition, some Jews survived—or had their chances of survival increase—precisely because they were not persecuted *as Jews* (at least not at all times), which had implications for their postwar lives. Schochet, who was likely spared from death in Dachau by the "political" Polish inmates, was such a case. (Perhaps because of his mental abilities, political inmates pulled him, at a crucial point, from the Jewish population and gave him a clerical post in one of the offices staffed by prisoners.) Speaking perfect Polish and German, he could have subsisted in postwar Munich as a Pole. (Despite their boasting, Germans, as he and others reported, could scarcely tell who was a Jew.) And there was a small number of German Jews in the student group who could have carried on as Germans but instead identified after the war with displaced and stateless Jews.

A whole category of survivors, moreover, had passed as Christians, which created its own stresses and predicaments. Very young children, especially when integrated within non-Jewish families, might essentially forget having been Jewish, functionally convert to Catholicism, or otherwise choose after the war to retain a Christian identity.[93] Tanay, a teenager during the war, expressed well the existential burden of posing as a non-Jew: "My life depended on subterfuge . . . I could not be 'me' and live."[94] Even after the war, as the necessity for subterfuge to avoid anti-Semitism persisted, he wondered, "Would there ever come a time when I could safely be myself?"[95] Like Sabina Zimering, he eagerly reclaimed his Jewish identity at the first chance. Even for adolescents the internal confusion could be profound. In his memoir Tanay describes crossing with a group of Jews into Czechoslovakia in hopes of making it into Germany and beyond. Among them was a teenage girl who in the course of posing as a Christian had become a believing Catholic, and proudly wore a cross. Torn, she asked Tanay if she should make the passage. He explained that she would have to hide her Christianity from Jews if she left and her Judaism from Christians if she stayed. He recommended that she stay behind, interpreting her anguish in Orwellian terms as a sign of the oppressor's conquest of the consciousness of his victim.

Many of the alumni had a strong sense of Jewishness growing up, which the war did not unsettle. And all the members of Union, by definition, resolved any conflicts over identity on the side of their Jewishness. The internal pressure to do so, moreover, may have been so strong that the resolution did not feel like a choice. Nonetheless, the war created incentives and possibilities for disclaiming, concealing, or muting one's Jewishness in its wake. At least one UNRRA University student, Eduard Alperovitch, was Jewish but neither joined the Jewish Students' Union nor identified primarily as a Jew after the war, at least among his fellow university students. Originally from Latvia, he survived by passing as a "half Jew" (according to Nazi designations) and then in a concentration camp. After the war he embraced universalistic humanism—and not Zionism—as a leader of the UNRRA University Students Union. He promoted this ethic both as a repudiation of the national and racial particularism behind fascism and war and as a potential basis for sustaining the UNRRA University after the Allies shut it down in 1947.[96] Members of the Jewish Students' Union, he recalled decades later, criticized him for "associating with Ukrainians and such people, who are to be shunned and avoided."[97] Conceivably other Jews at university—if likely in very small numbers—made similar identifications and were unknown to the Union.

Letting go of a sense of "home" was another challenge, even as survivors resigned themselves to continued displacement and looked toward Palestine as a new home. Jews in prewar Europe had greatly varying relationships to their host countries. Those in Germany and Hungary, by and large, had a strong sense of national belonging. In Poland there was a great spectrum whereby some Jews saw themselves simply as Jews in Poland, others as both Jewish and Polish, smaller numbers as Polish Jews, and some, at a rare extreme, as Jewish Poles. The members of the student group from Poland, in general terms, were of a higher social standing than most other Jews. They were therefore both more integrated and inclined to feel a sense of national fealty—even as they experienced anti-Semitism firsthand and knew well or at least intuited the place of Jews in the society. As a consequence their sense of betrayal by their Polish countrymen could be intense. Tanay complained, "To hide my identity from the Germans was a badge of honor. To conceal my Jewish identity to avoid the hatred of Poles during and after the war was reprehensible."[98] All these decades later some alumni in the United States marvel, when in each other's company, that only in Poland were Jews killed after the war; they exude a sense of permanent exile.[99] The war and its aftermath, in short, not only rendered them stateless but made them feel homeless—a wound with the power to persist.

The formation of the Student Union ultimately was an expression of the unity in its members' ranks. That bond can be described by its positive attributes: their shared ambition to be students; their shared identity as Jews; and their shared sense of *Eretz Yisrael* (the "Land of Israel," as Jews commonly referred to the broad territory that would become the formal state of Israel) as the preferred destiny for Jews. At the same time that unity was a function of a common privation born of personal loss, displacement, statelessness, homelessness, and the uncertainty of their futures. Their lives, and the life of the Union, therefore existed under the dual signs of self-possession and dispossession, self-reliance and dependence, restored capacity and continued fragility.

The Jewish DP World

The Jewish Students' Union in Munich was formed in the winter of 1945 to facilitate a process that was already taking place. Individual Jews had found their way into the nascent UNRRA University. Word of the chance to study was spreading throughout the DP camps, among Jewish "free livers" in Munich, and beyond. And opportunities were opening for study at German universities. This process, intense in Munich, was playing out elsewhere in the American Zone. Around the same time twenty-five or so students in Heidelberg formed a Jewish students' union that later claimed to be the first in the American Zone to be recognized by the Military Government and German university officials.[100]

The Munich Union entered into a rapidly evolving matrix of institutions that organized Jewish life, represented Jewish interests, funded Jewish initiatives, and set expectations for Jewish consciousness and conduct. The students' individual decisions existed within a range of choices, each of which was ascribed political meaning in the pressure-laden world of displaced Jews; from its inception, the Union was in dialogue with opinion in that world regarding what was appropriate for young Jews to want and to do. This institutional and discursive landscape is the final context for understanding the Union's formation and initial self-representation.

The most important Jewish DP organization was the Central Committee of Liberated Jews. It served as the primary forum for the students' appeal for recognition within the Jewish world and the main source of their frustration with responses to their paths. The seeds of the CK (as I will abbreviate it) were sown even before the war's end, when survivors of the Kovno ghetto in Dachau and nearby Kaufering, Zionist cells in Buchenwald, and others began planning for the war's aftermath. By August 1945, following the gathering of survivors at St. Ottilien, an organization with elected leaders was formally established. Among them were Dr. Zalman Grinberg, Dr. Samuel Gringauz, and Jacob Oleiski—all "direct survivors" and men of accomplishment. In Mankowitz's description, "their protracted immersion in a world of suffering and pain strengthened their devotion and deepened their sense of historical responsibility. It was this willingness to work for the commonweal that helped them gain the respect of their fellows and endowed them with moral authority."[101]

The practical authority the Central Committee sought was to serve as the official representative body of all Jews in the American-occupied zone and to be acknowledged as such by the Americans. Strongly Zionist, the Committee agitated for a Jewish state in Palestine. Wary of the geopolitical implications of such activism, US officials limited its prescribed powers to forms of self-government and the dispensation of social aid, and barred it (rather unsuccessfully) from political advocacy as such.[102] The CK also assumed great responsibilities for the immediate welfare of Jewish DPs, helping to erect a Jewish society, in skeletal form, on German soil. It ran a tracing service, medical facilities, schools for the thousands of surviving children and youths, and vocational training programs, organized through formal departments. The CK employed thousands of workers inside and outside the camps, whether as CK officials, political leaders, medical personnel, teachers, or budding craftsmen and farmers, compensating them largely in the form of donated rations. In addition it sponsored the Historical Commission to document the recent devastation and published a weekly newspaper in Yiddish, *Unzer Weg* (*Our Path*). Separating from a parallel group in the British Zone, and with its functional dominion initially restricted to Munich, the Committee worked in late 1945 and 1946 to bring the Jewish refugees flooding the American Zone into the fold of its care and in line with its political goals.

Zionism infused the CK's rhetoric and nearly all its functions. Its leaders stressed the importance of discipline, industriousness, self-sacrifice, and the value of practical skills in preparation for a national future. Much of the education it sponsored focused on the Hebrew language, Jewish history, Zionist ideology, and "spiritual" edification.[103] The Jewish youth received a special charge. "First and Foremost, the youth must be trained for productive work to prepare for life in Eretz Yisrael," exhorted Jacob Oleiski.[104] "Only you, Jewish youth . . . awaken in me energy, in order to further build the foundation . . . [and for me to] fulfill my social duties to the Jews. . . . [L]earn a trade, for your spirit, for your soul—become good and useful people, as our people expects from you."[105]

If the Central Committee articulated the Zionist duty of DP youth, the aforementioned *kibbutzim* appeared to represent its fulfillment. Tens of thousands of Jewish youths joined *kibbutzim* in post-liberation Poland, with more than 30,000 eventually coming west with the Bricha.[106] *Kibbutzim* also flourished in occupied Germany (often with the aid of leaders from Poland and even Palestine) as collectives both within and outside the DP camps and in the several dozen *hakhsharot*, or agricultural collectives, established on German soil with the help of occupation authorities and aid agencies.[107] According to Avinoam Patt as many as one-third to one-half of Jewish DP youths (ages fifteen to twenty-four) "removed themselves from the network of assembly centers and DP camps . . . to actively prepare for migration to Palestine."[108]

The Central Committee strongly supported the *kibbutzim* as a "Zionist framework for youth" that would enable them both to avoid the dangers of "demoralization, black market activity, and idleness" and to serve the Jewish future.[109] Though young Jews joined *kibbutzim* for complex reasons often having to do with material and emotional needs, the collectives functioned as a Zionist vanguard. They provided young "pioneers" to establish the Jewish state and Zionist impetus among Jewish DPs. They would, in the view of the DP leadership, "also have to represent the DP community as a whole, providing spiritual and moral support to the broader public."[110] The *kibbutzim* represented a crucial point of reference for the students and their very different goals—to study at university; to obtain broadly professional and humanistic educations, not vocational training and Zionist rearing; and to organize as students, not "pioneers."

Displaced Jews organized as well into smaller associations, often on professional lines. Thus engineers, doctors, artists, and actors formed their own groups. Notable among them was the Writers Union of Liberated Jews (*Schriftstellerverband der befreiten Jüden*), which formed shortly after the Student Union.[111] It was comprised of journalists, publishers, essayists, poets, and writers of professional standing prior to the war. These writers played a great role in resurrecting the Jewish press and literary life in occupied Germany, in effect creating a public sphere for Jewish DPs. Much like the students, they argued that intellectual and cultural pursuits were a defining aspect of Jewish heritage and an integral part of the Jewish future.

The final, vital fixture in the DP world was the American Joint Distribution Committee (as noted earlier, commonly referred to as the JDC by officials and by DPs as the "Joint"), a private Jewish charity established in 1914 and pledged to helping world Jewry. Initially stalled in negotiations with the US Army, the Joint arrived late on the scene, sending its first permanent teams into the American Zone only in August 1945, months after the war's end.[112] As it built its operations, the Joint incurred the frequent complaint from DPs that it was excessively bureaucratic and deferential to military authority, insufficiently Zionist (as an officially "apolitical" organization), and insensitive to DPs' wartime suffering and current plight.[113] It took its charge very seriously, however, which was to aid DPs in most every way imaginable. The organization built separate divisions for education, employment, emigration, religion, medical care, supply, and legal services, and conducted frequent surveys to determine the size and needs of the fluctuating Jewish DP population.[114] With the de facto backing of the US occupation authorities, it also mediated among the US military, UNRRA, the Central Committee, other DP bodies, representatives from Palestine, and even the German government.

Perhaps most crucially, the Joint invested massive material resources in helping DPs. With a workforce that grew to 700, and drawing on a budget of 200 million dollars, it delivered food and clothing to tens of thousands of Jews (often to supplement UNRRA aid) inside and outside the camps and distributed de facto currency in the form of cigarettes and other goods.[115] The group essentially financed the Central Committee, providing stocks of tradable commodities as well as cash payments. The Joint also funded the *kibbutzim* and *hakhsharot*, whether for their rehabilitative or, more tacitly, political value.[116]

From the outset education was a priority. In October 1945 the Joint sent two "outstanding educators"—Koppel S. Pinson, a professor of sociology at

Queens College in New York City, and M. Jacob Jaslow, a high school principal in Ludlow, Massachusetts—to head its education division.[117] Their task was daunting. They quickly determined that their work would require securing Yiddish reading material, other basic texts, film projectors, and suitable films; establishing kindergartens, a primary school system, and vocational training; finding qualified teachers for each; assembling libraries inside and outside the camps; and providing adult education in the form of lectures and evening classes.[118] Over time, and in conjunction with the Central Committee and teachers from Palestine, it substantially succeeded in its goals.[119]

The Joint, finally, took immediate interest in the more elevated sectors of Jewish educational and cultural life. A January 1946 memo, which proposed a program for its educational work, counseled the "seeking out of exceptional literary, artistic, musical, and scientific abilities . . . this is an extremely important function, especially in view of the almost complete annihilation of the European Jewish intelligentsia. Individuals of such abilities must be sought out, encouraged and sponsored."[120] On the basis of such sentiments, the Joint pledged its "support of Jewish Students in Universities in Germany."

The Jewish Students' Union

One can now only guess at the precise sequence by which Jews in and near Munich first sought to register en masse for university study. A plausible account holds that Jews interested in studying approached members of the Central Committee, whether at its office in the Deutsches Museum or on Sieberstrasse—the Munich street where major Jewish institutions, including the Joint, would cluster, and where the CK would open new headquarters. The Committee likely assembled lists of prospective students and then referred them to the JDC. In Yehuda Knobler's account, the prospective students were initially offered little help; the kindly Josef Silberman, however, provided them a personal "card" and a moment's hope. In this way, the seeds of the Union were planted.

Its blossoming was, however, a halting process. Felix Korn remembers being approached in September or October of 1945 outside the Deutsches Museum by Silberman, who suggested that they form a union.[121] Busy with schoolwork, he declined. Robert Nenner also met other Jews in the fall at the UNRRA University but recalls that "everyone was guarded at that point."[122] Nonetheless, Silberman soon found collaborators, among them David Fund, Edmund Feuerstein, and Knobler, whose recollections decades later fill out the picture of the Student Union's founding. According to Knobler, in the fall and winter of 1945, Silberman wrote to UNRRA students, or aspiring

Early leading figures of the Jewish Students' Union in Munich in 1946 or 1947. Josef Silberman, the Union's co-founder and first president, is on the left; Israel Borenstein is in the middle; and Roman Ohrenstein is on the right. (Courtesy of Roman Ohrenstein)

students, at the DP camps and organized a meeting of between fifteen and twenty people, followed by a second and a third. Out of these meetings the Munich Union was born.[123]

What little we know about Josef Silberman comes from memorial essays penned by his friends in the posthumously published booklet of his writings, from the writings themselves, and from the testimony of the small handful of living alumni who have specific memories of him. Born in December 1921, he grew up in Sokolov-Podolski, a small town east of Warsaw, whose Jewish population was eventually sent to the Treblinka extermination camp. One essay describes him as a "child of the village," and an essay of his own presents village life in idyllic terms. His father, a man of "Hasidic enthusiasm and intensity," was a leader of the local Jewish community and a Zionist organizer. At age six Silberman attended a Tarbut (Zionist) school in Shedlitz, a regional center of Zionist organizing. He later became an activist, serving as a delegate in national Zionist conventions in Poland. Presumably having completed his *Matura*, he attended a teacher's institute in Warsaw. But his studies were cut short by the German invasion, which quickly claimed his father's life. Deported to the Soviet interior, Silberman survived with the remainder of his family in Tashkent. He briefly attended university in Leningrad, perhaps during the war or just after, and came to Munich no later than the fall of 1945, months earlier than most of the deportees.[124] At the University of Munich he studied law.[125]

I earlier described youth as a major asset of the prospective students. It both helped in their actual survival and lent them a striking vitality after the war. But relative maturity was also an asset. Age twenty-four at the war's end, Silberman was comparatively old among the students; he had by then developed leadership skills and completed some university study. Others of the Union's first officers—Feuerstein, Fund, and Michael Linwer—were born in 1912, 1916, and 1916, respectively, making them much older than most of the rank-and-file.[126]

To the younger students, Silberman conveyed maturity, worldliness, and savoir-faire. Schochet recalls addressing him, along with others of the Union's "elders," as "Sir." They were, he stressed, "very capable and dedicated people. . . . When they decided to do something, it was done, [always] with a lot of energy and thought."[127] Alumna Lucy Fink recalls that the Union leaders were "hard-driving people . . . who were altruistic."[128] Ohrenstein describes Silberman as handsome, kind, and charismatic. And though Silberman was very much on the political left and Ohrenstein on the right, such differences never got between them. Evidence of Silberman's central role in the Union abounds in its records. The group's early activity reports are largely a chronicle of Silberman's personal efforts on the group's behalf. One such report declares outright that he "especially is to thank that the union exists."[129]

The first document generated by the Union was its constitution, titled the "Statute of the Union of Jewish Students in Munich."[130] Its preamble makes reference to a December 1945 meeting at which the group was founded and its core "declarations" ratified. There is no indication of the meeting's location, though it likely took place at the UNRRA University or the offices of the Joint. Neither are the statute's authors mentioned, though Knobler credits the document to Silberman, with assistance from Feuerstein.

The main purposes of the constitution, written in German and running five-and-a-half typed pages, were to state the Union's goals, fix conditions for membership, and establish an administrative structure. The document is largely bureaucratic, and little in it betrays the extraordinary circumstances that gave rise to the Union. Korn recalls that the constitution "wasn't part of our everyday life. Once it was done, it was done. I doubt it was of any importance" to the Union's ongoing life.[131] Nonetheless, the statute says a great deal about the Union's identity, functions, and self-perception, and about the context in which it formed.

The first of the core declarations asserts, "The Jewish students in Munich regard it as necessary, in this transition period during which the Jewish people live in conditions of diaspora, to continue their studies, and therefore form a Union of Jewish Students."[132] The second states that the Union is made up of "all Jewish students and is built on a democratic basis." The final declaration holds that, "as part of the Jewish people, the Jewish students share its aims and wish to serve as fellow-fighters [*Mitkampfer*] in its goal—the resurrection of the country of Eretz Israel." On the one hand, the document shows that the Union is a contingent response to a temporary circumstance; the pursuit of education in occupied Germany is subsumed within the Zionist project, to which the organization proclaims its ultimate fealty. On the other hand, the students here insist upon their need and, by implication, their right to study, even on German soil. The elaborate organization the statute then describes suggests a dogged commitment to the challenges of the here and now, and not just preparation for a national future. Already evident are the dual wishes the students so desperately wanted reconciled: to be taken seriously as students—and have their choice to study viewed as valid—while also being seen as proper Jews, supportive of the Zionist imperative. In psychological, existential, and even political terms, their most essential appeal is not to occupation authorities, other DP students, or Germans, but to other Jews.

The statute echoes the dual goal by declaring that the central tasks of the Union are "the material and cultural support of Jewish students" and "a massive cultural campaign [*Aufklärungsarbeit*] to enlighten the Jewish population," to be carried out through presentations, assemblies, and speeches, as well as the publication of various writings. Here the Union asserts its desired role of contributing to the intellectual and cultural uplift of the Jewish people. Animating the Union's entire history is the struggle to make the student life possible for its members while at the same time making good on the pledge to serve their larger community and national cause.

The statute indicates that the Union was funded by seed money, income received through membership dues, and "fixed subventions and gifts." These gifts would come in the form of cash payments and rations from international relief agencies, Jewish DP organizations, and Bavarian state agencies. The Union's members were to be the students themselves, entitled to whatever aid the Union secured and to participate in the organization. The constitution also allows for "honorary members"—friends and patrons worthy of special recognition and who might add to the organization's prestige.

The highest organ of the Union was the General Meeting (*Generalversammlung*). Consisting of all members and convening once a semester, it had the power to legislate by simple majority, elect officers, and set the agenda for the group as a whole. The Union's leadership was the Executive Committee

(*Vorstandschaft*) comprising a chair and six other members, entitled to pay as staff members. Committee members headed distinct departments (*Referenten*) such as finance, cultural education (*Ausbildung*), and social welfare. In addition, there was a Control Council (*Revisionskommission*), which reviewed the organization's books and periodically assessed the work of the Executive Committee and the state of the Union as a whole. Finally, there was the Honor Court, whose function was to settle internal disputes, recommend the censure or even expulsion of offending members, and, most broadly, guard against corruption.

The statute concludes with a revealing provision specifying that, should the Union dissolve, all its property would go to the Hebrew University in Jerusalem. Established in 1925 and boasting Albert Einstein, Sigmund Freud, and Martin Buber among its first board of governors, Hebrew University was a leading center of Jewish thought and learning, and a place of pride for Jews worldwide. To the students in Germany, it was a place of near-reverential regard and longing, in which their identities as Jews and as students—indeed, the desired unity of their identity as *Jewish students*—were affirmed.

Conceived just months after Germany's surrender and in a chaotic environment, the Union's structure is conspicuous for its complexity. This sophistication reflected both the seriousness of the students' endeavor and the initiative of Jewish DPs in general, who practiced traditions of Jewish self-reliance and organizing as part of their "return to life." At least one of the Union's early leaders, in the recollection of alumnus Rafael Nenner, had been "a big organizer of the Jewish community" before the war.[133] Silberman had a background in Zionist politicking. Jews' wartime experiences, moreover, likely fed the organizational dynamism of DP culture. As Anna Holian points out, "organizing" in Nazi camps—which ranged from developing clandestine resistance networks to "procuring what one needed to survive without actually stealing"—imparted skills "valuable in the postwar context," where taking advantage of opportunities to improve one's condition was at a premium.[134] The term "organizer," reports Schochet in *Feldafing*, had an important place in the DP lexicon. Whatever the precise origins of their skill sets, the Union's leaders were organizers par excellence. The Union's complex administration reflected, in addition, the elaborate constitutional arrangements of prewar Jewish political and cultural organizations in Eastern Europe, evident also in other DP organizations.

In principle power within the Union was distributed among departments and controlled through internal checks and balances. In practice, however, the members of the Executive Committee had tremendous responsibility and, hence, authority. The elaborate structure also encouraged rivalries among parts of the organization, and thus invited the return of the heavily factionalized quality of prewar Jewish political life. In general there seemed two experiences of the Union. The key officers engaged in ceaseless organizing, advocacy, negotiations, meetings, and record-keeping, and indulged occasional power struggles on political and personal lines. To them also fell the bulk of what might be termed the "ideological" work of framing the student endeavor within the shared struggle of diaspora Jews and inserting the Union within DP discourse. Their efforts had an aura of self-sacrifice and strategic finesse. Many in the rank-and-file, by contrast, enjoyed the material and social benefits of membership and the cathartic sense of belonging the Union provided but had little direct role in its extensive work or political intrigues. A near constant in the Union's life was the officers' pleading with the broader membership to be more active, especially in the Union's cultural program, and to help realize the exalted mission the founding statute proclaimed.

When asked to define decades later what the Union essentially was, the alumni commonly describe it in terms of social welfare or "self-help."[135] The Union's core functions of securing enrollments, food, clothing, shelter, and academic supplies squarely fit these labels. The Union could, however, provide such aid—or self-help—only through the assistance of others, leading it to clamor relentlessly for more of everything from anyone in a position to give. As a result the deceptively simple label of "interest group," with its emphasis on advocacy and institutional relationships, may best describe the Union, as it may the countless other DP associations (not just Jewish ones) throughout occupied Germany.[136]

Most basically interest groups represent and advocate on behalf of a collective interest. As part of this, they seek formal and informal grants of recognition or legitimacy in the eyes of others. Paradigmatically, this recognition comes from the state, which has the singular power to confer legitimacy (legal or political) and, of course, dispense resources. Yet American-occupied Germany had no discrete state function, no seamless and stable system of governing authority or sovereignty. Rather it featured a mélange of authorities who variously claimed, disavowed, and competed over responsibility for diverse population categories, which were themselves highly fluid. This condition made the scramble for recognition, resources, and power among DP associations—each with its agenda—so dynamic.

The Military Government (MG)—the Americans—legislated through occupation policies, had police power over refugees in designated settings, and ultimately underwrote all other authority. There was also a functioning Bavarian government, with a parliament, state agencies, and a police force with dominion over the German areas (though conflicts over jurisdiction often arose). In the mix as well were international relief agencies such as UNRRA and the JDC. The Jewish DPs had their own associations, most notably the Central Committee. It both sought the legitimation of the Americans and itself conferred legitimacy on and distributed resources among Jewish DP groups. Finally, there was the Jewish Agency or "Sochnut"—the government in formation of the Jewish community in Palestine—which sent representatives to occupied Germany, worked closely with the CK, and staked claims, growing bolder as the Israeli state emerged, to the loyalties and decisions of Jewish DPs. Complicating this dizzying picture, the relative distribution of power, responsibilities, and resources among such entities frequently shifted in the first years after the war, as American priorities, geopolitical realities, and material and political conditions on the ground changed.

The Union appealed for formal recognition, legitimacy, and aid to these and other authorities simultaneously. Hence it placed great stress on bureaucratic competence and rectitude to demonstrate that it was a reliable representative and negotiating partner. Equally important, its appeals for recognition and assistance were always accompanied by an argument, explicit or implicit, about the worthiness of their endeavor and what was owed them, both by virtue of their wartime persecution and their status as Jewish students. The nature of the appeal varied based on what was being sought and from whom. The students' pragmatic pursuits, by extension, were always overlain with political meaning organized around issues of Jewish identity, German guilt and responsibility, and international obligation. The students' involvement in these issues, and how they negotiated them, are much of what gives the group historical significance far beyond its small size.

The Union and the Politics of Recognition

After its founding, the Jewish Students' Union stepped up activities already underway on behalf of existing and prospective students. Its most urgent task was securing additional enrollments. The first point of entry was the UNRRA University, where demand greatly exceeded available opportunities for study, making the Union's advocacy important. As early as the fall of 1945, several dozen Jews throughout the American Zone had successfully enrolled, sometimes with the help of the Joint, in the winter term of German universities.[137] No sooner did the Union form than it began negotiating for additional enrollment slots.

The first such school to enroll Jewish students during this time was the Ludwig-Maximilians-Universität (the LMU, also referred to as the

University of Munich). Established by a papal concession in 1472, the school was Bavaria's oldest university, retaining its Catholic character through the centuries. The university was never closed during the war, and its administration was implicated in the Nazi regime; it was the site of the famous White Rose resistance, made up largely of LMU students, which LMU administrators helped to mercilessly smash. The school had already begun its 1945–46 winter semester in January when a small number of enrollments became open to Jews. Soon thereafter opportunities for study opened up as well at the Technische Hochschule, an elite polytechnic university (likened by one alumnus to America's prestigious Massachusetts Institute of Technology) that had been badly damaged and closed during periods of the war.[138] Some months into the Union's existence, three broad paths existed for Jews wishing to study: enrolling in the UNRRA University; enrolling directly in a German school, including conservatories and art academies; or transferring from the UNRRA school to a German one.

The Union's advocacy entailed meeting, corresponding, and negotiating with Bavarian state officials and university administrators. The success of this advocacy depended on the Union's ability to establish legitimacy in the eyes of its interlocutors, for which various allies and patrons played a crucial role. Among the earliest documents in the Union's archive is a January 11, 1946, letter from the Central Committee to the director of the UNRRA University requesting admission for fifty-nine students.[139] The letter refers to a previous meeting attended by a representative of the CK, an educated professional with an engineering degree who spoke on the students' behalf.

Soon the Union began communicating on its own behalf. In mid-January Josef Silberman and David Fund personally met with the University of Munich rector, Herr Professor Röhm; Röhm held a position of extremely high status in Germany, likened by one alumnus to a "cardinal or a four-star general in America," and bearing the exalted title "Herr Magnifizenze."[140] Later in the month the Union corresponded with the head of the Bavarian Ministry of Education and Culture, whose oversight included all German (public) educational institutions in Bavaria, including the universities, which were under state control. These actions alone show the determination, or even audacity, of the young survivors. They also convey the Union's raison d'être as an interest group. Reflecting on its essential roles, alumnus Mark Hupert explained that the Union "enabled all of us to start studying. . . . Obviously we couldn't go [as individuals] to the Cultural Minister [to say] that we want to be admitted. . . . As a body, you have some influence. As one person you are nobody."[141] From the outset the leaders of the Union acted as if they and their constituency mattered.

A great deal of the Union's power came from the way it presented itself to officialdom. More specifically, the Union consciously played on its members' victim status and Germans' attendant obligation to them. The letter to the cultural ministry, sent on JDC letterhead, reads:

> The Union of Jewish Students in Munich, which comprises all [Jewish] students in Munich colleges, requests the retroactive admittance of 25 Jewish students to the University of Munich.

> The candidates consist exclusively of former Kzler [inmates of concentration camps, or *Konzentrationslager*] who, as a consequence of their health condition, are still under medical care in various hospitals, and individuals who, as residents in DP camps in the provinces, were unaware of the registration times. . . .

> Because the first steps of the National Socialist government were directed against the Jewish intelligentsia and for 12 years no development [*Nachwuchs*] was possible—to the contrary, nearly the entire Jewish intelligentsia was systematically annihilated—we ask that you respond favorably to our request and thereby fulfill the dream of those who for years in concentration camps longingly waited for the resumption of their studies.[142]

Such words are complex self-representations. They offer revealing—if also subtly misleading—descriptions clearly crafted to serve the Union's strategic goals.

The opening assertion is that the Union included all Jewish students in Munich. This is more aspiration than fact, as the Union, just a few weeks into its life, hardly counted all Jewish students in the city as formal members. Nonetheless, the claim enhances a sense of the group's importance as a body representing Jewish interests before German institutions. Doubtful as well is the implied claim that the candidates were made up entirely (or almost entirely) of concentration camp survivors. As we have seen, far from all Union members had been in camps. As a way to reinforce Jewish entitlement with respect to German authorities, this self-description had important standing in the occupation world.

Jewish and other DPs generally wanted the maximum amount of aid from occupation authorities and relief organizations. For a Jew in the American Zone, the surest way to secure such aid was to be recognized as a concentration camp survivor, ideally one liberated by the Americans. Liberation by the Soviets would mean that the DP was an "infiltree" and possibly arouse the suspicion from the Americans that he or she had some connection to communism. Many thousands of Jews in the American Zone right after the war had in fact been camp inmates, and had little or no trouble having this substantiated. When processing the liberated prisoners, the Americans often issued documents verifying individuals' status. Other ex-inmates had retained their *Haftlings-Personal-Karte*, or prison registration, and could use this document to prove their status. Yehuda Knobler, for example, had saved his registration from Buchenwald, which recorded basic biographical data and the "reason" (*Grund*) for his incarceration. (This section stated simply "Political-Polish-Jew"—"three strikes," he joked, when showing Bella Brodzki and me the original document.)[143] Some former inmates, however, did not have such documents. These individuals went to US military officials, the DP Commission set up to screen DPs, UNRRA eligibility officers, and even to German notaries to prove their status as former inmates. Such proof might require that they produce one or more witnesses to verify that they had been in a given camp. Simon Schochet, who saw countless inmates at Dachau, recalls trying to help others by serving as a witness. The Americans, he stressed, felt sympathy for the Jewish victims, and their first inclination after the war was to help Jews get aid, not to question their stories.[144]

Over time increasing numbers of Jews who had not been concentration camp inmates came into the American Zone, causing the Americans, UNRRA, and German agencies to vet more closely the DP population. One historian bluntly states that "postwar conditions encouraged the use of false identities," whether for illegal movement across borders or to secure aid.[145] As in the case of Emanuel Tanay and countless others, some falsely reported that they had been inmates to gain official DP status, admission to hospitals, and various dispensations. Like other survivors, the alumni did not see this claim as dishonest in a pejorative sense. First, the concentration camp experience, thought by the Americans to define Nazi terror, was an exceedingly narrow template for understanding Jewish victimization. An understanding of the systematic nature of German persecution—indeed, of "the Holocaust" as a comprehensive and intricately executed assault on Europe's Jews within numerous locales and by varied means—did not yet exist in the consciousness of the liberators. Many survivors had suffered enormously in ghettos, conventional prisons, labor camps, and in disguise or in hiding, but had never been in a concentration camp as such; they hardly felt less "worthy" of help after the war. Even those deported to the Soviet interior had suffered at German hands (and often had first experienced German occupation).

Second, as the alumni and other DPs explained, Jews "did what they had to do" to survive after the war as during it. Misrepresenting their status, in their view, fell into the realm of acceptable duplicity in the face of continued adversity, about which one need have little or no moral qualm. Misrepresenting one's wartime experience was in fact one among a host of common transgressions performed by Jewish DPs (including many students), whether by illegally crossing borders, falsifying one's age and nationality, trading cigarettes and other goods given as aid on the black market, or remaining registered at DP camps to receive rations even while also receiving aid as a "free liver." Myers Feinstein concludes that Jewish DPs "rejected the notion . . . that they were criminal" by virtue of any of this.[146]

The Americans eventually recognized the near-universality of Jewish victimization, formally considering all Jews persecutees, regardless of nationality or wartime experience, and dropping the designation of "infiltree" for those coming from the east. This shift did not, however, happen all at once, and there could be a lag between policy and practice. In April 1946 the Union complained to the welfare officer at the UNRRA University that a student had been refused accommodations at the Deutsches Museum because she had earlier been designated an infiltree; current directives, however, mandated that infiltrees receive the same treatment as registered DPs.[147] Some Union members, for their part, continued to press false claims many months after the war. As late as March 1946, UNRRA Team 108 sent a letter to the Union complaining that it had sent them an individual who insisted that he had been an inmate in Buchenwald. Yet "two persons who know the camp well . . . confirm that this man could never have been [there], as his information about the camp w[as] entirely wrong."[148] How many of the Union's members misrepresented their status in this way is impossible to say. Early in the Union's life, it is likely that a large percentage of members had been in camps, but this number surely dropped, as it did among Jewish DPs as a whole, as Jews came west.

The letter to the ministry insists as well that it grant the request for admissions to help restore the near-vanquished Jewish intelligentsia. On one level this plea indicates that the students saw the opportunity to study in a German university as a form of reparation—something Germany now owed them, given what the Germans had done to them. That Jewish academics were among the first targets of Nazi racial policies lent great pathos to the students' cause. On another level the framing of the plea conveys how the students deliberately appealed to German guilt: their substantive guilt for crimes against Jews, as well as their consciousness of the consequences of that guilt. In no sense did the Union leaders expect that the German university officials would feel authentically remorseful and voluntarily work to fulfill the dreams of study of the young, forlorn survivors. Rather, such references were an act of rhetorical shaming, crafted to make it harder for the officials to refuse the students' demands. The alumni uniformly report that the German university administrators—aware of the watchful eye of the Americans—were extremely compliant in their dealings with the Union. "It was a different Germany," Mark Hupert explained. The Germans "knew that . . . they did something horrendous and terrible. So obviously nobody would dare to object. . . . They had to take you. See, it wasn't from the goodness of their heart. . . . There was no question [that] there was a place for the . . . survivors of German concentration camps. . . . There was no point [for them] even to argue about it."[149]

Bearing out this logic, within four days of the Union's appeal for admissions, the Ministry of Education and Culture instructed the LMU to retroactively admit twenty-five Jews. Parroting the Union's letter, it explained that the prospective students had missed the scheduled registration in hospitals and distant DP camps.[150] As if to seal its sense of victory and to announce its emergence on the occupation scene, the Union sent a letter of introduction to the LMU rector the following day. It declared that "in December 1945 under the auspices of the AJDC in Munich the Union of Jewish Students in Munich was founded" and requested that "Herr Magnifizenze" direct any questions concerning Jewish students to the Union, which could be reached in its single-room office in the JDC headquarters on Sieberstrasse.

Brief reference to the students' wartime experiences and the broader context of German crimes became a standard feature of the Union's initial formal interactions with German and other authorities. Shortly after the appeal to LMU, the Union sent a letter to the rector, lamenting that "these students had no opportunity to study during the Nazi regime" and stressing that their admittance would "contribute to the rebuilding [*Neuaufbau*] of the Jewish intelligentsia."[151] A Union post to the UNRRA University rector declares that "almost all" of its members were "former concentration camp inmates [who] were persecuted in unbelievable ways."[152] An added subtext to such language was the intense competition for scarce postwar resources and opportunities. The claims of Jews as one victim population existed alongside those of others, such as the self-identified "political persecutees" from nations occupied by or even allied with Germany during the war. The Germans, for their part, generally saw themselves as victims under the American occupation, frequently alleging that food, housing, and other resources went to DPs. Such resentment, as Atina Grossmann, Margarete Myers Feinstein, and others have shown, was a source of considerable friction, and even some-times violent conflict, between Germans and DPs.

The Union's push for recognition extended as well to the Jewish world. Here the essential appeal was for material aid to make the student life pos-sible. Among the groups to which the Union introduced itself was the *Isra-elitisches Kultusgemeinde*—the reconstituted Jewish community in Munich headed by the German Jewish rabbi Aaron Ohrnstein.[153] The correspondence explains that the students, as concentration camp survivors, "lost entirely their ways and means [*Hab und Gut*]" but could no longer live in DP camps due to their studies; they therefore needed money, clothes, and, ideally, a group residence.[154]

Securing aid was an enormously important Union function, which had its own complex dynamic and rhetoric. The first step, engineered early in the Union's existence, was assessing the institutional landscape to determine to whom the Union should reach out. In late February the Union called for the creation of a formal "patrons' council" to alleviate "the extremely difficult circumstances in which the Jewish student community in Munich finds it-self."[155] Those invited to participate included the Joint, UNRRA, the Central Committee, the Kultusgemeinde, the Hebrew Immigrant Aid Society (HIAS, another US-based Jewish relief organization), and the State's Commission for the Care of Jews (*Staatskommissariat für die Betreuung der Juden in Bayern*)—a Bavarian state agency created in October 1945 and charged with assisting Jews not under UNRRA's immediate care.[156] Though such a council never quite coalesced to set and execute policy, the call identified the organizations that would help shape the students' destiny in occupied Germany.

The letter of invitation to the patrons' council has other significant fea-tures. For the first time Union correspondence is marked with a circular stamp bearing the English words "The Jewish Students Union—Munich." Likely furnished by the Joint, the stamp signifies that the Union had the backing of the Americans and must therefore be taken seriously. In addition, the letter indicates the address of the new Union office, 19/1 Gewürzmühl-strasse, which it would maintain until the mid-1950s.

Having an office was a practical necessity for everything from receiv-ing prospective members to conducting the Union's voluminous correspon-dence, holding meetings, and stocking and dispensing clothing, food, cig-arettes, and other items donated to the Union. The Union envisioned it as well as a social hub where students might read the newspaper and discuss their academic work. But more than that, a physical address had immense symbolic importance for the Union's effort to establish its legitimacy within the occupation world.

The office was most likely provided through the State's Commission for the Care of Jews. Run out of the Bavarian interior ministry and explicitly tasked with dispensing reparations, the commission provided housing and furnishings to Jews and had the power to requisition physical space.[157] The Union was given four or five rooms in a single floor of a multistory residential building.[158] The task of refurbishing and outfitting the space fell to the Union leaders. They dealt directly with German contractors and merchants for such things as building renovations, the servicing of an Olympia typewriter, and the acquisition of light bulbs, window shades, and office furniture.[159] In certain instances, the state commissioner, Hermann Aumer (a "half-Jew," by Nazi-era designations), simply instructed German companies to provide the needed items to the Union.[160] The money to pay for such things, as well as rations packets and other items, came from the State's Commission, the Joint, and the Central Committee.

By the middle of March the Union had a telephone and its own letterhead with "The Jewish Students' Union in Munich" printed in English, German, and Yiddish (in Hebrew letters).[161] In addition the Union hired the first of two secretaries, a German woman, through the Munich employment office.[162] These seemingly innocuous transactions could tap into troubling aspects of the recent past. A letter from the commission alerted the Union that the plumber they had been dealing with was, according to the Kultusgemeinde, a "horrible Nazi activist" who was using his son to front the company. It urged the Union to turn over any information it had on the plumber and to consult with another new agency, the Bavarian Fund for Those Affected by the Nuremberg Laws (*Bayerische Hilfswerk für die durch die Nürnberger Gesetze Betroffenen*), to find a plumber without a tainted past.[163]

"We Create"

Into the spring of 1946, the Union continued to matriculate students into area schools. The process involved submitting lists of prospective students to the LMU and then the TH to fill the quota of twenty-five students each university allowed. The numbers grew as additional slots opened for Jews.[164] By the middle of March, the Union boasted that Munich had 250 or so Jewish students in institutions of higher learning, with more than half attending the LMU.[165]

Accompanying such lists was typically some version of the following statement: "The candidates in question were given an entrance examination by our union, which assessed their level of knowledge. The exam demonstrated that they are truly capable students."[166] Here the reference is to the

Verification Commission (*Verifikations-Kommission*) that stipulated the candidates' readiness for university study. Set up to address the consequences of wartime persecution, the verification process was one of the most vital functions the Union performed, providing as well the most tangible evidence of its influence.

A great many of the prospective students had no proof of their *Matura*. This was especially true of camp survivors, who were apt to possess no personal documents. Moreover, many of the aspiring students had not completed *gymnasium*. The UNRRA University initially required a *Matura* for admittance to its college curriculum.[167] The German universities, in addition, sought to maintain credible admissions standards. Given the Jews' lack of documents, some system was needed to qualify them. Otherwise the great majority would be functionally excluded from university study.

The Verification Commission filled this breach by administering what amounted to college entrance exams and otherwise validating students' credentials. Documents indicate that the commission was already in operation in 1945, and likely predated the advent of the Union.[168] It first functioned under the auspices of the CK, and may well have been devised when Jews first began presenting themselves to the CK in 1945 in hopes of attending universities. The CK announced its existence to the UNRRA University director Halina Gaszynska in early March 1946, explaining that "since the greatest portion of Jewish students have lost their documents in concentration camps, a Verification Commission . . . has been founded"; further, "all the Jewish students [under the auspices of the Students' Union who are accepted at university] have been vetted by the commission." [169] The examiners, drawn from among Jewish DPs, were university lecturers and docents. Crucially, the commission's determination of candidate readiness was accepted by both the UNRRA University and German schools.[170] In this way the work of the Union, which soon played the leading role in the exams' administration, enjoyed formal legitimacy.

By the early spring of 1946, the momentum of the Union was palpable, as were the challenges it faced. Both were expressed at a session of the General Meeting held in late March. Preserved in detailed minutes, the meeting conveys not only the nature of the Union's work but also its internal culture and the pressures surrounding it.[171]

The meeting was held at the Café am Isartorplatz, with the members gathered by written invitations sent to their addresses at DP camps or the apartments they occupied. The session began with Emanuel Tanay leading a moment of silence in honor of the Holocaust's many victims among the student ranks. The specific nature of this remembrance shows how deeply

The General Meeting of the Jewish Students' Union in Munich in an
auditorium at the Ludwig-Maximilians-Universität in 1946 or 1947.
(Courtesy of Roman Ohrenstein)

the members identified specifically as Jewish *students*, which they thought of
as a social and cultural category. Josef Silberman, the Union's president, then
gave an address.

Silberman first implored colleagues without documents—whether basic
identification or verification certificates—to obtain them, as it was important to determine "who can truly be a student, and who cannot." He stressed,
"Only those should be sent to study [who are] learned and serious about
their education." Deceit about one's qualifications, whatever the claims of
some of the earliest students, would not be sanctioned by the Union going
forward, and could in fact badly damage its standing. And in no sense was
the Union intended for Jewish DPs who simply wanted to gain material
benefits by affiliating as students.

Through the Union's advocacy, Silberman reported, dozens of slots had
been opened for Jews at German universities. He also noted with pride the
procurement of an office, which had entailed extensive efforts to have the
Union legally recognized by the relevant authorities. Silberman confessed,
however, significant difficulty in obtaining "understanding and aid" from
the Jewish community. Efforts to establish a *gymnasium* course at the Foehrenwald DP camp fell through because "a Jewish institution in the camp decided against and prohibited such a course." In all likelihood the CK blocked
the initiative out of concern that it might drive young Jews away from their

Zionist duty as potential pioneers. Union efforts to establish a dormitory, in consultation with the Joint, the CK, and the State's Commission, had also fallen through, whether for reasons practical or political. The Union did, however, manage to secure special rations for four of its Executive Committee members, equal to what CK officials received; with such compensation, work for the Union was acknowledged as a contribution to the Jewish DP commonweal.

A good portion of the gathering dealt with expectations for the members' conduct, stressing the need to maintain integrity and solidarity in all affairs. The Union leaders blasted what they insisted was a member's false accusation, conveyed in a letter to a DP newspaper, that the Union had inequitably distributed aid to its members and had, in both its informal business and official announcements, used the Polish language. The latter charge speaks to the complex linguistic politics of the group and of the Jewish DP community more broadly. Union policy favored German for official business, given both its formal dealings and the fact that all its members had to function in German. It also conveyed the seriousness with which the students took their participation in German-language institutions. With very few exceptions, all of the Union's voluminous documents are in German, including those directed to the membership.

In principle Yiddish was reserved for the Union's internal dealings and some dialogue with Jewish groups such as the CK, which often used Yiddish in its affairs. (In the summer of 1946 the General Meeting in fact decided that the Executive Committee's meetings and office hours were to be conducted in Yiddish, though long-term compliance with that edict is doubtful.)[172] Yiddish cut across Jewish DPs' national origins and thus approximated a lingua franca. Equally important, the use of Yiddish—the "authentic" vernacular language of Eastern European Jews—was itself considered an affirmation of Jewish identity. (Hebrew, the language of Zionism and Jewish observance, was presumably too little known to be viable on a broad scale, although the kibbutzim used it; Hebrew instruction was also a priority in schools for Jewish DPs and was promoted by the DP leadership.) The Jewish DP press was overwhelmingly printed in Yiddish, thereby emphasizing the distinctiveness of Jewish culture and institutions. The continued use of Polish, by contrast, might convey estrangement from Jewish identity and attachment to one's national origin; hence the Union and others sought to limit its use. In truth, however, the alumni confess they commonly spoke their native languages with their peers, with those from Poland, Hungary, and so forth clustering with one another. Moreover, use of Polish terms such as "zwiazek" (association) for the Union and "zarzad" for the Executive Committee was nearly universal in the group.[173] The students were far from alone in struggling with linguistic expectations and proscriptions. The Joint's Koppel Pinson observed, "Although the vast majority of the East European Jews know and speak Yiddish, the greater number of the young people as well as a considerable number of the middle-aged lapse more naturally into Polish, Russian or Hungarian. In many camps, official signs in the offices, posted by DPs themselves, are in Polish. So widespread was this state of linguistic assimilation that the DP leaders adopted an official line of propaganda based on the slogan 'Speak Yiddish, learn Hebrew.'"[174]

Addressing the "tone that should reign" within the Union, Silberman indicated that there was "no place for rumors and vague accusations." The meeting also discussed the case of a Russian student who had been provided papers by the Union, which he then took to the DP commission. When it came out that he was not in fact a Jew, he was stripped of his membership. Silberman expressed, finally, his hope that the students' stay in Munich would not last much longer, and he pointed to the Union's joint efforts with international Jewish student organizations to have the students emigrate and study elsewhere. The meeting ended with dancing accompanied by a "jazz orchestra" made up of Union members. Although many Jewish DP gatherings, especially those that were explicitly Zionist, concluded with the singing of "Hatikvah," the Jewish national anthem, the students concluded their meeting on a note of cosmopolitan refinement befitting a European *Studentenbund* (student association).

Silberman's hope for a speedy exit from Germany proved to be wishful thinking. In early 1946 the students had little idea of what was in store for Jewish DPs, and they greatly overestimated the extent to which those outside their orbit cared about their plight. The next months were filled with frustrations as their pleas for assistance and plans for emigration were unmet, and the constant grind of subsisting with meager resources wore on.

As their time in occupied Germany lengthened, however, the Union also made great strides. It increased its membership, level of activity, and status on the occupation scene. Jews studying in other cities formed their own union chapters, represented collectively by an umbrella organization. By the fall of 1946, the students' cultural program was more robust, as evidenced by the publication of the first issue of their newspaper. Running twelve large pages, the paper's title, *The Jewish Student*, was printed in Yiddish (using Hebrew type), with this heading repeated beneath the main title in English, Hebrew, and German. The paper's lead editorial, titled "We Create" (*Mir szafn*) and written in Yiddish by Yehuda Knobler, provides an additional story of the Union's origin. It reads, in part:

Not only did the moral wounds burn during the Churban ["the destruction"], but also the physical wounds, when the first groups of the remaining intellectual Jewish youth took upon themselves the difficult measures necessary to obtain an education. From the villages, camps, and cities in which they found themselves by virtue of tragic destiny; across zones, lands, and borders the youth made their way to Munich, where they hoped to find temporary opportunities to begin or complete their studies.

In the Jewish community, there were [as yet] no signs of a constructive, civic-minded organization, there was no call for productivity and schooling for the youth, and so scores took it upon themselves to find their way to institutions of higher learning. . . .

There are by now hundreds of us in the American Zone. We are no longer weak ingénues, but academics who can successfully compete with peers from other nations. Today, we have the recognition and support of the Joint and the Central Committee, and we have fought for our place among academic and civil institutions. . . . This is the success of the Union, . . . [which] organiz[ed] the Jewish academic youth into a constructive, creative, administrative body, bringing pride to the *She'erith Hapleitah*. The Union aided in creating the prototype of a Jewish intellectual who knows clearly the falsehood of our enemies' reproof . . . of Jewish laziness and inertia. The difficult material life, the embittered struggle of Jewish students . . . [are] proof against those who would like to see in us the speculators of the black market. . . .

A substantial, enthusiastic, constructive portion of us stands before the Jewish community to say: We, the youth in school, a limb of the body of the *She'erith Hapleitah*, come to you to inform you of our lives, struggles, sufferings, aspirations, and demands.[175]

The Union used the newspaper to introduce itself primarily to the Jewish community in another appeal for recognition—one hinging on respect. As if to answer skepticism about the students' motivations, the editorial frames the Union's achievements as contributions to a larger social body, exemplifying Zionist values such as youthful vitality, productivity, and national pride.

The editorial also includes a telling reflection on language: "Taking into consideration the fact that many of our students, as well as non-students, are not familiar with the Yiddish language, we have decided—with much de-bate—to issue our publication in all of the languages in which our students can write." Indeed, the paper is a mix of Yiddish, Polish, German, Hebrew, and even English. The editorial insists, however, that the students "think and feel in Yiddish," as if to stress their spiritual connection to the Jewish collective. Telling as well, the paper's penultimate page features the lyrics and musical notation of "Hatikvah."

In powerful ways identity was established in the occupation world through perception—both self-perceptions and those of others. The agency the students enjoyed, by extension, depended on their ability to define them-selves as survivors, displaced persons, students, Jews, and Jewish students.

CHAPTER 4

"The New Life"

Education and Renewal
in Occupied Germany

The Jewish students continued to thrive, as evidenced by the growing numbers in their unions. Membership in Munich increased from approximately 250 students in October 1946 to 405 by February 1947, hitting as many as 460 by the fall.[1] Unions also formed in Frankfurt, Stuttgart, Heidelberg, Marburg, and Erlangen, bringing the number of Jewish students in the American Zone to more than 650 in the summer of 1947.[2] In a parallel development, Jews entered, though in comparatively tiny numbers, German universities in the British Zone, formally establishing a union in the spring of 1947.[3] Demand in the American Zone skyrocketed as well. In October 1946 the Joint reported that 1,400 Jews had registered, zonewide, as candidates for university study.[4]

Chief among the factors driving these numbers were new influxes of refugees from the east. To accommodate increasing demand, additional slots opened up in Munich and other German cities, aided by the Union's advocacy and the more committed patronage from various organizations. The State Commission for the Racial, Political, and Religious Persecuted (into which the State's Commission for the Care of Jews had morphed) offered key support. So too did the Joint through its Office of University Affairs, created in the summer of 1946. This department's charge was to assist students in enrolling at university and to advise them once they began matriculation; to supervise Joint aid given to the students; to help graduates find postgraduate work in universities; and, over time, to help "talented students finish their studies abroad" by securing scholarships.[5] The Joint hired University Officer Alexander Piekarczyk, a Jewish DP with an academic background in Poland.[6] He acted as a liaison among the students, the universities, and the Joint's education division. Though most active in Munich, his office tracked the progress and tried to meet the needs of students throughout the American Zone. The Joint was active as well in supporting students in the British Zone.

Accompanying the increase in students in Munich was their shift away from the UNRRA University and toward German schools. This transition reflected both the students' growing ambitions and changes in the occupation landscape, chiefly the scaling back of Allied governments' relief efforts. Like other DPs, the students became—and were forced to become—more self-reliant, and they began to cultivate new sources of support. The Union grew to be a fixed part of the shifting occupation scene in Bavaria, known to international agencies, German institutions, and the Jewish DP community. Its maturation spoke to a central tension for DPs: disappointment at being in limbo balanced by investments in the here and now that pointed past stasis and indeterminacy. The very reality of constraint drove efforts to break beyond it.

Wrapped into and transcending the institutional narrative was the students' more comprehensive restoration. As for other survivors, this process involved the continual interplay between the individual and the collective, conceived in multiple ways. The Union enabled the students' personal goals. Their increasing confidence and vitality were experienced in and through the community they formed with one another. And they sought to integrate their academic and professional goals within the larger framework of Jewish identity. All this played out in the German setting, complicating decisions of how to engage community and culture, as well as the stakes of the choices one made.

The Decline and Fall of the UNRRA University

Those Jews who attended the UNRRA University were grateful for its existence, as it helped them reassert dormant passions and functioned as a bridge to a new life. Yet they scarcely took the institution seriously as a university and coveted the chance to study at one of Munich's established schools. Making one's way through the German system—with whatever added adversity, and knowing the corrupt role of the universities in the Nazis' reign— was ultimately preferable to weathering the limitations of an experimental occupation institution.

The UNRRA University, in one alumnus's generous characterization, proved "too narrow" for the students' purposes.[7] It did not offer a full complement of courses of study. Nor did it initially offer advanced classes, poorly accommodating those who already had some university education.[8] Drawn from within the DP ranks, the professors lacked the range and quality of a proper faculty. Only three faculty members were Jews.[9] There were also the problems of overcrowding and insufficient books and laboratory equipment. That German was the language of instruction could itself create problems. Karl Eislander recalls a Russian professor named Sirotenko, who stammered through his lectures. He joked to the class, "One day you will pass a cemetery and you look. [A gravestone will read,] Here lies Sirotenko. He died of German language."[10]

In addition, the students questioned the worth of a degree from the fledging school. For the most part they approached university study not simply as a way to serve their love of learning but as a means of credentialing. "I wanted a profession," one alumnus bluntly stated.[11] And they knew well, or soon learned, the superb academic reputations of the LMU and the TH.

Fellow classmates at the UNRRA University appeared to make little positive impression on the Jewish students. Even at this international institution, the Jews socialized almost exclusively with one another. One reason for the separation was their assumption regarding just who their classmates were. In the Union letter to Einstein, the students complained that they were "forced to study with those who just yesterday had been our murderers (with Germans in the University of Munich, the Technische Hochschule, etc.) and with Lithuanians, Poles, Ukrainians, Slovaks, etc. who, in the great majority, served as efficient helpers to the Germans."[12] The comment about the Eastern Europeans is plainly a reference to the UNRRA University. Such a generalization is inaccurate, as many of the UNRRA University students had been opponents of the Nazis. The Jewish students, however, may have neither known nor appreciated this fact. Nonetheless, at least one student saw her classmates at the UNRRA school as less intimidating than their German peers. This was, she speculates, one reason she took so long to transfer to the LMU.[13]

The Jewish students also did not feel terribly committed to the internationalist ideals articulated by their classmates and UNRRA administrators. This tepid response was not necessarily an explicit rejection of internationalism in favor of a Zionist ideal. With rare exception, the Jews never felt the instinctive sense of solidarity that might serve as the foundation of such a commitment; indeed, they did not even see their non-Jewish peers as co-sufferers who might share a common perspective. Further, the students most certainly thought of themselves—in what Anna Holian characterizes as a "liberal," as opposed to a "cosmopolitan," outlook—as part of a distinctly Jewish intelligentsia, whether pan-European or proto-national.[14]

The Ludwig-Maximilians-Universität student registration card of Roman Ohrenstein, first issued for the Winter 1946/47 semester. The card marks him as a "foreigner" (Ausländer). (Courtesy of Roman Ohrenstein)

The students questioned, finally, if the UNRRA University would survive long enough for them to finish their degrees. The Allies' overarching goal remained the repatriation of DPs. They hardly wanted the instability wrought by expatriates agitating against the governments in their countries of origin or de facto economic refugees seeking greater opportunities in the west. To drive refugees homeward, UNRRA in fact tried to shut down the elaborate system of primary and secondary Polish schools built in the camps by Polish DPs.[15] So too, institutions like the UNRRA University, and even UNRRA as a whole, could be seen as working against repatriation.

For all these reasons attendance at the UNRRA University represented a noble start on, or return to, the student path for the Jewish DPs, but little more. At the very least attendance would help one's chances to enter an established college. In early 1946 the Union reported that dozens of students would soon be enrolled in German universities, lamenting that the others were "obliged to enter the UNRRA University, in spite of its low level, only in order not to lose the possibility to study."[16] Whatever the university's limitations, 139 Jews still attended the school in the summer semester of 1946,

Roman Ohrenstein, a student at the
Ludwig-Maximilians-Universität in
Munich, in 1946. (Courtesy of Roman
Ohrenstein)

and the Union continued to submit new lists of prospective students for
admission through the fall.[17]

Entrance or transfer into a German university could work in a number
of ways. Alumnus Louis Braude recounts that he and two fellow Jews, with
German notaries attesting that their documents were destroyed, attempted to
register in the TH in the fall of 1945; their pleas at first were ignored by the
rector. After three requests, they were let in, provided they passed a preparatory
course; this would require that Braude travel from Gauting hospital to Munich.[18] Already registered at the UNRRA University in 1946, Roman Ohrenstein was admitted to the economics faculty of the LMU on the basis of his
verification exam the prior December.[19] For the winter 1946–47 semester, he
attended classes at both institutions, as did others, before moving exclusively
to the LMU. While at the UNRRA school, working on his *Abitur* (secondary
school degree), Robert Nenner was accepted to the LMU, which required that
he take additional science courses and excel in his first semester.[20] A scholarship
paid for by UNRRA funded this transitional semester, after which he entered
the program in medicine. Other students simply finished out semesters of
university-level study at the UNRRA University and began the next at
Munich schools, lobbying to have their credits transferred. By January 1947
nearly all the Jewish UNRRA students had shifted to German institutions.[21]

From the standpoint of the UNRRA University, the challenges were immense, underscoring the complexities facing occupation institutions. Team 108 had been trained to deal with a refugee crisis. With the advent of the university, it was asked to run an educational institution with a large and diverse student body. Simply supplying books, furniture, and other equipment, as well as paying the faculty, required cumbersome administrative procedures. Providing food, transportation, and recreation further strained the staff, which was still responsible for the "traditional" DP population.

The culture clash between transient DPs and the more permanent student population compounded problems. A team report complained, "Historically, European University students [sic] groups have been intellectually aristocratic, feeling superior to the 'man in the street.' Such feeling is evident here and to handle a students' group on the one hand and non-student DP's on the other has required mental and administrative acrobatics defying description."[22] The nonstudents, for their part, were a gruffer bunch, much more likely to be involved in black market activity. This attracted the intervention of security officers at the Deutsches Museum, with students sometimes caught in the middle.[23] The two populations, in the opinion of UNRRA staff, were ultimately "psychologically distinct," with "vastly different . . . hopes and aspirations and problems."[24] By late summer 1946, the staff implored, "[T]he University and the other facilities of this [DP] Center should be completely separated, both from an administrative and physical standpoint."[25]

Housing was another challenge, raising the fraught question of who was entitled to scarce resources. Some students lived either at the Deutsches Museum or in DP camps; others lived privately in apartments they rented on their own; the great majority, however, lived in units in Munich billeted by UNRRA. (In May 1946 the DPs in these categories numbered 92, 287, 234, and 1,167, respectively).[26] These students technically remained under UNRRA's care, and were, in principle at least, to retain their rooms even if they transferred to German universities. The US Office of Military Government for Bavaria required that the city of Munich set aside the rooms for the students, and as of the spring of 1946 the US Army itself provided rental payments. [27] Conflicts occasionally broke out when the German housing authority, sometimes with the help of German police, claimed rooms billeted by UNRRA for students and gave them to Germans. Extensive negotiations among UNRRA, the US military, and Munich authorities were required to codify housing protocols. Feeding the students was also daunting. Messing facilities at the Deutsches Museum were limited. Those students registered at DP camps were to receive their midday meal in the camps, which were far from the university. As a result special arrangements were needed to have their lunches on campus paid for. Some students, finally, wanted so-called dry rations—food they could prepare themselves, to give them greater flexibility with their mealtimes and a greater semblance of adult autonomy.

UNRRA, in sum, struggled just to meet the practical, day-to-day requirements of the university and its students. By its own admission greater focus on its "educational aspects" was needed, from "course composition and content," to "instructional techniques," and "standards and accreditation."[28] Even while its own university was open, UNRRA staff helped DPs enroll in German universities, offering assistance with applications and, for some, scholarships and housing.[29]

Despite the enthusiasm of university director Halina Gaszynska, a Polish-American UNRRA welfare officer, and the loyalty of many of its students, the university was not permitted to make the improvements it sought.[30] In November 1946, the Munich Union regretfully informed candidates that the school was taking no new admissions.[31] In January 1947, at the end of winter break, the UNRRA University's doors were shuttered, under the guard of UNRRA police. At last deemed a barrier to repatriation, the university had been terminated.[32] Students responded with protests, including a hunger strike and vigil at the Deutsches Museum, as well as a march to the Office of Military Government for Bavaria.[33] They appealed to UNRRA and the Military Government to keep the university going, citing the school's promise of a new internationalism. In response the university stayed open through the end of the winter term, but then officially terminated.[34] Whatever its promise, the school had been done in by geopolitics. In late winter 1947, and under the same pressure, UNRRA itself was dissolved by its participating governments, with remaining responsibilities for DPs taken over by the International Refugee Organization (IRO).[35]

"Exquisite Meaning for Our Youth"

The shift in the Jewish students' path was accompanied by an increase in those seeking to study, as the Jewish population in the American Zone swelled in 1946 and 1947. The grand political narrative propelling Jews' westward migration was the effort to go to Palestine and establish a Jewish state there. Even those simply fleeing the dangers of Eastern Europe became implicated in that narrative as they struggled to settle their status and began to dream of a Jewish state. Individual destinies, however, remained driven by a combination of ideology, circumstance, and personal ambition. In the case of the students, the social and political odyssey of postwar Jewry was intertwined with their own educational odyssey.

Two students of similar backgrounds show how that entanglement manifested. Eva Siebald was born in 1929 in Stanislawow, Poland. Raised in a Zionist household, she attended a Hebrew school. With the Soviet occupation in 1939, the school converted to Yiddish as the language of instruction. Unfamiliar with the language, Siebald focused on math and science. For three years following the German invasion in 1941, she "did not see a school, not the inside, not the outside."[36]

After escaping the Stanislawow ghetto, her family managed to survive in hiding. Even as she existed in a frightful limbo, she nonetheless developed the desire to become an engineer. Liberation came in 1944 with the Soviet's reoccupation of eastern Poland. She then attended a Ukrainian school, where she was the sole Jewish student; she also served as a private tutor for farm children in exchange for cheese and milk. In the spring of 1945, Siebald's family pushed on to Krakow, where she hoped to attend *gymnasium*. Because she lacked the requisite schooling, her admittance depended on an exam that happened to be administered by a teacher who came from her hometown and knew of her family. Among other exam questions, the teacher asked her about the status of Jews in prewar Poland. Insisting, falsely, that Jews had "special privileges," he failed her for answering "incorrectly" on that portion of the test but ultimately admitted her out of hometown loyalty. She completed her *Matura* in May 1946 at age seventeen.

Siebald's family was then transported by the Bricha to Munich, where their hopes of making it to Palestine stalled. She applied to the Technische Hochschule in the fall of 1946. Intent on first accommodating the backlog of students whose studies were interrupted by the war, the TH was only taking students born in 1925 or earlier.[37] Siebald therefore claimed she was four years older than she truly was, and retained this adjusted birth year for the rest of her life.[38] She was initially both the only Jew and the only woman in the mechanical engineering program. Her father, having had some university education in Vienna and Berlin, entered the LMU to pursue a PhD in economics. In his mid-forties, he was among the oldest members of the Union.

Fred Reiter, from a largely Ukrainian part of Poland, survived the war with his parents. After liberation he journeyed to Krakow, where he entered university to study agriculture. While there he was active in a Zionist organization and was among the very few students who admitted to being Jewish. In time he and the others received letters strongly suggesting that they leave the university. Anti-Semites, anti-communists who assumed that all Jews were communists, or even Zionists eager that Jews in Poland go to Palestine may have been behind the threats. Whatever the case, Reiter recalled, "I heard in Krakow University that there's a [student] group in Munich, a

Jewish group, so I was going."[39] When other Jews in Krakow objected to his departure for Germany, he answered, "I am not going to Germany; I am going to [the] American Zone." In 1947 he entered the LMU's dentistry program. For Reiter and Siebald, as for so many of the students, the endgame of transit to Palestine was not so much displaced as deferred, as Zionism continued to hit political barriers.

As these examples suggest those who joined the Union in late 1946 and 1947 were generally more settled in their life paths, and often had already resumed *gymnasium* or university education. A fair number, especially those who had been sent to Siberia, had at least one living parent and, if their parents had property, jobs, or money, private resources on which to draw. Yet some who came to study in Munich among this "second wave" arrived more or less entirely alone and seeking to build the foundations of a new, autonomous life.

Rochelle Eisenberg was just sixteen when she was liberated by the British from Bergen-Belsen, to which she had been driven from Auschwitz. She was also orphaned. The cruelty and despair in Auschwitz, she reports, prevented any semblance of normal dialogue. In Bergen-Belsen, however, she did talk with other young people about their dreams for the future, and they tried to discuss ideas and literature. She and the others "keenly felt the[ir] lack of education."[40] She emerged from her ordeal feeling "intellectually deprived [and eager to] know about everything." Her education resumed at a Jewish parochial school in the Bergen-Belsen DP camp set up by the Jewish Brigade (Jewish soldiers from Palestine who had fought with the British). She and her classmates rued the fact that the school had Saturday (the Sabbath) off, and they "begged the teachers" to take no vacations so they could learn more.

Eisenberg spent nearly two and a half years in the camp. "Nobody was ready to begin life as a normal being" among her orphaned peers. Change for her came when the camp was demobilizing and a female pharmacy student from Munich, who took her vacations in the camp, suggested that she too come to Munich to study. Eisenberg arrived in Munich in the fall of 1947 with a sole contact, a "diploma" from a camp school that had little standing, and the need for more schooling to be eligible for university. After taking preparatory courses designed for former Wehrmacht soldiers, she passed the Union's verification test and enrolled in the LMU program in pharmacy.

Arnold Kerr was liberated in the summer of 1945, one day after his seventeenth birthday.[41] He had survived the war in Vilna and then in horrible camps in Estonia. His parents and two younger brothers were killed. After journeying for months in Germany and Poland with a ragtag group of survivors, he made it to the DP camp near Berlin, where his dreams of studying emerged. The trigger was being quizzed on Hebrew vocabulary by a teenage girl he fancied. Impressed with his skill, she suggested that he attend the camp school.

Within a few months of taking lessons—now living at the Eschwege DP camp near Frankfurt—he had completed the equivalent of middle school. He then found a German *gymnasium* instructor near the DP camp in Berlin with whom he could take private lessons, which he paid for with sacks of oatmeal he took from the camp cafeteria. Five days a week he learned math, physics, and chemistry, studying deep into the night. By the spring of 1947, he had completed the equivalent of a *gymnasium* education. In August he set out for Munich, where, he had heard, there was an exam by which Jews could be made eligible for university. He entered the TH's engineering program in the winter semester.

Eisenberg's and Kerr's experiences, while pointing to the young Jews' determination, also point to a practical obstacle so many prospective students faced: they not had completed *gymnasium* and thus were not yet ready for collegiate study. Catching up required some means. One option, however rare, was attending a German *gymnasium*. Yehuda Knobler did just that at the LMU, which offered *gymnasium* courses after the war. The courses sought mostly to accommodate the great numbers of young German men who, called away to the military draft or otherwise unable to attend school, wanted to complete *gymnasium*. Knobler graduated in July 1946 from the "Maxgymn.[asium] München" and was admitted to the university proper to study chemistry.[42] The first *gymnasium* for Jews in Munich was established, with help from the Joint, only in the fall of 1946, and it did not at first offer all requisite courses.[43]

Most commonly the aspiring students received formal or informal tutoring. Advanced students in the Union held *Abitur* classes. To get more qualified instructors, Roman Ohrenstein and others asked LMU administrators whether any professors might be available. The reply was that the school could offer only professors who had been relieved from teaching positions under denazification, which sought, however imperfectly, to bar former Nazi party loyalists from public life, including the universities.[44] The Union delegation, in Ohrenstein's recollection, gladly accepted the Nazi professors as tutors, as they were intent on getting from the Germans what they could.

The initial goal of preparatory study was to pass the exams administered by the Verification Commission, which winnowed down those simply desiring university study to those truly eligible. The commission's evolution speaks volumes about the development of the Union, the DPs' capacities for initiative and adaptation, and the growing sophistication of occupation institutions and relationships. Union records and the alumni's recollections suggest that the commission, in its initial incarnation, did not in all cases administer tests. Instead it "verified" some candidates by attesting to their professed credentials. Philip Balaban applied to the UNRRA University in the winter of 1945. Just sixteen, he had not completed *gymnasium* but had continued his studies in Tashkent during the war.[45] He nonetheless told the university that he was much older and had completed high school, taking care not to show them his Russian transcripts, which would have revealed him as an "infiltree." The commission accepted the various documents and stories he told as proof of his eligibility.[46] In other cases the commission signed off on fully credible "original documents," which candidates might obtain by writing to the *gymnasia* and universities they had attended in Eastern Europe.

Stepwise the testing regime grew both more stringent and more elaborate. In the spring of 1946, the commission had five members, among them three seasoned academics and two members from the Union; they tested twenty-nine candidates for the coming term.[47] By the summer of 1947, the commission boasted five academics of considerable pedigree and a battery of student assistants of high academic standing.[48] The 1947 chair was JDC university officer Alexander Piekarczyk. Among his titles were magister of mathematics, *Diplom-Ingenieur* from the Technische Hochschule in Warsaw, and state's architect in Poland. He engaged the Union in the details of academic life and consistently advocated on its behalf, especially to the Joint. (His ability to write reasonably well in English, the language used by the Joint, likely figured into his gaining the post.) Union members recall that Piekarczyk, in his mid-thirties, was serious, genial, and deeply committed to them; he cut an impressive figure in his Joint uniform, which added to his air of official authority. The Union made him an honorary member, praising his "exceptionally willing support [in] all our affairs."[49]

The vice-chair of the Verification Commission was Baruch Graubard, the director of education of the Central Committee. Graubard had been trained in Vienna in history and literature and was a longtime lyceum instructor. His presence on the commission shows the continued involvement of the Central Committee, whatever its ambivalence toward the students, in their efforts. Other commission members were similarly credentialed, and included the first chair of the Jewish doctors' union in the American Zone. Diverse both in their fields and national origins, the examiners were able to take into account the language and academic culture of the candidates' home countries. And crucially, the commission was designed as a "fully autonomous body, independent of the Student Union."[50]

VERIFIKATIONS-KOMMISSION

für Jüdische Hochschulkandidaten

München.

Herr/Frau/Frl. *Ohrenstein - Seifkopf Roman*

geb. am *12. VI. 1920* zu *Słomniki (Polen)*

der sein im Jahre *1939*

an der *Krakauer Handelsgymnasium*

...rbenes Reifezeugnis nicht mehr besitzt, hat durch Ab-

...ng der Verifikations-Prüfung gemäß M. E. des Bayerischen

Staatsministeri... für U...t und Kultus vom 9. 9. 1947 Nr. VI 39428 und vom 12. 4. 1948

Nr. VI 20978 im *Dezember* 194*5*.

mit Gesamturteil

gut

die wissenschaftlichen Voraussetzungen für das Hochschulstudium erfüllt.

Die Einzelergebnisse der Verifikations-Prüfung sind in dem nachfolgenden Auszug der

Prüfungsniederschrift zusammengestellt.

München, den *22 Juni 1948*

Der Vorsitzende der
Verifikations-Kommission

The Verification Commission certificate of Roman Ohrenstein, issued by the Bavarian Ministry of Education. The certificate was issued in June 1948 to indicate, retroactively, that he had passed the verification exam in December 1945. (Courtesy of Roman Ohrenstein)

The exams, administered in two cycles per year, had sections on math, physics, chemistry, history, and literature (both world literature and one's national literature). Candidates also needed knowledge of colloquial German, as well as the ability to read texts and follow lectures in the language. Yiddish and Hebrew were accepted as foreign languages, along with dominant European languages. Latin was a sticking point. Early on it was required for all candidates, partly due to the theological tradition of the heavily Catholic LMU.[51] Eventually, strong Latin was required only of candidates in pharmacy and medicine. Success on the exams did not guarantee admission but would only make one eligible. By early 1947 universities throughout the American Zone recognized the commission's results, and candidates came from distant cities and DP camps to take the tests.[52] Nearly 140 candidates applied for the March 1947 tests for the summer term, with 76 taking the exams.[53]

The alumni recall that the tests were demanding, and in each cycle some candidates failed (including 20 of the aforementioned 76). The Union took the exams very seriously. In the fall of 1947, aid workers organized an *Abitur* course for Jews at Gauting sanatorium—a medical facility near Munich where as many as 500 Jews, along with Germans and other DPs, were treated for tuberculosis and other serious diseases.[54] The welfare officer reached out to the Union to inquire what the exams entailed for those who wanted to continue on to university; stressing the patients' hardship, she specifically asked about the most important subject areas, which could be taught most expeditiously.[55] The Union replied with an unsparingly detailed description of the array of knowledge the candidates, no matter their infirmity, had to master.[56] On occasion Union members complained that the verification process was too rigorous, discouraging the very people it should help.[57]

This complaint reveals a tension in the Union's work and the competing pressures faced by DPs more broadly. On the one hand the Union wanted to open up opportunities for fellow Jewish DPs. This might entail actively assisting in misrepresentations, such as the falsification of one's age. On the other hand the Union fashioned itself as a proper *Studentenschaft*, whose members were committed to their academic work. Laxity in Union standards, academic and otherwise, would undermine both this self-conception and the Union's credibility in the eyes of relevant authorities.

Among those authorities was the State Commission on Victims, which also recognized the Verification Commission. Providing compensation to the Nazis' victims, the commission was intent on determining the veracity of individuals' claims. Poles and other Eastern Europeans met with the greatest scrutiny, but Jews—including the students—were hardly spared. On one occasion, the commission sent a skeptical letter to a prospective student who claimed he had been in Auschwitz and Buchenwald. Noting that he had no number tattooed on his arm and that information he gave about his transport from Buchenwald was implausible, the commissioner indicated that he would consider his petition for assistance only if the candidate could produce an "irreproachable witness" who had seen him in the camps.[58]

In January 1947 the State Commission declared that the Union's apparent concern to "exclude frauds from studying fully matches our own intention" and therefore decided to "refer anyone, even when they have original documents from middle schools and universities, first to your Verification Commission for examination."[59] Its hope, expressed in harsh tones, was to stop "unsavory elements [*unsaubere Elemente*] from entering the universities and to make study possible for those who have the right." Whether by virtue of this pressure or to fulfill its autonomous desires, the Union moved toward requiring all prospective students, even those with diplomas, to take the exams.

Practical difficulties also drove this shift. For all the attention the Union and the German universities paid to admissions criteria, the admissions process remained somewhat arbitrary, underscoring how the chaos of occupation settled neither easily nor quickly into reliable administrative protocols. A Union audit in late 1946 revealed that some candidates who had passed the exams were denied admission; others who had failed or done poorly were accepted; and the presence or absence of academic transcripts played no consistent role in admissions decisions.[60] Leery of having unqualified students enter university, and concerned that universities were not recognizing original documents, the Union voted to accept as members only those students who passed its tests.[61] (Even so, irregularities persisted. Emanuel Tanay recalls that a friend of his named Borenstein failed the verification exam. The following day the disappointed Borenstein took a train to Landsberg, on which he upbraided a group of Jews who were being rude to a German woman. As he left the train, an elderly man—by chance the rector of the LMU—thanked him and gave him his card. Borenstein followed up with the rector and was admitted, without an exam certificate, to the LMU, where he thrived as a political science PhD student.)[62]

The German authorities took the testing seriously as well. At stake for them was the composition of their student population, the standards of their universities, and their relationship with the American authorities demanding DP access to German institutions. The universities moreover played an essential role in training a skilled professional (German) labor force in a rebuilding economy. Enforcing rigorous admissions criteria would be an ostensibly nonprejudicial way to limit the numbers of Jewish students and thus reserve more slots for Germans.

In the summer of 1947, the Bavarian Ministry of Education and Culture formally recognized the commission.[63] By the winter of 1947–48, the ministry became directly involved in its work, dispatching Government Director Buck to assess the exams' rigor. Impressed with the commission, he nonetheless urged that candidates who failed not be permitted to take the tests a second time.[64] He further counseled: "The purpose of the test is not only to see whether the candidate has demonstrated sufficient intellectual readiness, but also whether the candidate is cut out for collegiate study. One surely knows cases in which someone has acquired an *Abitur* not in order to pursue additional study in a university, but because it is required for various professions. (Banking, large-scale industry, etc.) The test should, so to speak, represent the 'guidance of youth' because, in Bavaria for example, there exist few opportunities for young people in the academic profession, and it is well known that unfulfilled academics are a miserable lot, who can be described as the 'intellectual proletariat.'"[65] The commission responded defensively that "the Jewish students are relatively few" and possess great "internal motivation," evident in their usually high marks.[66]

The comments of the director betray an unmistakable German academic arrogance. In practical terms Buck was likely trying to limit the numbers of DPs in an overtaxed university system. Indeed in January 1948 it was announced that the 10 percent mandate of DP university admissions was lifted in most of Germany, including Bavaria, putting admissions decisions entirely in the hands of German officials.[67] Even so, the director's admonition betrays a stunning lack of appreciation for the young Jews' circumstances: their experience of true misery during the war; their efforts to compensate for the interruption of their education and to mentor one another; and the fact that none of them sought to make a career in Germany.

In the wake of education ministry visits, the Verification Commission grew still more formal. In early 1948 it issued new exam certificates on watermarked paper bearing the ministry's stamp. These were issued both to new candidates and to existing students, recording when they first took the test and their grades in all exam subjects.[68]

For the Jewish students the verification process was a source of considerable pride. Emanuel Tanay, who had had little formal education when admitted to the UNRRA University, was eventually required to take the test. Passing the exam "reduced my feeling of shame for not having attended a *gymnasium*"—a feeling he credited to his European upbringing, with its stress on educational achievement. (Americans, he later discovered, cared little about his pedigree.)[69] The verification certifications are among the documents the alumni most commonly saved from their time in Germany, and they frequently presented them to me as markers of their postwar achievements.

The ministry's affirmation of the commission meant that the candidates' hard work was valued not only by fellow Jews but also by Bavaria's "highest educational authorities."[70] The commission emphatically thanked the government director, whom it credited with "enhanc[ing] the [students'] trust [in] knowledge and humanity." Such sentiment has its own evocative subtext. The students knew well that the German academy had been complicit in National Socialism. They were familiar with the influential Jewish DPs' charge that the European Enlightenment had failed Jews. Their sense of worth, moreover, did not depend on winning the approval of "the Germans." Nonetheless, they preserved a reverence for learning and academic and professional culture. And their own knowledge of the hardships they had endured surely added to their satisfaction in meeting those standards. Perhaps for all these reasons the commission declared that the verification tests had an "exquisite meaning for our youth."[71]

"The Hardest Examination"

Additional perspective on testing and the circumstances that drove it comes from an American Jew, Marie Syrkin. Originally from Russia, Syrkin's parents were prominent socialist Zionists who attended university in Switzerland and met during the Second Zionist Congress in Basel, convened in 1898 by Zionist leader Theodor Herzl.[72] As she grew up in New York City, *Eretz Yisrael* was presented to her as a socialist home for persecuted Jews. A gifted writer well connected to New York's literary left, Marie Syrkin tried to educate her comrades at *The Nation* and elsewhere about labor Zionism and its utopian promise. She first traveled to Palestine in 1933, where she observed what seemed to be its incipient realization. She traveled there again at the close of the war to research a book on Jewish resistance to the Nazis. Engaged in the plight of Europe's Jews during and after the war, Syrkin figures prominently in Hasia R. Diner's research demonstrating the concern some American Jews paid at the time to the decimation—contrary to recent representations of American Jews' belated and heavily politicized interest in the Holocaust and its survivors.[73]

Syrkin came to the American Zone of Germany in January 1947 to gather "firsthand information on the DP problem [and] to screen suitable candidates for admission to American colleges, who would be allowed to enter" beyond existing immigration quotas.[74] In the latter capacity she interacted with the Munich Union and the students. Her essay about her efforts, "The Hardest

Examination," is among the most vivid external accounts of the students' situation, and unique as an American perspective on the student group.[75]

Syrkin offers the impressions of an outsider struggling to comprehend the circumstances in which she finds herself. She stresses the sadness and pathos of the applicants' lives, depicting them all as victims of horrible persecution, and likely underappreciating the confidence and agency many had reclaimed. In a voice at once earnest and overwhelmed, her account says as much about the dissonance between the helpers and the helped as it does about the students themselves. It is therefore of a piece with the reflections, amply recorded in DP research, of UNRRA, JDC, and other aid workers, while lacking the strained judgment that so often informs those reflections. By the same token, Syrkin's impressions provide a reminder of how difficult the students' situation remained, and they thus serve as a counterpoint to the equally partial image of prowess the Union projected.

Herself a teacher, Syrkin came to the DP camps hoping to find up to fifty Jewish DPs throughout the American Zone who would be "suitable applicants" for college scholarships offered by Hillel, an American foundation promoting higher education for Jews and humanistic Jewish values. Part of the Union's charge was to secure opportunities for its members to study abroad. Union records make reference to Syrkin's presence, as it instructed members from all over the zone about how to apply.

Her trip became an exercise in unexpected frustrations. However shocking or heart-rending to her, her experiences recapitulate the kinds of challenges the Union had faced since its inception. The first hurdle was posed by the fact that the United States would grant student visas only to those applicants who could prove residence in the American Zone since December 23, 1945, thereby excluding more recent arrivals. And any applicant might be rejected by the US consul for bureaucratic reasons. The bigger struggle commenced when Syrkin visited a DP camp to interview candidates, requesting that they bring credentials:

> People of various ages appeared. Then the ludicrousness of my request became apparent. If the youth was of normal college-age entrance, 17 to 20, then he had no preparatory schooling. In the years when he should have been attending high school he had been in a concentration camp or a ghetto. Those in the middle twenties had been old enough to graduate from a *gymnasium*. . . . But when I asked for diplomas, they smiled. How could they have diplomas? Everything was burned, destroyed together with their homes and families. . . . Their teachers had fed the crematoria. Could they pass

an entrance examination? . . . "We didn't memorize formulas in Dachau," one boy said to me angrily. There was no countering that answer, yet its truth did not relieve me of the need of instituting some objective standard of judgment.[76]

The testing process, worked out in consultation with the Joint's Piekarczyk, was also beset with challenges, starting with format and language. Syrkin decided to administer an exam consisting of "comprehensive questions in literature, history, mathematics, and physics" much like, one may presume, the Union's verification exams.[77] Syrkin and Piekarczyk further agreed that the students must provide biographical data in English, which the students would need to know minimally to study in America. German, Yiddish, French, and Russian (all languages in which Syrkin had facility) were accepted for literature and history, and Polish and Hungarian (both spoken by a second examiner) were suitable for math and science. An added bureaucratic difficulty was securing a day's provisions for the test-takers, who needed various permissions to travel within the American Zone. "The mere listing of the problems connected with the preparation of a simple examination," Syrkin marveled, "indicated something of the complex and tortured world into which this academic paraphernalia was making its somewhat incongruous entrance."[78] That entrance, she seems unaware, had long since occurred when the Verification Commission was first devised.

Settling on an appropriate pool of applicants ultimately brought Syrkin to the Union. Her initial hope was to offer scholarships only to those not already in university, as their need was presumably greatest. Yet she quickly discovered that "the small number of genuine students . . . had, for the most part, already been admitted to German universities."[79] She thus solicited the Union for candidates, but again ran into trouble. Many members objected that the scholarships were for study in the United States, not Palestine, and some refused her offer outright. "Nothing was going to deflect them from their goal of Palestine," she observed, "[and] they were skeptical of the assurances of their colleagues that they would be pioneers 'later.' These were the 'deserters' who permitted personal advantage to obscure the national interest. Naturally, it was not my business to deconvert the zealots."[80] Providing a fascinating glimpse into DP debates, Syrkin's recollection confirms strong Zionist conviction within segments of the student group, while referencing the gravity with which they assessed the consequences of various choices.

The test itself provided the greatest pathos. Some applicants, when first seeing the questions, walked out. A "bright mathematics and science student" from Poland who had been in Ravensbruck lamented, 'I did not realize how much I had lost' . . . , her fine gray eyes filling with tears."[81] Most stuck the test out and, to Syrkin's surprise, their work was "average to excellent, except that the number of mature and able discussions was higher than the norm." What most affected her were answers to the application question, "Why do you think you should receive a scholarship?" It elicited, often in broken English, compressed tales of suffering and idealistic tributes to "the idea of mankind, knowledge, and progress."[82] Most poignant was the answer of a "handsome Hungarian boy" whose family had died in Auschwitz. He wrote, "I should like to hope that I am not quite abundant in this world." "It took me a little time," she confessed, "to figure out that 'abundant' meant superfluous."[83] Whatever their postwar accomplishments, some students still clearly struggled with feelings of worthlessness.

Another applicant added desperation to the mix of sentiments. Having done poorly on the test, he begged to know from Syrkin when he might take it again. To prove his merit, he volunteered to play a Mozart concerto for her on the violin, in the Joint office noisy with typewriters. She recalled: "I have no idea how well or badly Peter played, because the performance was too painful for ordinary aesthetic appreciation."[84] Choosing the candidates proved agonizing, as some distinguished themselves by their high marks, but others who scored merely well would be selected on the basis of age, relative hardship, and the subjective determination of promise. Some scholarships were offered (including to candidates not already enrolled in Germany universities), with some among those chosen successfully studying in the United States. Others, however, were unable to obtain the proper visas.

Philipp Auerbach
and the State Commission on Victims

For Jewish university candidates, being declared eligible was one challenge; being admitted was the next vital step. If admitted, the students also needed some means to pay tuition. On both counts the young Jews found their great patron in the State Commissioner for Political, Religious, and Racial Victims, Dr. Philipp Auerbach. In its extensive dealings with Dr. Auerbach, the Union interacted with one of the more colorful, controversial, and important figures in the early postwar period. Auerbach's activities on the students' behalf further highlight the complexities of the postwar world: the tensions within the German government over the treatment of Germany's victims and the differing agendas among Jews.

A German Jew, Auberbach held positions in the Social Democratic Party before the war.[85] In 1933 he fled to Belgium, where he worked as a medium-scale industrialist. Captured in 1940, he was later interned at Auschwitz and Buchenwald. First employed in the British Zone, he became the head of the Commission on Victims when it formed in the fall of 1946. He also served as the head of the Jewish Kultusgemeinde in Bavaria from 1949 to 1952 and as president of the State Reparations Bureau (*Landesentschädigungamtes*) from 1951 to 1952. By virtue of these roles, he was uniquely conversant in the worlds of German Jewry, Jewish and other DPs, the occupation government, and Bavarian state power.

A tall, corpulent man, Auerbach had an imposing physical presence and a manner to match. He was a zealous advocate for the Nazis' victims, taking an adversarial role with parts of the very government he served. He was vociferous in denouncing German claims of victimization, inveighing against the postwar attitude that "what the Allies were doing to the German folk today was much worse than anything that had been done in Auschwitz."[86] He was also was prone to rule by fiat, giving him the aura of a potentate and attracting suspicion and resentment.

After protracted conflicts with Bavaria's interior minister, Auerbach was accused in 1951 of a host of crimes, including extortion, filing fraudulent reparations claims, and falsely claiming the academic title of doctor. (In Germany there is strict regulation of the title, which connotes far more than an American PhD.) He was thus the subject of the first major trial of a Jew in the Federal Republic of Germany. Though local Jewish authorities, fearful that Auerbach had undermined reparations efforts, now distanced themselves from him, other Jews—both in Germany and abroad—rallied around him as a purported victim of anti-Semitism. In 1952 Auerbach was convicted and sentenced to two-and-a-half years in prison. Upon learning his sentence, he committed suicide.

Though the State Commission assisted many categories of victims, Jews were the favored recipients of its aid and attention. Auerbach had repeated quarrels with Polish DPs seeking benefits as political persecutees. He accused them of falsifying their status and of anti-Semitism; they charged him, in turn, with anti-Polish prejudice and Jewish favoritism.[87] For Jews the commission secured housing and employment, as well as funds for cemeteries, recreation centers, hospitals, and, in one of its major commitments, university study.

Union members describe Auerbach as "very intense." Himself a victim of National Socialism, he commanded great moral authority. As a German, he knew how to deal with "the Nazis" and, by force of will and standing, get what he wanted. One alumnus quipped that the Germans were "more afraid of Auerbach than the entire occupation army. . . . When you mentioned Auerbach, the Germans . . . they drop to their knees."[88]

Largely through Auerbach's efforts, the quota on Jewish students in Munich universities was lifted altogether at the end of 1946, permitting Jews, in principle, limitless enrollments.[89] Auerbach was also the chief architect of direct state aid to the students. An official edict issued at his insistence in late 1946 mandated that the Bavarian Ministry of Education and Culture grant the full remission of tuition for university students who are "political and racial victims, as acknowledged by the State Commissioner," as well as pay each student a monthly stipend of two hundred Reichsmarks during the school year and 100 Reichsmarks during vacation periods.[90] Racially and politically "aggrieved" (*geschädigten*) students—those who had been in hiding, partisans, deportees, and so forth—had half their tuition waived and were instructed to seek additional support through the commission.[91]

The measure made sponsorship of the students a de facto form of reparation. The stipend was modest, given the devaluation of the Reichsmark after the war, when cigarettes and chocolate counted for far more than currency. Nonetheless it meant some income, and had symbolic significance for the students. The payment of tuition was a more meaningful material benefit. Though the edict had the force of law only in Bavaria, it set a precedent that students in other states could cite when lobbying for aid. Significantly, it distinguished between degrees of victimization while making all Jews reparations-worthy. To sort its members into the two categories, the Munich Union instructed those with concentration camp registrations (*KZ Ausweisen*) to verify their status with the commission.[92]

Commissioner Auerbach intervened in another major way on the students' behalf. In the fall of 1947, panic set in at the Union when the Technische Hochschule announced that all TH students would be required to work for six months in construction squads to repair wartime damage to university buildings. To the Jews the directive was doubly onerous: it would delay progress in their studies and require, in an inversion of the concept of reparations, that they help to rebuild a society that had sought their destruction. Auerbach, meeting with the TH rector, secured the Jewish students' exemption.[93] In addition, even when the 10 percent quota on DP students was lifted, Auerbach remained personally involved (as did his counterpart state commissioner in Hesse) in ensuring the admission of qualified Jews.[94] Auerbach, finally, lent assistance on much smaller matters, revealing the scarcity of the postwar environment and how institutions, for all the pomp and power they might project, were involved in the details of everyday life.

The Union submitted a list of members who needed tableware to Auerbach directly, as well as a request for coal and a window for its office.[95]

More than any other Jewish authority figure, Commissioner Auerbach lent the students sympathy and support. He sometimes attended their meetings and personally responded to their many pleas with great speed and effectiveness. As to his motives, Auerbach clearly had academic pretensions, and he personally identified with the students' plight. The commission he headed, moreover, sought to mete out justice—to exact payback, both literal and figurative, for Jewish victims. Assistance to the students thus was a form of justice. Finally, as a native German still committed to German society, Auerbach had no qualms about Jews participating in German institutional life and likely saw that participation as a moral victory. In this he clearly differed from the Central Committee, whose main goal was building a Jewish state. Both for his advocacy in dealing with the Germans and his support among Jews, Auerbach earned the students' enduring gratitude. Saddened by his very public demise, Union members still in Germany attended his funeral.[96] As its own kind of tribute, among the possessions Simon Schochet brought from Germany to the United States in the early 1950s was a multivolume LP recording of Auerbach's public trial.[97]

Existential Restoration

By early 1947 the Union's major goals with respect to academic matters had been achieved. Hundreds of students were enrolled in universities in Munich and elsewhere. In Munich basic expenses such as tuition were met for most students through a formal law. And through the Verification Commission a system was in place to process additional candidates. Through regular elections, new officers assumed positions within the organization's many-faceted operation. The Union issued all members registration cards, which served as their defining postwar documents. (Almost all the students were officially stateless and therefore had no passport or other state document.) These cards bore the member's picture, university affiliation, and Union stamps, and the instruction in German and in clumsy English: "As it is a very important document you will please keep it careful."[98] The Union also secured free transit for the students on trolley cars and buses along designated routes from their residences to their universities.[99]

The Munich students were also woven into the residential fabric of the city. While the DP camps offered safety and solidarity, they were physically cut off from the universities. To the independently minded students, they were also places of stasis and restriction. This view was hardly their exclusive

A special card granting Roman Ohrenstein free transit on public transportation between his residence and the Ludwig-Maximilians-Universität campus. (Courtesy of Roman Ohrenstein)

conceit. The Central Committee worried about the danger of idleness in DP camps and that the dependency they bred would work against the Zionist imperatives of initiative and self-reliance. By the middle of 1946, nearly all Union members were living in apartments. By a common arrangement, they were assigned rooms in residential units by Munich's various housing authorities upon presentation of papers indicating their DP and student status.[100] These were typically single rooms in German households, with rent paid for by the State Commission. As securing housing was an integral part of becoming a student, the Union also brokered living arrangements.[101]

In the summer of 1946, the Jewish Students Federation in the American Zone of Germany (*Jüdischer Studentenverband in der Amerikanischen Zone Deutschlands*) came together.[102] Individual chapters had adopted constitutions modeled on the one establishing the Munich group. Based in the Munich office, the federation had its own charter, letterhead, and administrative structure, and held regular, if infrequent, zonewide meetings.[103] The group took initiative on such issues as funding, emigration, outreach to Jewish organizations worldwide, and the mobilization for a Jewish state. At times the activities of the Munich chapter and the larger organization virtually merged. In late 1946 the officers in Munich bought a car—an Opel, complete with a German driver ("probably a Nazi," speculated one alumnus)—to facilitate the relay of communication among the chapters (as postal correspondence was unreliable).[104] Though students in various cities complained of the dominance of the Munich chapter, the *Studentenverband* added cohesion to the far-flung student community, increased its legitimacy, and helped advance collective goals.

Meanwhile young Jews in the British Zone had entered university as well. Holding nearly half of the Jews surviving in Western Europe at the war's end (largely by virtue of the twelve thousand or so liberated at Bergen-Belsen), the British Zone was not a favored destination for Jews coming west, and Britain worked to bar Jewish entry.[105] Its Jewish population remained small—around 16, 000, of whom 12,500 were DPs—as did the numbers studying. The first student in the zone attended the University of Hannover in December 1945, and was joined by a second in the spring term.[106] Their numbers grew to forty-five (with fifteen German nationals) as students took up coursework in such cities as Kiel, Hamburg, Bonn, and Göttingen. As was the case for their counterparts in the American Zone, life for the mostly orphaned students was initially a great struggle, as they lacked proper housing, sufficient food and clothing, and books and other supplies. Over time, however, they garnered support, with the Joint providing stipends and rations, and the Jewish Relief Unit and Inter-University Federation of Jewish Students in Oxford assisting with clothing and school materials. The advent of their union likewise represented a great achievement.

Having recorded the students' organizational achievements, I now pursue a more comprehensive understanding of their lives by exploring what their experiences at university were like, what broader functions the Union assumed, and what their student existence, both in subjective and historical terms, meant. In these questions I reengage a major theme of this study: existential restoration. By that I mean the process by which individuals, in the wake of trauma, establish again a sense of meaning and purpose. To the extent that the students experienced this process like other Jewish DPs, they add to common frameworks of Jewish renewal. To the extent that their experiences were distinct, they have their own place in that narrative, demanding that it be complicated or even revised.

The theme of existential restoration has been addressed, if not always in explicit terms, in existing literature on Jewish DPs. That research presents three main contexts in which Jewish renewal took place and by which DPs forged a post-Holocaust identity. The first is Zionism. Zionism was a potent ideology and political cause. It helped sustain countless Jews during the war and was a primary basis for organized resistance. After the war Zionists helped to bring Jews to western Germany, created political and social institutions there, established *kibbutzim* and vocational programs, and helped build a military through quasi-formal conscription. Such efforts drew on a staple of new converts: "Zionists of the catastrophe" now convinced that there was no future for Jews in Europe and that a Jewish state was a practical necessity.

But for DPs, as more recent research stresses, Zionism was more than a movement. In Grossmann's description it also "worked as a kind of therapeutic ideology that could offer a sense of collective identity, hope, and a future to those who had lost both family and home." And "[f]or young people who had lost their families, the Zionist peer culture, in all its passionate intensity, offered self-affirmation and community."[107] Patt amplifies this understanding of Zionism as a comprehensive identity, freighted with psychological need. Orphans especially benefited from the "camaraderie and companionship" of the *kibbutzim*, the substitute families they represented, and the satisfaction of working for a "higher goal."[108] (Patt also argues for the practical achievements of DP Zionist youth in advancing political goals.)

A second context for Jewish renewal, both within and outside the DP camps, was the revival of Jewish cultural and spiritual life. This revival encompassed religious worship, social rituals, theater, dance, literature, and press activity—all of which provided continuity with Jews' prewar existence. Though such culture was largely based in Yiddish (and not Hebrew), it was compatible with Zionist goals insofar as it helped consolidate a sense of collective identity and establish a Jewish commonweal in postwar Europe as an added basis for a national existence. DPs' practices, moreover, were themselves dynamic, working to link the Jewish past, the recent devastation, and the Jewish future. Myers Feinstein reveals how "rituals of remembrance" performed by Jews helped to create "a collective memory of the Holocaust that included resistance and an affirmation of Zionism," as well as to "revive the survivors' commitment to Jewish traditions."[109]

A last context for existential restoration was childbearing, marriage, and domesticity. Jewish DPs, by spontaneous and irrepressible desire, married and had babies in enormously high numbers. Such children served as emblems of physical survival and vitality, sexual recovery, and literal Jewish rebirth. For women especially, becoming a parent could mean reconnecting with an identity or aspiration they had had before the Holocaust. Postwar babies could also be both substitutes for and memorials, of a sort, to dead children. The hard work of parenthood gave one an other-directed sense of purpose and structure to daily life. Grossmann thus presents "fertility and maternity" as corollaries to "therapeutic Zionism." They "provided a means both of claiming personal agency and an intact individual body, and of constructing a viable new community. . . . [C]aring for an infant could perhaps initially offer the most direct and primal means of reaffirming the self."[110] DP women also made great investments in domesticity. In the crowded and often unsanitary camps, this meant trying to secure privacy, maintain cleanliness, and procure more and better food to supplement the camp diet. While reinforcing traditional gender roles, such activities helped reestablish a sense of normalcy and stabilizing routine.[111]

The Jewish students participated in these contexts, but only to a degree. All were Zionist insofar as they supported a Jewish nation, with some deeply committed to the cause. Yet shared Zionist belief and activity were hardly their primary bases for affinity, and they quarreled at times with Zionist authorities. The students sought to contribute to a Jewish cultural revival. Yet they did so largely outside the setting of the camps. Moreover, they proffered a version of Jewish identity rooted in educational achievement, professional ambition, and cultural elevation, whose primary arena in the postwar context was the German urban environment. Finally, although some students married and had babies, establishing families was a secondary impulse. To a great extent student life was itself the decisive context for their restoration.

Toward a More Secure Future

The chief task of the students was to study; a portrait of their lives must therefore begin with their academic commitments. At all times and in all settings, their studies gravitated heavily toward medicine, engineering, and the sciences. In late 1946, 85 of the 132 students at the LMU were part of the medical faculty. Another 16 were in pharmacy and the natural sciences (physics, chemistry, biology). All 57 students at the TH studied engineering or natural science. Forty-two of the 209 students in German schools in Munich at the time pursued economics, philosophy, art, and music. And only two students, both among the 42 still at the UNRRA University, studied law.[112]

This distribution continued, with some dropoff in the difficult field of medicine. One year later, of the 413 Munich students, 18 percent were in medicine; 15 percent in dentistry; 5 percent in pharmacy; and 1 percent in veterinary medicine. Engineering students at the LMU and TH made up 24.8 percent of the cohort, and another 5.5 percent studied in a special engineering school. Eight percent specialized in natural science and 2.5 percent in agronomy. Political science had 5 percent of the students, and those pursuing art, music, literature, and photography together comprised just under 14 percent of the total.[113] In July 1947, 320 of 402 Munich students studied medicine, dentistry, pharmacy, veterinary medicine, engineering, chemistry, agronomy, and physics, with medicine (82 students) and mechanical engineering (81 students) the most popular fields.[114]

This pattern was echoed in other cities. All but 11 of the 83 Union members in Erlangen University studied medicine, dentistry, or engineering (including textile engineering, a strength of the school).[115] Nearly two-thirds of the 39 students in Heidelberg studied medicine; just four were in the humanities.[116] In Stuttgart, where there was no program in medicine, all but four of the 34 students pursued engineering and the natural sciences.[117] This preference of fields is echoed among the 45 Jewish students in the British Zone, for whom medicine was the leading choice, followed by chemistry and natural science. Small numbers also studied music, psychology, theater, philosophy, and law.[118]

The Jewish students' distribution of fields, dramatically clustered in medicine, engineering, and the sciences, very much matched that among other DP and German students. At German universities roughly a third of

Germans pursued engineering, as did an equal ratio of DPs at the UNRRA University.[119] A quarter or so among each group favored medicine. Whereas for Germans philosophy was the third most popular choice, for DPs it was the natural sciences (in part, one may presume, because the UNRRA school had no philosophy program), followed by law. This pattern reinforces the notion, stressed throughout this study, that university training in Europe was overwhelmingly designed to cultivate both professionals and an educated elite, defined more by technical knowledge than humanistic pursuits as such.

Beyond this pattern the Jewish students' specific choice of fields had reasons both organic and practical. Some among them had a special aptitude and fondness for math and science, and had long dreamed of careers in medicine or engineering. Others developed this interest during the war. Several alumni confess that seeing so much death and dying nurtured their desire to be doctors—part of a helping profession, on the side of life.[120] Mark Hupert credits his decision to go into civil engineering, at a "subconscious" level at least, to the knowledge of building he developed as a slave laborer. Most important was the students' determination to learn a skill that could form the basis for a career in another society. This intention strongly favored fields like medicine and discouraged humanistic studies. (A medical degree was honored internationally, such that students immigrating to the United States were potentially eligible for advanced training or immediate employment. To their great frustration, the dentistry students had to essentially repeat their programs in America.) Law students, for example, learned German law—training largely irrelevant outside of Germany. A degree in history or literature would prepare one for little besides a career in academia where, in most places to which one might immigrate, job opportunities and demand for expertise in European subjects were limited. For similar reasons Polish and other non-Jewish DP university students also favored technical and professional training.[121]

Sabina Zimering, a medical student, summarized the predominant attitude: "We were in Germany temporarily and if we [im]migrated to another country, we had to come with something practical [from which] you could make a living . . . not what you were very excited about or loved—it would have been a foolish lifestyle." The students, she stressed, were not "dreamers" prone to dwelling on life's "big questions"; the exigencies of the present dominated their attention. Dov Steinfeld, an engineering student in Munich, had grown up in Silesia on the Polish-German border. When he and his family were incarcerated in a ghetto, his father hired a private math and physics tutor so that Steinfeld might have a solid foundation if he survived. (Steinfeld survived mostly as a laborer at a textile plant in Germany; his mother and sister were killed in Auschwitz.) He explained: "Most of the students in Munich studied practical things, not lawyer[s], only physicians or engineers. Every one of us . . . was a kind of type of people. . . . [We] saw only one thing: to study and go out.[122]

Some students, however, made concessions to the practical at great pains. At first a political science student, Emanuel Tanay looked down on his peers who pursued a pre-professional path. "We in the social sciences," he explained, "viewed medical students with disdain. They were parochial, preoccupied with passing examinations."[123] Concerned about his future, he nonetheless shifted his focus to medicine, and later became a psychiatrist.

A determined minority stayed true to their love of the humanities. Simon Schochet emerged from Dachau overwhelmed—intent to observe, absorb, and feed his curiosities about the human condition through broad-ranging study. The first classes he took at the LMU were on subjects such as the philosophy of history, the sociology of Russia, the French language, Shakespeare, and "the world of the fairytale."[124] In the United States he became an accomplished historian of the massacre at Katyn, especially of the Jewish officers killed there.[125] While studying in Munich he drew close to others with a humanistic bent. Perhaps not by coincidence, several among the group's leaders, including its "visionary," Josef Silberman, studied socially engaged subjects such as law and economics.

Women, although a minority, made up a significant part of the Jewish student cohort. The Munich Union in the summer of 1947 was 29 percent female (115 out of 402). This nearly matched their proportion among Jewish students in the American Zone as a whole, which stood at 31.6 percent (207 out of 655).[126] Some chapters were strongly female. Female students in Frankfurt approached 50 percent in June 1948 (46 out of 103).[127] The numbers of women students are all the more impressive given the preponderance of males among Jewish DPs. Although this imbalance—reflecting the higher number of male survivors—surely declined with the influx of refugees from the east, men likely remained a strong majority.

Gender differences existed with respect to fields of study. In Munich the ratio of men to women in medicine was roughly two to one, similar to the balance in the group as a whole. Women's numbers in dentistry, music, and philology (literature) were nearly equal, indicating their preference for—or at least openness to—these fields. In pharmacy, a somewhat "softer" science, there were twice as many women as men. All four students in the art academy were women. Male dominance was strongest in engineering (100 to 5), political science (15 to 2), chemistry (13 to 4), and agronomy (8 to 2).[128]

As the data reflect, there clearly was an educational and professional culture among women in Europe, including the Eastern European countries from which the students mostly came. In places like Russia, medicine was primarily a female profession.[129] Although in Poland, as Lucy Fink testifies, "it was uncommon for women . . . to want to pursue higher education," there were exceptions, as she and her peers attest. Indeed, the core motivation and expectations of the female students, based on my impressions of the alumni, were identical to those of the men. Gender equality hit its limit with respect to the Union leadership, which at all times was heavily dominated by men. Fink and other women recall, however, that they were treated with great fairness within the group.[130]

The percentage of women among the Jewish students perfectly reflected that among DPs at the UNRRA University, where women comprised exactly 30 percent of the student body.[131] In German universities only 13 percent of students were women.[132] Anna Holian speculates that DP women—unmoored from their native cultures and let into university under a special quota for DPs—were less subject to the biases favoring male professionals (and breadwinners) than their German counterparts were.

In an ironic twist, educational opportunities for Jews were likely greater in occupied Germany than in their native lands. This was especially the case for women. Academic opportunities were limited for *all* Jews, given university quotas and the barrier imposed by the costs of *gymnasium* and university education. But young women faced added barriers, as parents might make the education of their sons their priority. Although this does not seem to have been the case for the female alumni—from childhood, their parents largely supported their academic ambitions—the structural inequities within their respective societies might have curtailed that ambition had the war never broken out.

Romantic longings and intrigue were also part of the students' world. Some had barely reached puberty when the war broke out, and so were eager to engage in the rituals of adolescence and young adulthood, as well as to reclaim a sexual self. Relationships formed within the group, and some student couples married. (Having a partner outside the group was extremely rare—a subject I address in the next chapter.) But these were not the near-spontaneous post-liberation weddings that characterized the marriages of so many Jewish DPs, who wed in Bavaria at a rate ten times that of the surrounding population.[133] The students typically married several years into their studies, once their academic trajectory in Germany was well established, or after they had completed their degrees and emigrated. Student couples, moreover, tended to be supportive of each other's professional goals.

Even so, alumna Sophie Schorr reports, "My mother was terribly afraid that I will get married before I finish medical school. Well, I didn't."[134] Dov Steinfeld recalls that a colleague in Munich got married, and "we looked at him like he was somebody lost," someone who would put his studies in jeopardy with the responsibilities of family.[135]

The students, by extension, did not participate in the DP baby boom, and almost always started families only after leaving Germany. Focused mostly on their studies, the female Jewish students existed outside two prevalent idealizations of postwar Jewish womanhood: what Myers Feinstein terms the "partisan girl," defined by physical vigor, sexual freedom, and the readiness to (again) fight, and the "Zionist mamale," figured as the "protector of the young, manager of the home, and transmitter of Jewish culture."[136] The women in the group were less likely than the men to finish their degrees or, if they did, to enter the professions for which they were trained. This was, however, a minority among them, as most of the women indeed pursued a professional path after leaving Germany. For both men and women, their vitality and even Eros were initially directed toward to their education, which was closely guarded against the pressures of other desires and expectations.

The alumni recall that the academic work was demanding and made harder by circumstance. "Don't forget we were hungry," Fred Reiter remarked. "I used to say, we are the most religious people. We eat like [on] Yom Kippur" (a day of fasting in Judaism).[137] Textbooks, whose production during the war had virtually ceased, were in short supply—in general, and for DPs especially. As early as December 1945, the Joint wrote the chief editor of the *Journal of the American Medical Association* in the United States to request medical textbooks for the Jewish students.[138] A major initiative of the Zone Federation that yielded some success involved writing to private German booksellers throughout the American Zone to ask for donated texts.[139] Lydia Eichenholz recalls going to East Berlin on the Union's behalf to purchase texts that, though poor in quality, were in decent supply and comparatively inexpensive.[140] Obtaining such simple things as pencils and notebook paper was also a struggle, requiring that the Union lobby UNRRA, the Joint, and the CK. Ingenuity helped as well. At one point the students brought sacks of financial records scavenged from the bombed-out office of an abandoned business to a paper supplier who recycled the material; in return, he gave the students clean notebook sheets.[141]

Students whose German was weak faced added difficulties. Several alumni recall initially writing their lecture notes in their native Polish and taking days to read texts that students fluent in German could get through in hours. "They didn't fuss around," Mark Hupert said of the professors. "You had to be up to [speed]."[142] The German system, with its notoriously remote faculty and concern with rank, created challenges both serious and comical. Balaban recalls that "a German professor never talked to his students. He used to come, give his lecture. . . . You couldn't interrupt him, couldn't ask any questions."[143] Assistants provided the hands-on pedagogy. He recalls also a "Professor Doctor Engineer Graf Von Schulenberg," who taught electro-medicine. Balaban joked that at the oral exams, "if you called [him] Herr Professor Doctor Graf, you got an A. If you missed one of these [titles], you got a B. You miss two of these, you got a C."[144]

An English-language essay in the Union's newspaper from 1947 enumerated more soberly the hardships the students faced. After complaining about the lack of books and classroom space which all students felt, the piece noted that "there is something [the Jewish students] still miss more: It is the personal contact with Jewish scientists from who [sic], they might receive inspiration as the German student does from his professor."[145] ("Scientist" was likely derived from *Wissentschaftler*, which also translates as "scholar.") They also keenly felt the absence of family and home: "There is no father to give them any financial help, nor mother to make them comfortable in the small practical ways. Her place has [been] taken by the German landlady—distrustful, prejudiced . . . reluctantly doing little services for food and cigarettes."[146]

Despite all this the "progress of the Jewish students," the essay boasted, was "astonishing," with many students ranked at the tops of their classes. A Union member recounted that "the strictest" of his professors would occasionally say to the German students when giving a test, "It is difficult to understand how the Jewish students, in spite of language difficulties, far outclass their German colleagues."[147] Asked years later how they performed at such a high level, Hupert confessed, "I really don't know."[148] The complex nature of their drive is key to understanding their postwar restoration.

Fear of failure was surely one factor. One had to pass rigorous exams early in one's program or face termination, destabilizing an already fragile existence. The students thus supplemented individual study with group sessions, private tutoring, and enrichment courses, with the instructors paid in cigarettes, meat, and milk.[149] Above all they were extremely diligent. Hupert recalls that his friend Arnold Kerr could study "24 hours a day." Hupert could study "only eighteen."[150]

The quiet, largely private drama of their scholarly pursuits was perhaps the most "normal" aspect of their lives. Hard work was hard work, irrespective of one's background. Nonetheless, their efforts at times led them to dramatically charged situations. Kerr's first landlady in Munich had been a guard supervisor at Dachau. She and her husband raised a young child from the camp, the daughter of a Russian inmate who had likely been killed. Kerr's tiny room had space for only a bed and a small desk, and was without heat during a famously cold winter. He borrowed a small electric heater from his landlady, which he put directly below his chair, and studied for hours at a time this way. Once nearly starved to death and consumed by the Nazis' inferno, he was now feeding his mind and his future atop a plume of nourishing warmth in the house of a camp guard.[151]

The striving for "normal" can be pressed further in framing the students' motivation. Kerr recalls, "The moment I became a student at the [TH] I became a normal person."[152] This transition marked the end of the chaos and radical dependence of his existence as a DP to that point. As a student his life was defined by autonomy, purposiveness, and grounding routines; these paralleled the "therapeutic" effects of Zionism, childrearing, and domesticity experienced by other DPs. Emanuel Tanay recalls, "In Munich we lived an almost normal bourgeois existence. . . . To live a normal life was our goal. We avoided the reality that we suffered from emotional scars that affected our interactions with people and undermined our self-esteem."[153]

Normalcy had an aspect of defiance as well, further propelling the students to excel. Reflecting on their achievements, Hupert remarked, "First of all, we overcame the [pressure] to be slaves, to be down. We decided we are not going to be down, we're going to be like normal people, [and] continue our life" as if the Holocaust had not happened. "Ninety percent" of the students, he stressed, "knew [before the war] that they're going to go to school." This continuity represented not just self-affirmation but a mediated form of revenge—a repossession of the self in spite of persecution.

For all the students' emphasis on professional development, learning also provided a personal validation connected to its intrinsic pleasure and value. "I loved reading and if I could get a hold of something, I would read it," recalls Rochelle Eisenberg. "I didn't have a very good self-image until I started studying." There was a more directly psychological aspect, felt at least at a subterranean level, to immersion in study. Grossmann discerns in the lives of DPs a "productive forgetting" born of purposive activity that focused them on the present and away from the painful past.[154] Within this model the students' schoolwork, in its intellectual challenge and even monotony, was therapeutic. One alumnus remarked, "We were so busy studying and succeeding that it eased our existence."[155] More vivid confirmation of this diversion of energy comes from an unlikely quarter. Arnold Kerr has the exacting mind of an engineer, and is little prone to sentimentality or self-reflection even when intricately narrating his loss. Years after the war, he read a review of a book by C. P. Snow, one of whose stories was about someone "who in order to escape his problems" devoted his time to his studies. "When I read it, I said maybe this is also me. . . . I found a niche that was not emotional, that was very clear-cut, and contributed to a more secure future."[156]

Rubin Zimering, also an engineer who showed little emotion in our interview, further articulates the processes of productive forgetting and the sense of legacy the students might nonetheless feel. Learning at the war's end the fate of his murdered parents "affected me then [but] I didn't, I didn't fall apart."[157] At university "I kept my mind away . . . from despair and despairing about what happened. I felt that the best thing I could do is restore, try to restore the members of my family, replace them in a way. In other words, recreate, not, not by reviving anybody, but by procreating a new life." His studies—the very activity that diverted his attention—at the same time elliptically referenced, and even made symbolically present, who and what he had lost. "Forgetting," in short, was a means of remembering.

There is a sense, finally, in which the hard work itself was the students' essential accomplishment. On reflection numerous alumni indicate that they could have taken a softer, easier path, especially in the DP camps. Reiter spoke with great disappointment of a well-educated childhood friend who, in a DP camp in Austria, was content to take his meals, play soccer, and see movies.[158] This perception of the camps as places of complacency had broad echoes. Members of a kibbutz in the DP camp at Buchenwald, trumpeting their own dedication, declared that "everyone knows that since liberation one could live a life of comparative ease in Buchenwald. Plenty of food, and nothing to do."[159]

There was also the temptation of the black market, which the students mostly resisted. To be sure the Jewish students, like countless DPs, illegally traded cigarettes and other small goods for both necessities and small luxuries. (One might pay for a nice restaurant meal with a pack of cigarettes and tip the waiter an individual cigarette, Schochet remembers. Dov Steinfeld recalls that, at a time when paper money was near-worthless and price was a function of need, he bought a Leica camera for twenty cigarettes.)[160] The Union itself stockpiled tradable goods to acquire items for shared use. In the students' minds there was a distinction between these justifiable, low-grade exchanges and large-scale trading or speculation on the black market for the purpose of individual enrichment.

In the students' somewhat censorious view at the time, the latter activity was narrowly self-aggrandizing, dishonorable, and inimical to Zionist goals. An editorial in the student newspaper declared with political fervor: "A large portion of the youth has chosen to follow in their elders'

footsteps . . . [and] dedicated themselves, body and soul, to the black mar-
keteering which blooms today in Germany, and at which our brethren are
so adept. . . . These young people are basically committing suicide." The student path, by contrast, offered a "fruitful" life of "work and study."[161] Mark
Fintel recalls in more personal terms, "We were different than [the others],
because most tried to make a living on the black market. And we decided to
hit the books."[162]

Such a claim surely exaggerates how many Jews were speculators in the
market, minimizes the Union's practical reliance on it to help fulfill basic
needs, and contradicts the recollections of some alumni that a small number of students in fact sought to make money by exchanging goods.[163] This
sense of superiority, moreover, could smack of elitism. One alumna recalled
that while she respected her fellow students, she found their self-impor-
tance, seemingly dismissive view of the less educated, and somewhat forced,
sophisticated air off-putting.[164] In chiding tones Georg Majewski, head of
the Berlin Union, said of the Munich students, " 'Good manners' and an
aristocratic appearance had to suffice as a mask for their ignorance. Whoever could not express this was not worthy of being acknowledged as a
member of the Jewish Students' Union."[165] Whatever their pretense, most
of the students lived at a bare subsistence level, devoting their greatest en-
ergies to studying. In more positive terms, Ohrenstein stresses the students'
determination to "become somebody" and "stand on our own feet." [166]

Whatever the students felt at the time, the alumni later recognized that
others struggled to overcome difficult circumstances and faced constraints
they did not. This recognition qualifies their sense of accomplishment while
putting their dedication in another light. Even shorn of families and material
possessions, many of the students had—and were aware of—an enduring advantage relative to other Jewish DPs by virtue of their prewar education and
broader upbringing. To follow through on that promise after the war was to
fulfill, in part, an obligation born of privilege. Acknowledging the students'
advantages, Hupert and others in hindsight reject the idea that the group was
supremely special, and extend equal or greater plaudits to those Jewish DPs
who, without a cultivated skill and the "the luxury to study for three or four
years," nonetheless made it in new societies.[167]

The New Life

The student life also entailed extracurricular learning, socializing, and cultural activities. Important to students anywhere, these had added significance for the DP students given their experiences of deprivation, loss of

family and home, and relative isolation in occupied Germany. The various Jewish student unions not only pursued academic ends but also sought to facilitate diverse aspects of the students' lives. In the alumni's recollections the Union and the student community often run together as nearly equivalent dimensions of the same broad experience. Examining what filled out that lifeworld reveals the self-generated quality of the students' existence—how the unions and broader peer communities, like the actual families and collectives formed by other DPs, themselves gave coherence and meaning to life.

Jewish DPs had strongly collectivist impulses. These were most pronounced among the youth *kibbutzim*. Their members lived communally, defined themselves through shared dedication, and, especially when organized on socialistic lines, might renounce personal property and individual decision-making. In some cases even the choice to leave the kibbutz was subject to approval by the members, and "I" was replaced in group dialogue by "we."[168] Aid workers sometimes complained about what seemed the coercive conformity and near-military organization among Jewish DPs, as well as the apparent likeness of much DP schooling to Zionist indoctrination. Notably, the Joint's Koppel Pinson inveighed against their excessive "discipline, a monolithic conception of group life . . . [and] the widespread resort to agitation, propaganda and indoctrination."[169] Scholars seeking to understand the pressures behind such behavior conclude that Jewish DPs, for sound practical, psychological, and ideological reasons, were apt to trade individual autonomy for camaraderie and a sense of direction.[170] "The *kibbutzim*," as one DP bluntly described, "gave a framework to kids who didn't know what to do with themselves, who had no family."[171] Moreover, the *kibbutzim* continually struggled against members' resistance to collectivist demands.

From its inception the Munich Union saw itself not simply as a group of individuals with shared goals but as a community bound by a sense of collective belonging. Hence it valued having a physical space in which a group spirit could flourish. Sometime in 1946 the Union secured a midday gathering spot, the Café am Isartorplatz. Funded by the Joint, it was in truth a modest cafeteria that served a kosher lunch. (The students referred to it by the German word "Mensa," for student cafeteria, or more commonly by the Polish equivalent.)[172] Students might spend a couple hours there on weekdays, studying and talking, and informally conducting Union business. The cafeteria, which looms large in the alumni's memories, was a primary locus where they bonded—a place of comfort and safety away from the Germans.[173] The students developed a second café on Viktor Scheffel-Strasse, used primarily by students at the nearby TH.[174]

Jewish university students outside their dining hall in Munich. Sabina Zimering is the young woman holding the railing on the left. (Courtesy of Sabina Zimering)

Maintaining a connection to religion was another of the Union's goals.[175] A rabbi working with the Joint marveled in late 1945 that "the survival of the Jewish spirit and religious sentiment among these people [the DPs] is an even greater miracle than their physical survival."[176] Enabling Jews to practice was, however, another daunting task for relief efforts, entailing everything from securing kosher food, matzah for Passover, torahs, and prayer books; to building synagogues and mikvahs (ritual baths); reconstituting the rabbinate; providing religious education, including yeshivas; and performing marriages and proper funerals.

Most of the students grew up moderately observant, participating in Jewish custom but lacking strong religious conviction. They therefore adhere to the documented pattern by which more secular Jews engage in religious practice for reasons of ethnic and family solidarity whereas religious Jews do so for reasons of religious belief.[177] The Holocaust had no uniform impact on survivors' observance and faith. Some became more observant or faithful, and others less so. Research suggests that one's prewar religiosity—not wartime experience—was the greatest determinant of one's religiosity after the war. The alumni reflect this range of possibilities. Sabina Zimering remarked: "I wasn't too great a believer before the war and I became even less [so] after. Because, if there was a God, where was he?"[178] Fred Reiter, observant both early and later in life, did not go to synagogue for ten years after liberation and "didn't miss it."[179]

Other students remained steeped in religious belief and language, and interpreted their collective plight partly through these frames. The inaugural issue of the Union newspaper featured on its front page a special *kaddish*. The Jewish prayer for the dead, the *kaddish* was important for survivors, who commonly wove into it reference to the recent destruction, individual tributes, and hopes for the Jewish future.[180] Drafted in Hebrew by Roman Ohrenstein, the prayer read:

> The Nation of Israel—the pure souls of its sons and daughters, the students of the rabbinical institutions, the Yeshivot, and the universities, their teachers, and rabbis.

> The holy and faithful ones who were burnt, murdered, and strangled in the name of the Lord, the Torah, and the [Jewish] Nation. . . . May Israel be elevated and sanctified with its seed, the blossoms of purity and holiness, which fell beneath the hatchet of the Nazi animal.

> Remember and fight until the Nation [of Israel] returns to live in our land, and the wishes of millions whose souls departed with these prayers on their lips are fulfilled.[181]

The text is noteworthy for its specific remembrance of communities of learning and teaching, reinforcing the students' sense of carrying on their legacy. Combining the languages of biblical destiny and modern Zionism, as did so much early survivor discourse, the prayer was signed "The Munich Diaspora." In a final convention, it situates the creation of Israel as the fulfillment by the living of the wishes of the dead.[182]

Whether religious or not, the students generally saw Jewish tradition— and the celebration of the holidays especially—as an important affirmation of their Jewish identity. The holidays, however, exposed the fact that so many had lost their families, and they turned to the Jewish community and relief agencies to gain some semblance of belonging. In 1946 the Union was given more than a hundred seats at a Passover seder dinner organized by the US Army rabbi Abraham Klausner for Jewish US military personnel and DPs.[183] The Union requested that UNRRA supply special packets (likely containing matzah) for each student whose "relatives were murdered in the concentration camps."[184] By the fall of 1947, the student representatives lamented: "Under the conditions in which the Jewish students live in Germany, it is impossible to celebrate the holidays in a festive manner. Most of the students

Roman Ohrenstein officiating at a Chanukah celebration in 1948. (Courtesy of Roman Ohrenstein)

are without families. . . . In order to sustain the beautiful tradition of the Jewish holidays, the students should have the chance to spend, at the very least, a few hours celebrating, in a joyful mood, with each other."[185] It recommended that all chapters reserve the final days of *Sukkot* (the Feast of the Tabernacles) for a "celebration" (*mesiba*) with presentations on "the role of Jewish tradition in the maintenance of the Jewish people" and "Jewish holidays in the 'old homeland.'" There is no evidence that the chapters followed through on this suggestion, but student groups afterward organized Chanukah festivities, and clusters of friends sometimes held Sabbath dinners and holiday celebrations together.[186] In sum, religious practice—even in its more cultural guises—did not easily survive the students' alienation, bereavement, and displacement.

The Union's greater investment was in its cultural program, organized both at the chapter and zonewide levels, by the Cultural Department. The program's internal aspect focused on the students' own development (*Selbstbildung*); the external aspect comprised efforts to "enlighten" the Jewish community (*Aufklärungsarbeit*). The former included deepening the students' knowledge of Jewish culture and the Hebrew language, building a library, holding lectures, and organizing sports and group outings. The latter entailed publishing a newspaper and bringing cultural events into the

DP camps.[187] The two initiatives often merged, as activities for the students' benefit might also be enjoyed by the community and vice versa. Efforts geared toward the students' own enrichment had at their base the higher purpose of crafting a new intelligentsia as a part of the Jewish social body. I focus here on the internal program, given its relevance to existential themes.

The Jewish students did not by and large participate in their universities' extracurricular academic life, such as lectures and symposia, nor in the associational life of their fellow students (whether Germans or other DPs). Rather, the Union developed its own program to advance knowledge of specifically Jewish topics. The Munich Union organized a "knowledge circle" that featured afternoon discussions and student lectures on such topics as "Zionism and Socialism" and "The Place of the Intelligentsia in Jewish Society."[188] The gatherings sought in part to combat the "intellectual lethargy" that, by the Union's admission, befell much of the hyper-studious group. These gatherings had only limited success, as the same few individuals attended most of the sessions. In the summer of 1946 the Union requested ten public seats at the war crimes trials in nearby Nuremberg, which it hoped could be given to law students.[189] Language courses in English, valuable for immigration to the United States, and in Hebrew, valuable for immigration to Palestine and for Zionist acculturation, never materialized due to a lack of interest.[190] The Cultural Department came under repeated criticism from other parts of the organization, while it complained about the passivity of the membership with respect to its efforts.[191]

Recreational activities were more successful. In early 1947 the Union organized a chess tournament for its members.[192] Sporting events also drew great interest. Sports played an important role in community life for Jewish DPs.[193] Jewish sports clubs formed both inside and outside the DP camps. Often sponsored by Zionist parties, these replicated the self-organized quality of Jewish life in much of prewar Europe. For DP Jews, athletic activity at once aided and confirmed physical recovery, offered healthy competition (both among Jews and with Germans and other national groups), and provided pride of achievement. Finally, the DPs' physical development squared well with a muscular Zionism trained on "reshaping the male Jewish body" away from the Orthodox archetype of the slender scholar.[194] This "new Zionist man" possessed a robust body poised for the physical work of building—and fighting for—a nation.

Incrementally the Union built its own athletic program. Ping-pong and volleyball teams soon formed, as did a ski club that made use of the nearby Alps.[195] Individual students entered, and sometimes won, athletic competitions among Jewish DPs.[196] In late 1947 the Munich Union, with the help of

Jewish university students on a ski trip to the Bavarian Alps in 1946 or 1947.
(Courtesy of Sabina Zimering)

the CK's Center for Physical Education, formed the Jewish Academic Sports
Club. It boasted separate sections for swimming, ping-pong, ice hockey, and
other sports; worked with local clubs to coordinate competitions; and built
an impressive stock of equipment, from boxing gloves to hockey sticks.[197]
One may speculate that the students appreciated sports for its intrinsic pleasure and for the relief from mental labor it offered; sports also permitted
these otherwise bookish students to embody the physical ideals of Zionism.

The Union also sponsored "dance evenings." Among the first dances was
a November 1946 event in the Foehrenwald DP camp.[198] The Union printed
a program, issued tickets, contracted with a Jewish restaurant in Munich
for catering, and hired a small orchestra.[199] Ever intent on building support
among fellow Jews, the Union heralded the event as a success, largely for
the positive impression the group made on the camp population.[200] In time
these events became proper balls held at venues in Munich, including the
famous Regina Hotel.[201] In preparation for the event, the Union organized a
dance course, and Commissioner Auerbach himself attended one of the evenings.[202] The elegant affairs accorded well with the students' projected image
of cultural refinement. They had a practical purpose as well: to raise money
for Union members with special financial needs. The Jewish community eagerly bought the pricy tickets because, as one alumnus remembers, "there
was always this reverence [for] somebody who learns, who goes to school."[203]

Jewish university students by the Isar River in Munich in 1946. (Courtesy of Sabina Zimering)

Part of the appeal of being a student was living freely in Munich, where one had easy access to its cultural life. (DPs wishing to travel from the DP camps to take in the city's culture had a much more difficult time.) The students had a mandate to expand their cultural horizons as part of their *Ausbildung*. In this spirit the Munich students, like those in other cities, frequently attended classical music concerts, operas, plays, and the cinema, often with discounted tickets given to the Union.[204] It was as if a whole world they had never known was opening up, one seen only in glimpses or sorely missed during the war years. Some students—especially those from cosmopolitan centers and of a high social standing—had the early foundation that allowed them to immediately connect with the city's many offerings. For students from rural areas or who had been very young when war broke out, their time in Munich might offer their first substantive exposure to elevated culture. Arnold Kerr recalls seeing his first opera in Munich and complaining that the actors kept singing to one another; if they had something to say, he wondered, why didn't they just say it? Kerr quickly overcame his cultural naïveté, eventually becoming an opera buff. Almost uniformly the alumni describe

Jewish university students in Munich in the spring of 1946. (Courtesy of Sabina Zimering)

their cultural explorations as integral parts of their education and broader postwar evolution.

The students' consumption of culture in occupied Germany tapped into a question deeply dividing postwar Jews, about the relationship of Jews to the European Enlightenment. The question arose most urgently in debates over whether Jews from Germany or elsewhere should try to rebuild a place for themselves in German society—a cradle of the Enlightenment into which Jews had been thoroughly assimilated. More broadly, Jews struggled over how the Enlightenment should figure into conceptions of contemporary Jewish identity and whether it was any longer appropriate for Jews to participate in the Enlightenment's cultural heritage.

Jews had in many ways benefited from, and shaped, that heritage. Its postwar defenders argued that an Enlightenment universalism stood both above and against the racial and cultural particularism of National Socialism. Jews, by extension, might be the bearers of an enduring humanism and help reeducate Europe in the best of its own ideals. Whatever the future, the Enlightenment was their culture too, to which they retained a rightful claim.

An opposing view, proclaimed loudly by DP leaders from Eastern Europe, was that European modernity had not only egregiously failed but also betrayed the Jews—that Jews' assimilation and contributions to European society had not immunized them against prejudice and, ultimately, savage attack.[205] To the contrary, where the Enlightenment was most developed—in the land of Goethe and Schiller—the contempt for Jews had found its most violent expression. Jews' investment in the Enlightenment's false promise is what Central Committee leader Jacob Oleiski, in an influential 1945 treatise, termed "the Great Disappointment." Along with other prominent DPs, he urged Jews to end their tragic involvement with European culture and commit to a Zionist future predicated on a distinctly Jewish culture.[206] Indeed, the Central Committee, in the characterization of historian Anthony Kauders, "frequently condemned community members who intended to stay in Germany, a stance that received the backing of the Jewish Agency in Palestine."[207] The powerful CK president Samuel Gringauz issued especially caustic denunciations of Europe, highlighting the hypocrisy of its humanism:

> We do not believe in the 2000 year-old Christian culture of the West, the culture, that *for them*, created . . . the wonder gardens of Versailles and the Uffizi and Pitti palaces in Florence, the Strasbourg *Münster* and the Cologne cathedral; but *for us*, the slaughters of the Crusades . . . [and] the gas chambers of Auschwitz. . . . How was [the Holocaust] possible . . . after Michelangelo, and Leonardo Da Vinci, after Molière and Victor Hugo . . . after Alexander von Humboldt and Immanuel Kant? How was it possible that professors and writers, priests and philosophers, artists and judges—how was it possible that almost the entire intellectual elite of Germany cheered on the blood-drunk murderers?[208]

Such sentiments might function as an indictment of the students' very presence in German universities. Here my concern is with their implications for the students' regard for the European culture around them.

The students voted substantially with their feet, declaring the legitimacy of their cultural engagement by attending performances, enjoying art, and, for some, undertaking the academic study of Europe's cultural lodestars. They typically took the attitude that they had been deprived of enough in their short lives; they did not want to be told there was more they must do without—certainly not by virtue of a position they did not share. One student recalls that a lead performer of a play she wanted to attend was a reputed Nazi. Rejecting a boycott of the performance, she reasoned that a German would buy the ticket and enjoy the performance, thereby defeating the political gesture and foreclosing her own pleasure in the play.[209]

The Union articulated no formal position about how its members should regard European culture. However, an opinion piece in its newspaper plausibly frames the students' core response to implied or explicit criticisms:

Here in Germany, there are possibilities to raise [our] cultural level. Theater, opera, music, art are accessible. True, it is German art; but if Heine was for Germans an "unknown poet," for us Schiller and Goethe are well-known. Because of that, though they may be the grandfathers of the hangmen and murderers of our people, we will not boycott them. Our people raised us on the foundation of national tolerance and social equality.

We will never forget what Ameleck did to us.[210] The blood of our martyrs demands: do not forget! But just as we will hear lecturers in German auditoriums and glean wisdom from German professors, we will also benefit from German art. . . . That which is human is not foreign to us.[211]

The statement declares that the students were entitled to seize opportunities for enrichment wherever they might emerge. Further, the Enlightenment was part of their own makeup and not something they could in any way reject. Finally, they insisted that connecting with its humanistic essence was not a concession to the Jews' historic enemies or, by implication, a repudiation of Zionism. Such views ultimately found echoes among the DP leadership. Gringauz himself took the eventual position that "the renunciation of Europe in no ways signifies for us the renunciation of European culture."[212] He counseled that Jews be the champions of a revitalized humanism, bearing the imprint of that culture in a new setting.

Among the cultural activities the alumni recall their nature outings with the most fondness. The beauty of the Bavarian landscape made a deep impression on them, as it did for other area DPs. A favored destination was Berchtesgaden, the vast nature complex in the Bavarian Alps where Hitler had his mountaintop "Eagle's Nest" retreat. The trips there, with twenty or so students staying for up to two weeks during vacation time, were major undertakings. For weeks in advance the Union negotiated with the Joint, the CK, and private hostels to secure their room and board.[213]

On these trips the students experienced camaraderie, the thrill of discovery, and the restorative power of nature. Emanuel Tanay, the leader of the first such excursion in the summer of 1946, gave a written account of the trip just after returning: "[E]ach day brought something new and worthy of beholding [Sehenswürdiges]. . . . The mood of the group was good, and it could not be otherwise, for there are few places where one may find so many wonders of nature." Taking in the lakes, mountain peaks, and salt pits, "even

Jewish university students in Berchtesgaden in 1946 or 1947. (Courtesy of
Roman Ohrenstein)

Jewish university students in Berchtesgaden in 1946 or 1947. (Courtesy of
Roman Ohrenstein)

the worst pessimists among us must concede that life can be beautiful."[214] Without referencing the Holocaust, the account captures the students' re-awakening to creation and to a positive faith in life's possibilities.

The alumni also experienced what might be called "liberating abandon" as a complement to their productive forgetting. "We were so happy to be alive," Sabina Zimering reports, "that we were doing all kinds of crazy things," like climbing imposing mountains.[215] She recalls a canoe trip to a vast lake where the students began splashing about and recklessly hitting one another's boats, as if to release the pent-up energy from years of deprivation, arrested growth, and emotional suppression. Felix Korn stressed the joy both of new experiences and of discovering his own capacities: "We lived. We had vacations. We learned how to dance. . . . To go to a movie was a treat. Being able, for the first time in my life, to go to an opera, even though it was a German one. Going skiing, putting on a pair of skis and tying the laces and looking at myself [in] haggard, terrible, torn clothes, but I skied down. I broke a leg, but I skied down."[216]

The students felt, finally, a special satisfaction in standing at the key sites representing Nazi power. They enjoyed the symbolic revenge commonly felt by Jews on postwar German soil. Actual physical acts of revenge against German persons and property were rare (though far from absent).[217] Much more common was the survivors' triumphant sense that "we are here," alive in a defeated Germany. Jewish DPs "made it their business to visit the historic symbols of the Nazi regime" and engaged in the "calculated appropriation of Nazi 'shrines' and German space for their own practical and symbolic purposes."[218] Among the most striking acts of appropriation was the establishment of a collective farm on the former estate of Julius Streicher, the anti-Semitic propagandist. Hitler's compound at Berchtesgaden was ripe for symbolic appropriation. The Central Committee held a special council session there, noting the locale's significance. To the delight of Judah Nadich, President Eisenhower's adviser on Jewish affairs, Jewish Brigade soldiers left Hebrew graffiti on "what had been Hitler's stronghold, his fortress and his pride."[219]

Sabina Zimering recalls that during one student trip to Berchtesgaden, the Joint had rented them rooms in the area's "top hotel." "In the beginning it was spooky [to] realize that only a few months ago all these important generals and Gestapo, whoever, were vacationing there." The mood shifted to glee: "[I]f those spiffy generals could see us now!" Sophie Schorr recounts that one of the "high moment[s]" of her life was standing in Hitler's villa (into which hikers could traipse) and thinking, "Here I was, a free Jewish student attending university, and he was dead."[220]

"The Chain Was Broken"

In a sermon on Yom Kippur in 1945, Samuel Gringauz instructed survivors—and young survivors especially—not to bear the crushing burdens of sorrow but instead to "show the world that we live. You must create and build, dance, and sing, be happy."[221] The students embodied this difficult mandate, if in improbable ways, without thought of a global audience, and in a setting that the deeply Zionist Gringauz had not intended. "We just enjoyed life in a tremendous way, as unlikely as it may seem today," one alumnus recalled.[222] Some spoke of their time in Munich in terms of "fun," "happiness," and even "ecstasy."

The meaning of so much in the students' lives, however, had been transvalued, freighted by circumstance. Emotions such as "happiness" stood against and were partly defined by loss. So too, the pleasures of their largely belated youths were the products of collective struggle. Felix Korn provided another, more ambivalent recollection that gives voice to that effort. One summer a group of students went to Starnberger See—a massive lake at Feldafing where a nineteenth-century Bavarian king had drowned, but whose body, in Korn's telling, was never found.[223] It was there, in Schochet's novel, *Feldafing*, that the playful survivors morphed into drowning men. Korn and a female companion rowed a small boat into the middle of the lake. Policing the waters, American soldiers caught sight of the wayward vessel and tried to topple it by making waves with their motorboat. When he suggested to his frightened companion that they jump in the water, she exclaimed, "But I don't know how to swim!" "You never told me," he answered. "And then I realized she doesn't know how to swim, so I [later on] taught her."[224]

The remembrance serves as a rich allegory for so much in the students' postwar experience. They are making their way, alone and somewhat adrift, in a setting at once beautiful and forbidding and where, by the Nazis' genocidal designs, they are not supposed to be. The legacy of Nazism, like that of the Bavarian king, lurks below the surface, threatening to pull them into the undertow of crippling pain or surviving German hostility. The Americans, as well-meaning but naïve occupiers, strain to distinguish friend from foe, and nearly do harm even as they try to help. The students are in the same boat, irrespective of differences in their backgrounds. Finally, in their moment of need, they reach out to help each other stay afloat.

The anecdote's conclusion summons a final association the alumni use to describe their time in Germany: their experience of togetherness, the power of the group itself, and its likeness to a family. By extension the alumni tend to invoke their collective rather than personal achievements. "We needed each

Jewish university students in Munich in 1947. (Courtesy of Roman Ohrenstein)

other," Mark Hupert explained. "Think of it this way. There was this terrible war, and none of us knew if he's going to survive. The war ended and most of us didn't have any family. Here was a group of people, and all of a sudden you were free. We did what we wanted to do."[225] He spent his time "only with this group. We went on vacations together, we went dancing together, we went eating together. We did everything together." Philip Balaban recalls: "We are friends, we are peers. . . . This was my family in Munich, I didn't know anybody else . . . this group made me."[226] Straining to describe what ultimately propelled the students, Felix Korn declared, "We were the purpose."[227]

Such reflections indicate how the group was both the key to the students' vitality and the basis of the connection they felt to larger narratives. "The New Life," the title of the students' newspaper, is an apt reference to their individual revival. But, as an editorial in the paper explains, "with this name, we wish to symbolize our hope that the Jewish student will take a meaningful part in the lofty work of the rebirth of the Jewish intelligentsia . . . and form it into a uniform, energetic, educated strength for the good of Jewish revival."[228] This dialectic between the individual and the collective was bridged by the group they established as a mediating collectivity. To be self-serving, in the sense expressed by Korn, was not in their view to be selfish; it was instead to serve higher purposes. The students, as we shall further learn, struggled with external censure and private doubt. Against this stood their sense of responsibility, in the words of Roman Ohrenstein, to "continue the chain" of learning—so important to the Jewish psyche—because "the chain was broken."[229]

CHAPTER 5

"Surviving Survival"

Living with the Holocaust
and among the Germans

Mark Hupert, who studied civil engineering in Munich from 1947 to 1952, was liberated from Dachau on April 29, 1945, suffering from malnutrition and tuberculosis so severe that he spent a year recovering in Gauting hospital. Dachau was the end of a grueling line of persecutions and sorrows, which included his digging graves at Plaszow, internment in Buchenwald, and the deaths of his mother and sister. He arrived in Dachau by means of a ten-day death march from Flossenbürg, during which SS men mercilessly shot the "stragglers." At one point Hupert scrambled with a friend to a roadside ditch to gather rotten food left behind by harvesters. Hupert quickly jumped back to the road, but his friend did not and was shot dead. "It's not that I was smarter than he was, it was just luck." Barely 2,000 of the 18,000 marchers survived the journey. "We must have been a sore lot when we arrived," he recalled, "because even the inmates in Dachau felt sorry for us."[1]

Soon afterward a piece of bread given to Hupert was stolen from beneath his head as he lay. "I wasn't able to stop it, I was a goner." Had the Americans come a day or two later, he is convinced, he would have been dead. Accounting for his survival through his years-long ordeal, he explained, "All the people who survived . . . somehow believed that they were going to survive, for whatever stupid reason. I won't say that all of them survived. . . . The people who said 'we will never survive,' I don't know of one of them who survived, [at least] among my friends." Hupert could find "no reason" for his faith in his own perseverance. "I just said I'm going to survive."

As US soldiers paraded SS guards around Dachau, Hupert tried to throw stones at them but did not have the energy. Many other prisoners died just after being freed. Speculating on how one lived and when one died, he allowed, "You wanted to survive to see that the Nazis and Hitler are fin-ished. . . . Otherwise there was no point in anything. And, lo and behold, the first weeks after the war ended, an incredible amount of people died. . . . [A] lot of it was, 'I accomplished what I really had to accomplish. . . . There's nothing else that has to be done.'" Hupert then made an effort at cleansing: "I decided it's time to take a shower. . . . So, I walked . . . to where the show-ers were, that took me a day. I came to the showers, you know, things are better, forget that life. I turn on the water and the water knocked me down. The stream of water from the shower. I was on the floor."

Some aspect of the comfort his body could not bear was provided by a religious service in Dachau conducted by Rabbi Judah Nadich, the special adviser on Jewish affairs to President Eisenhower. Years later in New York City, Rabbi Nadich presided over the bar mitzvah of Hupert's son at a Park Avenue synagogue, by which time Hupert was a successful engineer and family man married to a fellow Munich student. When informed of the coincidence, Rabbi Nadich replied, "Thanks to God that I [now] meet Mr. Hupert under different circumstances."

Hupert's experience, in both its raw facts and rich metaphors, speaks to the horror, heartache, and contradictions of the Holocaust, one's survival through it, and the remembrance of it. Hupert first describes his own sur-vival as a miracle of probabilities, not providence; the reward of luck, not will or smarts. Yet in another, contradictory breath, he strains for some ra-tional account, deciding that the decision to live—for whatever reasonless reason—proved decisive. And in a third recounting, the determination to triumph over the Nazis drove victims to live past the German defeat. Each explanation—each a story the self tells itself to give sense to unexplainable events—cuts through the other in a cross-hatch of impossible causality.

Hupert's body proved too weak for physical revenge. His hope of quickly washing away the nightmare proved equally strenuous, illusory; his body and this frail hope were knocked down by the "cleansing" water. In another reversal God—seemingly absent through the trail of bodies and tears—appeared to return in a happy miracle: the reunion of Hupert and the Dachau rabbi, who proceeded to bless a new generation—the embodiment of survival as a living legacy. The Holocaust, on this celebratory occasion, seemed well in the past.

Hupert's narrative, especially in the interplay between possession by and relief from the past, is an ideal starting point for this chapter. The chapter initially departs from the documentary reconstruction of the students' time in Germany to reflect on the place of the Holocaust in the alumni's lives over a longer arc. It then moves between their immediate postwar experiences and relevant aspects of their existence since leaving Germany. The first theme, which sets up the others, is the condition of survival itself as it has been articulated in relation to the Holocaust. I elaborate a model of survival as a combination of restoration and ruin and argue its salience for the student survivors. I further argue that survival is powerfully conditioned by context, requiring that broadly psychological dynamics be understood in relation to historical circumstance.

The second theme concerns the relationship that survivors and other Jewish DPs had to their pasts in the period just after the war. My central finding is that the students appeared to deviate from other survivors in occupied Germany in that they were conspicuously silent—certainly among themselves—about their Holocaust experiences. I try to account for that silence, urging an appreciation for the variety of approaches to the past employed by survivors, and of the relative benefits of various strategies, including silence. In concluding I address at length the students' attitudes toward and interactions with Germans after the war, tapping into a robust and richly varied dimension of scholarship on Jewish DPs. As was the case for other Jewish DPs, the students' dominant experience of distance was also often complicated by moments of engagement and even intimacy.

"This Is All a Cover-up"

For decades now, psychologists, historians, literary theorists, and others have made extensive study of the lives, psyches, and words of Holocaust survivors. Such research has yielded tremendous insight into the dynamics of survival through traumatic experiences. Lawrence Langer, in a work that revolutionized ways of "hearing" testimony and understanding the Holocaust through it, highlighted how certain experiences—in which death appeared essentially arbitrary, choice meaningless, and the world unremittingly cruel—are preserved as "anguished," "humiliated," or "unheroic" memory. These memories, such as Hupert's recollection of his friend's death, disrupt the efforts of survivors to provide rational, moral, or existential coherence to the Holocaust and their own survival. For Langer the Holocaust remains an "erratic universe void of meaning, spiritually adrift, remote from empathetic understanding, [and] bereft of value."[2] "Common memory," which seeks to "mediate atrocity" and reassure both the teller and the listener, crashes against this dismal core. Survivors are thought to suffer an infinite dissonance of self and narrative, manifest in breakdown, paralysis, guilt, and despair.[3] The Holocaust, in Langer's "listening," is a wound that cannot be healed, a searing mark on the body and in the psyche that cannot be effectively washed away, covered over, or even "worked through," whether three days or thirty years after liberation.

Henry Greenspan, a psychologist and a playwright, elaborated Elie Wiesel's framing of the special affliction of the survivor as at once "to be *and* not to be."[4] Greenspan casts survival as "not a living beyond, but an ongoing life and an ongoing death, a living after and a dying after, in some kind of permanent irresolution."[5] The effect, near-universal among survivors, is a doubling of the self, paradigmatically expressed in a survivor's reflections: "It is hard enough to live in one world; we are destined to live forever in two. . . . I talk to you and I am not only here."[6] Another spoke of living on "two levels . . . the so-called normal, and the not."[7] At root Greenspan sees in survivors the combination of restoration and ruin, normalcy and catastrophe in an insoluble dialectic. "Despite all the efforts to make psychological sense of survivors' experience," he insists, "[e]xisting concepts simply do not well enough explain how the obvious strengths, creativity, and engagement so many survivors demonstrate *can* coexist with a severity of injury that is also indisputable."[8] The analytic challenge is to appreciate both extremes by neither dwelling on the persistence of the injury such that "normalcy" fades from view (Langer's danger) nor marveling at survivors' success such that their overcoming of the past appears implausibly complete (the hazard of ubiquitous tributes to survivors' resilience).

Greenspan's observations speak to the lives of the students, which very much have an "on the one hand, on the other hand" quality. Both while in Germany and thereafter, they are conspicuous not only for their strength and engagement but also for their resolve—even within a survivor population remarkable for its accomplishments. Their student existence was at once their therapy and the foundation for futures defined by professional achievement and the positive adaptation to full, autonomous adulthood. At times they described their lives in Germany as virtually indistinguishable in habit and sensibility from those of any university students, at any time, and in any place. It is easiest, then, to see in the students the triumph of the imperative "to be," the ascension of the normal and the quotidian satisfactions of "the new life."

Yet the alumni also suffer the enduring shock of irredeemable loss, no matter whether they readily acknowledge or try to minimize its power. Robert Nenner, whose story includes his taking food from Buchenwald "patients," spoke to common dimensions of the survivor experience, such as feelings of shame, which others have addressed only with great hesitation, if at all. Neither did he hesitate to stress the damage. About a trip to Auschwitz he took at his American wife's urging in the 1990s, he said, "I don't want to remember. When you see those things, you know they're part of you. And then the guilt comes back. Horrible guilt. Not good. I'll never go back. I'll never go back. If I could erase that from my past, I would love to. Because I'm scarred. To this day. I mean, if anybody tells you that he's okay, he's full of crap, don't believe him. Nobody can come back well from this experience, unscratched. It's impossible."[9] By his own admission some of the searing anger he felt toward the Germans he later took out on his medical residents in the United States, whom he trained with merciless rigor. Even now, he confessed, he has difficulty forming attachments, which he learned can be shattered in an instant.

Felix Korn's first impulse when I interviewed him was to assert his ability to will the past away. Sent in 1942 to the Lodz ghetto, Korn declined to talk about his experiences from then until the end of the war. He did share however, with palpable pride, accounts of his brother—a technological wizard who saved himself first by fixing radios for his Gestapo captors and then by working for Nazi broadcast operations in Lodz. The brother was held in such high regard by the Germans that a car was sent to the ghetto to pull his parents out just before a liquidation. Korn's melancholy immediately returned when he reported that his brother was killed, allegedly for transmitting messages to the resistance, and that his parents later perished, most probably in Treblinka.

When asked about coping with loss, Korn first stressed the pragmatism of self-preservation: "I know your question. . . . How could you live? [You] just shut yourself up—this is my past, it doesn't exist, if I want to live I have to look ahead. . . . [The Holocaust] was a gradual degrading . . . and you become, not immune but you become . . . resistant to it. You gradually get into this state of mind. To me this whole thing ended, a new life started. A lot of people committed suicide, of course. Whoever couldn't take it. But the ones who made it . . . I think they're perfectly normal people. After all these years, they try to ascribe all kinds of things to having survived all that trauma. But I basically don't believe that."[10] Coping requires no special trick save mentally erasing the past, and is worthy of no great psychologizing. But as Korn continues, the sense of a seamless recovery unravels: "Of course you never forget it. You live with your dreams . . . the nights are probably the worst, where you cannot, you never, you never stop dreaming about those days. But during the day, it's normal." Normalcy, rendered more fragile by shattered nights, still has the upper hand, only to give way to Korn's chilling invocation of the doubled self, which divides him even by day: "How do I manage now? . . . You sitting here, you talking, you seeing me, *but this is all a cover-up.*"

More directly than Korn, Mark Hupert conceded the power of the past to disrupt one's life. I asked: "You survived . . . and your father did too, but then you also lost so much. How did you psychologically try to come to terms with what you had lost, your mother, your sister?" He answered in broken, repetitive speech, with shifts in voice, tense, and setting:

> We never come completely to terms with it. No. I don't dream much, but whenever I dream, I dream about the war. Always. Always being chased, death, and I scream. . . . Wherever you go you remember. [My wife and I recently] went to a concert . . . there was a flying piano and all of a sudden from nowhere [I saw] my sister. In the intermission . . . we went home. . . . She was playing piano, Jadja [an accomplished pianist]. . . . You go on and you think you enjoy. I have my sons and my granddaughter and my friends and we laugh and we joke and some got used to it but you didn't get over it. That's something nobody gets over. Nobody told us that we should, must be crazy. They didn't know about trauma, [like] Vietnam trauma . . . no, you don't get over it. The only time I, I dream, my dream was really a nice dream, when we were at the first [international survivors] reunion in Jerusalem [in 1981]. . . . And there in my dream I was liberated. . . . Never again and never before.[11]

In his dreams, only once did the Holocaust end; in waking life, it breaks through in near-hallucinations that evoke loss, and as a subterfuge that makes normal pleasures seem an illusion.

For Isaac Minzberg, the scar was real: the infamous Auschwitz tattoo on his arm represented possession by the past. Years after liberation a colleague of his at Chicago's Mount Sinai Hospital asked, "You want to have that number?" With the explanation that "it's a nuisance . . . because I have to tell, I was in a concentration camp," Minzberg had the number surgically removed. (Some children, he added, assumed that if he had been in "prison," he must have done something wrong.) The procedure nonetheless left the scar of a scar.[12]

Many of the students, as direct survivors, embody the coexistence of the normal and the not normal through the arcs of their lives, and it is precisely my ambition to try to understand this duality better. Central to my effort is the conviction that the intertwining of restoration and ruin, of the "normal" everyday and life at its most aberrant, is best seen not as a static condition that defines survivors as such. Rather the terms of this coexistence are forged by circumstance and will, by distinct individuals and groups, and in response to different pressures. As something produced in time and space, survival changes in its balance, texture, and effects. We need to understand better, in sum, not simply the psychology of survivors, but also the contexts in which they were embedded, how they functioned within those contexts, and what means they used for dealing with the past.

> "There are as many ways of surviving survival as there have been to survive."
>
> Philip K., *Holocaust Testimonies*

Surviving survival, for the postwar students, meant surviving the past. After the war they did this substantially as individuals, insofar as their personal determination to excel provided both salutary distraction from difficult memories and a new sense of purpose. So too was dealing with the past in part a deeply internal and lonely challenge. Yet their commitment to study was also a collective achievement, whether through the advocacy of their student unions or by together facing a shared academic challenge. The more anguishing challenge of survival—to at least tame the hurts of the past in order to seize the future—was also something they faced as a group, insofar as they developed a common, if surprising, strategy for dealing with the past *together*. This strategy was a condition of possibility, perhaps *the* condition of possibility, for their achievements in Germany.

Among the most important questions I posed to the student survivors was whether they talked about the Holocaust among themselves and others in occupied Germany. Absent any specific expectations, I nonetheless assumed they engaged in some group effort to recount, memorialize, and work through "the war years." (The alumni rarely used the terms "Holocaust" or "Shoah" to frame their own stories; more commonly they spoke of "the war" to encompass events we now mark as "the Holocaust.")

That assumption had historic support, further validated by recent research. As Myers Feinstein has documented, mourning, memorializing, and (re)burying the dead in both sacred and secular rituals were among the first collective acts of Jewish DPs and a sustained part of DP life.[13] Jewish survivors also formed "mourning academies." Both advertised and reported on in the DP press, these were typically made up of former residents of particular towns or ghettos who gathered to share memories of life under the Nazis. *Yizkor*, a special Jewish remembrance, was incorporated into religious holidays, while annual *Yahrzeit* ceremonies commemorated the death dates of those murdered. Playwrights, for purposes of catharsis and education, staged theatrical productions—for Jewish and non-Jewish audiences—that directly addressed the Holocaust. And tributes to partisans, which referenced Jewish victimization but also resistance, were ubiquitous in DP life. In sum, Jewish DPs developed rich commemorative practices. Through them, Myers Feinstein concludes, "survivors could speak about the past, recount experiences, and share memories"; Jews "formed a collective memory of the Shoah and found ways both to narrate their experiences and to incorporate them into their personal and communal histories."[14]

In a more documentary vein, as early as November 1945, the Central Committee of Liberated Jews in Bavaria set up a Historical Commission to assemble materials on the Holocaust, for which they used the Yiddish term *churbn* (destruction; from the Hebrew *churban*, typically referring to the destruction of the Second Temple). These included "testimonies, pictures, 'documents of historical value for current and future Jewish historians,' ghetto and concentration camp songs and lore, evidence [of] Nazi crimes, and names of murderers."[15] Questionnaires, printed in German and Yiddish and distributed in the DP camps, inquired into prewar life and details about the Nazi terror, such as the erection of ghettos, specific methods of humiliation, like wearing the yellow star, and the killing operations. Headquartered in Munich, the commission developed more than fifty departments throughout the American Zone.[16] In its first year of operation more than two thousand questionnaires were filled out. From August 1946 to September 1948 the commission published a newspaper, *Fun Letzn Churbn* (From the Last Destruction), which printed its findings.[17]

Jewish DPs, moreover, seemed spontaneously to provide stories of the past to each other and to aid workers. After spending a year in occupied Germany as the Joint's educational director, Koppel Pinson concluded that the Jewish DP is "preoccupied almost to the point of morbidity with his past . . . [and] always ready to recount in minutest detail the events of his past or the past of his relatives. In their entertainments and in the education of their youth there is the constant preoccupation with their experiences under the Nazis—gruesome recapitulation of concentration camp incidents combined with vows of undying loyalty to these memories."[18] He also chastised adults for allegedly pressuring children, "whose rehabilitation to normal childhood should emphasize obliteration of these memories, . . . to share in such demonstrations."[19]

According to a late-1945 JDC education report covering much of the American Zone, "It was confirm[ed] by personal interview that [Jewish DPs] live in the past referring constantly to their days in the concentration camps and to their treatment at the hands of brutal Nazi guards."[20] A contemporary scholar of the Historical Commission concluded that "the past was omnipresent in the lives of survivors . . . [who] in general were eager to render their pasts the subject of public discourse."[21] Finally, in an oft-cited reflection, Primo Levi spoke of survivors' near-obsessive need after the war to speak about their experiences—a need reinforced by others' indifference to their stories. Many survivors have described this indifference and the silence it imposed as a second exile that enhanced their sense of alienation from themselves and the world.[22]

The students, as a cohesive, closely bonded group of survivors, seem to have been spared this added exile (at least while together in Germany). Especially in light of the impulse to remember and the commemorative practices cited above, they might be expected to have taken advantage of their special circumstance to share stories about difficult times. The universal recollection of the students was therefore shocking: among themselves, they *never* talked about the Holocaust in any detail, no matter how intimate they had become as friends or as a substitute "family." From both the ardor and nuance of their responses, the complex origins, dynamics, and effects of this group silence come into view.

In our interview Roman Ohrenstein described the silence with panicked insistence: "No. No. No, we didn't talk [about] what we went through. Nothing, not a word." Asked how this worked—"Did you ever agree to not talk about it or was it just so obvious that you shouldn't?"—he was equally certain: "No, no, we didn't agree. We, no, it's just, we didn't."[23] Mark Hupert reports that the students generally learned only very basic things about each other's backgrounds, such as what town they were from, and only the barest outlines of their war experiences. For years he had weekly dinners with Arnold Kerr, yet he never knew in which camps Kerr had been interned.[24] Marion Glaser confirmed, "We didn't talk among ourselves about [the war years], we put a red line . . . it's a very odd affair."[25] She knew only that one of her dear friends had been in Russia, another somewhere in Germany, but "that's it." "It's not about sharing," Hupert explained, "because we would share everything with each other." Sharing about the war, however, was another matter. The students refrained even from collective acknowledgments of loss, which might had have a lesser emotional charge. As the former editor-in-chief of the student newspaper, Ohrenstein recalls one published tribute to the Holocaust's victims—the *kaddish* referenced earlier—and, beyond that, nothing.

These recollections suggest that within the group the ban on talking about the past had the status of a taboo—one spontaneously created, tacitly agreed upon, and collectively enforced. What gave this taboo, which mandated the absence of dialogue or a collective working-through, such automatic appeal

and force? Some students described the silence in pragmatic terms, suggesting the operation of "productive forgetting."[26] Fred Reiter said tersely, "We
had no talk [of the past]. The show has to go on."[27] Having witnessed terrible violence in the Krakow ghetto, Cessia Hupert explained, "Because they
were painful memories. Because they were unproductive."[28] After graduating
from medical school in Munich, she trained in the United States first as an
anesthesiologist, a professional dedicated to literally blocking out pain. Dov
Steinfeld also testified to the lack of dialogue about the past among the students. When asked if he grieved privately, he conceded that he did so with
his father just after the war, in consideration of the grim fates of his mother
and sister. Visibly uncomfortable when the topic came up, he switched in
our interview from English (a distant language of his) to Hebrew (he had
settled in Israel) to explain, "You cry and cry and cry and then you can't do
it anymore."[29]

Other alumni described the silence in a more comprehensive way. "We
wanted to erase [the past] from our memory," Ohrenstein recalled. "Because
otherwise we couldn't live. How are you going to live? . . . [U]nder these
conditions, amongst the Germans. So we didn't, we didn't talk about it. . . . I
[now] have [nightmares] . . . but at that time, I don't recall having night-
mares. It, it somehow, there was a kind of defensive mechanism within us
to put it out of our minds. It wasn't conscious, but subconsciously probably
we felt that . . . we're not going to be able to live if we're going to continue
to delve into the past."[30] Mark Hupert, puzzled by the task of accounting
for his postwar silence, said, "You really have to ask a psychologist. I don't
know. . . . It was impossible to talk about. It was just impossible. This was
someplace . . . buried." The temporal distance, he confessed, has made it
only a little easier to express basic memories, even to his family. Toward the
end of our interview, he remarked, "[My wife] Cessia"—herself a survivor—
"doesn't know half of that what you [now] know."[31]

In psychological language, Hupert and Ohrenstein plainly describe the
outright repression of the past, indicating a process more elemental than
"productive forgetting." The repression was both willed—the students
wanted the past erased—and driven by hidden psychic forces; it was a repression, in Ohrenstein's case, so powerful that at first it did not allow for even
dreams, the presumably irrepressible stuff of the unconscious and a common
locus for traumatized memories. In his dramatic telling, the repression permitted not merely a higher level of functioning but a chance for *life itself.*

The repression of the past within the group seemed to mirror the repression within the individual, and vice versa. Burying or bracketing traumatiz-
ing experiences and memories was something the student survivors had to

do, often when radically alone, during the war. After the war they collectively reinforced an imperative that they felt personally. The silence extended even to those who had been in the Soviet Union and may therefore not have had any direct traumatic experiences. Guti Kanner survived with her entire family in Kazakhstan. When explaining what made life in postwar Germany so hard for the students, she first stressed the weight of the past, volunteering that "nobody spoke about what they had, how they were during the Shoah. Nobody. . . . I cannot understand it." Though she was intensely curious about her friends' experiences—and began reading voraciously about the Shoah as soon as memoirs, histories, and other literature began to appear—"I never asked. I never pushed them to tell me."[32] Minutes later in our interview, she reversed herself, stating, "I think I understand [her colleagues' silence]," attributing it to the pain they felt and how difficult it must have been to articulate. To amplify her conjecture, she recounted how, in 1987, as a nurse in Israel, she tended to Abba Kovner—the famous resistance fighter, Bricha founder, and poet—when he was on his deathbed in the Ein Hahoresh kibbutz. Kovner related to her disturbing wartime episodes that, he claimed, he had never told anyone.

The students, then, rather than seeing in each other a sympathetic audience for speaking about the past, appeared to use one another to avoid talking or even privately thinking about it. In doing so they experienced the relief of not feeling compelled to share, and thus burden themselves or others with, their pain. Ohrenstein elaborated, "Since we are all in the same boat, we had nothing to add to each other. What am I going to talk about? I'm going to tell them what I went through, what my family went through? He has his own story."[33] With each other, as with the many marriages among survivors, they enjoyed the company of those who understood *without having to be told*.[34] Merely being together, committed to shared goals, appeared a way to share the past, even if it remained in shadows and muted tones. In contemporary language, the silence, the repression, was the therapy.

An additional comment of Mark Hupert's, coupled with Ohrenstein's image of the student as "all in the same boat," discloses a last dimension to the silence. "There was," Hupert recalls, "no, 'I had a worse time in camp than you had.' There was no competition. We just didn't talk about it."[35] Properly speaking the students were not in the same boat with respect to their wartime suffering; not all stories were equally bad, and some students who survived in Soviet exile never even faced the Germans. The silence about the past rendered these distinctions irrelevant. It thus warded off a potentially divisive hierarchy of suffering that might skew the distribution of sympathy or induce feelings of jealousy (such as toward those with living parents) and guilt (potentially felt toward those without parents). The solidarity of the students was rooted in the presumption—in fact a tenuous one, amounting to an enabling fiction—of an essential congruence of experience. Yet at another level this presumption reflected the recognition among a group of victims that the suffering they each experienced was absolute, not relative, entitling them to equal measures of compassion. However counter-intuitive, group silence—and not just communal acts of remembrance—could be a way of crafting a shared identity and a collective, future-directed narrative.

"My Pain, My Fears and My Distress"

It would be inappropriate to draw any sweeping conclusion from a small group of survivors regarding the question of the extent to which DP survivors shared about the Holocaust just after the war. Rather, the students provide occasion to address the question with added nuance and to suggest possibilities not taken into account by scholarship that stresses the alleged ubiquity of talk of the past. At a minimum the students contest Levi's insistence on survivors' universal inner need to share about the past. To the contrary, they confessed an equally desperate need *not* to talk about it, with some indicating that certain memories could not even be accessed or brought into language. So too Pinson's observation of the survivors' impulse to recount—one now quoted in so much research on DPs—needs qualification. Pinson's comment was based largely on his visits to DP camps. It may be that for those living outside the camps (or in bounded environments like the *hakhsharot*), where the presence of Germans and the challenge of functioning were greater, the cost of sharing could be prohibitively higher. And it is possible that aid workers, so taken aback or even put off by talk of the past, especially among child survivors, exaggerated its extent among DPs as a whole. (Adults, moreover, may have been more easily able to screen off traumatic memories.)

It is also possible that the students engaged the past in contexts outside their group bond, such that their silence was only partial. Unfortunately, I interviewed the group before recent research had made me aware of the mourning academies, *Yizkor* ceremonies, and other commemorative practices. I did not therefore inquire about the students' knowledge of or possible participation in these observances. However, at no point in my research did alumni mention such practices or indicate involvement, for instance, with the Historical Commission. The one exception was Leon Weliczker Wells, who had been a student in Munich; Wells was the author of the popular Holocaust memoir *The Janowska Road*, and a witness at the 1961–62 Eichmann trial, as well as others. As he reported in his survey response, he had worked with the Historical Commission.[36] Otherwise, the alumni stressed the group's silence.

Also germane are differences in the kinds of memories and their contexts. Myers Feinstein focuses on collective, often ritualized remembrances and their role in establishing shared narratives. But there are likely limits to the value of such acts for confronting one's individual trauma and loss. (By very approximate analogy, a funeral may be an initially cathartic and constructive way to honor the dead and reconcile oneself to their absence; yet it hardly ends internal processes of grieving.) Consequently, even if the students and other survivors participated in such public rituals, they still faced the challenge of dealing privately with their wartime experiences.

Historian Laura Jockusch speaks to differences in modes of sharing while also recording resistance to memory. She recounts the impressive work of the Historical Commission. Yet she reports that only a small minority of DPs offered materials to the organization. The "moral imperative to bear witness, document, and testify" driving the commission's appeal to survivors ran up against, as its "greatest obstacle," the "psychological burden of documenting the past."[37] Jockusch contrasts what she deems the comparative ease of private sharing and public performance about the past with the more challenging—and potentially more confrontational—work of forensic, scholarly documentation. But it may be, as the students' experience suggests, that even private sharing could meet a psychic barrier. The impulse to remember, in sum, existed in tension with productive forgetting and what I have described, more forcefully, as an enabling repression.

Finally, certain forms of remembrance might come at the expense of others, again pointing to the difficulty for some of sustained, *personal* engagement with the past. This dynamic is suggested by Boaz Cohen's essay about the Historical Commission's efforts to document the experiences of child survivors.[38] Leading the commission's effort was Israel Kaplan, an accomplished intellectual of the prewar period who chronicled the history of the Kovno ghetto while still interned there; he became the academic secretary of the commission's journal. Collecting the testimony of children with great dedication, he appeared conspicuously unable to engage the memories of his own son. His son had been hidden with a Lithuanian woman just before Kaplan's wife was killed; Kaplan had already been transferred to a work camp and did not see his son again until 1946. With evident bitterness, the son recalled that at their reunion his father "talked and talked, but he never asked me: 'What happened to you son[?]' . . . He was already working in the Historical Commission. . . . [H]e didn't need me to tell him about the Ghetto. But as to . . . my experience, my pain, my fears and my distress, my worries and my apprehensions—these he never knew because he didn't ask."[39] That estrangement was never bridged. One may speculate that the father's concern with the suffering of other children in part compensated for his lack of attention to that of his own son, which might have summoned in him terrible feelings of guilt.

My conclusions are threefold: that the students, by repressing so strongly their memories of the recent past, were outliers with respect to other Jewish survivors in postwar Germany; that survivors' public acts of remembrance did not preclude the need for private strategies—including silence, as one option—for dealing with the past on a more individuated basis; and that memory varied greatly in form and function, mitigating any uniform assessment of what survivors gained through confronting the past.

"It's Much Better to Live in the Present"

If determining the extent to which DPs engaged the past is difficult, more daunting still is discerning the psychological impact of that engagement. Aid workers in Germany held the bias that that too much sharing about the past was detrimental. Whether based in seeming common sense or the clinical assumptions of the time, the view was that such sharing would impede true recovery and keep survivors connected to a past from which they needed distance. This is analogous to Pinson's admonition regarding survivors' "constant preoccupation with their experiences" and "undying loyalty to the[ir] memories."[40] In a study of émigré survivors just after the war, Beth B. Cohen reports that social workers and doctors in the United States likewise felt it best for survivors to suppress the past.[41]

By now there is a vast clinical and theoretical literature that cautions against the blanket repression of traumatic memories and which advocates instead that they be directly confronted so as to be "worked through." In this light Pinson's view appears naïve and even wrongheaded. Recent DP scholarship has argued for the value of the commemorative practices of postwar Jews. Speaking mostly in a historical-discursive register, Myers Feinstein credits these observances with helping Jews to develop a shared narrative, a stronger collective identity, and a way to link past, present, and future. At times, however, she also addresses issues of individual psychology directly, as if to rebut the prevailing views of aid workers some sixty-five years ago.

This is most explicit in her treatment of an episode in the children's section of the Kloster Indersdorf DP camp, where a group of children, responding to a roll call by UNRRA staff, protested by acting out concentration camp scenes. Donning their camp uniforms, the children had mock stormtroopers beat or "shoot" those who did not give their names quickly enough. Myers Feinstein credits the children with performing "a scene from the past in order to have themselves understood better by the staff. . . . [They] instinctively realized what recent scientific studies have confirmed": that "converting intense emotions into narratives through writing or talking about traumatic experiences can result in improved health and a reduction in the effects of post-traumatic stress."[42]

Myers Feinstein is careful to qualify her claims, noting that the *unprocessed* repetition of traumatic scenes can be debilitating, and that sharing about the past may facilitate, but does not guarantee, a stronger recovery. Even so her assessment illustrates the difficulties of retroactive psychologizing. Without knowing, for instance, more about the particulars of certain practices, the participants' individual histories, the circumstances of their postwar lives, and their psychic states over time, definitive judgments as to what was more and less therapeutic for survivors remain elusive. Disagreement, moreover, existed among DP survivors themselves. As Myers Feinstein also records, some felt that the past could be depicted too graphically. Such was the objection of a Jewish theater veteran to a play developed by an ensemble in Foehrenwald: "[O]ne saw on the stage . . . a crematorium, how a Jewish child, torn from its mother, was thrown into the oven. . . . Our bloody wounds are still too fresh to allow them, in such brutal forms no less, to be exposed on the stage."[43]

Similarly, it would be inappropriate to offer sweeping clinical judgment of the functions and effects of the internal silence the student group maintained. My mandate is historical understanding, not diagnosis or prescription. The alumni, reflecting on their states of mind and dynamics within the group, commonly offered the qualification (however phrased), "I am not a psychologist." This was not true without exception. Marion Glaser earned a medical degree in Munich and then immigrated to Israel, where she established a pediatric practice and later became a psychiatrist. She was therefore in a position to offer a professional perspective on her survivor cohort and both the benefits and costs of varying relationships to the past.

Glaser's torment had been severe, as had her apparent need to cordon off its memory. In June 1941, she and her parents were placed in the Kovno ghetto.[44] Already interested in medicine, she was set to work in a hospital; before she could, the Nazis set the facility on fire, burning alive the patients and physicians. She later survived the "Great Action" of October 29, 1941. As SS Master Sergeant Helmut Rauca made the selections with a gesture she did not at the time understand, he casually threw a stick to his German shepherd. That night, her sleep was broken by screams from the adjacent "small ghetto," from which "grandmothers, grandfathers, little women with little children in their arms"—nine thousand people in all—were marched away and shot.[45]

Glaser's daring escape from the ghetto hardly ended her ordeal. For a time she boarded in Kovno, posing as a Lithuanian Christian, with a Sorbonne-educated Persian Jewish woman named Lena Houmini.[46] Married to a Persian Muslim living in France, and herself posing as a French Christian, Homiuni also sheltered her brother, his children, and two children of her own. (Homiuni was later captured, and her family killed.) Thereafter, the originally shy and bookish Glaser continued to draw on her recently discovered mastery of deception to stay just ahead of her persecutors. Though the death rate of Jews in Lithuania was the highest among German-occupied territories, she and her parents survived.

Like her story, Glaser's description of the strength and persistence of the "red line" separating the present from reflection on the past was striking. After the war even she and her parents did not talk with one another about their experiences. The intervening years scarcely increased her knowledge of what her colleagues in Munich—some of them her very best adult friends—had been through. Not until 2004, when helping to set up interviews with university alumni for my research in her home city of Haifa, did she learn basic facts about their stories. She began tentatively sharing information about the Holocaust with her daughter only in the 1990s, and she never told anyone her comprehensive story until an Israeli service organization for survivors videotaped her testimony in 2001. The day was September 11, and her account of horrible events was surreally interrupted by reports of a new catastrophe half a world away.

Among my great curiosities was what became of her wartime self—that person, in my phrasing, who showed the "savvy of a spy or a guerrilla fighter." Confessing that she "astonished" herself—especially in her ability to lie her way past danger—she insisted, "I returned being what I was before. I didn't need [that person]." Her goal all along had been to study medicine, and that reserved, focused young woman returned when her studies resumed. So too did her sense of ethics and faith in its rewards: "I knew a promise is a promise. I knew you don't lie to anybody. . . . I knew you have to be very diligent in order to be, to go farther." Desperate to be "finished with that crazy world," she appeared to live as though the wartime past, to recall Korn's words, "doesn't exist."

When asked about what she and her colleagues did with their pain, she layered clinical judgment on her personal experience: "As a psychiatrist I can tell you, a normal mourning time, if you are losing a partner or somebody

very near to you, is let's say half a year or the year. . . . People going on with
an endless mourning, they are disturbed. That is, that is pathological. And
something of that happened to all of us. To all the young people who stayed
alive. The father of my friend . . . [who] got killed later on, he stayed alive.
He was an old man, he was broken, he couldn't find, he couldn't form a new
life." What she describes in the students is an impeded, and hence prolonged,
mourning, but with ambiguous effects. The students, it appears, barely
grieved at all after the war in any deliberate, sustained way. Possibly as a result, Glaser confessed that a certain "craziness" has never left her—a condition
that a more thorough postwar grieving may have at least diminished. (Clinical research, Myers Feinstein notes, shows that the "repression of traumatic
memories in the immediate aftermath of the experience leads to increased
problems of post-traumatic stress syndrome, such as intrusive memories.")[47]
The craziness comes out, she allowed, in the smothering anxiety she feels
when her adult daughter goes on everyday excursions in Israel or the great
worry she has for her country's safety. "The past," she conceded, "throws a
shadow over my future."[48] By the same token such enduring "pathologies"
must be measured against the evident benefits that she and the student survivors reaped by not allowing the pain to rush in and crush them (as it did her
friend's father)—by *not* taking the risk of grieving and instead devoting their
youthful energy to creating new lives. She dismissed, moreover, the idea that
by "talking and talking," at whatever stage in the life cycle, one can expel the
pain of this past or really step outside its shadow. Concluding that "it's much
better to live in the present," she wholly concurred in the interview with my
deepening sense that repression—with all the determinations of circumstance
and necessary qualifications—"has a very good side to it."

The alumni also conceded that the repression of the past proved over
time neither sustainable nor desirable. Cessia Hupert echoes others in reporting that the memories were initially "too painful" and "had to be buried."[49] The silence extended deep into her life in the United States with her
husband, Mark Hupert. "For many years we didn't tell our children what we
went through. . . . I cannot tell you . . . how old my boys were before they
learned that their father was in Dachau [and] on the death march." Only at
the meeting of survivors in Jerusalem in 1981 did she begin to unearth the
memories and, with others, "realize that it was important that we survived."

A shift in the focus of her medical practice crystallizes this transformation
in her relationship to the past. Trained as an anesthesiologist, she gradually
lost interest in the field and became drawn to the emerging specialty of pain
management. In Jerusalem she told a psychiatrist friend of hers, himself a
survivor and student in postwar Munich, about the change. Instantly seizing

on the metaphor, he replied, "Yeah! You know what that means? . . . You finally decided to face your pain."[50]

Among the Germans

Surviving survival for the students meant also enduring the burden of place. Their challenge was to live and thrive in occupied Germany and at German institutions. Try as they did to repress internally memories of wartime, everywhere around them were its evocations. The reminders, in part, were physical. Much of Germany had been decimated by Allied assault. In Munich nearly half of all buildings were totally or substantially destroyed, and nearly all structures suffered damage.[51] Physical ruin was an ambiguous image for Jews. The destruction served as a welcome reminder of German defeat but also as an emblem of past Nazi power. The denazification of public space was enforced only inconsistently. Occupation law mandated the demolition of structures symbolic of the Nazi Reich and the removal of Nazi insignia. Yet buildings of "essential public utility or great architectural value" were exempt, and much of the urban architecture of Nazism therefore was preserved.[52] In Munich swastikas remained in ironwork and other decorative details; and though they might be chiseled out of the stone *Hoheitszeichen*, the unmistakable Nazi eagles were often left intact.

But above all the students had to contend with the presence of the Germans themselves—their great tormentors and for many the perpetrators of their families' deaths. The details of what it was like for them to live and work among the Germans are especially engaging and historically important parts of their stories. Most centrally, the stories illuminate how two epically polarized groups—Jews and Germans, victims and victimizers—coexisted, collided, and interacted at a time when the wounds of persecution, war, and defeat were still so fresh. The students, moreover, were in a position to provide special perspective on this postwar moment by virtue of the extent and nature of their dealings with Germans. Those dealings at once enrich and qualify existing understandings of the imbrications of the lives of Jewish DPs and Germans.

To a great degree Jewish DPs and Germans existed worlds apart. Run by the Allies, the DP camps housing most Jews were both secluded and self-secluding environments. In them Jews mostly enjoyed solidarity with each other and distance from the Germans, with whom they had little desire to interact. This picture of separation has been reinforced by DPs, who in common recollections insist, as if asserting a point of pride, on the utter absence of contact with Germans. The Germans, in the standard trope, remained the enemy, and occupied Germany was merely a weigh station on the road to a better future. Even when outside the camps, Jews might cluster within specific enclaves and circulate within an emerging Jewish world.

Yet the boundaries were hardly so absolute. As much recent research stresses, numerous contexts existed for interactions between Jews and Germans. Germans frequently came into the DP camps, serving as caregivers or maids for Jewish families with newborns and helping with administrative work. Hospitals had both German and Jewish patients and even mixed staffs. Sexual relations between Jews and Germans, if often discreet, were not unheard of. The DPs, moreover, often left the camp confines for cultural excursions, to buy goods, to visit friends, or to partake in cultural offerings. And nearly a quarter of Jewish DPs lived outside the DP camps, interacting with Germans in places of residence, commerce, and work. Munich alone had as many as 7,000 "free-livers."[53] Documenting these close encounters, Atina Grossmann concludes that for Jewish DPs the Germans—"the so-called enemies"—were "part of everyday life."[54]

Although the students saw their stay in Germany as temporary, their degrees took many years to complete, keeping them there past the migration of most DPs in 1948–49. The classroom entailed unavoidable interactions with German professors and peers, and the Munich Union employed German staff and contractors. Many students boarded with German families. They shopped in German shops, rode mass transit, went to cafes, concerts, and the theater, and vacationed throughout the country. While by no means unique among DPs in this exposure to Germany, the students were nonetheless among a minority of Jews who stayed in the country for extended periods and participated thoroughly in mainstream German institutions and urban life. Further, as a pre-professional cohort with a shared path, an organization of their own, and an enduring bond, there is both a consistency to their experiences and a sense of collective identity that give definition to their recollections of life among the Germans. And through interviews especially, their experiences are accessible in ways that those of other "free-livers"—existing outside a bounded narrative while in Germany, scattered in the time since, and many long deceased—are not.

What were the patterns of contact—or avoidance—between the Jewish students and the Germans? Did the young Jews encounter or witness anti-Semitism? Conversely, did Germans convey any sense of contrition, empathy, or simple interest in their experience? Did any rapprochement occur between the two groups?

These questions go to the heart of postwar realities, with their special dynamics and modes of interaction. From the students' answers one might draw inferences as well with respect to enduring historical debates. The first concerns the nature and extent of anti-Semitism before, during, and after the war.[55] If, as some insist, anti-Semitism was radical and pervasive in Germany, it could not possibly disappear with the regime's defeat; if manifest in the postwar period, Jews in Germany might naturally be its focus, attuned to its subtler forms. [56] The second concerns the question of Germans' readiness or refusal after the war to acknowledge guilt—a topic endlessly engaged in studies of postwar Germany. When among Germans, Jews might discern both self-serving denial and moments of conscientious reckoning, and come to some firsthand judgment on their balance. The experiences of the students, however small a group, reveal how such issues played themselves out on the ground, just after the war, and in the fine texture of human interaction.

In addition to what the presence of Jews evoked in the Germans, my focus is on the perceptions and experiences of the students: how they regarded the Germans and coped with being among them; what cognitive frames and cultural associations they used to interpret German behavior; whether they thought it useful to engage Germans about the past; and what came of such encounters when they did take place. Answers to these questions came not only as the students shared their strongest recollections but also as they retrieved from the corners of their memories puzzling moments and sensations. These crystallized, but also sometimes upset, the dominant story they have created of their time in Germany.

"They Couldn't Fool Us, and We Couldn't Fool Them"

Whether liberated inside Germany or entering as refugees from German-occupied Eastern Europe or the Soviet Union, the students had no illusions as to what the Germans had done and were in no mind to be conciliatory. The decision to study there, they stress, was pragmatic, a way to accomplish something while in a stateless limbo. Even in occupied Germany, where the Americans were in charge, the students very much felt themselves behind enemy lines. Civility best served their goals, and beyond that they felt they owed the Germans nothing. Their bitterness must be the starting point for understanding their lives among the Germans.

Anger could swell with their first impressions of the cities in which they would spend their student years. Fred Reiter, as I came to know him, is a conspicuously gentle man, who takes pride in not being judgmental and bearing no grudges. It therefore pained him to recall: "Munich was very destroyed, and I am sorry to say that I was very happy to see it destroyed. It's not nice to feel that way, but don't forget the bitterness and the pain."[57] Marion Glaser felt a different regret upon first seeing the city: "It was much too little destroyed for my taste. I looked around and I saw still houses standing. I was very sorry."[58] Some students never shook their distaste for Germany, no matter what they accomplished on its soil. "I didn't like anything about it," Lucy Fink conceded. "I hated it, the German language, because it reminded me of [the SS men] . . . and to this day I still can't stand it."[59]

For Robert Nenner, even certain knowledge of the existence of truly good Germans did not diminish his contempt. While in Munich, he met a member of the storied White Rose resistance group, whose student rebels had, often at the cost of their lives, spoken out against the Nazi regime. And yet, Nenner recalls, "It really didn't make any difference to me because I was so embittered. . . . That was my attitude, at that point, 'So what.' . . . We still believed that the best German is a dead German."[60] Elaborating, the former Buchenwald inmate, for years shuttled with bureaucratic precision among the dead and dying, said, "They were so meticulous, what they did." He then recounted a postwar scene of his continued rage. In Munich he boarded in a damaged rooftop room exposed to the frigid night. Late one evening, a brigade of Germans came to remove nearby bricks for some reconstruction effort. As they methodically worked, rudely indifferent to his presence, Nenner cursed to himself, "My God, if you're so meticulous I should have been dead! And you didn't destroy me. *So I will live in spite of you.*" Nenner, like so many others, describes his survival and very presence on German soil after the war as expressions of defiance, of existential revenge.

Marion Glaser conveyed her anger by relating a story as wildly improbable as it is chilling. In late 1942 or early 1943, she left Kovno and went to Berlin to see her German (Christian) grandmother. Her hope was to obtain papers from German authorities indicating that she had no Jewish parentage. The ruse was to have a friend of her grandmother's claim that she was Marion's other grandmother and that her son, allegedly dead for some time, had had an affair with Marion's Christian mother.[61] The official, after stamping the papers, clasped Marion's grandmother's hand and said, "You did a good deed." Wise to the ploy, he took mercy on the family.

Marion's second task was to inquire into the circumstances of the Persian husband of Lena Houmini, thought to be living in Paris; Houmini, as we saw earlier, had sheltered Glaser. By that point Germany had "friendly" relations with almost no one, so dealings with places like Iran were handled from the embassy of neutral Switzerland. Confronted inside the embassy by a German official, Glaser claimed her name was Schmidt. "Curious," he replied, "everybody here is Schmidt, Schultz, or Müller." Outside the doors, she saw rows of plaintive Jews waiting to get in.

At the Iranian desk Glaser asked a Swiss official to make contact with Lena Houmini (still alive at the time) in Kovno, and urged, "But do it quickly." Her recounting of their conversation continued:

> "Why quickly? She's in danger? What's the danger?"
> "You know, Lithuanians are very homogenous people, and they
>   all look alike, and everybody looking a little bit different is in
>   danger of being thought of as being Jewish."
> "So what?" he says.
> "So what? . . . Don't you know? They are killing Jews."
> "Wait a moment," he says. He gets out, comes with another two or
>   three people. "Tell this once more."
> "Not long ago there was a big action, they took out ten thousand
>   people and killed them."
> "That can't be," he says. 'How can you kill ten thousand people?
>   It's impossible!"

She continued: "Tears came to my eyes [and] he started to believe I am saying the truth. I told them there are graves. 'The people have to lie down and a little bit shooting and the next, next, next,' and then, the same Swiss man said to me, 'If that is true, what you are telling, the Germans will pay for this very, very hard after the war.'" "That sentence," Glaser continued, "never left me during my whole life." It reverberated as she related, with wounded sarcasm, her impressions after the war: "When I came to Germany, I thought, 'Oh, they paid very much.'"

The comments of Glaser, Reiter, and Nenner reveal the survivors' desire that the Germans be made to pay some adequate price for what they had done. That desire was surely unsatisfied—regardless of the Nuremberg trials and lesser efforts to prosecute perpetrators; the removal under denazification of some party members from public roles in the new society; the occasional acts of retribution by Jewish DPs; and the material deprivations many Germans suffered, such as food rationing and a lack of proper housing, in the wake of their country's total surrender. Given the enormity of the crimes committed, there could be no righting of essential wrongs. The students therefore lived in a universe in which hope may have been partially restored but which dispensed little or no real justice. Each day among the Germans—who seemed to them eager to rebuild their world with few backward glances, scarcely any shame, and little genuine threat of retribution—affirmed this sense. Indeed, Jewish DPs and some aid workers expressed shock at how little life had changed for many Germans, especially outside major cities. Added to this was anger at the Germans' sense of entitlement to scarce recourses and their frequent complaints of the alleged unfairness *to them* of the occupation regime.[62] In one of the very few public statements of the students' impressions of life in Germany, a piece in their newspaper complained, "The alien milieu the Jewish student in Germany is forced to live in . . . emanates hatred and coldness—puzzling things to one who . . . [given] the terrible wrong done to him by these very people . . . has every right and reason to hate! He wonders, too, how it can be that there is neither awareness of complicity or co-responsibility, nor the least desire to make good in the average German."[63]

As these words suggest, the students appeared to pass a collective sentence on "the Germans," even if some had acted honorably toward them. Their inclination was to see "the Germans" as an enveloping, recently predatory, and still fundamentally hostile, if defanged, Other—not to make any effort to separate the guilty from the innocent or parse degrees of complicity. In this they echoed other survivors, "who often blamed all Germans for the atrocities committed against them."[64] Only rarely, such as when the Union extended special greetings to Munich chemistry professor Heinrich Wieland on the occasion of his seventieth birthday, did the students appear to make formal distinctions among Germans in the university setting. Wieland, a Nobel Prize winner, had extended aid and comfort to Jewish students during the Nazi ascent. In response to the students' well wishes, Wieland indicated his own vain hope that "in the near future the racial differences in the student community disappear so that a true community can be created, as before the Hitler era."[65]

Decades later, the alumni maintain—in one of their enduring, primary frames—a generalized ill-regard for Germans of their generation. Brian Bergman, who had lost his parents and lived alone for a time at the fringes of the Warsaw ghetto, is especially vocal in this dislike. When I asked him at an alumni dinner to sketch his Holocaust story, he answered, "The Germans had a nickname for me: shit. 'Hey shit,' 'little shit.' Need I say more?" At two alumni meetings Bergman upbraided the director of survivor affairs of the United States Holocaust Memorial Museum for referring to the Jews' persecutors in his presentations as "the Nazis" and not "the Germans." The director both times apologized, though scholars and others debate how broadly to indict the German populace. Bergman concluded his second reprimand by intoning, "There was no such thing as a good German!" (Some alumni supported his intervention, adding that Lithuanians, Poles, and others could be just as bad. The conversation ended when one alumna lamented that although the Germans and others did horrible things, they have tried to confront their pasts and change their attitudes; one cannot, she concluded, go on feeling so bitter forever.)

During the students' stay in Germany after the war, the main manifestation of their anger was a preference for sticking dearly close to one another and having as little to do with individual Germans as possible. This distance was their dominant experience, defining something of an "official memory" among the group which echoes the recollections of other DPs. The deepest reason for the separation was the identification they felt with one another as fellow Jews still left on the European continent. This bond reflected a sense of cultural, religious, and ethnic affinity, but also shared suffering. Lucy Fink, who married a member of the student group, spoke to both. Just twelve years old when the war broke out, she survived by posing for years as a Christian live-in maid in a Polish household. Her recollections bear both the horror and the sweetness of her young age: "I thought if I survive the war . . . there wouldn't be any Jews left, because it seemed everybody was gone. . . . I was brought up in Judaism, I went to Hebrew school from the age of seven to twelve, and I knew I was Jewish. . . . I thought if anybody survived who is Jewish, they'd all be my friends."[66]

As if in fulfillment of such a pledge, the Jewish students at the disparate universities quickly found and befriended one another and, again by silent agreement, kept distance from the Germans. "Nobody was fighting but nobody was socializing," Fink said of relations between the two groups. "It was cut and dry. We had absolutely nothing in common."[67] Simon Snopkowski stressed how the Union provided a welcome barrier: "As a student organization, we were completely separate from the German students—there were individual contacts here and there, but all in all they were very rare, on both sides."[68] Cessia Hupert explained: "I felt the Germans hurt us too much. We did not want to interact with them. Even though I went to a German university, it was only the professors that examined me that I interacted with. The German students, I would just ignore them."[69] "We did dislike them," Guti Kanner bluntly stated. For an entire year she sat next to a German classmate, with the two exchanging only perfunctory greetings.[70] "They didn't try and we didn't try" to share anything of consequence. Marion Glaser concluded with respect to this second red line: "We [Jews] lived together, we learned together, we had all the courses together. We had a student organization, we had our own feasts. . . . We had excursions together, we went to the mountains together. . . . We did not need the others. And we didn't want the others. And they didn't want us."[71]

Interactions outside the universities could be similarly proscribed. Walking home from Munich's opera, Rochelle Eisenberg noticed a sign outside a private dwelling offering the rent of a private chemistry lab. Its owner was a Nazi, revealed by the SS towels he displayed in the space. With much of the university lab space destroyed, the Jewish students were happy to rent the facility. They had only minimal contact with its owner, whose house adjoined the lab, and took great satisfaction that he was unable, perhaps due to denazification, to practice his profession.[72]

The students' comments suggest that the separation between the groups operated by an understanding that was mutual: Jews and Germans alike both intuited that they should stay apart and wanted it to remain this way. Crucially, the students' proximity to Germans did not necessarily translate into greater intimacy or even an openness toward the Germans. To the contrary, it appears that the absence of more formal boundaries between the groups made it all the more important for the students to erect and maintain informal barriers.

Added insight into the students' behavior, from a sociological perspective, comes from Lynn Rapaport's study of Jews in West Germany. Though focused on permanent Jewish residents in the decades after the war rather than DPs, she explains that "interactions with Germans, especially within a social context of potential intergroup conflict, generate unspoken understandings between Jews that allow them to play the same ethnic game—to include themselves into one group and draw a boundary that excludes the others. In such interactions there is a seemingly natural commonsense understanding that . . . one is from a community that is different from the Germans."[73] Further, in settings and moments of tension—which may describe the totality of the students' existence in Germany—"it is by maintaining social distance from Germans that Jews maintain a key sense of both personal and collective honor."[74]

Eva Frenkel, one of the handful of Jews from Germany who belonged to the Munich Union, provided special evidence of this dynamic. Observing her fluency in the language and her German demeanor, German students initially assumed she was simply German and attempted to socialize with her, even date her. She had little interest in doing so, however. She recalls accepting only one invitation from a young German man, and she refused to allow her German peers to address her with the informal "du." The distance she insisted on was rooted both in a sense of solidarity and in the ethical boundaries necessary for maintaining it. As she continued to spend time with the Jews, it became apparent that she was not available for, or worthy of, the Germans' company.[75] Though she came from the German world, Frenkel no longer felt she belonged in it nor sought to be a part of it.

The rare attempts by Germans to bridge the two worlds were generally met with polite reserve. Fred Reiter recalls that, while he was president of the dental students association within the Union, their German counterparts invited the group to a dinner dance. The Union decided that it was inappropriate for the organization to accept the invitation, though individuals were free to attend. Reiter, in his official capacity, declined to go.[76] Presumably the Union did not want to permit the Germans a sense of professional solidarity that, in light of recent events, could only ring false. The sum effect of the separation of Jews and Germans was a precarious coexistence, shot through with currents of suspicion, dislike, and self-protection. Fairly or not, Ohrenstein generalized, "Look, we knew they were all Nazis, and it was a very strange, hostile environment. I mean at least the way we looked at it. . . . They couldn't fool us, and we couldn't fool them. So, obviously, it was not pleasant."[77]

"Was He a Worker, an SS Man, You Didn't Know"

The Jewish students' sense that they were unwelcome came through means both direct and more subtle. Henry Miller heard of a physical threat being made against Jewish students in Munich. Miller had a classmate, a tough-minded Russian Jew from Leningrad named Weiner, who had been in the Soviet military. Weiner told Miller that a German student had approached him to say, "Aren't you afraid there's going to be a pogrom [at the university]?" Weiner replied, "You just try." The next day he brought a machine gun to school and warned the German not to say such things again. Asked if he had witnessed this episode, Miller replied, "Well, he showed me the machine gun," though he had no idea where Weiner had procured it.[78] Whether the German's threat was serious or, in nearly all likelihood, idle, its hostility is unmistakable, as is the seriousness with which Weiner took the intimidation.

More common were verbal slights. Though many regarded such slights as part of everyday university interactions, they could be painful. Sophie Schorr, in her own telling, had always been very short in stature. She would bring her own folding chair and sit just in front of the lecturer so that she could see the blackboard. One day as she was setting up, a German called out from the back, "Schau, Schau! Der kleine Jude! [Look, the little Jew!]." Schorr did her best to ignore the humiliating remark.[79] Sabina Zimering witnessed a more upsetting episode. To illustrate the symptoms of particular psychopathologies, her psychiatry professor brought in patients and conducted conversations with them in front of the class. Into the packed hall he one day called up a nondescript woman who first gave appropriate answers to basic questions. But, Zimering recalls, "All of a sudden she just raised her head and shouted 'And the Jews are buying out all our best chickens!' "[80] At the time food was scare for Germans, who commonly believed that Jews were treated better by the American occupiers and that they dominated the illicit trade of highly desired goods. "The response of the students," Zimering recalls, "was frightening. They were whistling, they were clapping, and they were agreeing with her one hundred percent. And there we were, maybe five or six of us [Jews] here, and five or six of us somewhere else, realizing who is surrounding us. I remember one German student . . . turned around, and he was very upset and he said, 'Those idiots. Don't pay attention to them. They are idiots.' Well, one person. So, that just reinforced what I was afraid of."

Zimering relates one of the paradigmatic scenes of the students' time in Germany: sitting in a lecture hall in small clusters with fellow Jews, surrounded by Germans. Under normal circumstances, German university classes are large and impersonal, with the students massed around the professor lecturing at the pit of the auditorium.[81] Just after the war the lectures were especially intimidating. The shortage of professors, coupled with a lack of classroom space, meant that classes were greatly oversubscribed. The pent-up demand for higher education among Germans who had been at war added to the numbers and potentially increased German resentment of the Jewish students who took coveted university slots.

The presence of German students returning from war added a chilling visual to the setting. With proper clothing scarce for the German population as well (especially in winter), some young men at first wore their military boots or even pieces of their Wehrmacht uniforms to class. It was an image oft-recalled by the Jewish students, who thus sat side by side with people in the military dress of their persecutors. Another surreal circumstance was seeing rows of German faces in the class and questioning: Who had been a Nazi enthusiast and who a reluctant conscript? Who had done something wicked and who had been far away from the killing fields? What did these Germans think of having Jews in their midst? Mark Hupert described the grim wonder of surveying the Germans: "Was he a worker, an SS man, you didn't know. They all look the same. So, that . . . was a terrible time to be there."[82] The tumble of silent questions was typically followed by the realization that one risked making oneself crazy by speculating in a void. Hupert's memory also provides a revealing complement to Myers Feinstein's summation that many survivors "saw their parents' murderers in every German face."[83] Here Hupert struggles to "see" differences in the Germans, but cannot. The episode Zimering described was so disturbing for her because it seemed to confirm a suspicion the Jews had about German attitudes that normally went untested. And her reaction shows just how isolated the students felt: she was not impressed that at least one German had privately chastised his peers but was distressed that it had been only one.

Instances of overt hostility were, however, very rare within the students' experience. Many, in fact, recall no such instances whatsoever during their time at university or in Germany more broadly. Emanuel Tanay, who spent four years in Germany after the war and traveled throughout the country, reports being treated with near-uniform courtesy. To him the Germans had a Jekyll-and-Hyde quality: oddly gracious in defeat, but monsters during the war. Elias Epstein, a survivor of Buchenwald, reports experiencing not only "no form of any anti-Semitism" but demonstrable German decency while he was a dental student in Munich. The Germans, whom he had told he was Jewish, lent him books and lab equipment and even held doors for him. When his ten-day-long "half-diploma" examinations overlapped with Yom Kippur, his professor excused his absence, "[explaining to the] German students that Mr. Epstein is taking two days off in order to celebrate the highest Jewish holiday."[84] Epstein, moreover, made genuine friendships with one German and one Pole among his classmates. Mark Langer, who had endured the Stanislawow ghetto, similarly described the postwar Germans as friendly, even solicitous.[85] And he was careful to stress, when describing postwar Germany, the exhilaration of at last being physically safe; intimations of lingering hostility were simply not comparable to the fear and perils of the ghetto.

"I Was His 'Good Jew'"

The students did not interpret the lack of brazen anti-Semitism as a sign that the Germans now accepted them. Though no precise gauge of the Germans' postwar attitudes exists, a 1946 survey taken by the US Military Government concludes that anti-Semitism persisted. The surveyed reported that nearly 40 percent of the population was intensely (18%) or moderately (21%) anti-Semitic.[86] According to historians Michael Berkowitz and Suzanne Brown-Fleming, what had changed was its mode of expression, as "many if not most Germans understood that it was no longer appropriate, at least outside their confidants, to refer to the Jewish remnant in their midst by the racial terms that were ubiquitous in the Third Reich. Informal and later compulsory restraint on public speech and publications did not mean, however, that well-entrenched stereotypes were ubiquitously quashed."[87] In particular, exaggerated claims of Jewish involvement in the black market fed German perceptions of endemic Jewish criminality. "It was acceptable" after the war "to label Jewish DPs as crooked, as responsible for and profiteering from the sea of crime in which the Germans felt themselves to be immersed, and as exacerbating German misery."[88] German actions consistent with this view included church and public mobilization against the alleged confiscation of German property by Jewish boarders; efforts to forcibly remove Jews from housing; "overzealous raids" by German police on Jewish black market activity, both in DP camps and German cities; and the refusal of German merchants to sell goods to Jews.[89]

Given the new atmosphere of relative restraint, some students claimed to feel German resentment through a sixth sense. "All day long you are among Germans," Robert Nenner explained. "And sometimes, looking at the German faces you saw the Nazis in them. You know, blond, blue-eyed. And they look at you, and you know that they didn't really approve of you. They kept you there because you were there. . . . I felt the undercurrent. I felt, not overt, but some kind of a hostility."[90] He also recalls a common brusqueness or rude reserve as the Jewish students sought small forms of help from their German peers—vague answers to some query about a class; claims that a notebook had been left at home so notes could not be shared; seemingly feigned ignorance as to the location of a campus building. (The Union newspaper complained of an incident in which a German doctor refused a Jewish student a book he needed, explaining that it would have to go first to a German.)[91] In response Nenner says that he "made sure that I'm there, I'm there in every lesson. In every class. And I studied my butt off."[92]

Most commonly, the students discerned a grudging civility in the Germans. Their interpretations of that civility are intriguing, both for their potential insight into German motives and—irrespective of their "truth" as sociological or psychological observations—as expressions of the Jews' mindset. Above all the Jews regarded German civility as a consequence of fear. For several years after the war, it remained unclear how broad and deep Allied justice against the perpetrators and Nazi party members would go. The Germans, they surmised, did not want to tip off the authorities to their roles during the war by attracting the suspicion that they were anti-Semites. "Don't forget, they were scared to death," Fred Reiter stressed, despite the fact that punishment of former Nazis ultimately was quite restricted.[93] Felix Korn came to a damning conclusion about German attitudes. While in Munich he was placed in the home of a Nazi's widow, whom he sensed masked hatred for him with superficial respect. He explained, "They're scared, first of all, of the American occupation. To say that they woke up, no, they didn't really change, but they had to stop doing what they'd been doing. . . . I don't believe they became any different."[94] German civility, in short, reflected an instinct for self-protection, not any change of heart.

Oftentimes the students bundled inferences about German fear with broader generalizations about the way Germans *are*. Korn described them as "very subservient." Reiter elaborated, "The German follows the leaders, the rules. . . . [W]hen the leader tells them to do something, they close their eyes and do it. . . . They wouldn't dare to be different."[95] Now it was the Americans giving orders; cruelty, not kindness, toward Jews could get them punished, so they adjusted their behavior. Such views reflect in part what so many of the students had themselves observed during the war: the steely discipline and unquestioning obedience of the Germans as they intimidated and brutalized Jews and others. While being herded into a ghetto as scarcely more than a child, Nenner recalled, he met the Germans' expressionless dedication to their task. Contrasting his Russian and German occupiers, he elaborated, "We considered the Germans still Westerners. And we always thought [of] German culture, the music, the Mozarts. . . . And how can I consider those people crude and rude? You can't. And suddenly, the realization . . . [when] they beat you, they beat the hell out of you. . . . There was one saying, 'a good German is a dead German.' I mean even the 'good Germans,' as you may refer to, were bad. Because they were told to do something, and Germans are very Germanic, I mean you tell them what to do and they'll do it. Regardless if they disagree or agree."[96]

The students' critique of German conformism, while helping to explain the Germans' postwar behavior, also seemed a way for the Jews to cognitively invert the Nazis' moral hierarchy, with its assumption of Aryan supremacy. The Germans, by virtue of their passive, even servile nature—their choice to be "good Germans" before decent human beings—proved themselves the *weaker* "people" or "race," devoid of moral autonomy. (This inversion has persisted in subsequent decades, though in modified form, among Jews in Germany. They commonly feel both like a stigmatized identity and morally and culturally superior to the Germans, who are in their minds still tainted by the Holocaust.)[97] However compensatory, such a view added to the Jews' satisfaction in seeing the Germans subject to a coerced civility.

The civility ultimately offered the Jews little more than cold comfort, however, because they mostly saw it as insincere and self-serving. Germans' fear of reprisal, several suggested, tapped into a deeper denial of guilt. Ohrenstein first boarded in Munich in the house of a German woman with whom he exchanged only basic salutations. Prompted by the sight of the Auschwitz number on his arm, she one day tried to account for the Nazi phenomenon. In a common trope of German rationalization, she stressed the charisma of Hitler; to illustrate, she related how a friend of hers had been "so overcome" by the Führer at a Nazi rally "that she kissed his garment." [98]

Her point, Ohrenstein sensed, was to convey that *she* had not been a Nazi, only her friend. Ohrenstein scoffed, "Nobody in Germany was a Nazi. Each German would say, 'Ich habe ein guten Jude'. . . So there were about sixty million Jews, because each one knew one good Jew." Mark Hupert echoed this quip with greater sarcasm: "It was very hard to live amongst [the Germans] because nobody was a Nazi. . . . There should have been eighty million Jews because everybody at least saved one."[99]

German fear and self-serving denial could work to the young Jews' benefit. Brian Bergman had completed only one year of *gymnasium* prior to the war but sought admittance afterward to the University of Frankfurt. A panel of faculty, he recalls, inquired into his qualifications, which he greatly embellished. When they realized that he was Jewish from his (original) name, Baruch, they stood in line and "everyone put his arms around me and said, 'Ich war nie Nazi gewesen' [I was never a Nazi]. Each one of them," he sensed, "expected to be punished and they wanted me, in case anything happens to them, to defend them in court. So they were so 'good' to me, they made it possible for me to attend university."[100]

The myriad stories of the students suggest just how provocative their postwar presence could be for the Germans. It might activate surviving prejudices, or a sense of guilt, or the desire—self-conscious or not—to deny, minimize, or mask this guilt. Apparent gestures of conciliation or contrition might carry old hatreds, and shame might induce resentment. These, at least, were the conflicting impulses and sentiments the Jews saw in the Germans.

German university officials were generally accommodating of the Jewish students. The students, in turn, treated the officials with formal respect and even courtesy. The Union went so far as to send the university rectors written Christmas and New Year's greetings.[101] Nonetheless, the students' suspicions of the officials ran deep. Robert Nenner, an officer in the Union, discerned in them not only fear but also a deeply ambivalent and compromised guilt. "First of all, they felt guilt that we survive," he explained.[102] "And the second guilt was that they didn't want us to stay there. And they knew that when we finished the school, we will go home. Where home was, it was not Germany. So therefore, they wanted us to learn quickly and disappear." Nenner's analysis—typified by the provocative (if unattributed) postwar saying, "The Germans will never forgive the Jews for Auschwitz"—proceeds by an intricate sequence: The Germans recognized, with a stirring of shame, Jewish suffering at German hands. Yet they resented the surviving Jews, insofar as their presence served as an unwelcome reminder of German crimes; hence the desire—and with it the added guilt—that the students take care of their business in Germany and be gone. Korn amplified this view with the remark that the Germans resented them so because "they knew that we were typical" Jews.[103] That is, the students were neither the duplicitous, avaricious, syphilitic monsters depicted in Nazi propaganda, nor the self-serving loafers and criminals described in early postwar discourse. By being polite, disciplined, and decent—each one of them a "good Jew"—they only gave lie to the stereotypes and compounded the cause for guilt.

At times, according to the Jewish students, the Germans sought to use kindness toward them as a way to placate their own consciences. Pivotal in Ohrenstein's course of study at the LMU was a Professor Lucas, a bona fide Nazi who had been dean of the economics faculty during the war. Another professor had been hard on Ohrenstein during his matriculation exam, issuing a grade that would have blocked his degree. But Professor Lucas made sure that he received passing marks. Nearly fifty years later, Ohrenstein allowed, "I am very grateful to him to this very day. I know that he was a Nazi and I'm not going to defend him. But he gave me a profession."[104] Asked why he felt Lucas treated him so well, Ohrenstein explained that the head rabbi of Munich's reconstituted Jewish community was also named Ohrenstein (Aaron Ohrnstein, eventually the Bavarian state rabbi); the professor, assuming in error that there was some relation, presumably did not want to cross such a student.[105] Yet the ultimate cause of the kindness, Ohrenstein sensed, lay elsewhere. With a mixture of resignation and disappointment, he concluded, "I was his 'good Jew.' "[106]

Intimacy and Distance

In assessments of the postwar dynamic, nothing suggests that Jews and Germans now saw themselves as coequal members of a restored human family, or even of a modestly integrated social system in which the boundaries of group identity could be easily overcome. Rather, members of each group seemed to feel that they had their proper place, demarcated by silently communicated and intuitively obeyed norms. These governed appropriate or permissible forms of interaction, and strongly shaped perceptions. The norms were built on an edifice of primal emotions such as rage, hurt, and shame, making the situation one of perpetual tension, a shadowplay of entangled suspicions and resentments. Complicating matters were the facts that it never seemed transparently clear who was who, what an individual's experience had been, and what was in his or her head and heart. Stereotypes and untested assumptions often held sway at the limits of firsthand knowledge. Finally, there did not seem an established language with which the groups could meaningfully engage each other or systematically redraw the norms to narrow the distance between them.

Yet the norms, developed ad hoc, were ultimately unstable, and the boundaries often transgressed. Such moments could be uncomfortable or worse, confirming why the boundaries were in place at the outset. Yet new possibilities also emerged for exchanges not shaped so powerfully by Germans' self-serving fear and resentment and by the Jews' bitterness and attending distrust.

There was, nonetheless, a fundamental asymmetry of experience between the Jews and the Germans that made anything like an ethic of "mutual recognition" an unrealistic goal for or a moral-discursive telos of their interactions. The primary task of the Jewish students was to reestablish a sense of self and the future. This largely meant working on their studies, building community with one another, and keeping a safe psychological distance from the Germans. They felt no obligation and little motivation to revise their negative impressions of "the Germans"; to demonstrate what Jews are really like; to educate Germans about German guilt; or to aid Germans in coming to terms with it. To the extent that they did any of this, the value lay primarily in how it helped the Jewish students restore a sense of dignity and human fellowship. And sometimes defiance of the Germans best served these ends.

The Germans, by contrast, had a duty imposed by their past conduct to demobilize their hatred and meet the Jews in their midst as equals. This came neither quickly nor easily, as it ran contrary to cultivated instincts and contingent pressures. Apparent efforts at conciliation might remain stillborn, and boundaries inappropriately crossed. By the same token, small acts of courage and kindness could yield moments of genuine empathy and dialogue. A concluding series of encounters or vignettes, each with its illustrative subtexts and meanings, shows the range of possibilities within Jewish-German relations.

An especially intimate, though still circumscribed, variety of encounter involved sexual or romantic coupling between Jewish students and Germans. Such relations revealed at once how dramatically the red line between them might fall, but also—when it did—the complicated distance that might still be maintained. Both the male and female students were focused on their studies and, relative to other young Jewish DPs, little interested in dating, finding partners, and having babies. While wartime deprivation could enhance desire for attaining these, it could also have the opposite effect. Rita Schorr explained, "The idea of marriage was not even considered. I lost too much, I had too little trust in human beings and the world."[107] Nonetheless, relationships and marriages formed among many of the students. And around the edges, a small number of male students dated German or Polish women.

Recent research has begun to open up the controversial realm of postwar Jewish-German sexual relations. In general, sex for survivors could serve as an assertion of their survival, vitality, and, for the men, their masculinity.[108] Physical relations with Germans—often bartered for coveted goods—might satisfy basic desires but also be tinged with a sense of revenge. German women, moreover, had not suffered the physical degradation of their Jewish counterparts, and could be more appealing for that reason. Jewish women's coupling with German men appears to have been exceedingly rare. Though less rare, Jewish men's coupling with German women was perceived by many Jewish DPs as a betrayal, pushing it to the margins of DP life and the public memory of that time.

My dialogue with the alumni about the subject was informed by mutual caution, reflecting the sensitivities of history and circumstance. The alumni are decorous Europeans, in their seventies and eighties when I met them. I often interviewed them when their spouses were present, either at the interview itself or in the household. There were therefore limits to what I (or Bella Brodzki) felt comfortable discussing, and much of the scholarship about Jewish-German sexual relations had not yet appeared to give impetus to and help guide my inquiry into the subject. The alumni, for their part, rarely raised the issue themselves, and often left unclear what they knew firsthand or had merely heard—what they could or could not confirm had happened.

Sabina Zimering asserted, "I don't remember anybody" coupling with Germans, but stressed that her immediate circle of friends was small; she could not say for sure what the "personal lives" of the others were, and thus left open the possibility of such couplings.[109] Guti Kanner recalls that such trysts did occur; but they were, she insisted, strictly private and a function of "physiological needs," nothing more.[110] She added that she personally did not know anyone who "went with" Germans but nonetheless attested to the behavior. As to the Germans' motives, she marveled that "the whole country was with Hitler" and then, after the war, "you could buy [any] German girl for some cigarettes."

The male students' remembrances suggest that the couplings with Germans did not necessarily represent any conscious communion between Jew and German. Mark Langer reports that at no point did he and his German girlfriend even discuss the fact that he was Jewish and she German, let alone the implications of their bonding.[111] He was not in love with her, and he doubted even that he could have fallen in love with a German; that line was not so easy to jump.

Simon Schochet, who also had a German girlfriend, first invoked the attitudes of Jews toward one another when explaining his choice. After the war he sensed that "Jewish women . . . had a certain kind of a disdain for the Jewish men."[112] Years later, he encountered the scholarly thesis that the women did not see the men as appealing partners because of how emasculating the Holocaust had been—how little the men had been able to protect their wives, children, and girlfriends. Sensing this, he "did not feel comfortable with Jewish girls." Neither did he find it easy to accept the Germanness of his German girlfriend. She was from a prominent Berlin family of German Huguenots—descendants of French Protestants who came to Germany as long ago as the seventeenth century after being expelled by the French Catholic monarchy. During the war she had been interned in a camp in Bavaria. Schochet comforted himself by reasoning that "she was not actually German."

From these accounts one gets little sense that postwar romances with Germans entailed consciously confronting and working through differences. Rather, the tenuous or even instrumental romantic bonds seemed both heavily mediated by tensions within Jewish identity and predicated on the Jews ignoring, minimizing, or rationalizing away those differences. This rule had its exceptions as well, though not in the years just after the war. Simon Snopkowski was among the tiny handful of Jewish students who settled permanently in Germany, eventually becoming a senator in the Bavarian parliament. He married a German woman, Ruth Snopkowski, who converted to Judaism. She has played a central role in Munich's new Jewish community, working to preserve the public memory both of her late husband and of the Jewish students group.

In the less sensitive realm of academic life, as we have seen, Germans had difficulties embracing the Jewish students. The Union newspaper complained that Germans at the universities commonly attributed the Jews' conspicuous academic success to their allegedly superior living conditions.[113] One student faced this assumption head on. Mark Langer was a standout in the dentistry program, consistently at the head of his class. Before an oral exam his professor took favorable note of his German surname and inquired if he was German, to which Langer responded, "No, I am [a] Jew."[114] Shortly into the exam, the professor broke form to ask, "Can you tell me why the Jews do all things so much better than the Germans?" Langer stayed silent, and the professor quickly answered his own question: "Maybe [because] you have better life conditions than the Germans have now." Unflinching, Langer replied, "You know, maybe."

The episode is emblematic of the rich dissonance between assumption and evidence, in which the prospect of a breakthrough in understanding was thwarted. The professor, hoping to see a German excel, was forced to concede Jewish achievement. But he seemed incapable of following his thought process in a credible or remotely gracious way; perhaps the Jews were simply hard working and strongly motivated. As if not even considering this possibility, he attributed Jewish prowess, in the fashion of the stereotype, to unfair advantage. A wall of prejudice had begun to come down only to be reerected, with the Jew discursively returned to a subordinate place.

Sometimes Germans broached more sensitive matters with their questions, with greater stakes, and in more intimate settings. One such setting was the German household, where many of the students boarded. To punish Nazi families, an Allied-directed policy put Jewish DPs in the homes of party members (most often with widows).[115] The confined domestic spaces and ideological clashes, as Ohrenstein discovered, created unique discomforts, as well as opportunities for Germans and Jews to meet each other anew.

Liberation for Ohrenstein came at the end of a death march, following internment in Auschwitz and other perilous settings. The German family with which he initially boarded had some intimation of his ordeal. There was his Auschwitz number. More provocatively, his body was covered with sores not yet healed, as insects and infection had eaten at his flesh. ("We were rotting. You know what it means to rot?" he asked in the interview.)[116] The family looked on him with a combination of repugnance and curiosity, with the latter growing as the wounds healed.

Nazi ideology had a biogenetic component that deemed Jews a mortal danger because they were presumed to be physically degenerate and literally harmful to German blood. The Holocaust, in one aspect, tried to rid the world of the Jewish contagion, and so protect German blood, the German body, and German *Lebensraum*. The German household might be seen as sanctified space—the symbolic center of the Third Reich—as that domain which must, at all costs, be kept pure of Jewish contagion. And yet in this postwar scene, the always already diseased Jewish body—further depleted by persecution—was in the sanctum of the German home. With the Jew's penetration of the domestic sphere, an anti-Semitic nightmare had become real.

The family occasionally asked Ohrenstein about Auschwitz. Sensing, however, that their curiosity had more to do with voyeurism than genuine sympathy—worse, that it contained kernels of prejudice—Ohrenstein would speak only humorously about the notorious camp and otherwise say nothing. "I did not want them to have the satisfaction," he explained, of hearing stories of his degradation. No longer would he be available, as a

Jew and a human being, for easy degradation by others, whatever their confused motives. This small protest evokes Albert Camus' notion—developed through reflection on the horrors of the mid-century—that rebellion, at its core, entails saying "no" to the attempted crossing by others of the limit by which dignity is established. To defend that limit is to defend not only oneself but all of humanity, making rebellion a radical expression of solidarity.[117] Here *resisting* the German invitation to dialogue on account of its skewed terms, Ohrenstein helped to restore that fundamental bond which National Socialism had worked so hard to shatter.

Sometimes the Jews took the initiative of sharing, and the Germans listened with quiet decency, producing a more genuine bond. Mark Hupert, liberated in Dachau, found himself at the concentration camp site after the war. His return was the subject of an evocative story, which, he admitted, "may sound very strange."[118] Hupert was accomplished at ping-pong, and often played with a friend from the Jewish Students' Union. With tables scarce at the university, he was drawn to a ping-pong club in Munich, which let the students practice. There too tables were in great demand, and tension built one day as Hupert and his partner played game after game. Yet the Germans did not, by a tacit injunction, feel free to take the table from the two Jews. "There was always this delicate thing," he explained. "They couldn't say no."

Noting Hupert's skill, a German invited him to join the club's team. Now feeling that *he* could not say no, Hupert agreed, and toured with the club in regional tournaments. One competition took them to the former Dachau concentration camp, part of which had been made into a public facility. "Obviously I didn't play very well," Hupert recalls, and his teammates sensed something was wrong. After the match, the players had a beer and talked, as was their custom. But on this occasion, Hupert related what he knew of Dachau: "This was the only time I talked to them about my experience during the war. And they were young people, my age, they were probably in the army because they took them in at sixteen years old [by] the end of the war. But that's the only time I spoke to a German person about it." The young Germans, who had known few details of Jewish suffering, were visibly shaken up, prompting Hupert to feel pity for them. They, in turn, felt pity for Hupert, and thereafter related to him with special warmth.

The whole episode contrasts sharply with Langer's and Ohrenstein's experiences, starting with the behavior of the Germans. Rather than resenting Jews for their entitlements as victims—in this case something so small as the use of ping-pong tables—the players proposed the friendly accommodation of having Hupert join the team. Despite his reluctance, Hupert chose to regard the invitation as a gesture of kindness, not a disguised put-down. And, prompted by the surreal location of the match, Hupert himself chose to talk about the Holocaust. His listeners did not resist the truth, protest their innocence, or press Hupert in uncomfortable ways. The result was a moment of mutual empathy.

Good Germans

Hupert's story complicates the picture of Jewish-German relations and Jewish attitudes in the war's aftermath. Whatever the Jews' dominant impression, the Germans were not, as in Ohrenstein's declaration, "all Nazis." And by their actions, some appeared to be genuinely good—not merely "good Germans"—raising the question of how the Jews might respond to this reality and assimilate it within their view of Germans. Stories of benign engagement thus form a second thread coloring the fabric of their experience as a whole.

When they encountered German vulnerability and decency, many of the students faced a challenge or dilemma after the war which they had faced during it. Survival under German occupation all but required protection, aid, or fleeting mercy from members of largely hostile populations, whether German, Polish, or Lithuanian. Many students had passed as Christians, and so were either rescued outright (as when knowingly taken in by a Christian family) or otherwise spared by someone in a position to identify them as Jewish. Those in hiding typically benefited from having neighbors look the other way at key moments (though Holocaust stories of egregious betrayal abound). Even in camps, Jews might receive protection. Isaac Minzberg's life was saved by a forlorn German locksmith in Auschwitz.

The bonds of rescue could go deeper still. A German officer, recalled late in life into the military, developed a fondness for Eva Siebald's father—the first Jew he had ever really known.[119] He brought food to the Siebalds in the Stanislawow ghetto and later helped bring the family out. He continued to look after the family as it hid with other Jews—eighteen in all—in a nearby town. As the war worsened for Germany, the Siebalds begged him to stay with them in relative safety. He stoically declined, stating, "I am still a German." To protect him in turn, the family (as in the account in *Schindler's List*) wrote a letter in Hebrew explaining to any potential Allied captors what he had done to help them. Siebald wept—the only time during our interview—when she recounted that he was killed by a Soviet bomb. Here a German really had saved not just one Jew but many, and clearly made no distinction between the "good Jews" and the others.

Even when Germans showed them no kindness, the young Jews faced the issue of whether to recognize a common humanity in the Germans. Sabina Zimering, while working in southern Germany during the war, had contradictory feelings: "In my mind there were these two categories—the soldiers, which were usually scary but not quite as vicious as the Gestapo, the SS . . . . [B]ut the big contrast was observing the civilian Germans. I was shocked by how much they looked to me like other people. . . . [In a] couple of instances I outright felt bad for them. [I asked myself,] 'What's the matter with you? You know who they are.' "[120] On one occasion she saw an attractive high-ranking couple bidding goodbye at a train station, the man bound for "the dreaded Eastern front." Despite thinking, "Who knows what he will be doing [there]?" she "couldn't help" feeling sympathy for the distraught pair. She later observed a woman crying inconsolably among a group of women who were passing around a letter. "Her youngest son was badly wounded and maybe dying, again on the front. And when I looked at it, I just, I saw a mother in her." For Zimering empathy seemed less a choice than a feeling. In an insoluble dilemma, compassion for the oppressor competed with solidarity with her fellow victims.

For Mark Langer the question of pity arose as an agonizing decision just after the war. When Langer was a teenager, a doctor had nursed him through a severe case of pneumonia. Ever since then he had wanted to practice medicine. It was therefore propitious when his Soviet liberators put him to work in an infirmary, which housed Soviet soldiers and prisoners of war. One evening, a "beautiful German boy" (likely a very young conscript) close to death cried out creakily, "Wasser . . . Wasser."[121] Langer recollects, "And I was thinking, give the water or not . . . because only a few weeks before these people were killing us. . . . I was thinking maybe two, three minutes. . . . I came, I gave the water." Langer looked beyond the image of youthful innocence that had been corrupted by service to a genocidal regime; he saw at last a frightened young man, and he summoned a sense of duty, both human and Hippocratic, to offer help. (In a form of coda to this episode, Simon Schochet distilled the dilemma Jewish students faced by the real-life question of whether one should yield one's seat in class to a German student disabled by the war.)[122] Later in Munich, while a dental student, Langer treated German patients.[123] As his skill became evident, Germans sought him out for care; he had become for them a good dentist, whatever prejudices they may have still harbored.

Most of the Germans the Jews interacted with were not, of course, objects of such obvious pity or people seeking service from them. Under more conventional, everyday circumstances, how was it possible for members of each group to make a positive impression on the other? What prompted solicitousness and curiosity beyond the ordinary, which could serve as a touchstone for sustained, reciprocal interest or even friendship?

Though rare, friendships between individual Jewish students and Germans were not altogether uncommon, again contesting the memory of the strict separation between the two groups. Of forty-five survey respondents, eight report having had German friends, six had "few" such friends, and thirty-one had none. Sometimes the Jews initially had no idea what impression they had made on their German peers. And that impression, as Eva Siebald discovered, might be conveyed only years later. When she entered Munich's TH in 1946, Siebald was both the only Jew and the only woman in the mechanical engineering program.[124] Soon a German woman named Gaby joined, and the two shared a room when the engineering students went on educational visits to factories. (Gaby's father had not wanted her to study mechanical engineering, so she told him she was really studying chemistry, a subject more fitting for a woman.) Nothing about their interaction seemed remarkable to Siebald, and for years she gave it no thought. She therefore reacted with great surprise when she received a call from the German woman in Haifa years later, indicating that she was in Israel and would like to visit. (Gaby had come alone and had remained unmarried.) Gaby had made Israel "her project," learning "everything" about the country—far more than Siebald herself knew. Thereafter, she frequently came to Israel, and the two women became friends. Gaby often brought gifts to Siebald's friends and family, including a diamond ring for Siebald's daughter. The daughter at first thought it was inappropriate to accept such a thing from a German, but with her mother's explanation that it was probably stolen from a Jew anyhow, she accepted it. Whatever the entangled associations of the past, Siebald and her German friend "never, never spoke about the war."

Much in their symbolically rich relationship remains opaque, starting with Gaby's motivation to learn about Israel and reach out to Siebald. Perhaps she was working off a personal sense of guilt. Perhaps her interests were laced with a philo-Semitism. Perhaps she had a hidden history of kindness toward Jews. Perhaps the self-assured Siebald had been an early female role model for her. Whatever the case, her actions suggest an honest effort both to learn about the sustained life of a people once condemned by Germany and to engage Jews not as an abstraction but on personal terms. Siebald certainly responded to her overtures in this spirit.

Marion Glaser, finally, related a story of boundaries crossed and friendships formed that pushed toward an upper limit of what was possible for

Jews and Germans after the war. Glaser had grown up German, and her German classmates frequently "mistook" her for one of them. As a result, she "heard terrible things the [other] Jewish students didn't hear."[125] She sometimes took advantage of her ability to pass as a German—something she tried to do during the war—to probe further German attitudes. She made one such effort while sitting in a lab with ten or so medical students studying a cadaver.

> [Among them] was a very nice, very delicate-looking German. Blond, blue-eyed, she was a pianist before. And she started learning medicine. She, it turned out she came . . . from Sudetenland. And she was complaining endlessly what the Russians did to the Czechs [and] to the Germans in Sudetenland. And then I looked at her and said, "Why are you so astonished? Think about what we did to them?" I am talking as a German. "What did they do?'" "Oh, look, the Russian prisoners were killed. We took their country. And think about what we did to the Jews." And then she said, "Really, you are right, to the Jews we behaved very bad. We should have thrown out or [had] all of them killed." When I heard that, I was so shocked I started crying, I jumped from the chair, and I run away. And one German student ran after me. That was Peter Schily. And he caught me and said, "Marion that was a very ugly discussion. But why were you personally so hurt by that?" I said, "Because I am Jewish." He didn't leave me anymore. He was from a family who were anti-Nazi. Really, that was not a story. . . . He was an invalid, from the German war. He lost an eye and he was partly paralyzed.[126]

Glaser confirmed what so many of the Jewish students suspected: that German civility was largely a front, as here the purported absence of Jews freed the Germans to say, cavalierly, hateful things. The redemptive twist is the conscientiousness of the young, disabled German man who first tries to console a German peer and then—perhaps to atone for the shame of his countrymen—makes a Jewish friend. He quickly developed an interest in the Jewish experience and began learning Hebrew on his own. Schily then engaged in a ruse so that he could, from a different vantage point, hear what so many Germans still thought of Jews.

After the war, Möhlstraße, long one of Munich's upscale streets, became the city's center of black market activity, in which Jews were involved. Germans buying the marked-up goods, Glaser told Schily, cursed the black marketeers. Curious to see for himself, Schily one day went to Möhlstraße and stood with a "Jewish newspaper" (likely written with Hebrew letters), pretending to be Jewish. He reported to Glaser, based on the slurs he heard, "You are right. They are all anti-Semites." The ruse represents a fascinating reversal, wherein a German is now passing as a Jew. Nonetheless, the result is the same: confirmation of German anti-Semitism. However here the ambiguity of identity—the confusion of subjectivities and subterranean assumptions and prejudices—is also generative, as it helps Glaser and Schily bond.

After Glaser left Germany, the two lost touch. Many years later, when Glaser was living in Israel, she received a call from a German woman—Peter Schily's wife, and mother of their seven children—who was visiting Israel. Thereafter, the Schily family sent each of their children to spend time on a kibbutz, and one son eventually married a Jewish woman from India whom he had met in Israel. Glaser proudly reported that Peter Schily (since deceased) was the brother of Otto Schily—once a controversial attorney for the notorious Red Army Faction, later a Green Party politician, and eventually the minister of the interior in the government of Chancellor Gerhard Schroeder.

How much solace one may take from an isolated case of moral courage is a matter of perspective. How often individual Germans privately expressed such courage will never be known. At the very least, the friendship of Marion Glaser and Peter Schily set a standard—however improbably high—of good faith efforts at reconciliation and solidarity.

CHAPTER 6

"Pioneers, Not Scholars"

The Jewish Students and Zionism

For two weeks in August–September 1947, a delegation of students from the American Zone traveled to Brighton, England, to participate in the Second International Student Camp of the Paris-based World Union of Jewish Students. Never before had Union members travelled outside the American Zone to meet an international body of their peers, which included students from the United States, Italy, England, France, Switzerland, and Poland. As with all Student Union activities, the trip was a struggle; their journey was made possible only through outside financial support. Though twenty-seven students had hoped to go, only seven (five of them from Munich) were given the chance. A cluster of organizations worked to secure visas, and the Joint paid for travel. The World Union of Jewish Students covered other expenses, while England's Rabbi Bernard Moses Casper, who had been the senior chaplain for the Jewish Brigade, played gracious host, earning an honorary membership from the Union.[1] Also true to form, the Union came with an agenda: to describe the plight of Jewish students in occupied Germany and to appeal for both aid and scholarships for them to study abroad. A special session of the camp discussed the prospects for such support, yielding earnest, if vague, promises.[2]

For the Union, the centerpiece of the trip was the address to the entire camp by Stefan Hornstein-Haraszti, a twenty-three-year-old Hungarian medical student from Munich and general secretary of the zone-wide Student Federation. The speech began with an indictment of European anti-Semitism, highlighting assaults on the Jewish intelligentsia in the interwar years in Germany, but also in Hungary, Romania, and Poland. About the Holocaust, Hornstein-Haraszti described: "And so were our fathers, mothers, sisters, entire families gassed, so was in the firestorm of this grisly war the entire, noble tradition of the Jewish intelligentsia, including 90% of the European student community, annihilated."[3] After citing basic statistics about the postwar students, he intoned: "Colleagues, who in Germany and perhaps the entire world no longer have any relatives, live in a real sense in great misery. It soon became clear to us that the Central Committee of Liberated Jews in Bavaria would offer only modest support. . . . Our aid organizations bring to the concerns of the student community too little understanding. As a result of their—in our view—erroneous assessment of the future structure of Jewish society, we are the stepchildren of our people." He stressed that "the overwhelming majority of our students are committed Zionists" and ended by expressing the hope that the next gathering would be "in our free, independent homeland."[4]

The address and the entire trip speak to many of the issues integral to the Jewish students, with broad resonance in the Jewish DP world and bearing on historical reconstructions of the postwar period. For all the students' academic drive, the Union's enduring preoccupation was material: what amount of aid its members would receive, from whom, and for how long. At stake was their ability to subsist as students. But they also viewed such aid as the definitive imprimatur showing support for their choice to study. Far and away the greatest tension they experienced with Jewish authorities involved aid, given all that it signified. Their particular struggles provide a window into the complex system of relief efforts and how they were invested with political meaning.

The second burning question besides aid was emigration: When and how would the students exit Germany, and where would they go? Like other Jewish DPs, the students desperately wanted to leave. But they were also intent on finishing their studies. Securing scholarships abroad would permit them to do both, and the Union worked to generate such options. Yet these efforts remained paltry, creating an incentive—all but unique among organized groups of Jewish DPs—to stay in Germany after other opportunities for exit had passed, at least for as long as it would take to finish their degrees. The students' experiences therefore pointed up the ways DPs sought to reconcile personal goals with available opportunities.

The third great issue, laced through the first two, was the students' relationship to Zionism. Palestine/Israel was the preferred emigration choice for most students, but not if it meant suspending their studies and possibly derailing their educational goals for good. The students were thus caught between their hard-fought professional ambitions and Zionist duty, whether they felt it internally or externally. That duty, as communicated by the Jewish leadership, ideally demanded vocational or agricultural training, the readiness to leave when conditions dictated, and, eventually, conscription in the army.

The Union tried to square this circle by arguing that support for their studies was an investment in the Jewish future and an asset to Zionism. But such arguments failed to persuade the key Jewish bodies, who tried to force the students' migration by dramatically reducing their aid. This required that the students fight, in essence, for their claimed right to study. The question of what Zionist duty demanded divided some within the Union, and four Munich students in fact dropped their studies to join the fight for Israel's independence. It burned as well in the consciences of individual students, who worried that serving their personal goals meant failing larger obligations to the Jewish people. In this thicket of competing perspectives, claims, and agendas, one gains additional perspectives on controversial subjects within Zionist and DP historiography: the place of Zionism in the consciousness of DPs, the extent to which it was autonomously embraced by them or imposed, and the kinds of pressure applied to mobilize DPs in the cause of Jewish statehood.

This chapter explores the nexus of aid, emigration, and Zionism in documenting perhaps the most intense of the students' postwar struggles. Those struggles, resulting from their particular dilemmas, speak to the highly politicized nature of the DP world in general and the pressures for DPs created by the emergence of the Jewish state. No matter one's wartime misery, ideological boundaries were set to constrain and direct one's decisions about one's future. The contest over those boundaries, especially acute in the case of the students, concerned fundamental understandings of Jewish history, identity, and destiny.

Aid and Jewish Displaced Persons

Though resources in occupied Germany were scarce, not all Jewish DPs were destitute or equally dependent on relief efforts. Some had living parents with resources on which to draw, whether saved through the war or generated afterward. Some might also have received money or goods from relatives elsewhere in Europe and in the United States, or even on behalf of deceased parents. Arnold Kerr's father, killed in the Holocaust, had been a wealthy businessman with connections in England; for years after the war, his father's associates sent Kerr stipends from his father's assets.[5] Other students supplemented their aid with income from employment, such as guarding Joint facilities, performing clerical services in DP camps, and part-time work with the US military.[6] And some DPs, including students, had accumulated wealth through illicit activity. Just after the war, Mark Fintel was involved in a complex currency exchange scheme, yielding enough valuable paper money to fund his student existence in Munich for two years.[7] Guti Kanner, in her one failed attempt at illicit dealings, imported butter for resale, only to find that it melted in transit.[8]

Rafael Nenner (the cousin of Robert Nenner), a key Union officer, estimated that 10 percent of the students had little or no need for money or donated goods. As to the source of their means, he explained, "We never asked them, it's not our business to ask them because the more you ask them, the worse it gets."[9] By another unspoken agreement, the students did not press one another, whether to ward off potential jealousies or to tacitly sanction illicit dealings.

One could also take advantage of the aid system. Any number of students had family members or friends in the DP camps set aside rations for them, which they collected despite being free-livers technically barred from such aid; some even registered in two camps to get double rations. One alumnus joked that his friend and fellow Union member was a "thief" who, at the risk of US jails, would "steal American property" on the Union's behalf by bringing falsified registrations to the camps.[10]

Eking out even a modest existence, however, remained a challenge for most students. Housing was perhaps the least difficult necessity to secure. Through the intervention of Commissioner Auerbach, Munich students were commonly given at least habitable rooms, if in ex-Nazi households. Rafael Nenner recalled that his room was a "closet" with no access to running water, and that his landlord, a former Nazi military captain, would pester him by brandishing his certificate of clearance from a denazification tribunal. But Nenner was "happy" with his little dwelling.[11] The students nonetheless complained of the winter cold, given the poor condition of many buildings and the scarcity of heating fuel, and occasionally rejected the allotted rooms. While often citing physical damage in such cases, the Union on one occasion requested new housing for a student because, living in cramped quarters with several family members, he could not properly study for his exams.[12]

Obtaining clothing was a more fraught task. Virtually all the students' garments came via donations, whether from the Joint directly or from the Central Committee or Munich Committee as intermediaries. Union records teem with efforts to secure clothing, the exact number of shoes, socks, shirts, and so forth they had been given, and protocols for their distribution. Though making use of anything they could get, the students, judging from photographs, favored the somewhat elegant suits, skirts, and blouses typical of European students, and avoided as best they could the mix-and-match outfits, often including items of military dress, commonly worn by DPs.

Academic materials were in short supply. Stocks of donated pencils, erasers, and notebook paper were likewise meticulously recorded, and the Union sometimes wrangled with other Jews over such items. In one instance, the CK commandeered for its own administrative use supplies intended for the Union, prompting the Joint to intervene on the Union's behalf.[13] Securing books was a great priority, as it was for Jewish DPs in general. The Joint, intent on outfitting camp and city libraries with Jewish reading material, estimated in early 1946 that it would ideally need 600,000 volumes.[14] To print educational texts it made use of two German-owned printing presses in Munich, importing up to twenty-five tons of paper per month.[15]

Academic texts were especially hard to come by, prompting the Union's haphazard outreach to student and professional groups worldwide, which occasionally yielded small numbers of donated books. There were also tragicomic moments of dashed hopes. In August 1947 the Joint director of the American Zone personally wrote the Union staff to inform them that rumors of the existence of 60,000 medical texts, available for distribution to the students, were false.[16] The texts the students did secure were frequently traded or borrowed, and the Union built a small stock in its office, mostly of English titles. Outfitting a proper student library, ideally at a dedicated facility, was an enduring goal of the Union and a frequent demand it made of Jewish leaders.

The Union also had administrative costs, which included maintaining its office, paying its secretary, and sending mail. These were generally covered by the Joint, which made cash payments and provided special allotments of cigarettes, chocolate, and other forms of de facto currency. The items were stored at the Union office and most often "spent" by the Executive Committee on goods and services for mutual benefit.[17]

The greatest of the students' basic needs was food: the students needed to eat. For many survivors, in addition, the experience of starvation during the war caused them to crave sufficient food in the postwar era (even as it may have trained them to eat very little). Explaining this postwar obsession, Arnold Kerr vividly recalled that to survive the death march from the Stutthof concentration camp he had each day fed himself, on strict ration, two spoonfuls of sugar from a small supply he had hidden away.[18] Finally, as Atina Grossmann emphasizes, food was imbued with enormous symbolism in an environment where various victim groups, other refugees, and the German population competed for limited resources.[19] The amount and kind of food one received was commonly seen as the essential measure of how fairly one was treated in the occupation regime, with nearly all groups complaining that the food was "never enough and never good enough."[20] For the students, food was indeed the key metric for assessing support for their path, including within the Jewish community.

The students had no single supply of food, and arrangements varied by geography. Students throughout the zone generally received greater support from UNRRA, until its dissolution, than their Munich counterparts. Those in Munich had access to weekday lunches, paid for with Joint-issued meal tickets. The students could spend their modest stipends on food. They also may have garnered UNRRA rations from DP camps or even made use of standard German ration cards. Their lifeblood, however, was the monthly "Joint packets" they received starting in mid-1946, by which point most students were free-livers. (Those still in the camps received "half-packets.")[21] The packets were distributed out of the Union's office, after having been collected from the Munich Committee (called also the "Jewish Committee")— another major institution on the occupation scene.

Officially constituted in January 1946, the Munich Committee was a Jewish-run organization responsible for delivering aid and services, mostly provided or funded by the Joint, to Munich's free-livers.[22] Each Jewish resident registered with the committee and had the power to vote for the members of the organization, which enjoyed close links to the Central Committee. The committee's president, Hersch Schwimmer, became a powerful figure in Munich, helping to establish a Jewish enclave in Möhlstraße, brokering DP interests to both aid organizations and German authorities, and quietly supporting the Bricha. Equivalent committees existed elsewhere in the American Zone, though they served much smaller Jewish populations.

The Joint rations were at the center of tensions within the Jewish world and became a source of enormous controversy for the students. The Joint's ambition was to guarantee adequate food to all Jewish DPs, both inside and outside the camps. This meant issuing rations, including to those refugees cared for by UNRRA whose food aid was insufficient. The Joint's work was made more urgent by the dissolution of UNRRA in April 1947 and its replacement by the IRO, whose assistance to DPs was greatly diminished.

Throughout the American Zone, tens of thousands of monthly ration packets were issued as "payment" to various kinds of workers, with one's type of work (specified by category) determining the size of the ration, which was carefully measured by calories.[23] To incentivize service, work rations were substantially greater than standard aid. This also made them extremely prized, inviting manipulation of the aid system.

The Central Committee, both inside and outside the camps, largely set the number and classification of workers, who were defined very broadly. Doctors, nurses, teachers, rabbis, camp administrators, instructors in vocational schools, the staff of city and regional committees (like the Munich Committee), work project employees, and CK officials drew workers' rations. But so too did the leaders of political parties and youth organizations, as well as *hakhsharot* members and those in various associations. Kibbutz members also received special aid. Vocational students, subsidized by ORT (a worker-training program first organized in the DP camps by Jacob Oleiski), enjoyed the equivalent of workers' rations. Lesser rations were given under the rubric of "relief"; its recipients included children and the elderly, tuberculosis sufferers and the disabled, and pregnant women and nursing mothers. Some food aid was given, finally, to those falling outside any of the above categories.

The Joint and the CK, as Zeev Mankowitz reports, had intense, ongoing conflicts over who had the primary say in the allotment of aid, and it was often unclear who had the greater power.[24] Revising the aid system in the fall of 1947, the Joint complained bitterly to the CK that 20 to 40 percent of all those in camps, and an alarming percentage of those outside as well, had been receiving work rations, thereby limiting the aid for everyone else.[25] All but accusing the CK of padding employment rolls and politicizing aid, it set percentage quotas for workers, shored up the classification system, ordered greater oversight of aid distribution, and reiterated that the CK and the Jewish Agency must not, in serving their own ends, limit or deny rations to any worthy recipient. As 1948 approached, the Joint anticipated providing 85,000 fixed rations and many more irregular rations; this required, along with other Joint operations in the zone, 600 tons of food per month.

The students had a lowly place within this complex system. They were given limited rations under the category of "relief."[26] They were not, that is, considered full-fledged workers entitled to elevated aid. (Individual students might, however, receive worker rations by virtue of other activities.) The students' great effort, both in Munich and zonewide, was to have the students recognized by the CK as workers, and to be compensated accordingly. In symbolic terms, this would mean being acknowledged as a vital part of the Jewish social body, on par with agricultural trainees and those learning trades. The packets the students did receive, whose contents varied based on the availability of specific goods, included smallish amounts of cigarettes, meat, jam, butter, and other foods—just enough, the students claimed, to barely subsist, even with other aid.[27] Even so one alumnus described the packets as "manna from heaven," most valuable for the cigarettes, condensed milk, and occasional chocolate.

In the early spring of 1947, while illegal migrations to Palestine were in full force and just as UNRRA was dissolving, the number and contents of the Munich students' Joint packets dwindled. The sudden withdrawal of UNRRA support in March hit students hard in other cities. Those in Frankfurt were quickly "attached," with help from the Joint, "to the Zeilsheim [DP] camp for the purpose of drawing rations."[28] The Marburg students, now displaced from the UNRRA student hostel where they had been housed and fed, affiliated with a local kibbutz and scrambled to find new housing. The several dozen students in Heidelberg set up a community kitchen, which they supplied by using German ration cards and sporadic, "unfixed" Joint rations from the Joint committee in Stuttgart. Their union reported "great difficulty" in securing aid from the Joint, whose regional director denied the kind of "stable support" students elsewhere had enjoyed.[29] In Munich the students interpreted the reduction of their aid as an effort by Jewish authorities to force them to quit their studies. That decision, and the protest it prompted, represent the defining moment in the long-simmering conflict between the students and the Jewish DP community.

"The Old Jewish Intelligentsia Is Dead— These Students Are the Coming One"

The relationship between the students and the leading Jewish authorities— chiefly the CK, the Jewish Agency, and the Joint, which was prone to the influence of the other two—is among the most delicate, and at times opaque, aspects of the students' entire narrative. Most often the students maintained a formal posture of deference, whether out of diplomacy, a measure of genuine respect, or their own sense of Zionist exigency. Just after lamenting the lack of support for the students in his Brighton address, Hornstein-Haraszti explained, "It is far from our intention to criticize the politics of our authorities, because we know the difficulties they deal with daily," and he credited them, whatever their perceived failings, with "goodwill."[30] When noting difficulties with Jewish officials, the Union's early records tend to speak in generalities, or report that the relationship had improved, without specifying what conflicts had to be smoothed over. The tensions, in short, initially resided sub rosa, surfacing through such issues as whether a dormitory in Munich would be supported or if the students, during a trip to Berchtesgaden in 1946, would be permitted use of the CK's hostel. (The CK refused, insisting that the facility be reserved for convalescents.)[31] The students likewise complained to the CK that special rations for Union officers were not delivered as promised.[32]

The students had little doubt where they stood in the eyes of the Jewish leaders. Asked decades later to describe that regard, Felix Korn replied, "You want to call it disregarded or ignored? They called us 'die Studentenlein' . . . it's like a diminutive of a student, but in a very cynical [way]. . . . Why? Because, what did these guys [the students] do, they're studying instead of making a living or doing some trade or going to Israel. . . . It was very demeaning."[33] A Union newspaper column in the spring of 1947 complained that "the students' position is very difficult. Placed in a community of survivors [who were] anxious to rebuild the material foundations of their existence, crying out for craftsmen, for workers, for farm-labourers and in their shortsightedness rather indifferent to intellectuals—the students find neither the understanding for their aspirations, nor the support in their needs they would have expected. . . . No longer starving, they have been underfed all the same."[34]

The objections to the student path were twofold. First, as we have seen, some Jews felt that study in German universities was itself a betrayal. Second, and most important, was the sense prevailing among the CK and the Jewish Agency that physically healthy DPs should contribute to the building of a Jewish state by readying themselves for migration, physical labor, and military service. The students were thus in a bind, acutely aware that standing up for themselves as students could be seen as standing against Zionism. They were also conscious of the example set by the kibbutz members—Jews often of similar age who were heralded by DP leaders as representing the Zionist vanguard. How the students' justified their choices, framed criticisms, and, in essence, lobbied both officialdom and the broader Jewish community reveals both their self-understanding and the wages of various decisions DPs made.

The students' great rhetorical defense was to argue that academic and professional pursuits were integral parts of the Jewish past and future—indeed, of great utility to Zionism. To make this point, the Union distributed flyers showing a graph of the Jewish population before and after the war, and the proportion of professionals, with the caption, "Help Create a Jewish Intelligentsia."[35] The column cited earlier further elaborated: "The overwhelming majority of Jewish students study: Technics, medicine, natural sciences, agronomy and economics—practical branches, the application of which may help to make Palestine habitable for far more people than she could contain just now. It has been said of the German Jew Fritz Haber, the inventor of a new chemical process [instrumental to the manufacture of fertilizer], that he gave Germany more soil than all her field marshals together. And so Palestine will need every intellectual. . . . The old Jewish intelligentsia is dead—these students are the coming one."[36] In defending intellectuals, the Union makes a fascinating argument for the value of knowledge to power, with implications for the escalating conflict with the Arabs in Palestine: here science (chemistry, in service to agronomy) is credited with the functional acquisition of territory (in the form of arable land), beyond what even a military can deliver.

The Union's external program, pledged to raising the intellectual and cultural level of other Jews, was in part an effort to tangibly demonstrate the students' value to community life and to Zionism more broadly. In somewhat bombastic tones, conveying a thoroughly nationalized and elitist conception of intellectuals, a student essay asserted, "If our community is likened to a desert, we as students should be the oasis from which the masses draw their nourishment."[37] Students gave frequent lectures in the DP camps, and the Union held a concert in the Gauting sanatorium for infirm Jews.[38] The Union also played a leading role in Munich in efforts to help plant a million trees in Palestine, both to make more verdant the arid terrain and to honor the Holocaust dead.[39] Urgent calls that the members get more involved in cultural work clearly reflected the Union's awareness of its value to the students' reputation. With less fanfare individual students engaged in private acts of beneficence. Simon Schochet met a sweet, intellectually curious girl in a DP camp whose religious parents had had little schooling. Schochet persuaded them to allow their daughter to pursue secular education, and for a spell he escorted her each day from her camp dwelling to the school.[40]

The Union newspaper was another vehicle for contributing to the Jewish commonweal, as well as for explaining the students' position. Printed in Munich, seven issues of the paper appeared between the fall of 1946 and early winter of 1948. Copies were sent to Jewish committees throughout the American Zone for distribution (the retail price of the first issues was one Reichsmark), though the paper, dominated by Munich students, never quite functioned as an organ for students zonewide.[41]

The paper was conceived as an academic tribune that would feature work on history, literature, Judaica, science, economics, and student life.[42] The content was limited by the availability of research material and the students' time. As was often the case with DP publications, a small group crafted most of the pieces, and the paper printed excerpts of works by Jewish authors such as Martin Buber and Heinrich Heine. (In the second issue the Union, to solicit contributions, offered prizes for the best essays, with the top award set at 500 RM.)[43] Student-authored content included poetry, profiles of Jewish intellectuals and political figures, a two-part piece on "The Birth of the Jewish Brigade," cultural musings (feuilleton), various statements by the Union, and,

ווידערגעבורט

תחיה

פאריאדיעצ שריפט
«יידישע סטודענטן פארייניגונג»

Wiedergeburt

MÜNCHEN
APRIL—MAI • 1/4—5

1947

THE NEW LIFE

Itgadal weitkadesz...

Umfargeslech iz undz der nomen fun Ajch, welche hot nyt derlebt cu zeen di zun fun di felker-bafrajung. Tajer un nont iz undz jeder horch fun ajere farsznitene lebns. Hejlik der sztojb un dos asz noch ajere cezejte bejner.

In umfarleszlechn wejtik bojgn mir di kep un faln anider far di erd fun a gancn kontynent, welche iz geworn cu ajer gemajnzamen masn-kejwer.

Noch di windn, wos rajsn zich in ale fir ekn fun der welt, lojfn noch undzere blikn, zoln zej dertrogn cu ajch dos szeptszen fun di lipn undzere „Itgadal Weitkadesz...."

Wu Ir zajt, wu Ir rut, efszer do unter undzere fis, arum undz un wajt, wajt wu es szpanen zich ojs die ajzerne fedim fun di szines, ojf welche es zajnen gelofn di wagonen fun mojlech... Unter di felder wu men sznajdt dos korn, unter sztet farbrente ojf koji, unter gexrner wu es szprocn di blumen un unter plecer dort szrekn geszpentster fun farblibene flijes, es walgern zich resztlech fun elektriszn drot...

Cu Ajch szikn mir hajnt undzer tfile, in ir baheft zich alc wos iz geblibn in undz mit dem alem wos iz zwek mit Ajch....

Hajnt, in.trog fun zunike strale, in tog fun felker-friling un felker bafrajung brajbt undzer ort baj Ajch, buj Ajch undzere gedanken, undzere gefiln rajsn zich cu Ajch, arajn unter di szwarce sztub-muter-erd, wos hot fardekt mit ir lajb di szande fun ire zin.

Arajn in di tunkele lecher, wu es cerfojlt di reszt fun dem, wos iz nechtn gewen majn mame, dajn bruder un ir kind. . . .

Cu Ajch in di griber bort zich arajn dos gesztikte geszrej. Es muz dergejn cu Ajch wuahin es derlangen nyt undzere trern, trern fun ojgn welche hobn ojfgehert kenen wejnen, trern wos woltn muzn fardekn wi regn-wolkn dos gance himl fun Europe, az zejere tropns zoln faln umetum, wu men hot ojsgehakt kworim far undz....

Hajnt, kumen mir cu Ajch... Cu Ajch....

Mir, — cu Ajch .... Mir — welche hobn gefunen chesed in di ojgn fun szed, wen er hot getejlt ojf links un ojf rechts, mir, ojf welche es iz grod nyt gefaln der tojt-klap fun zajn hant — efszer, wajl er iz gefaln ojf ejnem fun Ajch ....

Mir — welche hobn fursztanen fun tog mach n nacht un fun nacht tog, cu derkenen dem ojs-weg ojch dort, wu far poszete ojgn iz gewen cojm un opgrunt ....

Mir — welche hobn zich arajngegrobn mit undzere negl in di glate want un zich on ir ongehaltn, — wajl zi iz grod ojsgefaln cugenglecher — wen far Ajch iz zi gewen fun glitszikn ajzn, fun kaltn beton ....

Mir — far welche es hot zich ojsgesztrekt mit hilf a fremde hant — wen ajch hobn fremde hent dersztikt. . . .

Mir — wemens odern, wemens harc hot noch geszlogn biz dem tog fun zun-ojfgang — wen ajer harc hot ojfn weg geplact.

Mir, mir kumen hajnt cu Ajch — in hunderter, tojanter, szarbns fun a folk, wos trogn ojf zich farflichtung un chojw kegn miljonen . . . A chojw wos lozt zich nyt arojszogn mit werter un nyt oncejchnen in mos, a chojw, welcher filt ojs undzer tojchn un lozt ojf kejn rega nyt fargesn wegn Ajch ....

Cwiszn di finger fun undzere hent grubn mir ajn far wejtik undzer ponim, far charpe iber a chojw, welchn mir hobn ajch nyt ojsgecolt ....

Ajer blut iz gechasmet far hafker — di sztrof far tojtn a folk iz nyt gekumen.' . . .

Ajere bejner zajnen nyt gekumen cu kejwer-Jisroel — wajt, wajt fun Erec-Jisroel . . .

Es brent nyt kejn fajer far dem umbakantn jidiszn held un martirer . . . .

Ajer denkmol iz der umbakanter denkmol unter der umbakanter fon . . .

Afile di dornike krojn nyt farginen . . .

5 Mk.

crucially, tributes to Zionism. In November 1947 the students took up the question of the proper language for the paper, with some insisting on Yiddish and others on German, arguing that the latter was important from the stand-point of the universities.[44] By the last issue in the winter of 1948, the newspaper compromised, with the first twelve pages printed in Yiddish (using Hebrew characters) and the remainder in German, with Polish dropping out entirely.[45]

The paper's editor, Roman Ohrenstein, described it as very "oriented to Israel." In early 1947 it published a statement of the solidarity of the "Academic Youth" with the 22d Zionist Congress in Basel, Switzerland.[46] The paper's consistent message, crafted by the passionate Zionists at its helm, was that the Union steered DP youth toward a productive path and that students' goals "when they finish their current studies [are] to work in Israel under any conditions and wherever they will be sent."[47]

For all the students' practical arguments and protestations of their Zionist loyalties, more complicated sentiments existed among them, rooted as much in experience as ideology. Union records include an unsigned letter, written in English in June 1947—just as tensions with Jewish leaders were exploding—and appealing for aid to an unspecified group of Jewish students in the United States. Explaining the need for aid, the letter conveys with uncommon depth the students' frustration and hurt:

> One has first to know the world in order to show anybody a new and better life, and this is perhaps the most important impulse, which induced us to study. . . . We have chosen this way with the deep hope that the time will come, when we will be recognized as a integral, positive part of the Judaism over here. . . . We have to describe why it was and still is possible, that Jews, who formerly were known as fanatics of science, parents of Jews, who sold their last property and ate dry bread to make their children's study possible now do not appreciate the studying youth. . . . The "Judische Gasse" (Jewish lane) is governed by the leaders of the Jewish agency, the first people in the American zone. As the emigration to be speeded up as much as possible, is the main point, and all other problems were replaced. Although a great part of us will go to Palestine, though being patriots, too, we have recognized that the time while sitting on our luggage . . . must not be lost, because we have already lost all the years of the war.[48]

The letter is a reminder of how young and vulnerable the students were: denied so much already, curious about the world, and not yet ready to join

234

the putative vanguard of a world-historical struggle—especially if it meant first being intercepted by the British en route to Palestine (and, perhaps for some, fighting an Arab "enemy" with whom they had no personal, historic quarrel). It also conveys how the contemporaneous denigration of academic study was at odds with the students' personal experiences of having grown up with the Jewish veneration of learning. According to Mark Hupert that regard survived among some Jewish DPs, who eagerly contributed to the Munich students' fundraisers. (The Heidelberg Union similarly raised money by holding balls and lotteries.)[49] Jewish tradition dictated that "you supported people who study. . . . The guy who is studying Torah, he didn't have to work."[50] The students' plight was evident to outsiders as well. In 1947 an American Joint official in the education division of the Frankfurt district, someone personally familiar with the students' travails, allowed, "The student groups, in the opinion of the writer, are a precious remnant of the intelligentsia of European Jewry, and their struggle to obtain higher education under the present adverse conditions in Germany must be encouraged and aided at every opportunity."[51]

The students' letter, along with Hupert's comments, suggest a psychosocial subtext to the students' often desperate pleas for official recognition and support, and their indignant sense of being wronged. Jewish survivors, as countless commentators have noted, were apt to feel a double betrayal: largely abandoned to the Nazi slaughter by the world's nations, they were then stranded in the land of their former oppressors, as the goal of settling in Palestine was initially thwarted. The students appeared to experience an additional betrayal, as the leaders of their community tried to undermine a path they had been raised to regard as valuable, even noble. Circumstance, one may speculate, compounded the students' bewilderment at the way they were regarded. Many were now orphans, so the Jewish authorities loomed especially large as societal parent figures and even caregivers. Yet for many students fulfilling the explicit wishes of their true parents meant disappointing—and even defying—their substitute elders. Craving the approval of the Jewish DP authorities, they sought to reconcile at once the values of their upbringing, their expectations of adult authority, their parents' legacy, their duty as Jews, and their wishes for their own futures.

"We Decided We Have to Do Something"

On May 21, 1947, the Munich Union's Executive Committee sent an urgent directive to the entire membership to protest the "hunger rations" the students were now receiving. The April allotment from the Munich Committee included only 319 Joint packets, although 405 students were in need of them.[52] The rations were missing jam and meat, and contained just 100 grams each of sugar and coffee, one kilogram of grapes, one tin of milk, two small tins of sardines, and two packs of cigarettes. The money for stipends (provided by the German state but doled out by the Munich Committee) had likewise diminished, while the clothing distribution had fallen to just fifty shirts and hats and ten winter coats (hardly needed as summer approached).[53] The Executive Committee refused to collect what it deemed a demeaning allotment and registered its "sharpest protest" with the relevant bodies, resorting also to sending a delegation to the Central Committee.[54]

The membership was now called on to act. A subsequent notice ordered all students to appear at the Union's office at 8 AM on May 27 to finalize plans for their protest. As the protest concerned "the very existence of the student community," students failing to show up would face "the severest consequences."[55]

The meager April aid brought to a head the increasingly volatile, and public, conflict between the students and key Jewish authorities. At the Munich Union's February general meeting, one student advocated "a more confrontational [*kämpferisch*] stand toward aid organizations, on account of their minimal support," while another counseled that they demand—and not merely ask—that such organizations fulfill their duty.[56] Soon thereafter the Union presented formal written demands in a letter to the Central Committee and the Munich Committee, which underscored demands they had made in "numerous, personal conversations." These involved the "inclusion of the students in the same worker category as the employees of the CK and Munich Committee," with appropriate rations of food and cigarettes; the expansion of stipends; the provision of academic books in German, better clothing, and an improved student facility, ideally one that would include a 500-seat lecture hall.[57] The letter blasted the "bluntly passive, indeed negative" attitude of Jewish DP officialdom toward the students. To close it noted that although the Second Conference of Liberated Jews in the American Zone had discussed the importance of raising the cultural level of DPs, the students were unable to make their demands at the gathering, because they had not been invited.[58] The zonewide union registered similar demands on behalf of students in other cities, adding the provision of a rest home (*Erholungsheim*) for those in poor health.[59]

The April–May edition of the student newspaper printed the Munich demands, along with a caustic article titled "The Idea of 'Productivity.'"[60] Aimed squarely at the Central Committee, it asserted: "If one makes the charge that the economist, the physiocrat has defined the idea of 'productivity' too narrowly, because they acknowledge only the cultivators of the land as the productive class, so can one also assert that among our aid organizations the idea has undergone a strange alteration and expansion: every form of work is defined as first, second, third or higher order productivity and earns special compensation. Not so the work of the students. The students, so it is argued, study only in their self-interest." After noting the obstacles put in the way of Commissioner Auerbach's and Alexander Pieckarczyk's sincere attempts to help them, the author asked: "Who will guarantee the minimum existence of the students, whose great majority are orphans?"[61]

Despite the students' long pleading for more aid, they had received just the opposite. Rafael Nenner, a key Union officer, recalls that for several months prior to April certain items and whole packets had gone missing, purloined by the Munich Committee. He had a dim view of the committee, describing it as self-serving businessmen and politicos who "had no need" for the students, wanted only their votes, and would spout "junk" about how Palestine had better doctors anyhow, precluding the need for more.[62] When the students first complained to the Munich Committee, he recalls, they were "laughed at" and referred to the Central Committee to take up their grievances.

The choking off of their aid in the spring of 1947 was an outrage to the students, but it did not come entirely as a surprise. Emanuel Tanay reports that at some prior point an official at the Jewish Agency asked to address the entire student membership, with a leading Joint official and Commissioner Auerbach also attending. "To our amazement the representative of the Jewish Agency told us it was shameful to be studying in Germany. . . . Instead, we should try to go to Palestine illegally. 'We don't need intelligentsia, we need chalutzim (Zionist pioneers to go to Palestine)' was the passionate ending of his speech."[63] Also in Tanay's account—with which some of the other students' recollections differ, and which is at odds with the public positions of the Joint and Auerbach's commission—the Joint official warned that in the future the students would not be receiving aid packages, while Auerbach made similar threats to withhold support.[64] Whether referring to this or other episodes, Sabina Zimering recalls that speakers "would come to our union that made us feel ashamed . . . [for] staying in Germany for selfish reasons, to study, instead of going to Israel, to Palestine."[65] The message, as she heard it, was not that the students should finish their professional training in Israel; rather, they should give up that training for good in service of a higher goal. Philip Balaban similarly remembers the Jewish Agency advising that the students "should join the Zionist organizations and try to work the fields."[66]

Indeed, the well-established aim of the CK and the Jewish Agency was to encourage DPs' migration. Such migrations, known collectively as "Aliyah

Bet" and organized largely under the auspices of the Bricha, sought both to bolster the Jewish population in Palestine and, as the world's powers debated the Palestine question, to create irreversible momentum toward Jewish nationhood.[67] The explicit purpose of the various youth movement groups and the *kibbutzim* they organized was to prepare pioneers, ideologically and physically, for *aliyah*. To prompt Jewish flight, the CK and the Jewish Agency made fervent appeals to DPs' patriotic duty and exerted various forms of pressure. The withholding of aid, Patt reports, was one such measure, broadly applied when formal military conscription among DPs began in the winter and spring of 1948.[68] The cuts in the students' aid appear to be an early instance of this tactic.

The timing appears powerfully related to context—chiefly the crisis into which Zionist efforts were slipping. Patt describes the first part of 1947 as a period of increasing demoralization among DPs, and prospective pioneers especially, as they languished in occupied Germany.[69] The numbers of those even able to attempt *aliyah* were severely restricted, limited by Jews' financial resources and logistical capacities and, most of all, by British policy that all but prohibited passage to Palestine. Those internally cleared for illegal *aliyah* might spend months just trying to leave the American Zone. If one did make it onto a vessel, it would most likely be intercepted by a British blockade, with its passengers then held indefinitely in Cyprus.[70] Kibbutz members who made it to Palestine were sometimes split up upon arrival, severing the bonds they had made while living collectively. And life in Palestine could be challenging, given the inhospitable landscape, hard pioneering work, and armed conflict with the Arab population. For all these reasons, *aliyah* might appear to DPs—and not just the students—to be a poor option, causing them to consider other emigration possibilities, even if *Eretz Yisrael* was their ultimate goal. Changes in the DP demographic further strained pioneering efforts. The Jews flooding into the American Zone from Eastern Europe included many either too young or too old to make *aliyah*; intact families loath to split up or face the hardships of Palestine; unaccompanied, but not orphaned, young people unwilling to separate so fully from their parents; and families who, even if joining *kibbutzim*, lacked the "pioneering spirit."

One may speculate that the pressure put on the students in the spring of 1947 was part of an effort to revitalize the push for *aliyah* just as Jewish leaders feared Zionist enthusiasm was waning. Notwithstanding their resistance, the students were ideal candidates for recruitment insofar as they were young, energetic, (mostly) able-bodied, without children, often emphatically Zionist, and highly functional. If born of a sense of despair, the pressure may have also been pegged to a moment of hope within the Zionist cause. In a much-anticipated decision, on May 15, 1947, the General Assembly of the newly formed United Nations created a committee (the UN Special Committee on Palestine) to take up the question of Palestine, spurring Jewish hopes that the UN would recommend partition and the de facto creation of a Jewish state. Finally, power struggles within the DP world, themselves implicated in Zionist politicking, may have been at play in determinations of the students' support. At around the time when the students' packages were diminishing, the Central Committee asserted greater control over the distribution of aid to Munich's Jews. Presumably trying to encourage *aliyah*, it scaled back support even to those who were ill, pregnant women, and nursing mothers.[71]

The Union chose to protest on May 27 by taking over the Joint's offices, an elegant compound on Sieberstrasse, while sending a smaller contingent to seize CK offices on Möhlstraße. In what one alumnus referred to as an "Italian strike" (a kind of labor action), several hundred students in effect held the Joint officials hostage and remained in the office until their demands were met.[72] As Tanay recounts, "A contingent of boys surrounded the building. An American military police vehicle in front of the building made us reluctant to storm the place. I climbed a tree and watched the villa, which was surrounded by high shrubs. Once the police vehicle departed, we entered the offices and forced our way into the [Joint] Director's office. He was told that we were not leaving until he cancelled the order depriving the students of the packages."[73] Turmoil ensued. "'I am calling the MPs, you better leave at once,' he yelled in Yiddish, and reached for the phone on his desk. 'No you are not,' I answered and ripped the phone cord off the wall. A few other fellows approached him in a threatening manner, letting him know that he should not get out of his chair. . . . He expressed his willingness to talk to Silverman, our president, if the 'hooligans' left his office."[74] Near-simultaneously, the offices of the CK also were occupied.

Perhaps the students' greatest leverage was the fact that they'd put the Jewish officials in a bind. "What are they going [to do]?" Ohrenstein asked. "Call German police to remove us? That would have been the biggest scandal in the world"—and something the students could surely publicize in the Jewish press.[75] Rafael Nenner recalls that several of the students were in fact arrested and held overnight.[76] But the students agreed to keep quiet about this fact as a bargaining chip in the tense negotiations.

The Union came with specific demands written in Yiddish and directed to "the Presidium of the Central Committee."[77] This suggests that the CK was dictating the newly harsh stance toward the students and that the Joint, if it was even fully aware of the reduction in aid, had been following the

CK's lead. As the source of aid, the Joint, however, had ultimate authority to override the CK. The students insisted that the committee "create a workers' category for students that meets their need for room, board, and clothing"; secure a student residence with work rooms; provide textbooks; and guarantee "a monthly stipend in the sum of 200 RM for the students who are not as of yet recognized by the State Commissioner [Auerbach] as 'political and racial persecutees.'" The text also listed stipulations the CK must accept, chiefly that "the students as future members of the intelligentsia are an important element in the Jewish people's existence." Asserting with a heavy hand the CK's paternal responsibilities, another stipulation held that "by not fulfilling the aforementioned demands, there is a danger that the students will quit their studies and resort to means of subsidy through undesirable channels."[78]

The CK was clearly angered by the audacious action, calling it in an official communiqué "brutal," "immoral," and "irresponsible."[79] The CK reported that it refused to negotiate with the students so long as the occupation of its office persisted; they wanted to demonstrate that nothing would be accomplished by coercive means. In their official account the students indeed relented and left the CK premises, after which dialogue took place.[80]

Whatever the particular sequence and dealings, the action proved successful with respect to the students' core demand. To end the daylong takeover at the Joint offices, Mr. Piekacz, a CK representative, issued a statement. After declaring the students "a productive group," he assured them that they "will be integrated into a work category that will allow every student to live a decent existence" (indeed, "on par" with Mr. Piekacz's own as a CK official).[81] Hammering out the details, however, proved difficult, with the students complaining of being marginalized in the deliberations. In the meantime, something of a public relations battle took place. The Jewish newspapers, several alumni recall, generally denounced the student action in its immediate wake. The Union, for its part, held an open house at the Isartorplatz café on June 10, where the Jewish public could enjoy a buffet and dance music while gaining a positive impression of the students.[82]

On June 18 the Munich Union proudly announced to its members that an agreement had been struck.[83] It mandated that the students would be placed in a worker category, qualifying for a "50 percent ration" (half of what a CK officer received); that twenty students (Union officers or those "socially active") would receive additional payment "in kind" for their service; and that the CK would make efforts to secure stipends from the State's Commission for students not currently receiving them. If those efforts failed, the CK was to cover the stipends. The Union also issued an apology of sorts to the

CK, declaring the protest a "happy and joyful event [that] bore no aggressive character. It casts no judgment on the C.K. . . . whose authority we respect." It further communicated that "if it so happened that there were individuals who behaved irresponsibly," they would be disciplined in-house.[84] The Union members who did not participate in the protest were merely docked a pack of cigarettes.[85]

The zonewide federation made gains as well as a result of the protest. In July it was agreed that students everywhere would be eligible for the new rations and that the CK would cover the administrative costs of all Union chapters, as well as fund a student initiative to obtain texts from German booksellers. The federation credited the increasingly favorable press coverage of the "student problem" with doing "much to change the formerly negative behavior of our officials."[86] By midsummer, many students in the American Zone were now receiving increased rations from the Joint.[87]

Student complaints of insufficient food, shabby clothing, and poor housing persisted, with acute hunger still a problem for some. Even after the student strike, Roman Ohrenstein was hospitalized briefly in the winter of 1948 for cold and malnutrition, and begged to stay at the facility so he could receive warm meals.[88] (He was also, he confessed, honest to a fault in consuming only provisions to which he was strictly entitled.) In its appeals for aid to Jewish students worldwide, such as the Brighton address at the end of the summer of 1947, the Union still spoke about making up the deficit caused by the Jewish authorities' weak support. Yet the strike had put the students on sounder material footing while making a powerful statement. The students had engaged in a high-stakes mass protest against the most important Jewish institutions in occupied Germany. They won at least grudging acceptance for the validity of their pursuits. Historian Juliane Wetzel concluded, "Above all, in moral hindsight, the [student action] can be described as a success, because the student community showed courage in consciously fighting for its rights."[89] In the recollection of the alumni, the protest was a moment of catharsis, both reflecting and deepening the solidarity among them. Speaking of the action, Rafael Nenner stressed, "We really were together. We liked each other, really liked each other . . . [and] we decided we have to do something."[90] They did.

"Somebody Trusted Me, Somebody Wanted Me, Somebody Cared"

The strike victory softened but did not resolve the students' dilemma over how long to stay in Germany. That dilemma sharpened again as the goal of a Jewish state grew closer to, and then became, a reality. In July 1947 the saga of the *Exodus*—a ship of Jews travelling from France to Palestine which the British intercepted and sent to Germany, to great public outcry—brought unprecedented international sympathy for the plight of DPs and the Zionist struggle more broadly. In September 1947 the UN Committee recommended the partition of Palestine into separate Jewish and Arab states, with the General Assembly endorsing the plan in late November. Though the plan was rejected by the relevant Arab bodies, Jews widely heralded its acceptance by the UN as the definitive step toward statehood, with spontaneous celebrations breaking out in the DP camps. The mobilization of DPs—to emigrate and ultimately to fight—intensified. As early as the winter of 1947–48, the Haganah, the official army of the emerging Jewish state, put out a special call among DPs for volunteers to fight in Palestine. After months of irregular battle between Jewish and Arab forces, and just on the eve of the expiration of the British Mandate, David Ben-Gurion declared on May 14, 1948, the establishment of the State of Israel. The Arab-Israeli War, regarded by Jews as a war of independence, immediately began.

These developments changed the equation for the students. It was one thing for them to resist suspending their studies—under duress from DP organizations—in order to migrate illegally to a land with a highly unsettled political reality. It was another to insist on staying in the face of the Jewish Agency's urgent call for service, when the state of Israel was in decisive formation and a war for its early survival was taking place. After May 1948 the US lifted restrictions on emigration from the American Zone to Palestine (with the brief exception of June to August), making *aliyah* much more viable.

If the students had to that point struggled chiefly with other DPs to validate their decision to study in Germany, they now wrestled internally—in their own organization and within themselves—over what to do. The dominant rhetorical position of the Union had been that Palestine, whether initially or ultimately, was overwhelmingly their desired destination. The undated Union letter to Albert Einstein indicated, "Were it possible for us to emigrate to Palestine . . . that would be an ideal solution. Should this not be possible, we appeal to you and Jewish authorities . . . to be brought to another country . . . where we could finish our studies and later go to Palestine."[91] In the face of pressure, some students held fast to their intention to get their degrees first, and then see what the future brought (including the possibility of a speedy exit to Palestine/Israel). Others chose to stay yet agonized over the decision, wondering if it made them less than true patriots. Finally, a tiny but determined minority dropped their studies and heeded the call for *aliyah*. This range shows both the power and the limits of postwar

Zionism, how circumstances comingled but also sometimes chafed with ideology in shaping individual DPs' preferences and decisions.

The Jewish students had long been on record as supporting a Jewish state. In April 1947, to whatever effect, they had sent a telegram to the United Nations Secretary-General, encouraging the international body to take up the issue of statehood.[92] A circular produced by the zonewide union reported on the telegram and instructed all chapters to help organize demonstrations in support of statehood.[93] The fall and early winter of 1947 was the high-water mark of the students' Zionist activism and the period of their greatest harmony with Jewish authorities. A zonewide union directive in November announced that the "sole solution to the Jewish problem and, along with it, the future of Jewish academics ultimately lies in Erec-Israel."[94] The students sponsored two high-profile events that both reflected the Zionist enthusiasm of the organizers and served to demonstrate, in the wake of the strike and in the midst of Israel's early creation, the Union's Zionist commitment. The first, held on November 7 at Munich's Bayerischer Hof (a theater hall), was a celebratory ceremony for the Gdud-Awoda, a short-lived, left-wing Zionist organization that sought to aid Jewish settlements in Palestine, and which operated in conjunction with Karen Kayemet LeYisrael, the Jewish National Fund. The event, as described in the DP newspaper *Unzer Welt*, "marked the debut of the Jewish students within the realm of national civil work." (Their tree-planting campaign in the following weeks was carried out with the Gdud-Awoda.) An impressive roster of officials attended, among them Mr. Piekacz from the CK, leading Sochnut, Joint, and Gdud-Awoda representatives, and Munich Committee head Hersch Schwimmer. The event concluded with a performance by She'erith Hapleitah, the orchestra of the CK.[95]

The second event was held on December 19 at the same venue. Organized this time by the zonewide federation, and attended by six hundred students from many cities, it was a robust Zionist rally just after the UN endorsed the partition plan.[96] The rally was prompted by the angry reaction to the UN decision by Arab students in Cairo, who rallied by the thousands to condemn the prospects of a Jewish state and pledged to fight to defeat it. At their event the Jewish students denounced the Arabs' "hooligan activities" while "appeal[ing] to the true Arab student and intelligentsia to find a unified way to work together and achieve a mutual understanding." In this they proffered an idealized—and naïve—sense of the power of academic fellowship to transcend deep divisions of identity, outlook, and interest. In addressing their Arab counterparts, they also sought to highlight their specific utility, as students, to the Zionist cause.

The recitation of the resolutions passed by the students met with "stormy applause." The students declared their support of the *Yishuv*, called on Jewish students everywhere to help create a Jewish state, and pledged to mobilize all their forces to build a united, nonpartisan front to achieve the goals of Zionism. The program, conducted in Hebrew, Yiddish, English, and French, was attended by an elite group of representatives from the occupation world: officials from the US military and French and Yugoslav consulates; Commissioner Auerbach and Chairman Schwimmer; representatives of youth movement organizations; a leading Sochnut official; and the chairman of the CK. The last two highlighted, respectively, the importance of the intelligentsia to the future of the Jewish state and the students' "readiness to serve" the Zionist struggle. The program concluded with the singing of "Hatikvah."

Internally, the Union supported, at least rhetorically, the preparation of its members for life in Palestine/Israel. Documents on the founding of its sports club in the winter of 1947–48 suggest that part of the group's goal was physical preparation for *aliyah*.[97] Further, a Union circular to all local chapters declared it a "pressing duty to support [the students'] learning of the Hebrew language.[98]

These displays of Zionist solidarity, while capturing the general spirit among the students, conceal a more complicated reality with respect to their investment in Zionism and, under their current circumstances, what they were prepared to do to support it. In this they mirrored—albeit from their distinctive standpoint—Jewish DPs as a whole. Among displaced Jews, Zionist sympathy was near-universal but did not necessarily translate into DPs' joining the Jewish state in Palestine at its inception.

The students' backgrounds and experiences inclined them to a range of sentiments. Some students, among the leadership especially, had grown up in Zionist households and long dreamed of settling in Palestine. They were most likely to pursue emigration to Palestine as their singular goal after the war. This describes the case for Josef Silberman, the Munich Union's founder. Yehuda Knobler, another of the Union's leaders and a dedicated Zionist, later eulogized Silberman by saying, "With his mother's milk Josef nursed the living value of national redemption. Songs of Zion, horahs, rousing speeches—this was his sustenance from childhood until the end of his life."[99] Though describing his father as "apolitical" (while giving financial support to the Revisionist movement), Eugene Miller had been part of the left-wing Hashomer Hatzair youth movement in Lodz, Poland. A survivor of Auschwitz, he served as the president of the Frankfurt Jewish Students' Union in 1947–48.[100]

Zionism, often nurtured from childhood, permeated the student cohort. Ziona Oberman, who joined the chemistry program at the LMU in 1947, was from a left-Zionist household in Lwow, and indeed named in honor of Zionism.[101] Surviving the war as a hidden child, she and her parents first entered occupied Germany in order "to go to Israel," which remained her ardent wish while a student. Mark Fintel had been part of Zionist youth groups in Rovno. He recalls feeling as a student, "It was clear that our road will lead us to Israel, to Palestine." First enrolling in the mechanical engineering program, he soon switched to civil engineering, reasoning that "in Israel construction will be a major kind of field."[102] Some students, in short, took seriously the Union creed that their study in Germany prepared them to serve a future Jewish state.

A small handful of the students had fought with Zionist cells as partisans during the war. Michael Okunieff grew up in Vilna, where he was a member of left-wing and centrist Zionist youth groups.[103] Surviving the liquidation of the Vilna ghetto in September 1943, he fled to the Rudniki forest, where he joined the partisans and fought for a time with the now-fabled Abba Kovner group. In July 1944 he was among the first fighters working with the Red Army to liberate Vilna. After the war he pursued medical studies at the University of Vilna, where he was one of only four Jews. Okunieff also worked to protect Jews from Polish attacks and aided their passage through Western Europe toward Palestine. In 1946, given his "preparation and experience" as a former partisan, he was selected by Bricha leaders to lead a large group of children on a perilous mountain trek to Czechoslovakia, even as they were shot at by nationalist Poles. From there he went on to Munich, enrolling as a medical student.

Other students became immersed in Zionist culture and longings after the war. In her mid-teens when the war ended, Cessia Hupert was first placed, along with her brother, in a Zionist-run orphanage/kibbutz in Eastern Europe, even though her parents were still alive. The group made it to Bavaria, with her parents following behind. The "orphanage," she recalls, "made Zionists out of us"; she soon wished "more than [her] life [to settle in a] Jewish country," where Jews would be "real people." Her brother was among the many DP kibbutz members on the *Exodus*.[104] Later making it to Israel on an illegal *aliyah*, he fought in the army and suffered a near-fatal battle wound in the 1948 war.

Others still affiliated with particular Zionist parties. Shortly after the war Rafael Nenner fell in with Betar organizers, initially enticed by the extra bread they offered as well as the prospect of quickly becoming a commandant.

While a student he engaged in clandestine military training, helped publish the underground Betar newspaper *Only by the Sword*, and worked to bring party members from occupied Germany to Palestine. His activism underscores both the Zionist passion of some DPs and how the prospect of greater aid and a little prestige could shape one's loyalties. Betar was extremely controversial within Zionism by virtue of its hard line toward the British and the Arabs, its belief in armed struggle as the sole path to statehood, and its militaristic culture. Nenner later chalked up becoming a "Betar man" to being "young" and "stupid," because the group, as he viewed it in hindsight, was "a terrible thing," with fascist tendencies "like Mussolini."

The most remarkable example of postwar Zionist involvement among the students was that of his cousin, Robert Nenner—the young man so terribly abused in Buchenwald and other places. His case shows how the Holocaust could induce a militant postwar Zionism in which the fight for a Jewish state, directed centrally against the British and the Arabs, was an explicit response to Europe's brutalization of Jews. It also shows, given his expressed fondness for his classmates and love of university life, how hard some students worked to balance their academic and Zionist commitments.

In our interview Nenner first mentioned his work with Irgun Zvai Leumi—an elusive and deeply divisive guerrilla organization with close ties to the Revisionist movement—just after testifying to the wrenching guilt of doing nothing for his fellow human being while he was a concentration camp inmate. In an abrupt shift in his somber narration, he recalled meeting by chance, while already a student in Munich, a representative of an Irgun network into which he had been loosely recruited. As if in a scene from a Hollywood thriller, the man, who wore an eyepatch, discreetly addressed Nenner's reflection in a store mirror: "You don't want to know me, because I'm now here on a mission. . . . I have to [make them] pay for what they did to us. And if you hear [that] something happened in the British Zone, that was me."[105] Two days later, reports Nenner, a train with British ammunition destined for Palestine was attacked, with the man dying as a result. "From that point on," Nenner recalls, he "got very active in the Irgun Zvai Leumi movement," as if to honor the sacrifice of this man, who himself had sought to avenge the Holocaust dead. By the terms of this cathartic episode, Nenner's activism and support for Zionist violence was in part an effort to expiate his own shame.

Nenner's initial recruitment had taken place months earlier as he searched for his parents in Krakow and then in Prague, where several Irgun members sidled up to him, expressing optimism that he would find his family. For the first time in years, "somebody trusted me, somebody wanted me, somebody cared." Later in the Ainring DP camp (where he found his parents), he was instructed by a deserter from the Jewish Brigade to continue on as a student in Munich, which would be "good cover" for clandestine work. Of his recruitment he explained, "They knew I wanted to get even with the Germans. . . . I really wanted the Jewish state because I felt that I don't belong in anything. Dispersed, my origin was dispersed. My identity, I didn't have [one]."

For more than two years, Nenner headed a cell whose task was to facilitate the passage to Palestine of high-ranking military officers from the Soviet Union, Poland, Hungary, and Czechoslovakia. This work brought him into the shadowy world of various undergrounds. Part of his job was to force the cooperation of ex-Nazi border officials by threatening to reveal their pasts or even by physically threatening their families. He claims to have had the help of US counterintelligence officials—American Christians who aided Zionism because they felt "the Jews have suffered enough." He took great satisfaction in this work, aspects of which he conceded were "not so nice" from an ethical standpoint.

For Nenner, simply being a student pledged to the Jewish future was an inadequate way to support Zionism. Neither did he feel the center-left Jewish Agency, which at times fiercely battled the Irgun on ideological and strategic grounds, was doing enough. To him his work with the Jewish Agency under an official position of Zionist unity was "good cover," but it did not "give me the impetus to say 'I'm living now.'" Impressed with the kibbutz and Haganah members, he nonetheless viewed them as "soft on everything." He saw Irgun—notwithstanding its reputation as terroristic and for carrying out periodic, grisly acts—as "much more devoted [and] aggressive, [which] was important to me. . . . I didn't want to be a patsy anymore, I survived and I want[ed] to do something for the people who died." To the extent that Arabs suffered Irgun violence, they were in part both victims of Jewish anger toward their European persecutors and displaced sacrificial objects, against whom aggression, in the minds of some of their adversaries, would help avenge the Holocaust dead. Throughout his tenure as a student, he kept his involvement with Irgun a secret, entirely unknown to his classmates.[106]

Robert Nenner was at the extreme end of Zionist commitment among the students. More commonly, the students believed in the value and necessity of a Jewish state, with some resolving to join it when they were ready. Instead of longing for Israel, however, some students—perhaps those with relatives already in the United States—were captivated at an early age by the idea of America and hoped to settle there after the war. Others had only a broad vision of life beyond their studies, with no particular attachment to place. Of this constituency, Rubin Zimering allowed, "Our interest was in getting on with our studies, finish and get a degree and settle someplace in the world where it's possible to make a peaceful, decent life." Still other students were adamant in defending their autonomy of choice. Denouncing the efforts of the CK and others "to ship us away to Palestine," Imek Metzger asserted, "They had no right to decide our future for us."[107]

The students were also differentiated by degrees of political interest. Some participated heatedly in the key debates of the moment, chiefly over how best to support Zionism and what politics should reign in a Jewish state. Battling for adherents and prestige, the various youth movement groups solicited the Union for its endorsement. As individual students formed loyalties and factions developed, the Union struggled to maintain basic unity in its ranks. Late in 1947 Knobler cautioned that its "social activities can be only broadly nationalistic and must remain non-partisan."[108]

Other students paid only marginal attention to politics. (By reputation, those in the very demanding engineering program at the Technische Hochschule were the least political.) Even as the Union ramped up its Zionist activism, the leadership still complained of "apathy," evident, for example, in the poor student turnout for an "*Exodus* demonstration" in the fall of 1947.[109] United in their academic drive, the students remained divided, as Israeli statehood approached, over how best to serve both their own and the collective Jewish futures.

"We Couldn't Have Good Arguments"

Having fended off pressure to quit their studies in the first half of 1947, the students again faced the question of *aliyah* in the early winter and spring of 1948. Specifically, the Sochnut, supported by the Central Committee, called on male and female Jewish DPs of eligible age to join the Haganah to participate in the escalating fight with the British and, centrally, the Arabs in Palestine. The mobilization, termed in Hebrew the *giyus* (often written in Union documents as *Gius*), combined a call for volunteers with a weak version of a compulsory military draft.[110] The initial appeal, beginning perhaps shortly after the UN recommendation of statehood in November 1947, was for willing recruits; its draft rhetoric stressed Jews' duty to support a Jewish state. By early spring an apparatus developed to administer, and ideally force, conscription. An independent state would mean the fulfillment of decades of Zionist longing, self-determination and (relative) safety for Jews, and an answer to the DP problem. Long seeking *aliyah*, kibbutz and youth movement members responded with the greatest enthusiasm.

Desire to join the fight was, however, far from universal among Jewish DPs. As with their prior resistance to illegal *aliyah*, some DPs did not want to risk breaking up their families, or wished to emigrate elsewhere, or feared being stranded in Cyprus, or were leery of the hardships of Palestine. And some could not bear the thought of another war. Lacking the standard means of a proper nation-state to force compliance (ultimately, jailing resisters), the Jewish Agency and its allies concocted other ways to sanction "shirkers." These included withholding their aid, removing them from employment, and, in an act of public shaming, publishing their names in DP newspapers.[111] At the same time Jewish authorities scrambled to carve out exemptions for categories of DPs, such as single parents and those in poor health. Organized haphazardly and under trying circumstances, the mobilization was a qualified success, yielding 13,000 DP fighters between May and November 1948, including 8,000 from Germany.[112]

As early as January 1948, the students debated how best to aid the recruitment of volunteers among its members, weighing personal appeals against using simple "circulars" (*Rundschreiben*) to publicize their goals.[113] By early spring the Union was contending with the *demand* to join the fight, as Jewish associations were tasked with ensuring their members' registration with the *giyus* and compliance with its requirements. After meeting with *giyus* officials in April 1948, the Executive Committee of the zonewide federation explained to the chapters: "All Jews among the *She'erith Hapleitah* who are ages 17–35 are to register for the *giyus*. Therefore, all of the members of the Jewish student unions, if they fall within these ages, are to register. By means of individual applications, the local draft commission can exempt students who are in their last or second-to-last semesters. . . . We regard it as an urgent task of the Executive Committee of local unions to see to it that all members without exception go to the draft commission."[114] Individual unions honored the directive, generating lists of *giyus* registrants as well as those requesting exemptions.[115]

For the students, however, the great drama of the mobilization had first played out some months earlier, when they faced the call to volunteer. Roman Ohrenstein recalls when the entire Munich membership met—datable from a Union record to January 12, 1948—to vote on the suggestion of Yehuda Knobler and others that they quit their studies en masse and volunteer.[116] The stakes, in his mind, were huge. Fearful of the likely tally and its damage to the students' legacy, he "warned Knobler" not to hold a vote because "it will appear, in terms of history . . . that the Jewish students refused to go." In a decision that was not binding for individual students, the group voted almost unanimously to stay in Germany.

Though no archival record exists detailing the students' collective decision, the tenor of the debate can be gleaned from the alumni's reminiscences

The cover of Roman Ohrenstein's Certificate of Registration with the Jewish Agency (Sochnut), issued in Bavaria in April 1948. (Courtesy of Roman Ohrenstein)

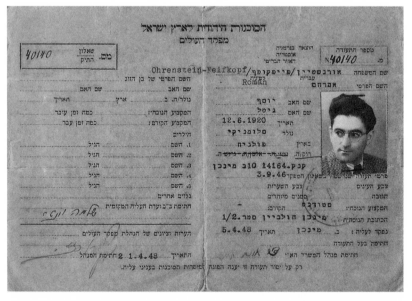

The interior of Roman Ohrenstein's Certificate of Registration with the Jewish Agency. (Courtesy of Roman Ohrenstein)

and other Union documents. In them one can observe both the pull of post-war Zionism and how DPs' individual circumstances and predilections conditioned their choices. Philip Balaban, the young bookworm who had spent the war in Soviet exile, recalls the students' core desire "to be professionals" as decisive in their resisting pressure from the CK and Jewish Agency in 1947. Soon the pressure came from within their ranks, led by Knobler, who left for Palestine in January 1948 shortly after the Union vote. "They were screaming, 'We shouldn't study, we should go home. . . . We should . . . fight for our land . . . otherwise we will die over here." To this plea, Balaban conceded, "We didn't have an answer. . . . We just didn't go. . . . We couldn't have good arguments." He elaborated, "Many people didn't want to go to Palestine . . . [and were] always planning to go to United States." *Aliyah* would likely mean time stranded in Cyprus and dim prospects, especially if without sponsorship in Israel, for ever continuing one's studies.[117] Of his own decision, he said, "I wanted to be a professional, no matter what, because that's what my mother taught me." Balaban confessed that he and others nonetheless felt guilty for not going. Asked if his choice seemed like a betrayal, he answered, "I felt that [Knobler is] a hero. I'm not."

Sabina Zimering reasoned that immigration to Israel would make "medicine just out of the question. And I think that's vastly been the feeling of most of us. If we wanted to get a degree, Germany, as much as we didn't want to be there, was the only realistic place to be. Because if we went to Israel, we'd be in a kibbutz." The choice "made me feel bad. . . . I thought well, why not wait the two years that I still have left and then go. . . . The idealists did go to Israel. They thought that this is higher priority for them than their own personal career and future." Mark Hupert, granted a draft exemption on account of his tuberculosis, recalls his fellow students saying, "[We should] finish and then go to Israel, more advantage for Israel to have people who are educated and have trades and doctors and engineers." For him, having suffered the last, gruesome days of Dachau, "[it] was very hard to decide, especially after what you just survive[d], the war, to drop everything again and go."

Other students admonished their colleagues. In March 1948 an uncommonly positional report from the leaders of the zonewide union declared, "When the student demurs or outright rejects the call to fight for our coming homeland—to give up comforts, however modest—and dedicate his life [this way], then the Jewish student community is not on the right path. . . . Conscience is the first duty of the student, diligent work and education follow, but each student must show that he is a Jew first and a student second."[118] This is a fascinating judgment in the life of the Union, which had

long insisted on the essential unity between one's Jewish and student identities; but here, in a moment of perceived emergency, the two are placed in
tension, with the higher calling made clear.

A second statement, likely penned by the same author or authors in late
November 1948, amplifies such criticisms. The authors first note that, during
the term covered by the report, the state of Israel had been founded. Its military victory in the war fills "every Jew on earth with happiness and pride."
"Each must ask himself: what did I do to bring it about? What was my sacrifice. [Opposite the fighters in Palestine] stand all those Jews—above all the
youth and especially the students—who made during this time the decision
to diligently pursue their *Ausbildung* but did not with heart and soul contribute to this great goal. They cannot put off an embarrassing self-examination."
The statement is telling in its construction. Upbraiding their peers for weak
Zionist commitment, the authors themselves had chosen not to join the
fight and instead to remain students. Further, for all the students' Zionist
defense of bookish pursuits, military sacrifice is held up as the apex of nationalist commitment. The guilt the authors counsel others to feel appears to
mask poorly their own. Still defending the choice to study in Germany, the
statement later pleads that the students must find a way, through a strengthened cultural program, to contribute to the Jewish collective.

A student newspaper essay was likewise caustic with respect to the students' Zionist commitments. Exhorting the students to action, it declared
that to "lose ourselves [in the] auditorium or laboratory . . . would be a crime
against our conscience and our people."[119] In the next breath, it complained
of weak Zionist commitment, aside from a flurry of activity to protest Arab
students' opposition to a Jewish state. Even that reaction was wanting: "Arab
students in Cairo shouted 'Let's go to Palestine! We will defend the land
against the Jews!' Did Jewish students behave [by comparison] honorably?"
The piece concluded that, "In the history of the few survivors, our chapter
will be a poor one." Ambivalence and even anguish with respect to Zionist
duty, in sum, continued to haunt some of the students.

Despite this handwringing, other students matched their Zionist rhetoric with action. Indeed, Knobler set a standard of heroism for many alumni
and looms iconic in their memories. Balaban recalls him as a scrappy young
man who, already bald at a young age, "knew he had to fight." Fighting
first on behalf of the Union against the CK, and then becoming a pioneer,
Knobler later struggled for greater acknowledgment for Holocaust survivors in Israel. The attitude of the *Yishuv*, as Balaban recalls from his own
time in Israel in the late 1940s and 1950s, was, "We are building a country,
we are a new generation . . . a new people, actually"; they looked down on

Holocaust survivors as people who "never fought." Knobler, finishing his chemistry studies in Israel, battled in the Knesset (Israel's parliament) for Yom Hashoah, the national day of recognition for the Holocaust dead and for survivors.

Given Knobler's stature in the group, it was with a special sense of expectation that Bella Brodzki and I met him, on a rare Israeli day of driving rainstorms, in his Tel Aviv apartment in the winter of 2004. Knobler was the last of the Union's living founders, as well as the last of those who made *aliyah* early in 1948; our encounter thus felt like a communion with both the origins of the student community and Israel's founding generation.[120]

In functional English impaired by a stroke, he shared his experiences as an inmate at Mauthausan, as a student in Munich, and as a pioneer in Palestine with exuberant intensity, as if to convey a legacy nearly lost to history. While casting no aspersions in our interview on those who finished their studies in Germany, he carefully wrote for us in Hebrew the names of the three students—Ze'ev Sachs, Adam Mandel, and Tavya Greenhauser—who joined him on *aliyah*. Knobler, though deep into his studies and loyal to a group he helped found, in essence left everything behind within weeks or even days of his decision to go. The group, still migrating illegally, was intercepted and sent to Cyprus, where they spent a year or so, effectively missing the war for which they had volunteered. Given this delay some students, having finished their studies, arrived in Israel at around the same time.

For Knobler his *aliyah* was not a repudiation of his student existence and Union arguments about the importance of the intelligentsia but instead an affirmation of them. On his journey to Palestine he was intent on adding an intellectual influence among his fellow boat passengers; elaborating, he recited the adage, "It takes only a little spice to flavor the soup." Knobler was given a special commendation by the Union, which he saved in his records, in March 1949 (perhaps for his use in Israel and to enhance the Union's standing). It read, "Jehuda Knobler in January 1948 interrupted his studies and in conjunction with the *giyus* left for Israel with the first transport of volunteers. Colleague Knobler led all the Zionist actions carried out by our union. As the first volunteer with the *giyus*, he serves as an example for many others to follow."[121]

Also fascinating was our dialogue with Roman Ohrenstein—Knobler's close friend and likewise a dedicated Zionist—about the students' decision to stay. Though defending the decision's validity, he remained anguished, all these decades later, at having abandoned Zionism in its hour of greatest need. At the mere mention of those who first made *aliyah*, he remarked, "I apologize and bow my head before them." He quickly offered, when discussing the draft, to show documentation of his exemption. And he resolutely refused to describe the pressure put on the students to leave as "Zionist coercion" or to categorically denounce the Jewish authorities in hindsight. Their message to the DP Jews, as he could also see it, was, "You're a vagabond again, they've locked you in. What are you going to [do], be with the Germans? What are they going to do with you? . . . [T]his has to be taken into consideration and not to condemn 'Zionist pressure.' It was a completely different order," in which concerns for long-term Jewish survival were paramount.

Further complicating the students' decision was a dynamic common among DPs. For some, although the Zionist struggle and the idea of Israel might be dearly important, other emigration options proved superior. Jewish DPs' strong preference was to settle in Palestine/Israel. The lion's share of Jewish DPs in fact migrated there, going in great numbers after the advent of the Israeli state and the easing of British immigration restrictions. From July 1948 to 1949, 86,000—or 72 percent—of the 120,000 Jews leaving Germany, Austria, and Italy made *aliyah*.[122] Parsing a complex statistical picture, Myers Feinstein estimates that a total of 177,000 Jewish DPs went to Palestine/Israel between the end of the war and 1952.

But nearly 135,000 others during this period went elsewhere, with roughly 100,000 immigrating to the United States. (The Displaced Persons Act of 1948, amended in 1950, greatly facilitated such migration.) Avinoam Patt, in a work that stresses DPs' Zionist dedication, asserts that by 1947, with efforts at *aliyah* largely bogged down, DPs were forced to consider other emigration options. Further he concedes that, "had immigration to the United States been a realistic option after the war, it is quite conceivable that a majority of Jewish DPs would have made the choice to move there."[123] Both he and Myers Feinstein suggest that the Sochnut and the CK overestimated DP enthusiasm for *aliyah*, especially in the context of the draft.[124] Finally, in judging the volunteer effort to have been a failure, some scholars assert that Zionists (largely from Palestine) manipulated the memory of the Holocaust among DPs to stress martial values and all but forced *aliyah* for some by applying sharply coercive measures under the auspices of the draft.[125]

The students, in the main, were long open to emigration opportunities other than Palestine, at least in the near term. In its outreach to Jewish students and institutions outside of Germany, the Union sought to place its members in fellowships for university study and possible permanent settlement abroad. The aforementioned Hillel scholarships for study in the United States proved, however, the only viable option (though a small handful of students did manage to study elsewhere in Europe). By the end of 1946, forty-seven students had been granted scholarships, with fifteen already departed for the United States (and four to other countries). Others from this group would follow. Several dozen more were selected via the test Marie Syrkin administered in the spring of 1947. Yet roughly a third of these did not meet the residence requirement and were barred from emigrating; for those eligible it could take months or more before they got the necessary clearances to leave Germany.[126] And some fellowship recipients, such as Philip Balaban—accepted first at the Colorado School of Mines and later the University of West Virginia—declined to go, preferring to wait to immigrate to Palestine.[127] Though Syrkin had hoped to bring forty to fifty students to the United States, her efforts likely resulted in twenty or so arriving there for study. In total, eighty young Jews made it to the United States on scholarships provided by the Hillel Foreign Student Service, as recruitment extended beyond DPs in Germany (including, for example, Jews in Budapest).[128]

Other apparent opportunities did not pan out. In the spring of 1947, the Student Federation complained that outreach to France, Holland, Switzerland, Scandinavia, and Australia had as yet yielded nothing concrete (prospects for Holland indeed proved a "a great bluff").[129] Though later granting twenty scholarships, Switzerland required that the students have relatives in the country and would not accept "stateless" immigrants, thus denying the necessary visas.[130] However content some DP students were to go to whatever country would take them, they largely remained stuck in the first years after the war.

"They Keep My Religion"

In the summer of 1949, thirty-three students (with twenty-six from Munich) went to Israel in connection with a gathering of the World Union of Jewish Students, the same group that had met in England two years earlier.[131] For the participants the trip represented communion with the reality of a Jewish state but also a chance to assess the viability of settling there. Eva Siebald, raised in a prominent and strongly Zionist family in Galicia, made the journey.[132] She recalls with humor that the students, eager to explore the country and Jerusalem especially, were typically placed in *kibbutzim* remote from urban centers. Escaping her kibbutz, she visited a leading political figure in Jerusalem who had been in Palestine since the mid-1930s and knew her family. After hearing her tales of Sochnut emissaries in Germany trying to pry the students away to Israel, he recommended that they stay in Germany to finish their studies and then emigrate. Without their yet knowing Hebrew, he feared, the students will struggle, and "the girls probably will get

Roman Ohrenstein in Israel in 1949, on a trip made by several dozen of the university students. (Courtesy of Roman Ohrenstein)

married." Everything the students had worked so hard for "will get lost." Heeding his counsel, she continued her engineering program in Germany, came to Israel in 1952, and immediately started working.

Other students received very different signals, creating great ambivalence about *aliyah*. Roman Ohrenstein, already with his PhD in economics, was exultant at being in a Jewish state and impressed with settlement efforts. The visit, however, left him "disappointed and depressed." Late in 1947 the Joint's Piekarczyk, himself a committed Zionist, had assured the anxious students that "each of you is an asset within the national capital and will be used."[133] Ohrenstein assumed that the fledging state would be solicitous of his expert knowledge, which led him to be critical of the country's socialist leanings. But in Israel he encountered the same attitude expressed by the Jewish Agency in Germany. "They did not need intellectuals. They needed kibbutzniks to . . . build up the land." Seeking employment, "I showed them my degree and was laughed at." Bucking the center-left ideology predominant in Israel, he speculates, also led him to be shunned.

Though initially hopeful of staying in Israel, he returned to Germany to start on a medical degree.

Emanuel Tanay likewise experienced a wrenching mix of feelings. In December 1946 he had sent a letter to a dear childhood friend, and longtime object of his affection, who had survived the Holocaust and settled in Palestine. In the letter he proudly reported his attendance at a German university but stressed, "Study is nothing but a means and not a goal. I can distinguish the two with mathematical accuracy and therefore it is a given that Emanuel Tenenwurzel [his birth name] one day will land in Eretz Israel."[134] Merely seeing the Israeli ship—draped in the national flag—that was to take him there in 1949 made him weepy.

In Israel he was hosted by an uncle who had settled in Palestine in the 1930s and worked on a kibbutz. When Tanay left the kibbutz, his uncle "insisted that I wear my American army surplus shirt and pants from the DP camp, instead of the elegant shirt and fashionable slacks I had bought for the trip," so as to look "like a Sabra."[135] Tanay soon realized that his uncle was trying to conceal the fact that he was a survivor. Holocaust survivors, he concluded, "were the disdained newcomers in Israel," expected to shed their backgrounds. "The pioneers transformed the desert into gardens; they expected to do the same with people." Unable to "disown" his survival and convinced that "my need to live a life of authenticity could not be fulfilled in Israel," Tanay too returned to Germany, feeling rejected by what was ostensibly his country (as well as by his love interest, whose ability to bury her European past shocked him).[136] He made his eventual home in the United States, where a lack of concern over one's origins proved welcoming to him. In his case, as perhaps for many other survivors, Israel represented the denial, and not simply the realization, of vital aspects of one's experience and identity as a Jew.

A dramatic perspective on such feelings of ambivalence toward Israel comes from Robert Nenner—the one student who all along fought as part of an Irgun cell for the Jewish state but ultimately declined to go there. "I'm still confused," he confessed from his American home decades later. "I have a strong belief in Israel [even though] . . . I hate those bastards there. Because first of all they're parasites [presumably for their reliance on American aid and military backing, as local conflicts go unresolved]. But I have this secular feeling that Israel must exist, otherwise the Jews in the world will never have peace. . . . Israel yes, I'll fight for the Israelis. I don't like them. They're obnoxious people. But I still will fight for them. Because they keep my religion." For Nenner Israel is above all a political vessel for the survival of important parts of the Jewish essence, worth defending irrespective of the desire to make one's life there.

Having seen in detail the students' varying attitudes toward and experiences with Zionism, we may now take stock of their implications for important historiographic debates. For years there has been a powerful and evolving divide within representations of DPs' relationship to Zionism. A group of scholars has asserted provocatively that Zionism was not a strong inclination of DPs. Instead, they hold, it was substantially imposed by militant Zionists, and representatives of the *Yishuv* especially. These Zionists allegedly exploited the emotional vulnerability of survivors to gain adherents; stressed, in their representations of the Holocaust, the value of violent resistance to persecution and the perils of passivity, encouraging a militaristic approach to the Zionist struggle; used survivors and DPs, in cases such as the *Exodus* affair, as pawns in geopolitical efforts to tilt world opinion; coerced compliance with the draft, including by aggressive and even violent means; and employed DP fighters in the 1948 war as "cannon fodder," who suffered disproportionately the burdens of mortal combat.[137]

There has been significant opposition to such representations, especially within recent DP histories. The scholars Mankowitz, Grossmann, Myers Feinstein, and Patt, on whose work I have extensively drawn, paint a very different picture. Zionism, in their casting, was the authentic commitment of the key organizations created by DPs, chiefly the Central Committee. Further, Zionism was broadly attractive to the DP masses, as evident in DP Zionist activism, youth movement participation, opinion surveys, and the culture and commemorative practices of DPs, so much of which was oriented to the national future. That Zionism's appeal could be as social, existential, and psychological as it was political did not make it less than genuine.

The newer histories also stress that the majority of DPs immigrated to Israel, but also argue that some Jews' migration elsewhere did not necessarily mean they lacked loyalty to Zionism. Zionist youth movement members from Europe, in addition, contributed to the Zionist enthusiasm on the *Exodus* and among other "pioneers." Charges of extreme coercion in the context of the draft were often overblown or politically motivated; and, finally (as other historians have argued), DP fighters bore no disproportionate percentage of casualties in the 1948 war.[138]

The case of the students aligns with neither position and complicates the very terms of the divide. The students were patently subjected to pressure from Zionist groups, which literally tried to starve them out of their student existence and force them to Palestine. The heavy-handed and even insulting message, as they largely received it, was not just that university study was inexpedient but that it was self-serving and selfish, making them less than proper Jews. Indeed, Zionism is broadly responsible for the irony that the main resistance to the Jewish students' attendance at university came not from the Germans but from other Jews.

In individual narratives, moreover, there is anecdotal evidence of what one may consider manipulation. One may think here of Rafael Nenner being lured into Betar by the promise of food and a rank, or his cousin Robert's recruitment into Irgun by members first extending to him emotional comfort to soothe his trauma. As to Zionist militarism, Robert Nenner's confession that fighting the British and the Arabs appeared to him a means to avenge the Holocaust dead supports the argument—laden with political implications—that the Palestinians paid, in effect, a terrible price for European anti-Semitism.

By the same token, the student unions were decidedly Zionist, with some of their members fervently so. Crucially, the students defended Zionist pressure to quit their studies largely *in the name of Zionism itself*. In part they argued that as a practical matter Zionism needed trained professionals to aid in nation building. But they also desperately wanted to feel included in the fold of Zionist longing and struggle, and to be seen as loyal to the cause. The question for them was not whether one was for or against Zionism but rather what within the Jewish experience and character—such as intellectual and academic pursuits—would be valued in a new Jewish society. In addition, some of the students' most ardent backers themselves joined the military mobilization in 1948. Many others wrestled with guilt for not having done so, even if they were exempted from the draft.

If Robert Nenner exemplifies the routing of anger at the Nazis into militant Zionism, he also shows that a strong and secure Jewish state could be an authentic goal of the survivors, cultivated—but hardly entirely imposed—by Zionist militants. Finally, some of the students, as we will soon see, embraced Israeli society and the challenge of developing it when they immigrated there.

Staying Put, Moving On

Into the summer of 1948 and beyond, the students in Germany continued to grapple with their obligation to Zionism and, specifically, the draft. If it was important to the students to continue their studies, it was also important that their conduct be sanctioned within mobilization efforts, which extended, remarkably, even to German authorities. The Union thus negotiated with various officials to determine the students' treatment. In July the students responded to the policy set by Commissioner Auerbach's office that stipends be given only to students whose exemption from the *giyus* was certified. [139] The Union's plan was to work with the State Commission and the Jewish Agency, which "in principle" favored an exemption for all those students requesting it, to guarantee stipends even for those without formal exemptions (e.g., those who were just beginning their studies). Further, the student federation decided to continue to distribute clothing to non-*giyus*–exempt members, because "we are a social institution which must represent the interests of all our needy members."[140] By the same token, the federation accepted the August 1948 policy that the Verification Commission, which certified candidates for entering university, would sign off only on those who secured exemptions.[141]

The Jewish authorities, for their part, appeared willing to accommodate the students so long as their Zionist loyalty was clear. The Central Committee, which played a key role in implementing the draft, once again forced the issue for the students. In early November the Executive Committee of the Munich Union held a "special meeting to take up the demand of the CK [that the Union] throw out all non-Gius exempt students in order to consider the group Zionist," likely with implications for continued aid.[142] (Some students, evidently, were either not eligible for exemptions or had failed to register with draft officials.) The committee confessed that addressing the demand was "the most difficult matter any Executive Committee had ever taken up." For the first time membership in the Union might depend on more than simply being a Jew and a university student. After strenuous debate, the committee accepted the proposal in principle, while recognizing that changing the terms of Union membership would require altering the "founding documents," which could be done only by vote of the General Meeting. It thus decided to dispatch members "known for their Zionist perspective" to lobby individual union chapters for this change.[143]

Later in the month, the CK delivered decidedly mixed signals to the students. A CK representative addressed a meeting of representatives of the zone federation. He reiterated, in keeping with the CK's current position, that "each individual should, through [external] support, have the opportunity to continue his studies." Further, the imminent dissolution of the *She'erith Hapleitah* in Germany should have no bearing on the goals of university students. He nonetheless stressed that the students had "done much too little for Israel," pointing to weak student compliance with draft protocols. (The same Union document reporting on the meeting indicates that 80 percent of all students, zonewide, had "registered for Aliyah," by which it may well have meant *giyus* registration.)[144] The CK was therefore "ready to work with the Union when the students promise[d] to fulfill their duty" to the Jewish nation. He suggested, with no mention of the CK ultimatum recorded earlier, that it was up to the Union to determine how to sanction those failing to comply with the draft. He added, finally, that little had come of Union promises to instruct its members in the Hebrew language and Jewish history and literature.[145]

No record exists indicating what became of Union efforts to require draft registration. In all likelihood the issue of draft compliance grew moot as the Arab-Israeli war came to a close, the draft abated, and Jewish DPs migrated en masse to Israel. The DP students would face a last moment of decision with respect to Zionism when, having completed or advanced in their studies, they immigrated—to Israel, the United States, or elsewhere. That moment came at different times for different students, depending on when they had begun their studies, what program they were in (as curricula varied by field), and what kind of degree they sought. So many of them had pledged—to themselves at least—to migrate to Israel when they had met their academic goals. This trajectory dominated the students' collective self-understanding and the Union's self-representation in the DP world; however, it only sometimes defined the destiny of individual students.

Conclusion

The students' staggered exit from Germany took place against the back-drop of the demobilization from late 1947 on of nearly the entire Jewish DP world, referred to by Jewish organizations as the "liquidation [*Liquidierung*] of the *She'erith Hapleitah*." Jews left Germany in droves. As of April 1948, just before the declaration of the state of Israel, 165,000 or so Jews remained in the American Zone. By September there were perhaps only 30,000.[1] The majority, as we have seen, immigrated to Israel. But the easing of immigration restrictions to the United States via the Displaced Persons Act of 1948 enabled others to leave for America. Initially restricting immigration to those DPs who had been in the American Zone as of December 1945 (and hence had not entered thereafter with the waves of "infiltrees" from the east), the act was amended in June 1950 to extend the residency cutoff to 1949, greatly expanding those eligible.

As Jews left Germany, the displaced persons camps that had housed so many of them were dramatically reduced in size or decommissioned altogether. By June 1950 only four DP camps remained in operation, holding about 9,000 Jews. The Landsberg camp closed in October 1950. The Feldafing camp closed less than a year later, with many of its 1,500 residents moved to the Foehrenwald DP camp.[2] The final haven for a Jewish DP "hard core," Foehrenwald closed in 1957.[3] Jews living still in Germany outside the camps worked to create what would become longstanding or even permanent communities.

The key institutions displaced Jews had energetically built also wound down and then exited the historical stage. Principally, the Central Committee disbanded in December 1950, holding its final meeting in Munich's

Deutsches Museum, where the DP saga had begun for so many refugees.[4] Much of its leadership, however, had already emigrated. With a dwindling Jewish population to serve, and many of their members now gone, other bodies and programs DPs had created—vocational institutes, newspapers, theater troupes, musical ensembles, and literary collectives—also disbanded. Among them was the school system for Jewish children built by DPs, educators from Palestine, and institutions like the Joint. Summing up its achievements, a Joint official remarked in August 1948, "I dare say that in the history of education one will not find so elaborate a program developed so rapidly, and certainly not under comparable conditions."[5] Despite plans to sustain the system for those staying behind, it too withered.

Intertwined with and accompanying this denouement were changes in the broader political landscape—above all, the creation of Israel. In Germany itself, both the US authorities and the German people prepared for the advent of an independent West German state, realized in May 1949. The US Military Government had already given way to US civilian authority in Germany. Eager to reconcile with the Germans and to help create the Federal Republic as a bulwark against communism, the Americans increased pressure for DPs to emigrate or integrate into German society. International relief efforts, scaled back when UNRRA was replaced by the IRO, fell even more to private entities like the Joint, which now dealt with frustratingly recalcitrant DP populations. In 1951 the German government assumed formal control over the remaining DP camps.[6]

In the midst of the dissolution of the DP world, the Jewish students pressed on. Despite hard-fought pledges of support from Jewish organizations, difficulties persisted. With the Central Committee disbanding, the students' main quarrel was now with their longstanding patron, the Joint. A panicked Union letter from February 1949, sent in rough English to the JDC's main offices in New York City and Paris, represented the students' situation as still dire. It detailed the modest (if improved) contents of monthly rations, claimed that the students suffered "headache anemia" from malnutrition, and demanded that the JDC both create "special Relief Funds" for the students and provide scholarships for study in the United States or Israel.[7] It also reported the "irony" that "Jewish maid-students must work as servants in German restaurants" to support their studies.

The Joint did not take kindly to the missives, questioning the validity of the students' claims and privately describing the students as now something of a nuisance. Samuel Haber, the Joint director for the entire American Zone since March 1947, personally weighed in, informing colleagues that the current level of JDC support, which included the payment of student fees and continued rations for nearly all Union members, was fair and that what likely motivated the letters was the hope for scholarships. The JDC had set up scholarships for medical personnel to practice abroad, prompting "the Central Committee, the teachers, the Rabbis"—and now the students—to request them also. Haber concluded, "I am shedding no crocodile tears over the conditions of the students."[8]

From the perspective of the students, external support was as necessary as ever, especially as so many were close to finishing their degrees. Their fear was that, with the dissolution of the *She'erith Hapleitah*, they would be forgotten. The Joint, in all its existing dealings with DPs, considered whether it should support with its shrinking resources only those who intended to leave Germany or extend aid to all needy Jews, regardless of their plans.[9] Tensions between the students and the Joint erupted again in August 1949. New Union letters claimed that life for most students was "unbearably hard" due to lack of support, alleged that their aid had been reduced, and demanded greater rations and financial assistance for the unions.[10] Director Haber's September 1949 response to Joint staff was still more dismissive, pointing to the continued distribution of Joint packages and remarking that the "Jewish students here now are no worse off than were thousands of American students during the depression years."[11] He asserted that there is "no need for maintaining the [student] organization as it has been operated," as it "now serves no constructive purpose. . . . Many of [the students], in our opinion, are ill-advised to continue their studies here because they will not be able to practice their chosen professions."[12]

However strongly the Joint had supported the students, this strife underscores the gulf that could still separate DPs from those seeking to help them. For all their practical concerns for their futures, the students also embraced university life as a comprehensive commitment, aligning them with elevated European and Jewish traditions. Simon Schochet perceived a cultural divide. Many Joint staff from the United States, it pained him to relate, were the kin of Russian Jews who had immigrated to the United States decades ago. They had, in his view, the mindset of social workers—well-meaning but able to understand neither the DP students' intellectual preoccupations nor what the "intelligentsia" connoted to them.[13]

To the Joint's American staff, it was entirely reasonable that students should take jobs to supplement their income, as was common in the United States. But to the DP students, employment in the regular German economy could appear lowly, with service work for Germans especially debasing. Most importantly, the students saw support for their studies as a matter of justice and an investment in the Jewish future, and their unions as indispensable ballast in their lives. By 1949, in sharp contrast, the Joint's deputy zone director regarded the Union as just another "pressure group" that "must prove to their constituents that they are 'kampfing' on their behalf."[14]

The fatal withdrawal of support the students worried about never materialized. Relations with the Joint bent but never broke, as the students continued to receive from it fluctuating amounts of rations, stipends, and cash. In October 1949 all Jewish DP associations in Munich—including the Student Union—were supposed to disband. Yet the students worked with the CK, the Joint, and other groups to "ensure the existence" of the Union through continuing support.[15] Additional aid came from the recently established Bavarian Bureau for Reparations (*Bayerisches Landesamt für Wiedergutmachung*), headed by Philipp Auerbach, as a successor to the State Commission for the Racial, Political, and Religious Persecuted, and the Auxilium Academicum Judaicum—a newly created organization devoted to support for the students. The latter was led by Munich rabbi Aaron Ohrnstein of the *Israelitisches Kultusgemeinde*, with whom the students had a longstanding relationship.[16]

As the 1940s came to an end, the Munich Union and others continued to hold meetings, elect new officers (if in reduced numbers), anchor the academic and social lives of their members, and, as we have seen, lobby for aid. Even so, the student community fell into its own soft decline, no longer enjoying the vitality it had during the first years of sacrifice and struggle, when the thrill of personal and collective renewal was most intense. Union documents grew still more administrative in character and trained on the issue of resources. In a small but telling indication of stress, the zonewide union decided in the summer of 1949 to sell its car, indicating that it could not be maintained given financial difficulties.[17] With the Jewish DP world disappearing around them, the students had fewer points of engagement with the broader community and fewer occasions to define themselves in relation to Jewish values, Zionist politics, and the collective future. Finally, the cohesion that was the hallmark of the student organizations began to fray somewhat, evident in renewed complaints regarding the Munich Union's power within the federation, political struggles among the leaders and organizational branches, laments of the passivity of the rank-and-file, and even accusations of the improper accounting and distribution of Union resources.[18] A Munich executive report from late 1949 remarked that the recent General Meeting had been dominated by colleagues who had been expelled from the Union but allowed back in, and that "the spirit of the Union" is scarcely recognizable, given that many students had emigrated and others appeared buried in their studies.[19] Indeed, alumni testimonials, whether in the research surveys I conducted or in interviews, stressed the pressure of passing exams and the stress of settling on emigration options when they described their last months in Germany.

Above all the student community's own denouement was a consequence of the students' success in fulfilling their primary purpose: to pursue their education and move on. In this they mirrored other DPs, for whom time in Germany was a bridge to a new future. In October 1948 Alexander Piekarczyk, the DP academic and Joint university officer who had done so much to support the students, announced that he would leave shortly for Israel. In formal but heartfelt prose, he wished the students a speedy end to their studies and that, wherever they wound up, their "specialties and knowledge would be put to ideal use."[20] In November 1949 the Union's crowning institutional achievement, the Verification Commission on which Piekarczyk had worked so hard, disbanded at the order of the Bavarian Ministry of Culture.[21] Perhaps the ministry sought to encourage the exit of DPs from what was now the Federal Republic. Regardless, the Verification Commission had achieved and arguably outlived its purpose. Nearly all those for whom it was intended—*gymnasium* graduates who had lost their documents during the war or aspiring students quickly finishing their secondary education through private study—had already matriculated into universities. By late 1949 new candidates would have had ample time to pursue university study through attendance at a proper *gymnasium*. The Union set up a "liquidation commission" to manage the process, securing Verification Commission documents and returning official stamps to the Bavarian government.[22]

The students began completing their degrees and thus were themselves ready to leave Germany. The majority finished their studies in 1949 or, much more commonly, in 1950. The alumni surveys record these years for nearly two-thirds of the graduates, with nearly all others graduating, or otherwise concluding their education in Germany, in the following years. In August 1949 Union documents estimated approximately 300 members in Munich, down from a peak of 460 in late 1947, and 560 zonewide, down from nearly 700 at the start of the year.[23] By the summer semester of 1950, the total membership had fallen to 308, with 210 in Munich.[24]

This dramatic dropoff does not strictly indicate graduations. Some students, especially those who finished *gymnasium* after the war and recently entered university, left Germany before earning their degrees, oftentimes completing them in the United States and elsewhere. And many others, such as those earning the *Diplom-Ingenieur* in Germany (roughly equivalent to a master's degree in the United States), added to their professional credentialing after emigrating. Whatever these variations, the early 1950s had an aura of closure for the students.

Despite the achievement they represented, graduations typically drew little fanfare from the Munich Union: no proud colleagues in attendance, no special celebrations sponsored by the group. In fact, the absence of family members could trigger recognition of the enormity of one's loss. Roman Ohrenstein had described the absolute need after the war to repress the memory of the "apocalyptic terror" he suffered and not dwell on still being in the Germans' midst.[25] Upon receiving his PhD in economics in July 1949, the dam of emotion broke. "At the official ceremony," he wrote years later in an American economics journal, "I was the only Jew. . . . After we were awarded the doctoral certificates, the German well-wishers embraced their graduating kin, and girls with flowers greeted their boyfriends, all former soldiers in Hitler's army. . . . I stood alone, bewildered, as if in a twilight zone. [My family] was all gone, murdered, perhaps by those very graduating celebrants standing next to me. Instead of being happy, it was the saddest day of my life. Dejected, I returned to my room and cried."[26] Perhaps no more compelling episode exists to underscore both the twisted circumstances of the students' academic pursuits in Germany and the duality defining the lives of DP survivors: the coexistence of life destroyed and life reborn.

The departure of friends and colleagues from Germany was bittersweet, as for any close student cohort scattering after graduation, but with added pathos and pride. "When Arnold [Kerr] left," his dear friend Mark Hupert related, "I was sad because I was with him for seven years. . . . [It left] a void. But, on the other hand I knew that he had to go."[27] The very future the students had crafted together destined that they part.

"I Did Not Want to Start Fighting for My Life Again"

Arnold Kerr was in fact among the very last Jewish DP students in Germany, leaving in 1954 after serving as the Munich Union's final general secretary. By that point the great majority of students were gone, meaning that they had faced the final decision when in Germany: where to go when they left.

There was, as scholars have documented, no fully predictable pattern as to where Jewish DPs ended up, with one's fate often determined more by circumstance than will. A committed Zionist might settle in the United States, while a DP open to a variety of possibilities might immigrate to Israel. Someone might settle first in Israel and then move to the United States, or vice versa. A portion of DPs left Germany and then came back to settle. And some DPs, initially intent on emigrating, might never leave.

The students embody this diversity. Roman Ohrenstein, an outspoken Zionist, returned to Germany after visiting Israel, lived in Germany for two more years, and then left for good for the United States. Mark Fintel first settled in Israel but then relocated to America in 1956, after the first Sinai War. Students Mark and Cessia Hupert left Germany only in 1959, having raised their daughter there for the first years of her life.[28] Simon Snopkowski met his wife (who converted to Judaism) in Germany and made his life there.

Nonetheless, the students as a whole exhibit certain propensities that differ from those of Jewish DPs as a whole. The majority of Jews immigrated to Israel, with the United States the next most common country. By percentage, the destinations of DP emigrants between the end of the war and 1952 are roughly: Palestine/Israel, 57.9 percent (177,000); the United States, 32.4 percent (99,000 or so); Canada, 5.2 percent (16,000); Australia, 2.6 percent (8,200); Europe, 1.4 percent (4,300); other, .3 percent (930). Some 10,000 non-German Jews remained in Germany, less than 5 percent of the total number of Jewish DPs.[29] No fully accurate data exist on the immigration choices of the students. The richest picture comes via the alumni rosters assembled by the German University Students Alumni Association in the late 1990s, when the group was most robust. A 1999 list of 282 addresses, with at least one alumnus in each household, shows 56.3 percent (159) in the United States; 34.3 percent (97) in Israel; 2.8 percent (8 each) in both Canada and in Australia; 1.8 percent (5) in European countries other than Germany; and 1.8 percent (5) also in Germany.[30] The percentages, based on common-sense assumptions about this rather large sample, represent a credible breakdown of the students' immigration decisions, if likely skewed somewhat to the United States.

As was the case among all Jewish DPs, students immigrated to Canada, Australia, and countries in Europe in small proportions, and the percentage of students staying in Germany was even tinier than that of the Jewish DPs as a whole. Most conspicuously, the ratio of students immigrating to the United States versus Israel (1.6 to 1) is nearly the inverse of the ratio among all Jewish DPs (1 to 1.8). Exploring the students' immigration choices both deepens our understanding of how and why Jewish DPs in general went where they did and helps to explain why the students deviated from broad patterns.

Here the alumni surveys, roughly 70 percent of which were returned from the United States and the others from Israel, offer insight. Among the questions were: "Where did you intend to go [when leaving Germany]?" "Did Zionism and moving to Israel appeal to you? If so, why? If not, why not?" "Where did you first go? Where did you settle?" The respondents typically provided short answers to these big questions, coming toward the end of a long survey. Yet even their clipped answers are revealing.

The most straightforward cases are those alumni who reported longstanding Zionist commitment, indicated Israel as their preference, and indeed first went and ultimately settled there. Matching this profile, Marion Glaser wrote: "After the Holocaust I wanted to live in a total Jewish surrounding to avoid for me and my family to feel like a second class citizen."[31] Several others credit the anti-Semitism of their native Poland, even before the German onslaught, as convincing them of the need for a Jewish state. Though retrospectively constructing their intentions, those settling in Israel (among those I interviewed as well) typically describe their decision as a matter of principle, even when facilitated by practical considerations such as the presence of relatives there. Georg Majewski had family in Israel dating back to the 1920s, but also an uncle in Detroit who invited him to the United States just after the war, signing an affidavit that he would look after his nephew. But Majewski refused to immigrate there, explaining that "for me it was only one place possible, Israel."[32] Former student Boldo Pinchas, whose parents had been part of the Betar movement and who became a partisan fighter, described Germany as simply "on the way to Palestine."[33]

Straightforward in their own right are the rare cases in which the alumni confessed that the prospect of settlement in Israel did not appeal to them at all. One alumnus allowed, "kibbutz, agrarian culture, etc. not my way of life."[34] Another conceded, "I was not dedicated and not willing to work hard in Israel."[35] Most interesting are the many cases in which the alumni indicate that they were attracted to Zionism and to Israel but made their new lives in the United States (or Canada).

Scholars have well acknowledged that Jewish DPs drawn toward Zionism might settle in the United States for reasons including immigration opportunities, familial concerns, employment prospects, war-weariness, or combinations thereof. Many students exemplify this dynamic. Any number had relatives already in the United States who could house and/or sponsor them when they arrived. Others were pulled toward America by their surviving or new families. Max Grieffez wanted to go to Israel. His twenty-one-year-old brother, however, was killed in the 1948 war, and his parents demanded that the remainder of the family go to America.[36] Eugene Miller relates that the father-in-law of his recent bride "insisted that we go to USA and finally he prevailed."[37] Fred Reiter, whose parents also survived, allowed, "Even though my family and I planned to go to Israel . . . my girlfriend and fellow student in Munich Dental School changed my mind. Her mother had two brothers and a sister in America. Since I could not nor would not part from my parents or brother, I finally after months of persuasion, convinced them to come to the United States."[38] The Holocaust inclined some to wish to settle in Israel but disinclined others. Representative of the latter, Joseph Heimberg, who had endured Auschwitz, Buchenwald, and Sachsenhausen, explained,

"I did not want to start fighting for my life again."[39] Alex White confessed, "After all the suffering and hardship I did not feel like going through it again. However, my sympathy was with Israel."[40]

Common among Jewish DPs immigrating to the United States, such reasons do not account for why such a large percentage of the students came to America. One structural explanation concerns the timing of their immigration. Huge numbers of Jewish DPs, finally released from their limbo and exultant at the new Jewish state, immigrated to Israel in 1948 and early 1949. During that period, and even with the 1948 Displaced Persons Act, immigration to the United States was comparatively much more difficult. However, by the time most students were finished with their studies (measured by varying thresholds), immigration to America had eased considerably via the 1950 amendment to the act. (Similarly, those already in the immigration pipeline had more time to be processed.) By simple logic, so many of the students went to the United States because they now could.

But a second factor, in some cases at least, was also at play: the importance to the students of continuing their professional or educational pursuits. More encompassing than the desire merely for employment, that priority goes to the heart of what made the students distinct among DPs and recapitulates the bases on which they resisted pressure to become pioneers while in Germany. Though a Zionist from youth, the medical student and Auschwitz survivor Isaac Minzberg "found out that Israel needed no physicians" and came to Chicago, Illinois, where he developed a medical practice.[41] Zionism likewise appealed to Arnold Kerr, who earned his *Diplom-Ingenieur* in Munich. "Since I lost my entire family and had to rely on myself," he explained, "the first priority was to complete my higher education."[42] He came to the United States in 1954, earning his PhD at Northwestern University five years later. For these and other students, the perception was that the United States was the better locale for realizing the very ambitions that drove them when in postwar Germany. No less a dedicated figure than Michael Okunieff, who fought with the partisans and again risked his life with the Bricha, immigrated to the United States to pursue a medical career. In sum, the decision of many students to come to America could be an extension of their postwar recovery of self, even as support for Israel was universal among them.

"The Future Is Not a Gift. It Is an Achievement"

As for nearly all Jewish DPs, the new life the students worked to create in occupied Germany was ultimately lived elsewhere, chiefly in the United States and Israel. That life could at first be difficult. In either country the student

271

émigrés might have to learn languages (English or Hebrew) with which they were substantially unfamiliar; struggle to earn livings, even when supported by families or sponsors, by taking nonprofessional employment; repeat portions of their education to procure necessary credentialing; and, for camp survivors especially, contend with cultures not receptive to them.

In Israel the survivors and their trials squared poorly with the vigorous, forward-looking personae and narratives of longstanding settlers, which were often already steeped in the mythology of Jewish passivity in the face of Nazi violence. The student survivors settling there typically kept their Holocaust backgrounds hidden among their co-nationals for years or even decades. Eva Siebald recounts that only after the 1973 Yom Kippur War, which caused Israelis to reflect on the range of responses to danger, did her dear friend—also a German university alumna—reveal to her co-workers in Israel that she was a survivor.[43] Siebald even encountered the view among Israelis that it would have been better if World War II had lasted longer so that Jews in Palestine could have extracted more concessions and resources from the British.

The immigrants to the United States relate that even well-meaning and curious Americans had little capacity to understand what they had been through. More sharply, their prior abjection and enduring "otherness" might chafe against the image of optimism and rectitude that American Jews, intent on assimilating into the Judeo-Christian culture integral to the "civil religion" of early Cold War America, sought to project. Roman Ohrenstein entered the Jewish Theological Seminary in New York City to train for the rabbinate when he came to the United States in 1951, despite having an economics PhD.[44] Serving as an assistant rabbi, he had bitter conflicts with his lead rabbi as he sought to address the congregation directly about the Holocaust.[45] Such struggles, in part, convinced him to leave the rabbinate and begin a career as an economics professor in 1963. Cessia Hupert encountered terrible sexism from a Jewish superior at a New York hospital. When his senior colleagues confronted him, confiding also that she was a Holocaust survivor, he replied caustically, "I don't give a damn . . . which hole she crawled out from."[46]

Irrespective of such disturbing episodes, the raw challenge of starting fresh in new societies, as well as the enduring psychic imperative to repress traumatic memories, kept the Holocaust largely at the margins of the students' post-emigration lives, even as it continued to mark their identities and their psyches. The primary continuity they asserted was with their prewar selves, with the devastation of the war years too great a rupture to be integrated into their postwar existence.

Even so, their new environments proved largely therapeutic. Those in the United States enjoyed Americans' relative absence of judgment and prejudice (even as they observed African Americans' great struggles for equality or, as professional women experienced, the sexism of colleagues). Decades after immigrating, Brian Bergman noted appreciatively that no one in America "ever called me a 'Jew.'"[47] The students settling in Israel took both comfort and pride in being in a Jewish state (though some also confessed sadness at the Israeli treatment of Arabs). With some exceptions, only with the massive interest in survivor experiences and testimony beginning in the late 1980s and early 1990s did the alumni thoroughly confront their pasts.[48]

Focused on the students' time in postwar Germany, my research has entailed only general knowledge of their post-emigration lives. Nonetheless, two aspects integral to the themes of this study have drawn my attention. The first is the evident determination with which the students followed through on their stated goals in Germany by pursuing the careers for which they trained. Of forty-nine survey respondents, only five indicate that they did not end up in a profession based in their postwar studies. Nearly all those I interviewed had similar trajectories.[49]

The students exited Germany with high-quality degrees and, in some cases, a battery of professional recommendations. For example, when he graduated in 1949, Fred Reiter was issued a Union certificate in English and German attesting that he had served as the president of the Munich Students' Union, an academic recommendation in English from the dentistry clinic at the LMU, and a special commendation from the office of the LMU rector, who had come to know Reiter in his capacity as Union head.[50] For some of the Jewish students, the transition into professional life was almost immediate. Alex White, graduating in medicine from the LMU in 1951, began an internship at a New York City hospital—facilitated by the cousin of fellow Munich student and Union co-founder Edmund Feuerstein—within days of arriving in the United States.[51] Feuerstein and several others soon followed, forming a "mischpacha" of Munich students in New York City. Struggling to meet the stringent admissions requirements for New York state boards in medicine, White relocated to Illinois, where he became an established physician, again joined by some of his Munich cohort.

Earning a medical degree in 1949, Michael Okunieff worked as a doctor at the Feldafing DP camp until 1951. Shortly after arriving in Chicago later that year, he began his medical career in the US.[52] Joseph Taler left Germany with a medical degree in December 1950. The Physician Placement Committee in America told him that, as a married man with a child, it was best that he seek a job in the "provinces" and not in New York City, which seemed every aspiring doctor's first choice.[53] By 1951 he had a residency at a hospital in Baltimore, Maryland, and in 1954 opened a family practice elsewhere in the state.

Some of those in Israel had similarly fluid transitions, no matter the perception that professional opportunities were scarce. Ziona Oberman, a medical student in Munich, immigrated in 1949. She worked for a year at the Wiezmann Institute of Science, continued her studies at Hebrew University, and next joined a Tel Aviv hospital, where she worked for more than thirty-five years.[54] Zwi Markus, an engineering student, came to Israel in 1951 and soon started working for a company called Water Planning in Israel, later founding his own construction firm.[55] In many other cases both in the United States and Israel, there was a lag of several years or more between the students' immigration and the start, in earnest, of their careers. In the interim they might have worked to establish themselves financially, dealt with familial responsibilities, or continued their schooling.

Over time the alumni enjoyed high levels of professional achievement. Those in medicine built careers as cardiologists, internists, ophthalmologists, obstetricians, general practitioners, family and medical dentists, neuropharmacologists, and researchers working in hospitals, private practices, and medical schools. Some became psychologists and psychiatrists, even developing specialties in the treatment of trauma victims. (Henry Krystal, practicing in Michigan, has published extensively on understanding and treating the trauma of Holocaust survivors.)[56] Other alumni worked as chemists or civil, mechanical, and electric engineers for the government, in the private sector, in academia, and at elite research institutes. Among the alumni are also successful architects and several humanists, who are distinguished as teachers and writers. In America, Simon Schochet was first employed by the Miami University in Oxford, Ohio. Recruited as an "exotic" foreigner, he educated provincial Americans in European history and culture before resettling in New York City.[57] His 1983 novella, *Feldafing*, stands as the preeminent work of fiction on the Jewish DP experience and is routinely quoted in DP scholarship. Finally, a small percentage of the students built successful careers in unrelated fields. Elias Epstein, leaving Germany in 1951 with a partial degree in dentistry, had learned that he would need to enroll in a four-year program to earn his doctor of dental surgery degree.[58] (Epstein was in fact told by the National Committee for Resettlement of Foreign Physicians in 1949: "It is difficult to get an admission to an American dental school since there are quotas for Jewish students and you would have the additional obstacle of being a foreign-trained student.")[59] Fred Reiter, a fellow dentistry student, lamented that "our Munich degrees were not accepted by the United States" and that "getting into Dental schools in the early 1950s was virtually impossible."[60] With a small child, and lacking any money to pay for dental school,

Epstein embarked on a career as a jeweler, winning international awards for his innovative designs.[61]

The alumni also include a fair number who performed military service, typically in the middle-late 1950s. The US government initially regarded the students with suspicion. Immigrating just as the Cold War was heating up, they were seen as potential communists, coming from a left-leaning foreign student association with a dubious name. The former partisan Michael Okunieff's immigration to the United States was in fact long delayed as the US government worked through its suspicion that he was, by virtue of his wartime involvement with the Red Army, a Soviet spy.[62] Several alumni recall being interviewed by US intelligence officials upon their arrival in the United States about possible communist affiliations and the broader European landscape. And a number of alumni concealed from immigration officials their deportation to the Soviet interior in order to avoid the glare of anticommunist fervor. Nonetheless, some students proudly served for spells in the US military, frequently as medical personnel.[63] Some alumni made good on the pledge to use their expert knowledge toward national ends through military service in Israel. Notably, the engineering student Joseph Zaphir worked for years in the top-secret electronic warfare division of the Israeli Ministry of Defense, earning the Israeli Defense Prize in 1967.[64] In sum, the vigilant sense of intellectual and professional purpose the students exhibited in postwar Germany carried over into their post-emigration lives.

Striking also is the close bond so many alumni retained after leaving Germany. In some cases they were able from the start to sustain close friendships with classmates who fortuitously settled in the same city. In others cases they discovered years later that fellow alumni now lived near them. They might revive prior friendships, draw close to students whom they had barely known in Germany, or befriend alumni who had studied in other cities. The areas in which the alumni clustered—New York City, northern New Jersey, Chicago, Minneapolis, Detroit, Los Angeles, Tel Aviv, Jerusalem, Haifa—typically had one or more such friendship circles, which might in turn overlap. The bonds ranged from private friendships, to regular meetings in private homes or restaurants, to large-scale reunions.

From at least the early 1970s the students made efforts, with haphazard success, to formally organize themselves as alumni.[65] A 1971 plan to purchase a property in upstate New York for use by New York City–area alumni fell through. The initial global reunion was to be in Israel in 1974, but the 1973 Yom Kippur War scuttled those plans. A subsequent planned reunion in Israel faltered when a key alumnus living in Israel, the Berlin student and Israeli resident Georg Majewski, suggested that the itinerary include Vienna, Munich, and Berlin. The first successful large-scale gathering took place in the United States in 1993, bringing together eighty or so students from the New York metropolitan area. In 1995 a reunion of global alumni was held at last in Tel Aviv, Israel. The event was followed by gatherings in Florida, where many US alumni had relocated or established second homes, in 1997, 2000, 2003, and 2005. The program at such events typically included *kaddish* prayers, reflections on survival and the student life, trips to sites of interest (such as Miami's Holocaust memorial), and presentations by a "second generation" working group made up of the alumni's children. New York City–area and Chicago alumni met throughout this period, sometimes joined by representatives from the United States Holocaust Memorial Museum. For several years in the 1990s the former students issued a newsletter, "Reunion: Holocaust Survivors Who Studied in Munich and Other German Universities," which reported on their gatherings and shared historical and personal reflections about their journeys.[66]

The enduring loyalty of the former students to one another begs explanation. College classmates often form lifelong friendships, and in this the postwar students are unexceptional. Yet surely there is more behind their bond. For those orphaned especially, the student community is a substitute family—one that partly replaced their original families and helped to make the creation of their actual postwar families possible. Felix Korn stressed, "We had no families. And this became like our family. Because we have so much in common, we have a common purpose and a common origin. And this really carried on all through life, we still keep in touch. . . . We feel good among one another, we understand one another."[67] That understanding is multifaceted and includes memories, whether sweet or bitter, of their upbringing in Poland or elsewhere; of their time in Germany; and of their wartime trials, about which the alumni grew increasingly comfortable sharing with one another. A 1999 alumni newsletter, in describing a recent reunion, recounted that "we talked and talked about our lives. We no longer needed to keep distance from our bitter past."[68] The need for that kind of intimacy was no less great in Israel. Eve Siebald, for example, explains that her fellow alumni (and survivors) were her best, indispensable adult friends, singularly capable of understanding her.[69]

In a telling image that suggests an additional kind of bond, the alumni reception in a Florida hotel in 2000 was held next door to a reunion of an American World War II military unit—a "band of brothers," similar in age to the students, sharing unique memories of their experience of war. The alumni, as a band of brothers and sisters in their own right, experienced independently the destruction of war and the Holocaust and collectively the extended drama of rebirth. The primary basis of their bond is thus not

Jewish alumni of German universities at a global reunion in Boca Raton, Florida, in 2000. (Some of their children and nonstudent spouses are in the picture as well.) The photo was given to me as an attendee at the reunion. I am in the upper right corner, wearing a badge.

what they mutually suffered but instead what they together accomplished. Indeed, the core lesson of their lives, as distilled by their children into a maxim printed on a second generation tribute, is "The future is not a gift. It is an achievement."[70] Physical survival, as so many alumni described it, was the consequence of fate. The success of their lives thereafter, for which university study in postwar Germany served as catalyst, was the result of their will, which was far more worthy of tribute in their minds.

Simon Schochet, in response to a call from the global alumni for reflections on his time in Germany, submitted a tender tribute to his friend and late Munich alumnus Natan Rosenbilt. Surviving the war in the Soviet Union (and loath to talk about his experiences out of recognition of the far greater suffering of those stuck in the west), Rosenbilt had as his greatest passions "philosophy, history, and literature," despite his skill at mathematics.[71] Rosenbilt eventually came to the United States and began a program in physics at the University of California in Berkeley. Doomed by a fatal illness, he visited Schochet in New York City not long before his death.

Schochet put the student experience at the center of Rosenbilt's life: "It seems to me that it would be proper to write these words on his gravestone, 'Natan Rosenbilt is survived by his friends in the Student Union with whom he shared his youth, their struggle, their dreams and search for justice and meaning. This was his legacy and nobility.'"

"Happily Ever After"

The ostensible unity the alumni share conceals an enduring and sometimes bitter division: that between those settling in the United States and those settling in Israel. Many among the former, as we have seen, felt guilty for not joining Israel at or near the birth of the state, whether by participating in the 1948 draft or immigrating there in the years afterward. Some of those opting for Israel judged that their American counterparts had indeed taken the softer, easier path, merely working to establish their own lives while they worked—in the face of economic hardship, physical challenge, and periodic wars—to establish a country. Their personal becoming was bound up with, and in some sense secondary to, the evolution of the Jewish nation.

The US immigrants felt that judgment, especially from the handful of "pioneers." Felix Korn explained, "We felt bad that we did not go. That group that decided to go, and went, they didn't talk to us."[72] When he visited Israel in the 1970s, they were "not too forthcoming, not too friendly." Guti Kanner, who for years worked as a nurse after immigrating to Israel in the late 1940s, gave the critical perspective of an émigré to Israel, echoed (though less sharply) by others. The failing of the students, she felt, began in Munich, where she saw little evidence of true Zionist commitment, or efforts to learn Hebrew or otherwise to prepare for life in Israel. Herself feeling that she could have done more for the Jewish state, it "bothered [her] very much" that others settled in America in pursuit of a "good life."[73] Only when the alumni in America were older and professionally settled, it seemed to her, did they "try to have any connection" with those in Israel. Moreover, in her view they displayed weak solidarity with Israel during its periods of crisis. For these reasons, she suggests, many of the alumni in Israel have been reticent to attend reunions in the United States, and she personally declined to go to the 1995 gathering in Israel. Though individual alumni in the two countries stay in touch, and segments in each camp feel little enmity, no collective reconciliation has taken place between the two groups.

As for Germany, the country receded in the narrative of the forward-looking students even before they left. By the same token, Germany and its people indelibly define the students. The students arguably had far greater cause for ambivalence toward Germany than most Jewish DPs. As was the case for other survivors, the Germans had been the primary authors of their persecution and, in many instances, the murder of their families. But the DP students participated to an uncommon degree in postwar German life and benefitted from German institutions, if for reasons having little to do with their former persecutors' genuine contrition. Their enduring bitterness stands against a heavily qualified gratitude.

Never resolved, that tension is periodically restaged. An especially resonant episode took place in June 2005, sixty years after the war's conclusion. The alumni had been invited to Munich by the Bavarian government. The occasion was the opening of the exhibit "'Hoffnung trotz allem . . .': Jüdisches Leben in Bayern, 1945 bis Heute" ("Hope in Spite of Everything . . : Jewish Life in Bavaria from 1945 to the Present") at the Bavarian parliament building. The primary host was Ruth Snopkowski, the wife of the late Munich alumnus and Bavarian state senator Simon Snopkowski, and the exhibit heavily featured the student community.

Bella Brodzki and I eagerly joined the trip in order to see the exhibit and the physical settings—such as the LMU campus—that had been so important to the students, and to witness how the alumni would react to their German reception. Yet just a tiny handful of alumni, all from the United States, made the journey.[74] Ruth Snopkowski, though clearly disappointed, graciously led a program that included a visit to the Ohel Jakob synagogue then under construction, meetings with leading Munich academics and administrators (including the current prorector of the LMU and the president of the Technical University, as the Technische Hochschule was renamed), and attendance at the exhibit opening, which featured a tribute address in the main hall of parliament.[75] The paltry turnout of alumni, Bella and I learned from those attending, was no fluke. At an impassioned meeting of New York–area alumni, influential members had insisted that their presence in Munich would be an insult to the memory of their murdered relatives, and that the alumni association as such should therefore refuse the invitation (though individuals were free to go). At root they did not want to encourage the misleading belief that Germany had done anything positive *for them*, given all that it had done *to them*. Even being honored by the Germans would mean conceding too much.

Several of those on the trip had returned to Germany earlier and already sorted through their complicated feelings around being in the country. But one of them, Brian Bergman, was returning for the first time. He had just come from a visit to his native Poland and raved about how gracious the Poles—knowing he was a Jew—had been toward him. Whether he genuinely encountered their empathy, or mistook philo-Semitism for solidarity, or merely needed to believe that the Poles had worked past their anti-Semitism, Bella and I could not say. By contrast, the Germans—who had historically done so much to confront and atone for their past—inspired his scorn. He was tempted, he confessed, to scream at random Germans of his age, "Your parents murdered my parents!"

As were rode in a taxi cab to our hotel, just before he was slated to appear on a public panel, Bergman descended into panic, fearful that he had only contempt to share. Speaking in English, Bella and I urged him to think of something constructive to say to an audience that would surely include young people far removed from the genocide and eager for perspective. The cab driver, likely in his thirties and listening intently despite his poor English, inquired into Bergman's identity and the subject of the event.

The panel was hosted by the Jewish-German professor Michael Brenner, head of the Institute of Jewish History and Culture at the University of Munich, and featured testimonials from Munich alumni Arnold Kerr and Alexander White, in addition to Bergman. Mixing German and English and struggling against tears, Bergman first spoke of the murder of his parents, the degradation he experienced in camps and Gestapo jails, and how, after liberation, he still felt like "less than a human being."[76] Mindful of his parents' wish that he attend university, he entered the University of Frankfurt to study literature, concealing that he had only one year of *gymnasium*. "From there on my life has changed. . . . I caught up with all the students and I felt so good, and my feeling of inferiority ha[d] disappeared, and this is the thanks that I have for the Johann Wolfgang Goethe-Universität in Frankfurt." Always a "book lover," he found his studies "beautiful, exhilarating," guided by "excellent teachers." With a rousing crescendo, he related that he did two years at university, immigrated to the United States (where he completed his schooling), and "lived there happily ever after." The rapt audience burst into applause. To our great surprise, those attending included the taxi cab driver and his children.

So much in the students' circumstances, sagas, and feelings percolated that evening. The attendance of the cab driver was symbolically resonant. In great contrast to the vast majority of Germans the students met when DPs, this young father seemed intent on exploring the meaning of individual, collective, and historical guilt; honoring the persistent imperative of empathetic engagement with victims; and modeling an inheritance for his family based on conscientious reckoning with the past rather than on efforts to avoid it or mark oneself as separate from it.

Bergman did not quite summon conventional praise for the Germans. But he could acknowledge the catharsis his time as a DP represented, driven at once by his sense of familial legacy, intellectual curiosity, and love of learning. National Socialism had substantially corrupted the whole enterprise of knowledge, along with the German university system. After the war, it was nonetheless possible for him while in Germany to participate in and enjoy, across profound divisions of identity, the universalism of intellectual and aesthetic pursuits.

Finally, Bergman concluded his address with the words "happily ever after" with both palpable irony and sincerity. Of course for survivors like him there is no such thing as a storybook conclusion to life. Later at the event he stressed that in no sense did he emerge from the Holocaust "normal," no matter the relative normalcy of the student life. Rather, over time and especially in his new, American setting, the difficult feelings simply lessened. To the extent that his happiness has been genuine, it was predicated not on mastery of an unmasterable past but rather, as he started his postwar existence, on recapturing positive aspects of his prewar self and individual, familial, and group legacies. The "new life" was thus an extension of the old, in a reinvention of both personal and collective destinies.

Notes

INTRODUCTION

1. The numbers of all types of refugees and displaced persons are approximate, though the US and British military, occupation authorities, and non-governmental agencies compiled detailed data on the postwar population in Germany. The figures of fifty thousand Jews and the total of eight million DPs come from Michael Brenner, *After the Holocaust: Rebuilding Jewish Lives in Postwar Germany*, trans. Barbara Harshav (Princeton, N.J.: Princeton University Press, 1997), 11, quoting Wolfgang Jacobmeyer, *Zum Zwangsarbeiter zum Heimatlosen Ausländer: Die Displaced Persons in Westdeutschland, 1945–1951* (Göttingen: Vandenhoek and Ruprecht, 1985), 421. A "Statistical Synopsis," compiled from contemporaneous sources, is provided by Leonard Dinnerstein, *America and Survivors of the Holocaust* (New York: Columbia University Press, 1982), 274–290. Dinnerstein estimates as many as nine million displaced (276).

2. After the war "displaced persons" was often shortened in Allied records to "DP's." Like other contemporary scholars, I use "DPs," without the apostrophe.

3. The figure of nine hundred assembly centers comes from Abraham J. Peck, "A Continent in Chaos: Europe and the Displaced Persons," in *Liberation 1945* (Washington, D.C.: United States Holocaust Memorial Museum, 1995), 106. Mark Wyman counts 762 DP camps throughout Italy, Austria, and all the zones of Germany (excepting the Soviet Zone) in 1947. Mark Wyman, *DPs: Europe's Displaced Persons, 1945–1951* (Ithaca, N.Y.: Cornell University Press, [1989] 1998), 47.

4. Dinnerstein, 273. Elsewhere Dinnerstein estimates that seven million had been repatriated from Germany and Austria combined. A US military report totals more than three million people repatriated from the American Zone alone by April 1946. Dinnerstein, appendix 2, 475. Other estimates give higher totals.

5. On the Old Testament origins and postwar uses of the term, see Zeev W. Mankowitz, *Life Between Memory and Hope: The Survivors of the Holocaust in Occupied Germany* (Cambridge: Cambridge University Press, 2002), 1–4.

6. On the Bricha (whose spelling in English varies), see Yehuda Bauer, *Flight and Rescue: Brichah* (New York: Random House, 1970).

7. Dinnerstein, 278.

8. After surveying statistical data and migration patterns, Yehuda Bauer concludes that "most of the Jewish DPs [in postwar Germany] were not Holocaust survivors, but wartime refugees in the Soviet Union." Yehuda Bauer, "The DP Legacy,"

in *Life Reborn: Jewish Displaced Persons, 1945–51—Conference Proceedings, Washington, D.C., January 14–17, 2000*, ed. Menachem Rosensaft (Washington, D.C.: U.S. Holocaust Memorial Museum, 2001), 25. This statement is mostly true but subtly misleading. Many of these refugees were Soviet, Polish, or Baltic Jews who had spent the entire war well east of the German advance, and therefore are not Holocaust survivors as such. Yet some of the refugees had experienced German invasion in 1939 or 1941 before escaping German occupation and fleeing or being exiled into the Soviet interior.

9. JSU, Aufstellung der jüdischen Studenten in München, 22. Oktober, 1947, YIVO 294.2, reel 85, 1196. The great bulk of archival material in this study is from the files of the Jewish Students' Union in Munich and, secondarily, the zonewide Jewish Students Federation, whose records are amalgamated with those of the Munich Union. The materials are available on microfilm in the collection "Record of the Displaced Persons Camps in Germany" (294.2, formerly MK 483), at the YIVO Institute for Jewish Research in New York City. Hereafter when citing Jewish Students' Union and Federation materials from this collection, I provide "JSU" as a prefix followed by identifying information from the given document as it appeared in the original (typically in German, with European dating). "YIVO" follows, and then the reel number and folder in which the document is found. Documents from the Student Union papers authored by other organizations are not given the prefix "JSU" but instead other identifying marks.

10. Determining with precision the combined peak membership figures for all the local unions is difficult, as individual chapters and the zonewide federation constantly revised their lists. As the unions gained new members, they lost others who may have suspended their studies, emigrated, or moved within or out of the American Zone. Given this turnover, as many as one thousand Jews belonged to various Jewish student unions in the first several years after the war.

11. Bernard Stone, Letter to the Jewish Alumni of German Universities, April 28, 1998, donated to author by Mark Fintel.

12. Munich Alumni Group, Program for Reunion of Jewish Graduates from German Universities after World War II, Boca Raton, Florida, January 1997. Donated to author by Mark Fintel.

13. *Wiedergeburt/The New Life* (April–May 1946), vol. 1: 2. Donated to author by Roman Ohrenstein.

14. The greatest attention given to the students is in Juliane Wetzel, *Jüdisches Leben in München, 1945–1951: Durchgangsstation oder Wiederaufbau?* (Munich: Kommissionsverlag Uni-Druck, 1987). Atina Grossman addresses the students briefly, and Avinoam Patt gives them passing mention (I cite their works below). Anna Holian's article, "Displacement and the Postwar Reconstruction of Education: Displaced Persons at the UNRRA University of Munich, 1945–1948," *Contemporary European History* 17: 2 (2008), discusses the Jewish students while they were at the UNRRA school. The students have also been the subject of periodic profiles in the German or Jewish press, such as Dietrich Mittler, "Wir waren alle Waisen: Wahlverwandtschaften dem Holocaust—Jüdische Studenten in München," *Suddeutsche Zeitung* (April 20/21,

1996), and David Bittner, "Schooling Survivors: Alumni of German University Recall Post-war Situation," *L'Chaim* (January 14, 1997), 1.

15. These impressions are based on my attendance at the conference, where alumnus Mark Fintel gave a presentation on the DP students at one of the many panels.

16. Elie Wiesel, "Keynote Address," in *Life Reborn*, 84.

17. Eva Fogelman, "Coping with the Psychological Aftermath of Extreme Trauma," in *Life Reborn*, 91.

18. Author interview with Mark Fintel.

19. Sabina Zimering, *Hiding in the Open: A Holocaust Memoir* (St. Paul, Minn.: St. Cloud Press, 2001), 161.

20. This broad tendency, often implicit, is present in the work of Lawrence Langer, Shoshana Felman, Michael Bernard-Donals, Richard Glejzer, Linda Belau, and the film *Shoah*, by Claude Lanzmann.

21. A first generation of studies includes, most prominently, Dinnerstein, *America and Survivors of the Holocaust*; Malcolm J. Proudfoot, *European Refugees: 1939–52: A Study in Forced Population Movement* (London: Faber and Faber Ltd., n.d.); and Mark Wyman, *DPs: Europe's Displaced Persons, 1945–1951*. Engaging specifically Jewish themes, Yehuda Bauer authored *Flight and Rescue: Brichah*, and *Out of the Ashes: The Impact of American Jews on Post-Holocaust European Jewry* (Oxford: Pergamon, 1989). A next set of forays into DP history, oriented toward institutions, include Jacobmeyer, *Zum Zwangsarbeiter zum Heimatlosen Ausländer: Die Displaced Persons in Westdeutschland, 1945–1951*; Frank Stern, "The Historic Triangle: Occupiers, Germans, and Jews in Postwar Germany," in *Tel Aviver Jahrbuch fuer deutsche Geschichte* 19 (1990); Angelika Koenigseder and Juliane Wetzel, *Lebensmut im Wartesaal: Die juedischen DPs (Displaced Persons) im Nachkriegsdeutschland* (Frankfurt am Main: Fischer, 1994); and Angelika Eder, *Fluechtige Heimat: Juedische displaced Persons in Landsbergam Lech 1945 bis 1950* (Munich: Kommissionsverlag UNI-Druck, 1998). Michael Brenner's *After the Holocaust* arguably marks the most modern phase of research, as it sought to bring DP studies into histories both of the Holocaust and postwar Germany. Important subsequent works include Mankowitz, *Life Between Memory and Hope*; Ruth Gay, *Safe Among the Germans: Liberated Jews after World War II* (New Haven, Conn.: Yale University Press, 2002); Hagit Lavsky, *New Beginnings: Holocaust Survivors in Bergen-Belsen and the British Zone in Germany, 1945–1950* (Detroit: Wayne State University Press, 2002); Jay Howard Geller, *Jews in Post-Holocaust Germany, 1945–1952* (New York: Cambridge University Press, 2005); William Hitchcock, *The Bitter Road to Freedom: A New History of the Liberation in Europe* (New York: Free Press, 2008); as well as the works by Grossmann, Patt, and Myers Feinstein cited below. Two important conferences in the early 2000s brought together scholars from around the world who were working on the immediate postwar period. The first was "Birth of a Refugee Nation: Displaced Persons in Post-War Europe, 1945–51," held at the Remarque Institute at New York University in 2001. Its proceedings were published as "Workshop Draft Papers," distributed to its participants. The second conference was "Beyond Camps and Forced Labor: Current International Research on Survivors of Nazi Persecution," held

in 2003 by the University of London and the Imperial War Museum. Its many papers were published in a CD-ROM volume: Johannes-Dieter Steinert and Inge Weber-Newth, eds., *Beyond Camps and Forced Labor: Current International Research on Survivors of Nazi Persecution* (Osnabrück: Secolo Publishing, 2005). The conference has been reprised in subsequent years. Various monographs, largely by German scholars, detail the reestablishment of Jewish communities in German cities and towns after the war.

22. This narrative runs throughout Mankowitz's text, though he addresses many aspects of the lives of Jewish DPs. Constructing a more or less unified story of DPs' contributions to Zionism, Mankowitz's work appears as a postwar corollary to what Amos Goldberg described as an "Israeli school of Holocaust research." According to Goldberg, this "school seeks to redeem the Jews from their status of mere objects of annihilation by reconstructing them as historical agents in their own right—at both the collective and individual levels. In Israel, this history was written within the Zionist national history paradigm . . . which views Jews not as a religious, cultural, or even ethnic group but as a national grouping." Amos Goldberg, "Forum: On Saul Friedländer's *The Years of Extermination*, (2) The Victim's Voice and Melodramatic Aesthetics in History," *History and Theory* 48: 3 (October 2009), 223–224. Mankowitz became the first director of the Diana Zborowski Center for the Study of the Aftermath of the Holocaust, established in 2009, at Israel's Yad Vashem.

23. Avinoam J. Patt, *Finding Home and Homeland: Jewish Youth and Zionism in the Aftermath of the Holocaust* (Detroit: Wayne State University Press, 2009).

24. Atina Grossmann, *Jews, Germans, and Allies: Close Encounters in Occupied Germany* (Princeton, N.J.: Princeton University Press, 2007). Patt, following Grossmann, discusses as well the existential and not merely political appeal of Zionism, especially among young survivors.

25. Margarete Myers Feinstein, *Holocaust Survivors in Postwar Germany, 1945–57* (New York: Cambridge University Press, 2010).

26. Geller, 5.

27. Avinoam J. Patt and Michael Berkowitz, "Introduction," in *"We Are Here": New Approaches to Displaced Persons in Postwar Germany*, ed. Patt and Berkowitz (Detroit: Wayne State University Press, 2009), 4.

28. See Tamar Lewinsky, *Displaced Poets: Jiddische Schriftsteller im Nachkriegsdeutschland, 1945–51* (Göttingen: Vandenhoeck & Ruprecht, 2008).

29. Professor Brodzki teaches at Sarah Lawrence College. She is the author of *Can These Bones Live? Translation, Survival, and Cultural Memory* (Palo Alto, Calif.: Stanford University Press, 2007). Its epilogue, which narrates a trip she took with her family to Poland in the 1990s, includes some biographical detail about herself and her parents.

30. I was serving as associate director of the Center for Holocaust and Genocide Studies, headed by the late Professor Stephen Feinstein.

31. I did these studies mostly under the tutelage of Professor Dominick La-Capra at Cornell University. LaCapra is the author of many influential books and essays on the Holocaust, focusing mostly on issues of trauma, the uncanny, and

representation. The attention in his work to processes of "working through" surely conditioned my interest in the post-liberation lives of survivors.

32. My parents met in the United States in the late 1950s, and their coupling is totally unrelated to Turkish migration to postwar Germany. After my mother's death, my father wrote a fascinating biography of sorts of my mother and her family: Bension Varon, *The Promise of the Present and the Shadow of the Past: The Journey of Barbara Frass Varon* (Xlibris Corporation, 2011).

33. Old age has since caught up with the alumni. Many of those I met and interviewed, including alumni leaders, have since passed on. In recent years their gatherings are less frequent and greatly reduced, with many living members now too frail or in too ill health to travel.

34. I continued to gather research from the alumni until 2008, sometimes conducting short interviews to clarify aspects of the students' archive or issues discussed in earlier interview sessions.

35. The newspaper article "Wir waren alle Waisen," by Dietrich Mittler, reports that Simon Snopkowski was the person who shipped the documents. Yet Kerr narrated in some detail how he personally sent the students' records. In one of our meetings, Kerr and I went together to YIVO where, once we explained that Kerr was the source for this part of its DP collection, the archivists were kind enough to pull the original documents, which normally can be viewed only on microfilm. Kerr explained that so many records exist because the student unions used carbon-copy paper for nearly all its typed texts, generating duplicates.

CHAPTER 1

1. Rita Schorr-Germain, Letter to Jewish University Alumni in Germany, 1945–55, July 5, 1998. Donated by Mark Fintel to author. Many of the female alumni took their husbands' names, and I generally use these when referring to them, even in their youths and before their marriages. When, however, they took hyphenated names in marriage, I do not use these names in the text, but only for identification purposes in the endnotes and bibliography. Instead, I use in the text the first part of their hyphenated names, which may themselves be altered forms of their maiden names. Alumni of both genders often adopted Americanized or Hebraicized first names (such as Brian for Bronek) or surnames (Kerr for Kierszkowski) after emigrating, which I also use, and they sometimes had nicknames among their student peers. Thus my naming of the alumni does not always conform to their given names, how they appeared in Student Union records, and how they referred to (or still refer to) each other.

2. Rita Schorr-Germain, Survey—The Jewish Students of Postwar Germany, 12/30/1999.

3. Schorr-Germain, Letter to Alumni.

4. Schorr-Germain, Survey.

5. Ibid.

6. Patt, 22.

7. Ibid., 22.

8. Ibid., 87. Pages 83–89 discuss what motivated young Jews to join and stay within a kibbutz.

9. Author interview with Roman Ohrenstein.

10. JSU, Bericht zur Generalversammlung—Tätigkeitbericht vom 3. Oktober bis 31. January 1947, YIVO reel 85, 1193. The document reports on the shift in numbers. An undated document, JSU, Aufstellung der Jüdischen Studenten, in München, gives the names and other data about exactly 254 students, and is therefore likely from October 1946. YIVO reel 85, 1196.

11. The figure 402 is from an undated document, JSU, Statistik ueber die Anzahl der juedischen Studenten auf einzelnen Universitaeten verteilt, YIVO reel 85, 1196. A separate document from July 1947 lists 402 students, suggesting that the former document is from the same time. JSU, Aufstellung der Jüdischen Studenten in München, 22. Oktober, 1947, YIVO reel 85, 1196, lists 460 students as members. Days earlier, the Union issued an internal document listing membership for the winter semester of 1947–48 at 413. JSU, Bericht der Vorstandschaft, 2. Februar 1947 bis 12. Oktober 1947, YIVO reel 85, 1234. Numerous lists of students in various locales are in YIVO reel 87, 1227 and 1228 as well.

12. JSU, Statistik ueber die Anzahl der juedischen Studenten auf einzelnen Universitaeten verteilt, YIVO reel 85, 1196.

13. JSU, Statistik der Jüdischen Studenten in München, July 1947. YIVO reel 85, 1196. The given figures for the breakdown in national origin add up to 400, though the document records 402 students in the Union. Two additional students are listed under a column headed with "sl." This could be an abbreviation for Slovakia, but I cannot say for sure.

14. JSU, Jüdischer Studentenverband in der Amerikanischen Zone Deutschland—Universität Erlangen, October 12, 1947, YIVO reel 85, 1196.

15. JSU, Undated list for Marburg, YIVO reel 85, 1196. The list has 38 students but legibly identifies the national origin of only 27.

16. JSU, Liste der Jüdsiche Studenten in Heidelberg, n.d., likely Summer 1947, YIVO reel 85, 1196.

17. JSU, Statistik der Jüdischen Sudenten in München; Bericht der Vorstandschaft, 2. Februar 1947 bis 12. Oktober 1947, YIVO reel 85, 1196.

18. Patt, 17; 278 note 9, from chapter 1.

19. Mankowitz, 17. He lists the nationality for 98 percent of the Jewish DPs in the survey. The other 2 percent likely came from an assortment of other countries.

20. Patt, 22.

21. Ibid., 22.

22. The number of surveys I reference throughout the text fluctuates mildly depending on the data I am culling. Some respondents did not fill out (or legibly answer) each question, such that the number varies. Also, they were returned in staggered fashion, and I did not thus always draw data from the full set of surveys.

23. JSU, Aufstellung der Jüdischen Studenten in München, YIVO reel 85, 1196.

24. JSU, Statistik der Jüdischen Studenten in München, YIVO reel 85, 1196.

25. If we add data from the above-cited lists for Erlangen, Darmstadt, and Heidelberg, we see that 32.8 percent of the students were born in 1924 or later, and those fourteen or younger in 1939 jump to 26 percent. The Erlangen list, it should be noted, is from October 1947 (nearly a year later than the Munich list), and that for Heidelberg is from the summer of 1947. The later lists generally show later birth years, as newly joining students had more time to complete *gymnasium* and study for exams after the war.

26. In a few cases, I detected discrepancies between the year of birth alumni reported in interviews and that recorded on old Student Union rosters, and some alumni admitted to falsifying their age.

27. Patt, 8.

28. Ibid., 8.

29. Author interview with Philip Balaban.

30. Alexander B. White, *Be a Mensch: A Legacy of the Holocaust* (Scottsdale, Ariz.: Self-published, Alexander Bialywlos White, 2004), 7, 14.

31. White, 32.

32. Author interview with Sabina Zimering.

33. Author interview with Mark Fintel.

34. Balaban interview.

35. White, 19.

36. Ibid., 33.

37. Author interview with Fred Reiter.

38. Author interview with Mark Hupert.

39. Author interview with Georg Majewski.

40. A 1931 census, subject to certain flaws, shows the following distribution— Poles: 69 percent, Ukrainians: 14.3 percent, Jews: 7.8 percent, Byelorussians: 3.9 percent, Germans: 3.9 percent, Others: .9 percent. Joseph Marcus, *Social and Political History of the Jews in Poland, 1919–1939* (Berlin: Mouton Publishers, 1983), 16–17. Records from 1938, less reliable still, report Poles: 64 percent, Ukrainians: 16 percent, Jews: 10 percent, Byelorussians: 5 percent, Germans: 4 percent, Others: 1 percent. www.kresy.co.uk/census_detail.html.

41. Norman Davies, "Ethnic Diversity in Twentieth-Century Poland," in *From Shtetl to Socialism*, ed. Antony Polonsky (London: Littman Library of Jewish Civilization, 1993), 237. Davies cautions: "In a very real sense, most people in early twentieth-century Poland lived in conditions which nourished their perception of being an exposed minority. . . . In particular, it would be wrong to identify automatically the majority population as social oppressors, and the national minorities as the oppressed. Both the Polish and Jewish communities displayed a wide range of social and economic standing, and in various times and locations groups of Poles and Jews could sometimes be regarded as advantaged, sometimes as disadvantaged, elements of society. The lines between rich and poor, or between privilege and underprivilege, did not follow the ethnic divide" (236).

42. Yisrael Gutman, "Polish Antisemitism Between the Wars: An Overview," in *The Jews of Poland Between Two World Wars*, ed. Yisrael Gutman, Ezra Mendelsohn,

Jehuda Reinharz, and Chone Shmeruk (Hanover, N.H.: Brandeis University Press, 1989), 101.

43. James Lichten, "Jewish Assimilation in Poland, 1863–1943," in *The Jews in Poland*, ed. Chimen Abramsky, Maciej Jachimczyk, and Antony Polonsky (Oxford: Basil Blackwell, Ltd., 1986), 121.

44. Szyja Bronsztejn, "Polish-Jewish Relations as Reflected in Memoirs of the Interwar Period," in *Jews in Independent Poland, 1918–1939*, ed. Antony Polonsky, Ezra Mendelsohn, and Jerzy Tomaszewski (London: Littman Library of Jewish Civilization, 1994), 66, and Annamaria Orla-Bukowska, "Shtetl Communities: Another Image," in ibid., 90.

45. Andrej Paczowski, "The Jewish Press in the Political Life of the Second Republic," in *Jews in Independent Poland*, 177; www.jewishvirtuallibrary.org/jsource/vjw/Vilnius.html.

46. Orla-Bukowska, 90.

47. Jerry Tomaszewski, "The Role of Jews in Polish Commerce, 1918–39," in *The Jews of Poland Between Two World Wars*, 147; Paczowski, 178.

48. Tomaszewski, "The Role of Jews in Polish Commerce," 142; Paczowski, 178.

49. The poverty of Poland and its Jews is a major theme in Marcus. More recent analyses have revised somewhat his rather bleak description of the economic standing of Jews.

50. Restrictions on Jewish employment are noted in Bronsztejn, 69, and Bina Garncarska-Kadary, "Some Aspects of the Life of the Jewish Proletariat in Poland during the Interwar Period," in *Jews in Independent Poland*, 247–248.

51. Paczowski, 178.

52. This is the conclusion of Yisrael Gutman after surveying arguments that Jews were subject to the same amount of discrimination as other minorities in Poland. Gutman, 101. It is affirmed by Bronsztejn, especially pages 74–86. Ezra Mendelsohn reviews the contentious debates about the extent of anti-Semitism in Poland in "Jewish Historiography on Polish Jewry in the Interwar Period," in *The Jews of Poland Between Two World Wars*, 3–13.

53. This did not preclude involvement in Polish politics and even alliance with Polish nationalist parties favorable to their interests. See Gershon C. Bacon, "Agudat Israel in Interwar Poland," in *The Jews of Poland Between Two World Wars*, 20–35.

54. The strongly urban character of the students is also likely a result of the patterns of killing in the Holocaust. The mobile killing squads known as the *Einsatzgruppen*, unleashed in 1941, were especially efficient in massacring Jews in Poland's many small towns. In general, opportunities for survival seemed greatest in the cities, and financial resources, most concentrated among urban dwellers, might be used to wager one's survival. By the same token, Jews in the countryside could more easily find safety with neighboring farmers.

55. The figure is from Orla-Bukowska, 95.

56. Balaban interview.

57. Georg D. Majewski, *Only a Dead Soul Is Forgotten*, trans. Gordon Shifman (Israel: Meida Techni, 1990), 105. Text given to author.

58. Henry Krystal, Survey—The Jewish Students of Postwar Germany, 12/21/99.

59. Sabina Zimering interview.

60. On both the elite and elitist characters of European students and intellectuals of the era, see Holian, "Displacement and the Postwar Reconstruction of Education," 186–190.

61. Schochet interview.

62. Frederick Reiter, Autobiographical Sketch, given to author by Fred Reiter.

63. Reiter interview.

64. Author interview with Lydia Eichenholz.

65. Interview with Henry Krystal, conducted on September 19, 1996, in connection with the Voice/Vision of the Holocaust Oral History Archive at the University of Michigan—Dearborn. The interview is online at http://holocaust.umd.umich.edu/krystal/.

66. Mark Hupert interview.

67. Joseph Heimberg, Survey—The Jewish Students of Postwar Germany, 1/20/2000.

68. Sabina Zimering interview.

69. Joseph Taler, Survey—The Jewish Students of Postwar Germany, 1/20/2000.

70. Sabina Zimering interview.

71. Krystal interview at http://holocaust.umd.umich.edu/interview.php?D=krystal&section=3.

72. Josef Furman, Survey—The Jewish Students of Postwar Germany, 12/30/1999.

73. Eichenholz interview.

74. Reiter interview.

75. "In Memory of Dr. Albert Genis, by Dr. Alice Genis, at the 1997 Munich Alumni Reunion, Boca Raton, Florida, January 12, 1997." Document given to author.

76. Fintel interview.

77. Krystal survey.

78. Balaban interview.

79. Fintel interview.

80. Sabina Zimering interview.

81. Author interview with Rubin Zimering.

82. On the impact of the depression on the Jewish economy and workforce, see Garncarska-Kadary.

83. Emanuel Melzer, "Antisemitism in the Last Years of the Second Polish Republic," in *The Jews of Poland*, 126.

84. Szymon Rudnicki, "From 'Numerus Clausus' to 'Numerus Nullus,'" in *From* Shtetl *to Socialism*, 332–358.

85. On the origins of the treaty, see Mark Levene, "Britain, a British Jew, and Jewish Relations in the New Poland: The Making of the Polish Minorities Treaty of 1919," in *Jews in Independent Poland*, 14–41.

86. Jerzy Tomaszewski, "The Civil Rights of Jews in Poland, 1918–1939," in *Jews in Independent Poland*, 121.

87. Ibid., 117–118.

88. Ibid., 121–122.

89. Ibid., 125–127.

90. Shimon Frost, *Schooling as Socio-Political Expression: Jewish Education in Interwar Poland* (Jerusalem: Magnes Press/Hebrew University, 1998), 21; Tomaszewski, "The Civil Rights of Jews," 125–127.

91. Frost, 21.

92. Ibid.

93. Poland's ministry of education made only one grant of public money to Jewish schools during the entire life of the Second Polish Republic. A bill proposing public schools for Jews with instruction in Hebrew or Yiddish was defeated in 1929. Frost, 25, 23–24. Education historian Shimon Frost concludes, "A Jewish educational system, supported by the state as a tangible expression of Jewish national autonomy and in fulfillment of the Minority Rights Treaty never came into being. Jewish education in Poland during the years of the Second Republic was destined to be an internally-motivated and self-propelled effort of the Jewish community itself." Frost, 26.

94. Frost, 23.

95. Ibid., 70–71. This schematic is based on Poland's 1932 "Revised National Education Act." My sense is that it hardly made education follow a uniform structure; as a result, various students—including some of the alumni—entered and finished (or were set to finish) primary and secondary school at different ages.

96. Frost, 30, 71. Where there were no Sabbath schools, Jewish children were exempt from Saturday and holiday attendance. Conversely, Jews enrolled in "regular" public schools were required to attend on Saturdays and holidays if there was a Sabbath school in the district, although they could not be forced "to write, draw, and participate in workshops" on those days.

97. Frost, 32. Part of the conservatives' motives was to drive Jews out of teaching.

98. Ibid., 31.

99. Opposed by Polish nationalists and anti-communists, and torn by ideological disputes, these fell into decline in the 1930s.

100. Frost, 35–51. This is only a sketch of a Jewish education system that in administrative, curricular, and ideological terms was enormously complex. Throughout the interwar years, negotiations with the state took place over such details as the hours and kinds of religious instruction and the degree of state supervision of Jewish schools. For more on such matters, as well as figures for Jewish enrollments in all types of schools, see Frost, 27–107. Marcus provides statistics on pages 149 and 151.

101. Marcus, 149.

102. The numbers are from Chone Shmeruk, "Hebrew-Yiddish-Polish: A Trilingual Jewish Culture," in *The Jews of Poland Between Two World Wars*, 294–295. The terminology regarding the status of institutions can be confusing. Shmeruk classifies, for example, the Tzisho and Tarbut schools as public, though they were not run by the state and were financed mostly by tuition, support from the Jewish community, and even outside aid via such groups as the American Joint Distribution Committee, along with occasional municipal moneys. "Hebrew-Yiddish-Polish: A Trilingual Jewish Culture," 293–294. On financing, see Frost, 34.

103. Shmeruk, 293. The figure is for 1930–31.

104. Frost, 33.

105. In 1934, only two of the Tarbut's secondary schools were authorized to administer the exams. Frost, 36.

106. Garncarska-Kadary, 245–246. For additional perspective on Jews in the Polish university system, see Natalia Aleksiun, "Ammunition in the Struggle for National Rights: Jewish Historians in Poland Between the Two World Wars" (PhD diss., New York University, 2010).

107. Garncarska-Kadary, 245–246.

108. Rudnicki, 361.

109. Bronsztejn, 72.

110. Rudnicki, 375.

111. Garncarska-Kadary, 246.

112. Rudnicki, 371.

113. Ibid., 375.

114. Elias Epstein, Survey—The Jewish Students of Postwar Germany, 7/19/2000.

115. Ohrenstein interview.

116. Author interview with Sophie Schorr-Reiner.

117. Author interview with Felix Korn.

118. Author interview with Isaac Minzberg.

119. Author interview with Henry Miller. I cannot independently confirm Miller's numbers.

120. Rudnicki, 366–367. Miller describes the National Democrats of his own day as comparatively mild and attributes the anti-student violence to still more hostile proto-fascist groups.

121. Author interview with Lucy Fink.

122. Sabina Zimering interview.

CHAPTER 2

1. Korn interview.

2. Schorr-Germain survey.

3. The survival rate of Jewish children is from Deborah Dwork, *Children with a Star: Jewish Youth in Nazi Europe* (New Haven, Conn.: Yale University Press, 1991), xxxiii.

4. Laura Jockusch and Tamar Lewinsky, "Paradise Lost? Postwar Memory of Polish Jewish Survival in the Soviet Union," *Holocaust and Genocide Studies* 24: 3 (Winter 2010), 390.

5. Norman Davies, "Introduction," in *Jews in Eastern Poland and the USSR, 1931–46*, ed. Norman Davies and Antony Polonsky (Macmillan: London, 1991), 3. Detailed population estimates are in Maciej Siekierski, "The Jews in Soviet-Occupied Eastern Poland at the End of 1939: Numbers and Distribution," in *Jews in Eastern Poland*, 110–113.

6. Davies, "Introduction," 3. In the fall of 1939, refugee totals, including non-Jews, were as high as 600,000. Siekierski, 113.

7. Not taking this last group into account, Zeev Mankowitz concludes that "two-thirds of *She'erith Hepleitah* were repatriates [from the Soviet Union] who had not been personally and directly caught up in the Nazi policies of terror, torture, and killing." Mankowitz, 19.

8. Timothy Snyder's acclaimed *Bloodlands: Europe Between Hitler and Stalin* (New York: Basic Books, 2010) tried, in part, to reorient understandings of the Holocaust and the war more broadly by placing great emphasis on the Soviet occupation of parts of Eastern Europe and the mass violence it entailed.

9. Davies, "Introduction," 13–15; Dov Levin, *The Lesser of Two Evils: Eastern European Jewry under Soviet Rule, 1939–1941*, trans. Naftali Greenwood (Philadelphia: Jewish Publication Society, [1989] 1995), 40–64.

10. See Ryszard Terlecki, "The Jewish Issue in the Polish Army in the USSR and the Near East, 1941–1944," and Klemens Nussbaum, "Jews in the Kosciusko Division and the First Polish Army," both in *Jews in Eastern Poland*, 161–171 (Terlecki); 183–213 (Nussbaum).

11. Jockusch and Lewinsky, 373. Siekierski, in an earlier estimate, gives a figure of 200,000 (113).

12. Davies, "Introduction," 30.

13. This is the thesis of Ben-Cion Pinchuk in "Sovietisation and the Jewish Response to Nazi Policies of Mass Murder," in *Jews in Eastern Poland*, 137. Davies affirms Pinchuk's portrait of Jewish distress, while doubting that the Soviet occupation was crucial in preventing a mass escape. "Introduction," 30–33.

14. Levin, 89.

15. Ibid., 90.

16. Ibid., 99–102.

17. Levin records the kinds and numbers of schools and verifies these rapid changes, 93–95.

18. Author interview with Marion Glaser.

19. Schorr-Reiner interview.

20. Rebecca Manley, *To the Tashkent Station: Evacuation and Survival in the Soviet Union at War* (Ithaca, N.Y.: Cornell University Press, 2009), 86–97.

21. Eichenholz interview.

22. Robert Nenner interview.

23. Balaban interview.

24. Manley details the intent of the evacuation on 24–41.

25. Manley, 43.

26. Manley, chapter 4, "Popular Responses" (77–114), discusses these dilemmas at length.

27. Manley, 46.

28. Ibid., 66. Two million people were evacuated from Moscow alone (63).

29. Jockusch and Lewinsky. The following summary is drawn from material throughout their article.

30. Jockusch and Lewinsky discuss the proliferation of such memoirs on page 392 and provide a partial list in note 86.

31. Balaban interview.

32. Author interview with Frida Karp.

33. Rubin Zimering interview.

34. Ibid.

35. Majewski, 4.

36. Ibid., 9.

37. Ibid., 22.

38. Ibid., 26.

39. Author interview with Guti Kanner.

40. These hardships are documented in Albert Kaganovitch, "Jewish Refugees and Soviet Authorities during World War II," *Yad Vashem Studies* 38: 2.

41. Jockusch and Lewinsky, 388.

42. Rubin Zimering interview.

43. Majewski, 60–61.

44. Author interview with Henry Miller.

45. Kanner interview.

46. Reiter interview.

47. Schorr-Reiner interview.

48. Author interview with Rochelle Eisenberg.

49. The family was liberated in Bergen-Belsen, to which they had been driven from Auschwitz.

50. Mark Fintel interview.

51. Author interview with Isaac Langer.

52. Trained in glasswork, White speculates that he was chosen by Schindler, whom he had never met, because the largely bogus factory needed some people actually skilled in trades, should real work be required. White, 141.

53. Ibid., 105.

54. White, after a brief internment in Groß-Rosen, began working in the Schindler factory in October 1944.

55. White, "Introduction," i, 135.

56. Minzberg interview. All quotes below from interview.

57. Author interview with Robert Nenner. All quotes below from interview.

58. *Wiedergeburt/The New Life* (April–May 1946), vol. 1: 2. Donated to author by Henry Frist.

CHAPTER 3

1. Yehuda Knobler, "A Few Words for Joseph," in *On the Road: Notes on the Lives of Survivors*, ed. Yehuda Knobler and Yirmiyahu Rabina (Tel Aviv, 1952). Silberman's name appears variously with an "S" and a "Z" (as it was translated here). I will generally use "Silberman," as the name appears in Union records.

2. Dinnerstein, *America and Survivors of the Holocaust*, 10.

3. The figures are from in Proudfoot, 258.

4. Grossmann, 133.

5. Wyman, 47. Proudfoot provides a detailed breakdown of the "division of responsibility" between the US military and UNRRA on pp. 230–302, summarized

in a table on pp. 231–234. Such formal divisions did not always, however, dictate the actual responsibilities each institution assumed.

6. Susan Pettiss, "The Story of a Museum," August 5, 1945, United Nations Archive-United Nations Relief and Rehabilitation Administration (hereafter UNA-UNRRA), S-0436-0031-02. (The last two numbers within the UNA-UNRRA archiving system indicate the box and file in which the document is found.) U.N.R.R.A. TEAM 108, "Report Nr. 9. September 12, 1946," UNA-UNRRA, S-0436-0031-03. The number of residents peaked in the first week of September. The week of August 18, 93 of the 533 residents were listed as Jews. U.N.R.R.A. TEAM 108, "Report Nr. 8. August 18, 1946," UNA-UNRRA, S-0436-0031-03.

7. U.N.R.R.A. TEAM 108, "Report Nr. 9. September 12, 1946," UNA-UNRRA, S-0436-0031-03.

8. Pettiss, "The Story of a Museum," UNA-UNRRA, S-0436-0031-02. Her book is Susan T. Pettiss, with Lynne Taylor, *After the Shooting Stopped: The Story of an UNRRA Welfare Officer in Germany, 1945–1947* (Victoria, B.C.: Trafford Press, 2004).

9. "Field Report. UNRRA Team 108—Deutsches Museum. 31 January, 1946," UNA-UNRRA, S-0436-0031-02.

10. U.N.R.R.A. TEAM 108, "Report Nr. 9. September 12, 1946," UNA-UNRRA, S-0436-0031-03.

11. Emanuel Tanay, *Passport to Life: Autobiographical Reflections on the Holocaust* (Ann Arbor, Mich.: Forensic Press, 2004), 183.

12 JDC, M. J. Jaslow, Report of Education Survey, December 26, 1945–January 5, 1946, JDC-NY [Joint Distribution Committee Archives, New York]; Record of the American Joint Distribution Committee Archives, 1945–1954, folder 335. Throughout this study, I cite extensively from Joint records, held at the AJDC archives in New York City, and specifically from the records of the Joint New York City office from the years 1945–1954. All such records will be marked as "JDC" when originating from the Joint, followed by the document title, then "JDC-NY," followed by the folder from which the document was culled.

13. Mankowitz, 101. The committee soon became the "Central Committee of Liberated Jews in the U.S. Zone," with a parallel group operating in the British Zone.

14. Susan Pettiss, "The Story of a Museum," August 5, 1945, UNA-UNRRA, S-0436-0031-02.

15. I have found no record of the number of Jews attending the fall lectures.

16. JSU, Aufstellung aller registrierten Studenten bis 2 Juni 1946, YIVO reel 87, 1227.

17. Anna Holian, "Between National Socialism and Soviet Communism: The Politics of Self-Representation among Displaced Persons in Munich, 1945–1951" (PhD diss., University of Chicago, 2005 [Ann Arbor, Mich.: UMI Microfilm, 2005]), 469. Holian's dissertation is the most authoritative, scholarly source on the UNRRA University. Much of the information and perspective on the university is reproduced in Holian's article "Displacement and the Postwar Reconstruction of Education" (referenced earlier). Her book, *Between National Socialism and Soviet Communism:*

Displaced Persons in Postwar Germany (Ann Arbor, Mich.: University of Michigan Press, 2011), also contains some material on the university and content important to this study.

18. Holian, "Between National Socialism and Soviet Communism" (diss.), 466. A condensed history of the university is also in Holian, "Displacement and the Postwar Reconstruction of Education," 171–177.

19. From "List of the Lecturers," n.d., UNA-UNRRA, S-0436-0031-03.

20. "Academical Section: Report from 11 September, 1945," UNA-UNRRA, S-0436,-0031-03. The numbers actually taking the courses were lower than the number registered, and grew over the fall.

21. Holian, "Displacement and the Postwar Reconstruction of Education," 191.

22. On the political and legal implications of both the condition of "statelessness" and that designation, see G. Daniel Cohen, *In War's Wake: Europe's Displaced Persons in the Postwar Order* (New York: Oxford University Press, 2012), especially 83–90, 129–131, 133–141.

23. These descriptions of the students are from a 1946 UNRRA report, quoted in Holian, "Between National Socialism and Soviet Communism" (diss.), 470.

24. "Memo: K. Richman to W.S. Rogers, Plans for a D.P. University at the Deutsches Museum, Oct. 31. 1945," UNA-UNRRA, S-0437-0031-02. The four-page memo outlines the challenges presented by the plans.

25. Ibid.

26. See Stefan-Ludwig Hoffmann, ed., *Human Rights in the Twentieth Century* (Cambridge: Cambridge University Press, 2011), especially the essay of G. Daniel Cohen, "The 'Human Rights Revolution' at Work: Refugees and Displaced Persons in Postwar Europe," 45–61. See also G. Daniel Cohen, "Between Relief and Politics: Refugee Humanitarianism in Postwar Europe," *Journal of Contemporary History*, 43: 3 (July 2008), 437–449, and Cohen, *In War's Wake*, especially 79. Recent scholarship, including Cohen, has complicated the origins and contested the extent of such a "revolution." Much of Cohen's work seeks to show how abstract notions of human rights developed at the time were partially, if imperfectly, realized in policies toward European refugees.

27. UNRRA Policy on Education for Displaced Persons in Germany, 20 November, 1945, YIVO reel 87, 1230.

28. Ibid.

29. George Woodbridge, *UNRRA: The History of the United Nations Relief and Rehabilitation Administration*, vol. 2 (New York: Columbia University Press, 1950), 526.

30. "Field Report. UNRRA Team 108—Deutsches Museum. 31 January, 1946," UNA-UNRRA, S-0436-0031-02.

31. Holian, "Displacement and the Postwar Reconstruction of Education," 181–186; Holian, "Between National Socialism and Soviet Communism" (diss.), 487–492.

32. Balaban interview.

33. JDC, M. J. Jaslow, Report of Education Survey, December 26, 1945–January 5, 1946, JDC-NY, 335.

34. UNRRA document with no cover page. Likely UNRRA Team 108 Field Report from Spring 1946, page 3. UNRRA S-0436-0031-02.

35. Holian, "Displacement and the Postwar Reconstruction of Education," 71; Tanay, 190.

36. "UNRRA University," in *DP Express*, February 16, 1946, UNA-UNRRA, S-0436-0031-04.

37. Ibid.

38. Patt, 15.

39. Ibid., 16.

40. Ibid., 14–15. Statistical table from Proudfoot, *European Refugees: 1939–52*, reprinted in Dinnerstein, 277.

41. Bauer, *Out of the Ashes*, 48, cited in Mankowitz, 15.

42. The figures are from the statistical table in Proudfoot, 238–239.

43. Wetzel, vii–viii. Additional statistics on the prewar and postwar Jewish populations in Munich are in Anthony D. Kauders, *Democratization and the Jews, 1945–1965* (Lincoln: University of Nebraska Press, 2004), 41–43.

44. Mankowitz, 17–19. A contemporary account of Jewish postwar migration is provided by Jacob Oleiski, a leader of the Central Committee, in an interview conducted by the American researcher Dr. David Boder on August 20, 1946. The interview text is at http://voices.iit.edu/interviewee?doc=oleiskiJ. Boder conducted 109 interviews with survivors in 1946, and is credited with recording among the very first Holocaust testimonies.

45. Patt, 98; Mankowitz indicates that as many as 250,000 Jews came via the Bricha into Italy and the American Zones of Germany and Austria by 1947 (17).

46. Patt discusses the "postwar organization of Polish Jewry" and the effort to establish *kibbutzim* especially, on 71–103. On Jewish repatriates in Poland, see also Jockusch and Lewinsky, 375–380.

47. Mankowitz, 18. Jockusch and Lewinsky put the estimate of repatriates as high as 200,000 (374).

48. Mankowitz, 18. On such violence, see especially Jan T. Gross, *Fear: Anti-Semitism in Poland after Auschwitz: An Essay in Historical Interpretation* (New York: Random House, 2006).

49. Mankowitz, 18–19. These migrations are discussed as well in Wyman, 143–145, and Bauer, 113–151.

50. Mark Fintel interview.

51. Tanay, 187.

52. The Harrison Report and its fallout are among the mostly widely discussed aspects of the history of Jewish DPs, recounted in nearly every major work. See especially Grossmann, Dinnerstein, Hitchcock, and Mankowitz.

53. Wyman, 145.

54. Holian, "Between National Socialism and Soviet Communism" (diss.), 103. For evolutions in policy, 89–103.

55. "CONFIDENTIAL- Extracts from a report made by Captain G. Weisz on field trip to U.S. Zone, 5 April 1946," UNA-UNRRA, S-0402-0001-01.

56. Holian, "Between National Socialism and Soviet Communism" (diss.), 103.

57. Mankowitz, 131.

58. Holian, "Between National Socialism and Soviet Communism" (diss.), 71–72.

59. Schochet interview.

60. Robert Nenner interview. All quotes that follow are from interview.

61. Mankowitz, 39.

62. Tanay, 173.

63. See Mankowitz, 30–31, 49–51.

64. Tanay, 190.

65. Sabina Zimering interview.

66. JDC, Report of the Educational Director of the American Joint Distribution Committee in Germany and Austria for November 1945, JDC-NY, 335.

67. Sabina Zimering interview.

68. Balaban interview.

69. Ohrenstein interview.

70. Korn interview.

71. Mankowitz uses the term "redeem the future" to describe specifically the Zionist aspirations of DPs, who concluded that "no redeeming purpose could be found in the destruction" (37). Grossmann uses the term frequently and more expansively to describe a variety of Jewish DPs' investments in the future.

72. Ohrenstein interview. For accounts of Gunskirchen's liberation, see the reports of US soldiers at www.jewishvirtuallibrary.org/jsource/Holocaust/Gunskirchen.html.

73. Patt, 20.

74. Central Committee, An Herrn Dipl. Ing. Suchenko, Director d. UNRRA Universität, 11. Jan. 1946, YIVO reel 89 1253.

75. JSU, Tätigkeitsbericht der Vorstandschaft fur die Ziet vom 13. Okt.47 bis zum 25. März 1948, YIVO reel 87, 1235.

76. Simon Snopkowski, *Zuversicht trotz allem* (München: Olzog Verlag, 2000), 51. Snopkowski narrates his Holocaust experience on 32–44.

77. Myers Feinstein, 65–67.

78. Ibid., 67.

79. Snopkowski, 59.

80. Tanay, 109.

81. Ibid., 184.

82. Ibid., 186–187.

83. Schochet interview.

84. Ibid.

85. Simon Schochet, *Feldafing* (Vancouver: November House, 1983), 53.

86. Henry Frist, Letter to the Jewish Alumni of German Universities, May 6, 1998. Donated to author by Mark Fintel.

87. Myers Feinstein, 210.

88. Ibid. On the 1946 Landsberg Purim festival, see also, Tony Blum Dobkin, "The Landsberg Carnival: Purim in a Displaced Persons' Center," in *Purim: The Face and the Mask*, ed. Shifra Epstein (New York: Yeshiva University Museum, 1979).

89. JSU, Letter to Albert Einstein, n.d., YIVO reel 85, 1197.

90. Observations of UNRRA and other relief workers are recorded in Grossmann, 142–159.

91. Mankowitz, 28–29.

92. Korn interview.

93. Myers Feinstein discusses the various fates of Jewish children after the war on 160–168, and the broader confusions, bureaucratic and existential, of adopting "assumed identities" both during and after the war, on 198–203.

94. Tanay, 111.

95. Ibid., 170.

96. Holian, "Between National Socialism and Soviet Communism" (diss.), 483–485.

97. Interview by Anna Holian with Alperovitch (later "Anders") in Holian, "Displacement and the Postwar Reconstruction of Europe," p. 11, n. 106.

98. Tanay, 174.

99. Korn interview.

100. JSU-Heidelberg, n.d. (only pages 2–4 in archive; reference in document to 1947), YIVO folder not recorded.

101. Mankowitz, 37–38.

102. The Central Committee's efforts at recognition are discussed at length in Wetzel, 144–213, Mankowitz, 101–130, and Holian, "Between National Socialism and Soviet Communism" (diss.), 422–434.

103. Mankowitz describes the committee's involvement in education in 131–160.

104. Quoted in Patt, 40.

105. Ibid., 80.

106. Ibid., 98–99.

107. Patt records the number of *hakhsharot* in appendix A, 270.

108. Patt, 2.

109. Ibid. 36.

110. Ibid., 51.

111. Lewinsky, *Displaced Poets*, 75.

112. Mankowitz, 112–113.

113. On complaints with the JDC, see Grossmann, 145, 154, and Mankowitz, 114–116.

114. The institutional structure is evident in the numerous reports the various divisions filed, and outlined in such documents as A.J.D.C. Organizational Chart U.S. Zone, Germany, Haber, 10/47. 30/315.

115. On budget and staff, see Grossmann, 154.

116. On JDC funding of the CK, see Mankowitz, 112–116; on support of *kibbutzim* and *hakhsharot*, see Patt, 60, 62, 146–147, 161, 310.

117. JDC, Letter from Joseph C. Hyman, Executive Vice-Chairman [of JDC], to Rabbi Philip S. Bernstein, October 30, 1945, JDC-NY, 357.

118. An early assessment of educational needs is in JDC, Memorandum on Work of Educational Division, A.J.D.C., January 15, 1946. The Joint's progress is recorded in numerous reports of its education division, e.g., M. J. Joslow, Education and Cultural Report, June–July–August, 1946, JDC-NY, 335.

119. In the summer of 1948, the Joint summarized its achievements, declaring "that in the history of education, one will not find so elaborate a program, developed

so rapidly, and certainly not under comparable conditions. The camps have schools, teachers, and supervisors; children are graded; there are text books and libraries; there are school facilities." It further asserted that the teachers brought from Palestine, financed by the JDC, were the "single most important factor in bringing about this situation." JDC, Judah J. Shapiro to Mr. S. Tarshansky, August 18, 1948, JDC-NY, 334.

120. JDC, Memorandum on Work of Educational Division, A.J.D.C., January 15, 1946, JDC-NY, 335.

121. Korn interview.

122. Robert Nenner interview.

123. Knobler interview.

124. This sketch is drawn from M. Ovadyahu, "The Milieu from Which He Came," and Levi, "Dr. Joseph Zilberman," both in *On the Road*, ed. Knobler and Rabina.

125. His field of study is recorded in JSU, Aufstellung der Jüdischen Studenten, in München, YIVO reel 85, 1196.

126. The early officers are listed in JSU, Protokoll der Gerneralversamlung, 24.3.1946, YIVO reel 87, 1233. Their dates of birth are drawn from a list of 254 Union members, JSU, Aufstellung der Jüdischen Studenten, in München, YIVO reel 85, 1196. The dates, I should stress, are not fully reliable. Silberman's year of birth, for example, is given as 1923, whereas the memorial booklet lists it as 1921.

127. Schochet interview.

128. Lucy Fink interview.

129. JSU, Protokoll der Gerneralversamlung, 24.3.1946, YIVO reel 87, 1233.

130. The constitution is titled "Statut der Vereinigung der jüdischen Studenten," prefaced by, "Einleitung: Zum Statut der Vereinigung der Judischen Studenten in München," YIVO reel 85, 1191. All quotes that follow are from this document.

131. Korn interview.

132. JSU, Einleitung: Zum Statut der Vereinigung der Judischen Studenten in München; Statut der Vereinigung der jüdischen Studenten, YIVO reel 85, 1191. All quotes that follow are from this document.

133. Rafael Nenner, from author interview with Rafael Nenner and Karl Eislander.

134. Holian, "Between National Socialism and Soviet Communism" (diss.), 23.

135. Tanay, 191.

136. My description of the Jewish Students' Union as an interest group is heavily indebted to Holian's theoretical discussion of interest groups and their practical role in occupied Germany. Holian, *Between National Socialism and Soviet Communism* (book), 11–19.

137. In November, when Education Director Pinson complained that "the achievements" of his division were "almost nil" due to a lack of basic administrative infrastructure, the Joint nonetheless boasted of having secured such admissions through an arrangement it brokered with the universities, the Military Government, and UNRRA. JDC, Koppel Pinson, Report of the Educational Director of the American Joint Distribution Committee in Germany and Austria for November 1945, JDC-NY, 335. The arrangement was not exclusive to Munich.

138. Nenner/Eislander interview.

139. CK, An Herrn Dipl. Ing. Suchenko, Director d. UNRRA Universität, 11. Jan. 1946, YIVO reel 89, 1253.

140. JSU, An Seine Magnifizenz, Herr Prof. Rohm, Jan. 19, 1946, YIVO reel 89, 1252. Tanay, 195.

141. Mark Hupert interview.

142. JSU, An das Kultusministerium, 24 January, 1946, YIVO reel 88, 1248.

143. Buchenwald "Häftlings-Personal-Karte," Yehuda Knobler, photocopy given to author.

144. Schochet interview.

145. Myers Feinstein, 200.

146. Myers Feinstein, 32–33.

147. JSU, An den Welfare Officer der UNRRA-Universität, 4 April, 1946, YIVO reel 89, 1253.

148. UNRRA Team 108, To: The Juedischen Studenten Vereinigung, March 12, 1946, YIVO reel 89, 1253.

149. Hupert interview.

150. Der Bayern Staatsminister für Unterricht und Kultus, 28 January 1946, to the MU Rector, YIVO reel 89, 1252.

151. JSU, An Seine Magnifizenz, Rektor der TH, Prof. Dr. Faber, 27 February 1946, YIVO reel 89, 1252.

152. JSU, An Seine Magnifizenz, Rektor der Universität UNRRA, 17 March 1946, YIVO reel 87, 1243.

153. On the formation and functions of the postwar Jewish community, see Wetzel, 3–34.

154. JSU, An die Israelitische Kultusgemeinde, 25 February, 1946, YIVO reel 88, 1248.

155. JSU, An den Staatskommissar für Betreung der Jüden in Bayern, 28 February 1946, YIVO reel 89. 1250.

156. See Wetzel, 50–53.

157. Ibid., 50–51.

158. Kerr interview.

159. JSU, purchase order for lamps, March 18, 1946, YIVO reel 89, 1250; Johann Croner—Schreibmaschinen to the JSU, March 2, 1946, YIVO reel 88, 1247.

160. Staatskommissar Hermann Aumer, An die Firm Schrey, 25 March 1946, YIVO reel 89, 1250.

161. The letterhead first appears on JSU, purchase order for lamps, March 18, 1946, YIVO reel 89, 1250.

162. JSU, An das Arbeitsamt, 21 March 1946, YIVO reel 88, 1247. Arnold Kerr recalls that the Union had, in time, two secretaries. Kerr interview.

163. Der Staatskommissar für die Betreuung der Juden in Bayern, An die Vereinigung Jüdischer Studenten, 26.3.46, YIVO reel 89, 1250.

164. For example, a list of ten additional students, which included Josef Silberman, was submitted to the LMU in early March. JSU, An das Rektorat der Münchner Universität, 10 March 1946, YIVO reel 89, 1252.

165. JSU, An Seine Magnifizenz, Rektor der Universität UNRRA, 17 March 1946, YIVO reel 88, 1243.

166. JSU, An das Kultusministerium, 24 January, 1946, YIVO reel 88, 1248.

167. The requirement is recorded in JSU/CK, Report—About the UNRRA University in Munich, n.d., YIVO reel 87, 1230.

168. A Union "Announcement," likely from October 1946, states that a given student "was accepted by our Verification Commission for university study. The Verification Commission has functioned since 1945 by virtue of an agreement between the Central Committee of Liberated Jews . . . and the Rectors of Munich universities." JSU, Bestaetigung, 15 October (no year given), YIVO, no folder recorded.

169. ZK - Kulturamt, An den UNRRA-University Director, Halina G. Gaszynska, 7.4.1946, YIVO reel 89, 1253.

170. ZK - Kulturamt, An den UNRRA-University Director, Halina G. Gaszynska, 7.4.1946, YIVO, reel 89, 1253. Recognition of the Verification Commission by the States Commissioner for Munich universities is recorded also in JSU, Protokoll, Sitzung der Vorstandschaft, 14. April 1946, YIVO reel 87, 1233.

171. JSU, Protokoll der Gerneralversamlung, 24.3.1946, YIVO reel 87, 1233. All material from the meeting comes from this document.

172. JSU, Protokoll der Vorstandschafts-Sitzung vom 7. August 1946, YIVO reel 87, 1233.

173. Emanuel Tanay, "Holocaust Survivors Who Studied at German Universities 1945–1951," 4–5. Presented at the USHMM conference "Life Reborn" (2000). Text of speech given to author.

174. Koppel S. Pinson, "Jewish Life in Liberated Germany," *Jewish Social Studies* 9: 2 (April 1947), 112.

175. Yehuda Knobler, "We Create," in *Der Jüdische Student* (October/November 1946), Munich. All quotes that follow are from this article.

CHAPTER 4

1. JSU, Statistik der jüdischen Studenten in München, 15.10.1946, YIVO reel 85, 1196; JSU, Tätigkeitsbericht der Vorstandschaft zur Generalversammlung vom 3. Oktober bis 31. Januar 47, YIVO, reel 85, 1193. Small discrepancies in the number of members exist in the Union's records. The former document, for example, counts 249 members as of October 15; the latter reports 254 as of October 3. JSU, Aufstellung der jüdischen Studenten in München, 22 October 1947, YIVO reel 85, 1196.

2. JSU, Statistik ueber die Anzahl der juedischen Studenten auf einzelnen Universitaeten verteilt, n.d., likely July 1947, YIVO reel 85, 1196.

3. JDC, Bericht über die Organisation und Tätigkeit des Verbandes jüdischer Studenten in der britischen Zone Deutschlands, 2, May 1948, JDC-NY, 335.

4. JDC, Report of the Education and Cultural Department for month ending October 31, 1946, JDC-NY, 335.

5. Ibid.

6. The hiring of Piekarczyk is recorded in JDC, M. J. Joslow, Education and Cultural Report, June–July–August, 1946, JDC-NY, 335. His office's duties, as they

evolved, are outlined in Alexander Piekarczyk, Condensed report for the period: January 1st–August 31st, 1947, YIVO reel 87, 1230.

7. Ohrenstein interview.

8. Marna Rehder, Student Services Officer, to Mrs. M. Kurth, Director of UNRRA Team 108, October 15, 1946. UNA-UNRRA S-0436-0031-02.

9. Holian, "Displacement and the Postwar Reconstruction of Education," 174.

10. Eislander from Eislander/Nenner interview.

11. Balaban interview.

12. JSU, Letter to Albert Einstein, n.d., YIVO reel 85, 1197.

13. Sabina Zimering interview.

14. See Holian, "Displacement and the Postwar Reconstruction of Education," 184.

15. Anna D. Jaroszynska-Kirchmann, "Patriotic Responsibility: Polish Schools in German DP Camps," in *Birth of a Refugee Nation: Displaced Persons in Postwar Europe, 1945–1951*, Workshop Draft Papers (New York: Remarque Institute at New York University, April 20–21, 2001). Wyman, 73. Wyman discusses the politics of repatriation at length in chapter 3, 61–86.

16. JDC, To the AJDC, c/o Mr. Josler, n.d., YIVO reel 88, 1248. Clues within the document suggest that it is from February or March of 1946.

17. JSU, Aufstellung an der UNRRA-Universität studierenden jüd. Studenten, YIVO reel 89, 1253. One such list of new applicants was from JSU, November 4, 1946, An die UNRRA-Universität, YIVO reel 89, 1253.

18. Louis Braude, "Recollections from Germany 1945–1951, June 17, 1998," donated to author by Mark Fintel. The text is a brief, unpublished account of Braude's time in postwar Germany, sent to the alumni association.

19. Ohrenstein interview.

20. Robert Nenner interview.

21. JSU, Tätigkeitsbericht der Vorstandschaft zur Generalversammlung vom 3. Oktober bis 31. Januar 47, YIVO reel 85, 1193.

22. Team 108 Field Report, Spring 1946, page 2. UNRRA S-0436-0031-02.

23. Team 108 Field Report, Spring 1946, pages 2–3. UNRRA S-0436-0031-02.

24. Team 108 Field Report, Spring 1946, page 4. UNA-UNRRA S-0436-0031-02.

25. Team 108 Field Report, Spring 1946, page 4-F. UNA-UNRRA S-0436-0031-02.

26. UNRRA UNIVERSITY MUNICH, Monthly Report, May 1946. UNA-UNRRA S-0436-0031-02.

27. UNRRA, Section 7. Living Quarters. Subject: UNRRA Lodgings, n.d. UNA-UNRRA S-0436-0031-02; UNRRA UNIVERSITY MUNICH, Billets in Munich for Professors, Students and Adm. Staff, 21 September, 1946, UNA-UNRRA S-0436-0031-02.

28. MD, Page 4, Section F.

29. Applications for Admission to German Universities Under German Auspices, n.d., YIVO reel 87, 1229.

30. On Gaszynska, see Holian, "Displacement and the Postwar Reconstruction of Education," 172.

31. JSU, Bekanntmachung, 13. November 1946, YIVO reel 87, 1238.

32. Wyman, 124–125.

33. Holian, "Displacement and the Postwar Reconstruction of Education," 176. Student response to the January "closing" of the university is recorded in Ehemalige "UNRRA" Universität Studentenunion, 21.2.1947, UNRRA Universität is als Universität ist nich aufgelost, YIVO reel 89, 1152.

34. Holian, "Displacement and the Postwar Reconstruction of Education," 176–177.

35. Grossmann, 260. On the IRO, see Cohen, *In War's Wake*.

36. Siebald interview. The following material is from the interview.

37. The TH's age requirement is recorded in JSU, Protokoll der Vorstandschaft, 16. Oktober, 1946, YIVO reel 87, 1233.

38. Siebald interview.

39. Reiter interview.

40. Eisenberg interview.

41. Arnold Kerr, USC Shoah Foundation Institute testimony of Arnold Kerr, 1/10/1998 (hereafter Kerr, Shoah Foundation interview). Kerr personally gave me a videocassette recording of the interview, which can be accessed via https://sfiaccess.usc.edu/.

42. Beglaubigte Abschrift: Auszug aus dem Studienbuch, original document, given to author by Yehuda Knobler.

43. JDC, Report of the Education and Cultural Department for month ending October 31, 1946, JDC-NY, 335.

44. Ohrenstein interview. On denazification efforts in academia, see Steven P. Remy, *The Heidelberg Myth: The Nazification and Denazification of a German University* (Cambridge, Mass.: Harvard University Press, 2003).

45. See, for example, JSU, An die Direktion des Handels-Lyzeums, Krakau, Poland—30 April, 1946, YIVO reel 89, 1252.

46. Balaban interview.

47. ZK - Kulturamt, An den UNRRA-University Director, Halina G. Gaszynska, 7.4.1946, YIVO reel 89, 1253; JSU, Bericht der Vorstandschaft, 14. April 1946, YIVO reel 87, 1233.

48. The following description of the tests comes from JSU, Verifikations—Kommission; für die Zulassung jüdischer Studenten zum Hochschulstudium, August 1, 1947, YIVO reel 85, 1191.

49. JSU, Tätigkeitsbericht der Vorstandschaft zur Generalversammlung vom 3. Oktober bis 31. Januar 47, YIVO reel 85, 1193.

50. JSU, Verifikations—Kommission; für die Zulassung jüdischer Studenten zum Hochschulstudium, August 1, 1947, YIVO reel 85, 1191.

51. Schochet interview.

52. JSU, Tätigkeitsbericht der Vorstandschaft der Jüdischen Studentenverbandes, Sommer-Semester 1947, 1. Oktober, 1947, YIVO reel 85, 1191. Individual confirmation of the validity of the test in Frankfurt going back to the fall of 1946 is in Hessisches Staatsministerium, An die Jüdische Studentenvereinigung, Frankfurt/Main, 11. November 1948, document donated to author.

53. JDC, Piekarczyk, Condensed report for the period: January 1st–August 31st, 1947, YIVO reel 87, 1230.

54. On the Gauting hospital, see Walter Fürnohr and Felix Muschialik, eds., *Überleben un Neubeginn: DP-Hospital Gauting ab 1945* (Munich: P. Krichheim Verlag, 2005).

55. I.R.O. Hospital—Team 1065, Gauting Sanitorium for D.P. Patients, An den Jüdischen Studentenverband München, 12. August 1947, YIVO reel 85, 1201.

56. JSU, An Welfare Officer z.Hd. von Miss Loerbel, 2. Oktober 1947, YIVO reel 85, 1201.

57. Such a complaint is recorded in JSU, Bericht—Generalversammlung, 2. Februar, 1947, reel 85, 1193.

58. Dr. Philipp Auerbach an Herrn Yerry-Isador Körner, Betr.: Ihre Zulassung zur Universität, 5. März 1947, YIVO reel 89, 1250.

59. Staatskom für rassisch, religiose, u. politische Verforlgte, An die Jewish Students Union, 8. January, 1947, YIVO reel 89, 1250.

60. JSU, Protokoll der Revisions - Kommission vom 15 Oktober, 1946, YIVO reel 87, 1233.

61. JSU, Bericht der Revisions Kommission, 3 Oktober 1946–31 January 1947, YIVO reel 89, 1250.

62. Tanay, 195.

63. Alexander Piekarczyk, Condensed report for the period: January 1st–August 31st, 1947, YIVO reel 87, 1230.

64. JSU, Protokoll der Sitzung der Verifikations-Kommission für Jüdische Hochschulkandidaten vom 10. Marz 1948, YIVO reel 85, 1192. This document is also in Folders 1191 and 1235.

65. JSU, Protokoll der Sitzung der Verifikations-Kommission für Jüdische Hochschulkandidaten vom 10. Marz 1948, YIVO reel 85, 1192.

66. JSU, Protokoll der Sitzung der Verifikations-Kommission für Jüdische Hochschulkandidaten vom 10. Marz 1948, YIVO reel 85, 1192.

67. The shift in policy is recorded in JDC, M. Jacob Joslow, Memorandum: From AJDC New York to AJDC Munich, Jan. 6, 1948, JDC-NY, 334. The policy is clarified in JDC, ZDN Letter No. 130. Re: Jewish Students in German Universities, Jan. 29, 1948, JDC-NY, 334.

68. Numerous alumni gave me copies of these documents.

69. Tanay, 193.

70. JSU, Protokoll der Sitzung der Verifikations-Kommission der Jüdische Hochschulkandidaten vom 20. Marz 1948, YIVO reel 87, 1235.

71. Ibid.

72. Marie Syrkin, *The State of the Jews* (Washington, D.C.: New Republic Books, 1980). This biographical sketch is drawn from the introduction, 1–8. Syrkin is also the subject of an appreciative biography by Carole S. Kessner, *Marie Syrkin: Values Beyond the Self* (Waltham, Mass.: Brandeis University Press, 2008).

73. Hasia R. Diner, *We Remember with Reverence and Love: American Jews and the Myth of Silence after the Holocaust, 1945–1962* (New York: New York University Press, 2009). Most centrally Diner's research is a rejoinder to Peter Novick's influential argument that contemporaneous American Jewish concern with the Holocaust was scant, and that the Holocaust figured only retroactively, and even opportunistically,

into American Jewish identity. Peter Novick, *The Holocaust in American Life* (New York: Houghton Mifflin, 2009).

74. Syrkin, 10.

75. The essay is included as "The Hardest Examination," in *The State of the Jews*, which is a collection of Syrkin's writings. Some first appeared in such venues as *The Jewish Frontier* and *The New Republic*, though there is no indication of where and when the individual essays were initially published.

76. Syrkin, 29.

77. Ibid., 30.

78. Ibid.

79. Ibid.

80. Ibid., 31.

81. Ibid., 32.

82. Ibid., 33–34.

83. Ibid., 34.

84. Ibid., 35.

85. The following sketch of Auerbach is drawn from Wetzel, 49–61; Geller, 81–83, 208–211; and Brenner, esp. 135–137.

86. Quoted in Grossmann, 173.

87. Holian, "Between National Socialism and Soviet Communism" (diss.), 305–306.

88. Eislander from Eislander/Nenner interview.

89. JSU, Tätigkeitsbericht der Vorstandschaft zur Generalversammlung vom 3. Oktober bis 31. Januar 47, YIVO, reel 85, 1193.

90. The text of "Edict No. 3567" is recorded in JSU, Rundscrheiben, n.d., YIVO, no folder recorded, likely reel 85, 1197. A notice of the policy to the students is given in JSU, Bekanntmachung 25. November 1946, YIVO reel 87, 1239.

91. JSU, Bekanntmachung 25. November, 1946, YIVO reel 87, 1239.

92. JSU, Bekanntmachung 5. December, 1946, YIVO reel 87, 1239.

93. JSU, Tätigkeitsbericht der Vorstandschaft für die Zeit vom 13. Okt. 47 bis zum 25. März 1948, YIVO reel 87, 1237.

94. JDC, ZDN Letter No. 130. Re: Jewish Students in German Universities, Jan. 29, 1948, JDC-NY, 334.

95. JSU, Protokoll der Vorstandschafts-Sitzung vom 28. Oktober 1946, YIVO reel 87, 1233; JSU, An den Staatskommissar für Opfer des Fascismus, Herrn Dr. Philip Auerbach, 6. Januar 1947, YIVO reel 89, 1250.

96. Mark Hupert interview.

97. Schochet interview.

98. Membership-Certificate, Lucy Fink, photocopy given to author.

99. Roman Ohrenstein, "Hochschulkarte: Nur für Fahrten von der Wohnung zur Hoschschule und zurück," photocopy given to author.

100. Correspondence with the Housing Authority is common in Union records. An example includes JSU, An das Hauptwohnungsamt 25. Juil 1947, YIVO reel 89, 1251.

101. JSU, Bekanntmachung, 20. Oktober 1946, YIVO reel 87, 1238.

102. The English "zone federation" is a somewhat awkward translation of the umbrella group's name, which the students themselves rendered in English on their letterhead as "Jewish Students' Union in the American Occupied Zone in Germany." On occasion I also refer to it as the "zonewide union" or the "Union," when it is clear I am speaking of the larger organization and not an individual chapter.

103. Individual chapters critiqued a draft of the governing statute in JSU, Rundschreiben—Nr. 3 11. August 1946, YIVO reel 85, 1197, suggesting that the zone federation formed sometime earlier in the summer.

104. Rafael Nenner from Eislander/Nenner interview. JSU, Protokoll: der Vorstandschaft-Sitzung vom 4. Juni, 1946; Protokoll der Vorstandschaft-Siztung vom 20. Februar 1947, both from YIVO reel 87, 1233.

105. On the Jewish population in the British Zone, see Lavsky, 60–62.

106. JDC, Bericht über die Organisation und Tätigkeit des Verbandes jüdischer Studenten in der britischen Zone Deutschlands, 2, May 1948, JDC-NY, 335.

107. Grossmann, 178–179.

108. Patt, 31–32.

109. Myers Feinstein, 81, 105.

110. Grossmann, 194–195.

111. Margarete Myers Feinstein, "Domestic Life in Transit: Jewish DPs," in *Birth of a Refugee Nation*.

112. JSU, Statistik der jüdischen Studenten, in München, 15.10.46, YIVO reel 85, 1196.

113. JSU, Bericht der Vorstandschaft—vom 2. Februar 1947 bis 12. Oktober 1947, YIVO reel 87, 1234.

114. JSU, Statistik der Jüdischen Studenten in München, July 1947. YIVO reel 85, 1196.

115. JSU, Jüdischer Studentenverband in der Amerikanischen Zone Deutschland—Universität Erlangen, October 12, 1947, YIVO reel 85, 1196.

116. JSU Heidelberg, An das Jüdische Studentenverband in der US-Zone, 22.5.47, YIVO reel 85, 1196.

117. JSU, Mitglieder liste der Jüdischen Studentenvereinigung in Stuttgart vom 15.10.1948, YIVO reel 85, 1194.

118. JDC, Bericht über die Organisation und Tätigkeit des Verbandes jüdischer Studenten in der britischen Zone Deutschlands, 2, May 1948, JDC-NY, 335.

119. Holian, "Displacement and the Postwar Reconstruction of Education," 173–174.

120. Schorr-Reiner and Langer interviews.

121. Jaroszynska-Kirchmann, 10.

122. Interview with Dov Steinfeld.

123. Tanay, 195.

124. Schochet interview; the classes are recorded on his LMU transcript, which he shared with me.

125. See, among his essays, Simon Schochet, "Polish Jewish Officers Who Were Killed in Katyn: An Ongoing Investigation in Light of Documents Recently Released by the USSR," in *The Holocaust in the Soviet Union: The Destruction of the Jews*

in the Nazi-Occupied Territories of the USSR, 1941–1945, ed. Lucjan Dobroszycki and Jeffrey S. Gurock (New York: M. E. Sharpe, 1993).

126. JSU, Tätigkeitsberict der Vorstandschaft der Jüdischen Studentenverbandes, Sommer-Semester 1947, 1. Oktober, 1947, YIVO reel 85, 1191.

127. JSU, Frankfurt am Main, Monatsbericht fur Monat Mai 1948, 4. June 48, YIVO reel 85, 1196.

128. JSU, Statistik der juedischen Studenten in MUENCHEN, n.d., probably July 1946, YIVO reel 85, 1196.

129. Balaban interview.

130. Lucy Fink interview.

131. Holian, "Displacement and the Postwar Reconstruction of Education," 173.

132. Ibid.

133. Mankowitz, 19.

134. Schorr-Reiner interview.

135. Steinfeld interview.

136. Myers Feinstein, 118–120; 152–153.

137. Reiter interview.

138. JDC, M. J. Joslow, Associate Education Director, to Dr. Morris Fishbein, JAMA, December 12, 1945, JDC-NY, 357.

139. The request to the booksellers, which included also writing materials, is recorded in JSU, Tätigkeitsberict der Vorstandschaft der Jüdischen Studentenverbandes, Sommer-Semester 1947, 1. Oktober, 1947, YIVO reel 85, 1191.

140. Eichenholz interview.

141. Kerr, Shoah Foundation interview

142. Mark Hupert interview.

143. Balaban interview.

144. Ibid.

145. J. Dabrowska, "The Situation of the Jewish Students in Germany," *Wiedergeburt/The New Life*, vol. 1: 6 (1947), 3.

146. Ibid.

147. JSU, Referat gehalten vom Kollegeb Hornstein-Haraszti Stefan am 29.8.1947 in Brighton, YIVO reel 85, 1201.

148. Mark Hupert interview.

149. The payment terms for the prep courses are recorded in JSU, Protokoll der Vorstandschaft-Sitzung vom 30. Nov. 1947, YIVO reel 87, 1234. The enrichment courses, designed especially for the TH students, are mentioned in JSU, Tätigkeitsbericht der Vorstandschaft zur Generalversammlung vom 3. Oktober bis 31. Januar 47, YIVO reel 85, 1193.

150. Mark Hupert interview.

151. Kerr, Shoah Foundation interview.

152. Ibid.

153. Tanay, 194.

154. Grossmann, 195–197.

155. Interview with Imek Metzger.

156. Kerr, Shoah Foundation interview.

157. Rubin Zimering interview.

158. Reiter interview.

159. Quoted in Patt, 32.

160. Schochet interview and Steinfeld interview.

161. "Paths of Youth," *Wiedergeburt/The New Life* (January–February 1947), 8.

162. Mark Fintel interview.

163. This is the recollection of Guti Kanner, who stresses that it was only a very small minority. Kanner interview.

164. The author of this remark requested that it go unattributed.

165. The quote is from Georg Majewski, "München IV. Quartal 1951," donated by author. Majewski formed such impressions when he at one point visited his Munich colleagues.

166. Ohrenstein interview.

167. Mark Hupert interview.

168. The most vivid portrait of kibbutz life is in Patt, especially 89–98 and 114–124.

169. Pinson, 113–114.

170. Mankowitz explicitly rebuts Pinson's comments on 142–144, and much of Patt's book addresses the complex roots of the collectivism of young Jewish DPs.

171. Quoted in Patt, 93.

172. Korn, Balaban, and Nenner/Eislander interviews.

173. This portrait of the cafeteria draws especially on the interviews with Balaban and Korn.

174. The second cafeteria is referred to in JSU, Bekanntmachung, 20. November 1946, YIVO reel 87, 1239. Its use by TH students is recorded in Eugene Miller, Survey—The Jewish Students of Postwar Germany, 1/6/2000.

175. On religion and Jewish DPs, see JDC, Rabbi A. Rosenberg, Director of Religious Affairs, "The Growth of Religious Life Among the Jews in the American Zone in Germany, 1945, JDC-NY, 335.

176. Ibid.

177. Myers Feinstein summarizes this and related research on 206–207.

178. Sabina Zimering interview.

179. Reiter interview.

180. On survivors' adaptations of the *kaddish*, see Myers Feinstein, 68–70.

181. "Remember," *The Jewish Student*, Oktober–November 1946, 1.

182. On this trope, see Mankowitz, 69, and Myers Feinstein, 102–105.

183. JSU, Protokoll über die erste Vorstandssitzung vom 26.III.1946, YIVO reel 87, 1233.

184. JSU, An den Welfare Officer d. UNRRA-Universität, 4. April 1946, reel 89, 1253.

185. JSU, Rundschreiben an alle lokal—Vereinigungen in der Amerikanischen Zone, 20. April 1947, YIVO reel 85, 1194.

186. JSU, Tätigkeitsbericht der Vorstandschaft für die Zeit vom 13. Okt. 47 bis zum 25. März 1948, YIVO reel 87, 1237.

187. The program is laid out in JSU, AN ALLE KOLLEGEN! 20. Februar 1947, YIVO 294.2.

188. JSU, Einladung—Die Erste Sitzung des Wissentschaftlichen—Kreises, 29. Okt. 1946, YIVO, no folder recorded, likely reel 98, 1238; JSU, Bekanntmachung—12. November 1946, YIVO reel 87, 1240; JSU, Bekanntmachung—2.1.1947, YIVO reel 87, 1240. The knowledge circle, chess club, and sport activities are discussed in JSU, Tätigkeitsbericht der Vorstandschaft zur Generalversammlung vom 3. Oktober bis 31. Januar 47, YIVO reel 85, 1193.

189. JSU, War Crimes Trials, Nurnburg, June 18, 1946, YIVO reel 88, 1247.

190. The first mention of a Hebrew course is recorded in JSU, Bekanntmachung, 23. Oktober 1946, YIVO reel 87, 1238. JSU, Tätigkeitsbericht der Vorstandschaft zur Generalversammlung vom 3. Oktober bis 31. Januar 47, YIVO reel 85, 1193.

191. JSU, Bericht der Vorstandschaft—vom 2. Februar 1947 bis 12. Oktober 1947, YIVO reel 87, 1234, and JSU, Auszug aus dem Protokoll der Vorstandschaftsitzung vom 19.6.47, YIVO reel 87, 1234.

192. JSU, Bekanntmachung—8. January 1947, YIVO reel 87, 1240.

193. See Philipp Grammes, "Sports in the DP Camps, 1945–48," in *Emancipation through Muscles: Jews and Sports in Europe*, ed. Michael Brenner and Gideon Reuveni (Lincoln: University of Nebraska Press, 2006), 187–212.

194. Myers Feinstein, 112–113.

195. On the ski club see JSU, Bekanntmachung. Ski—Gruppe, 27. November, n.d., YIVO, no folder recorded, likely reel 87, 1240.

196. JSU, Bericht der Vorstandschaft—vom 2. Februar 1947 bis 12. Oktober 1947, YIVO reel 87, 1234. Additional material on athletic activities on the zonewide level is in JSU, Protokoll der Zonenrats-Sitzung vom 14. Dezember 1947, YIVO reel 85, 1191.

197. JSU, Bericht des Jüdischen Akademischen Sportklubes, 21 März 1948, YIVO reel 87, 1237.

198. Organizing for the dance is indicated in JSU, Bekanntmachung, 3. November 1946, YIVO reel 87, 1238, and JSU, Protokoll der 2. Sitzung der Kommission für Organisierung der Tanzabende, 12. November 1946, YIVO reel 87, 1233. Subsequent dances, including one in Feldafing, are indicated in JSU, Bekanntmachung, 23. Januar 1947, YIVO reel 87, 1240, and JSU, Bekanntmachung, 11. Februar 1947, YIVO reel 87, 1240.

199. Catering, JSU, An das Restaurant Tel-Aviv 26. November 1946, YIVO reel 89, 1251.

200. JSU, Bericht vom Vorstandschaft zum Generalversammlung vom 3. Oktober bis 31. Januar 1947, YIVO reel 85, 1193.

201. A November 1947 ball is recorded in JSU, Tätigkeitsbericht der Vorstandschaft für die Zeit vom 13. Okt. 47 bis zum 25. März 1948, YIVO reel 87, 1237.

202. Dance course in JSU, Protokoll der Vorstandschafts-Sitzung vom 28. Oktober 1946, YIVO reel 87, 1233.

203. Hupert interview. A ball in the fall of 1947 raised 5,000 Reichsmarks for aid to needy students. JSU Protokoll der Vorstandschaft-Sitzung vom 30. Nov. 1947, YIVO reel 87, 1234.

204. The distribution of opera tickets is recorded in JSU, Bekanntmachung 18. November 1946, YIVO reel 87, 1239.

205. Such debates are the subject of Mankowitz's chapter, "Two Voices from Landsberg: Rudolf Valsonok and Samuel Gringauz," in *Life Between Memory and Hope*, 161–191, and Holian, "Between National Socialism and Soviet Communism" (diss.), 390–398. They are also taken up by Gay, with an emphasis on tensions between German and East European Jews. See 115–120; 124–129.

206. Jacob Oleiski, "Die Grosse Enttäuschung," 24 August 1945, YIVO reel 89, 1253.

207. Kauders, 45.

208. Quoted in Grossmann, 234, and Mankowitz, 178.

209. Siebald interview.

210. Ameleck is a biblical enemy of the Jews, often used by survivors as a metaphor for Hitler or the Nazis as a whole.

211. Ruben Abromowicz, "Three Aspects" from "Free Tribune," *Wiedergeburt/ The New Life* (January–February 1948), 6–7.

212. Quoted in Mankowitz, 180.

213. Documents concerning arrangements in Berchtesgaden include JSU, An den Leiter der Hotel Stiftskeller 28. August 1947, YIVO reel 89, 1250, among many others.

214. Emanuel Tenenwurzel, Bericht über den Studenten-Erholungsaufenthalt in Berchtesgaden, 15. Juni 1946, YIVO reel 89, 1251.

215. Sabina Zimering interview.

216. Korn interview.

217. On such acts, see Myers Feinstein, 36, 41–42, 114–115, and Mankowitz, 235–239.

218. Mankowitz, 240; Grossmann, 232.

219. Grossmann, 232.

220. Schorr-Reiner interview.

221. Quoted in Grossmann, 233.

222. Metzger interview.

223. The king was Ludwig II; his body was in fact found in 1886, though his death remains mysterious.

224. Korn interview.

225. Mark Hupert interview.

226. Balaban interview.

227. Korn interview.

228. "For the Second Issue," *Wiedergeburt/The New Life* (January–February 1947), 2.

229. Ohrenstein interview.

CHAPTER 5

1. Mark Hupert interview. All quotes from interview.

2. Lawrence L. Langer, *Holocaust Testimonies: The Ruins of Memory* (New Haven, Conn.: Yale University Press, 1993), 100.

3. Langer, 10.

4. Henry Greenspan, "Imagining Survivors: Testimony and the Rise of Holocaust Consciousness," in *The Americanization of the Holocaust*, ed. Hilene Flanzbaum (Baltimore, Md.: Johns Hopkins University Press, 1999), 47. Additional insights are contained in Henry Greenspan, *On Listening to Holocaust Survivors: Recounting and Life History* (Westport, Conn.: Praeger, 1998).

5. Greenspan, "Imagining Survivors," 48. Richard N. Kraft notes the prevalence of the frame of "doubling" in *Memory Perceived: Recalling the Holocaust*, Psychological Dimensions to War and Peace (Westport, Conn.: Praeger, 2002), 2.

6. Greenspan, "Imagining Survivors," 48.

7. Ibid.

8. Ibid., 49.

9. Robert Nenner interview.

10. Korn interview.

11. Mark Hupert interview.

12. Minzberg interview.

13. The dead included those deprived a proper grave before liberation and those who died afterward. Commemorative practices are summarized in Margarete Myers Feinstein, "Jewish Observance in Amelek's Shadow: Mourning, Marriage, and Birth Rituals among Displaced Persons in Germany," in *"We Are Here,"* 257–268, and elaborated in her *Holocaust Survivors in Postwar Germany*. On the mourning academies, *Yizkor* services, *kaddish*, and so forth, see especially 64–105. Unless otherwise indicated, I quote throughout the study from Myers Feinstein's book.

14. Myers Feinstein, 84, 77.

15. Yosef Grodzinsky, "Historic Commissions in DP Camps: The Resilience of Jewish Identity," in *Birth of a Refugee Nation: Displaced Persons in Postwar Europe, 1945–1951*, Workshop Draft Papers (New York: Remarque Institute at New York University, April 20–21, 2001), 7.

16. Laura Jockusch, "A Folk Monument to Our Destruction and Heroism: Jewish Historical Commissions in the Displaced Persons Camps of Germany, Austria, and Italy," in *"We Are Here."*

17. Grodzinsky, 7; Gay, 65. In late 1948, the archive of the Historical Commission was transferred to Yad Vashem in the newly created state of Israel.

18. Koppel Pinson, "Jewish Life in Liberated Germany," *Jewish Social Studies* 9: 2 (April 1947), 108.

19. Pinson, 109.

20. JDC, Report of Education Survey, American Zone, Third Army Area, Germany, December 28, 1945–January 5, 1946, JDC-NY, 335.

21. Jockusch, 40.

22. Greenspan, "Imagining Survivors," 52, 67.

23. Ohrenstein interview.

24. Mark Hupert interview.

25. Glaser interview.

26. Grossmann, 195–197.

27. Reiter interview.

28. Cessia Hupert interview.

29. Steinfeld interview.

30. Ohrenstein interview.

31. Mark Hupert interview.

32. Kanner interview.

33. Ohrenstein interview.

34. The likely role of this dynamic in survivor marriages is noted by Grossmann, 197.

35. Mark Hupert interview.

36. Leon Weliczker Wells, Survey—The Jewish Students of Postwar Germany, 1/3/2000. The memoir, published in many languages, appears in English as *The Death Brigade (The Janowska Road)* (New York: Holocaust Library, 1978).

37. Jockusch, 35, 41.

38. Boaz Cohen, "Representing the Experience of Children in the Holocaust," in *"We Are Here,"* 74–97.

39. Quoted in Boaz Cohen, 70.

40. Pinson, 108.

41. Beth B. Cohen, "Face to Face: American Jews and Holocaust Survivors, 1946–54," in *"We Are Here,"* 150–155.

42. Myers Feinstein, 185.

43. Ibid., 233.

44. Though her mother was a Christian German, only mixed families with a non-Jewish father were permitted to live outside the ghetto, and her mother initially chose to stay with her husband and daughter.

45. Glaser interview. The following quotes are from the interview.

46. I cannot be certain of this spelling, derived from Glaser's oral testimony.

47. Myers Feinstein, 186.

48. Glaser interview.

49. Cessia Hupert interview.

50. Ibid.

51. Gavriel Rosenfeld, *Munich and Memory* (Berkeley: University of California Press, 2000), 18.

52. As early as June 1945, the American Military Government ordered the removal of Nazi emblems from sites in Munich. The policy was extended nationwide in the May 1946 "Allied Control Council Directive No. 30—Liquidation of German Military and Nazi Memorials and Museums," from which the exemption is quoted. Rosenfeld, 79.

53. Brenner, 16.

54. Atina Grossmann, "Entangled Histories and Lost Memories: Jewish Survivors in Occupied Germany, 1945–49," in *"We Are Here,"* 15. Instances of "close encounters" suffuse Grossmann's *Jews, Germans, and Allies,* and are neatly summarized in the quoted essay.

55. For a textured study of the nature of postwar relations between Germans and Jews in postwar Germany, one that extends beyond the simplistic equation of anti-Semitism and the Final Solution, see Frank Stern, *The Whitewashing of the Yellow Badge: Antisemitism and Philosemitism in Postwar Germany* (Oxford: Pergamon Press, 1992).

56. This is a reference most obviously to Daniel Goldhagen's *Hitler's Willing Executioners: Ordinary Germans and the Holocaust* (New York: Vintage, 1997) and the debates it provoked. On the debates see, among many others, Geoff Eley, ed., *The "Goldhagen Effect"* (Ann Arbor: University of Michigan Press, 2000), and Fred Kautz, *The German Historians:* Hitler's Willing Executioners *and Daniel Goldhagen* (New York: Black Rose Books, 2002).

57. Reiter interview.

58. Glaser interview.

59. Lucy Fink interview.

60. Robert Nenner interview.

61. Glaser interview. Quotes that follow are from the interview.

62. Perception of German entitlement is a forceful theme in Grossmann; see esp. 47–49.

63. J. Dabrowska, "The Situation of the Jewish Students in Germany."

64. Myers Feinstein, 34.

65. JSU, H. Wieland, an die Jüdische Studentenvereinigung, 17. Juli. 1947, YIVO reel 89, 1252.

66. Lucy Fink interview.

67. Ibid.

68. Simon Snopkowski, "Jewish Organizations and Institutions," in Brenner, 123–124. The text is a brief interview Brenner conducted with Snopkowski.

69. Cessia Hupert interview.

70. Kanner interview.

71. Glaser interview.

72. Eisenberg interview.

73. Lynn Rapaport, *Jews in Germany After the Holocaust: Memory, Identity, and Jewish-German Relations* (New York: Cambridge University Press, 1997), 118.

74. Rapaport, 117.

75. Frenkel interview.

76. Reiter interview.

77. Ohrenstein interview.

78. Miller interview. Weiner, Miller reported, is long deceased, so I cannot corroborate this story.

79. Schorr-Reiner interview.

80. Sabina Zimering interview.

81. In a 2005 visit to the University of Munich, I saw some of the very auditoria in which the alumni had had their classes.

82. Mark Hupert interview.

83. Myers Feinstein, 34.

84. Epstein, Survey.

85. Langer interview.

86. Michael Berkowitz and Suzanne Brown-Fleming, "Perceptions of Jewish Displaced Persons as Criminals in Early Postwar Germany," in *"We Are Here,"* 168.

87. Berkowitz and Brown-Fleming, 168–169. Berkowitz documents the persistence of stereotypes pertaining to criminality in the chapter "The Lingering

Stereotypes and Displaced Persons," in Berkowitz, *The Crime of My Very Existence: Nazism and the Myth of Jewish Criminality* (Berkeley: University of California Press, 2007).

88. Berkowitz and Brown-Fleming, 168.

89. Berkowitz and Brown-Fleming, 172, 181–182, 184; Myers Feinstein, 41.

90. Robert Nenner interview.

91. J. Dabrowska, "The Situation of the Jewish Students in Germany."

92. Robert Nenner interview.

93. Reiter interview.

94. Korn interview.

95. Reiter interview.

96. Robert Nenner interview.

97. Rapaport, 118–120.

98. Ohrenstein interview.

99. Mark Hupert interview.

100. Brian Bergman, Panel Remarks at "Der Jüdische Studentenverband im nachkriegs München," at Gesellschaft zur Förderung jüdischer Kultur und Tradition, Munich, June 23, 2005.

101. JSU, An den Rektor der Technischen Hochschule, 20 Dezember 1946, YIVO reel 87, 1252.

102. Robert Nenner interview.

103. Korn interview.

104. Ohrenstein interview.

105. Brenner, 136.

106. Ohrenstein interview.

107. Schorr-Germain, Survey.

108. This summary of research is derived from Myers Feinstein, 112–122, 125–128, and Grossmann, 225–230.

109. Sabina Zimering interview.

110. Kanner interview.

111. Langer interview.

112. Schochet interview.

113. J. Dabrowska, "The Situation of the Jewish Students in Germany."

114. Langer interview.

115. Myers Feinstein testifies to the existence of this policy, mentioned by many of the alumni, on page 35.

116. Ohrenstein interview. All quotes that follow are from this interview.

117. Albert Camus, *The Rebel: An Essay on Man in Revolt*, trans. Anthony Bower (New York: Bantam, 1955), 13–23.

118. Mark Hupert interview. All quotes that follow are from this interview.

119. Siebald interview.

120. Sabina Zimering interview.

121. Langer interview.

122. Simon Schochet, letter to the author, September 2008.

123. Langer interview.

124. Siebald interview. The anecdote and quotes that follow are from this interview.

125. Glaser interview. Anecdote and quotes that follow are from this interview.

126. A brief account of the activities of the Schily family during the war is provided by Peter Schily's brother, Otto Schily, at www.shoahproject.org/daten/wehrmacht/debatte/debatte6.htm. Peter, his brother reports, had refused membership in the Hitler Youth and had tried to flee Germany, but was not successful. He later volunteered for the war and was badly wounded on the Eastern Front. Otto describes his father as a "declared opponent of the Nazis," who viewed the elder Schily with suspicion by virtue of his affiliation with anthroposophy—a humanistic movement persecuted by the Nazis.

CHAPTER 6

1. The twenty-seven students are noted in JDC, List of Jewish Students from the US-Zone, Germany for the Second International Students Camp in England, 1947, YIVO reel 85, 1201. The German cities from which the JSU delegates hailed are recorded in JSU—Erlangen, An den Jüdischen Studentenverband—Head Office, Munchen, 10. Oktober 1947, YIVO reel 85, 1201. The honorary membership is recorded in JSU, Letter to Rabbi Kasper, 27. September 1947, YIVO, reel 85, 1201. Casper's biography is at www.hcsjerusalem.org/our-founder.html

2. A thorough report on the trip is provided in JSU, Bericht über das Sommerlager in Brighton—England, n.d., YIVO reel 85, 1201.

3. JSU, Referat gehalten vom Kollegen Hornstein-Haraszti Stefan am 29.8.1947 in Brighton, YIVO reel 85, 1201.

4. Ibid.

5. Kerr, Shoah Foundation interview.

6. Eugene Miller, Survey. John Saunders, Survey—The Jewish Students of Postwar Germany, 12/27/1999, and Alfred Schneider, Survey—The Jewish Students of Postwar Germany, 1/8/2000.

7. Mark Fintel interview.

8. Kanner interview.

9. Rafael Nenner from Nenner/Eislander interview.

10. Rafael Nenner from Nenner/Eislander interview.

11. Rafael Nenner from Nenner/Eislander interview.

12. Complaints of damage are in JSU, An das Hauptswohnungsamt, München, 25. Juli [1947], YIVO reel 89, 1251; the situation with the family is in JSU, An das Wohnungsamt—München-Ost, 18. Sept. 1947, YIVO reel 89, 1251.

13. JSU, Tätigkeitsbericht der Vorstandschaft des Jüd. Studentenverbandes in der amerikanischen Zone, 24. Marz 1947, YIVO reel 85, 1198.

14. JDC, Joint Educational Division document; first page missing, n.d., likely early 1946, JDC-NY, 334.

15. JDC, M. J. Joslow, Education and Cultural Report, June–July–August, 1946, JDC-NY, 334.

16. JDC, An den Joint Muenchen, 10. August 1947, YIVO reel 85, 1199, and Sam Haber, Zone Director, To the Jewish Students Union, August 19, 1947, JDC-NY, 334.

17. Countless records of the Union's "Revisions Committee" record the Union's holdings, as well as its expenses.

18. Kerr, Shoah Foundation interview. Clothing, by contrast, was not a special concern of his during or after the war; he in fact regrets that he discarded early on his iconic striped concentration camp uniform, later recognizing its historic value.

19. Grossmann, 175–177.

20. Grossmann, 176.

21. The half-packet arrangement is in JSU, Protokotoll der Vorstand-schafts-Sitzung, 30 Oktober 1946, YIVO reel 87, 1233.

22. On the Munich Committee, see Wetzel, 206–212.

23. The following description of the aid system is drawn largely from the lengthy document, JDC, Memorandum to the Central Committee of Liberated Jews from Charles Passman, AJDC Munich, December 10, 1947, JDC-NY, 315. Though outlining a new arrangement for aid, it discusses extensively the system to that point.

24. Mankowitz characterizes the relationship between the two organizations on 114–116.

25. JDC, Memorandum to the Central Committee of Liberated Jews from Charles Passman, AJDC Munich, December 10, 1947, JDC-NY, 315.

26. The classification of the students under relief aid is recorded on page 7 of JDC, Memorandum to the Central Committee of Liberated Jews from Charles Passman, AJDC Munich, December 10, 1947, JDC-NY, 315.

27. The 319 "Lebensmittel" rations the Union received in February 1947, for example, included four tins of meat, one tin each of fish, milk, and jam, one pack of cigarettes, 100 grams each of butter and sugar, and 500 grams each of flour and pasta. JSU, Protokoll der Vorstandschafts-Sitzung vom 20. Februar 1947, YIVO reel 87, 1234.

28. JDC, Elaine S. Friedman, Educational and Recreational Activities in District II, March 1947, JDC-NY, 335.

29. JSU Heidelberg, An das Jüdische Studentenverband in der US-Zone, 22.5.47, YIVO reel 85, 1196.

30. JSU, Referat gehalten vom Kollegen Hornstein-Haraszti Stefan am 29.8.1947 in Brighton, YIVO reel 85, 1201.

31. The tussle over Berchtesgaden is recorded in JSU, An den Personal-Chef des Zentral-Komitees, 29. Mai [1946]; JSU, An den Personal-Chef des Zentral-Komitees, 11. Juni [1946]; JSU, An das Zentral-Komitee, 30. Juni 1946; ZK, An Jüdischen Studentenverband, 11.7.1946. All from YIVO reel 89, 1256. An explicit request for a dormitory is recorded in JSU, An des jüdische Komitee z. Hd. Herrn Schwimmer, 17. März [1946], YIVO reel 89, 1259.

32. JSU, An das Zentral-Komitee der befreiten Juden in Bayern, 3. Februar. 46, YIVO reel 89, 1256.

33. Korn interview.

34. J. Dabrowska, "The Situation of the Jewish Students in Germany."

35. Tanay, 192.

36. J. Dabrowska, "The Situation of the Jewish Students in Germany."

37. Ruben Abromowicz, "Three Aspects" from "Free Tribune," 6–7.

38. JSU, Tätigkeitsbericht der Vorstandschaft für die Zeit vom 13. Okt. 47 bis zum 25. März 1948, YIVO reel 87, 1237. The report indicates that around ten members had given up to eight lectures per month on various subjects.

39. Rabbiner Dr. Ohrnstein, "Das Rabbinat der Israel Kultusgemeinde für den 'Mifal-Hahaucach' in München," *Wiedergeburt/The New Life*, 1: 6 (1947), 8.

40. Schochet interview.

41. The price is recorded in JSU, Bekanntmachung, 18. Februar 1947, YIVO reel 87, 1240.

42. JSU, Bekanntmachung, 12. Dezember, 1946, YIVO reel 87,1239.

43. Ibid.

44. JSU, An alle Lokal-Vereinigung—politische Betätigung der Studentschaft, 2 November 1947, YIVO reel 85, 1194.

45. These characterizations are based on my review of a full run of the newspaper; from various alumni I received altogether a complete set of photocopies, as well as some original copies.

46. "Deklaracje fun der jidiszer akademiszer jungt," *D.P.Express—Wiedergeburt/ The New Life* (January–February 1947), 5.

47. "Paths of Youth" (in Hebrew), *D.P.Express—Wiedergeburt/The New Life* (January–February 1947), 8.

48. JSU, 21 June 1947, no title, YIVO reel 85, 1192.

49. JSU-Heidelberg, n.d. (only pages 2–4 in archive; reference in document to 1947), YIVO folder not recorded.

50. Mark Hupert interview.

51. JDC, Elaine S. Friedman, Educational and Recreational Activities in District II, March 1947, JDC-NY, 335.

52. JSU, Bekanntmachung, 21. May, 1947, YIVO reel 87, 1241.

53. JSU, Kurzer Bericht, 24. April, 1947, YIVO reel 87, 1241.

54. JSU, Bekanntmachung, 21. May, 1947, YIVO reel 87, 1241.

55. Ibid.

56. JSU, Bericht—Generalversammlung, 2. Februar, 1947, reel 85, 1193.

57. The demands, addressed to the Munich Committee, are in JSU, An das Präsidium des Munchner-Komitees, 21. März 1947, YIVO reel 89, 1257. The Central Committee was copied on the letter to the Munich Committee. A close version of the demands was publicly printed in N. Birman and A. Loewy, "Far undzere Recht," *Wiedergeburt/The New Life* vol. 1: 4–5 (April–May, 1947), 12.

58. JSU, An das Präsidium des Munchner-Komitees, 21. März 1947, YIVO reel 89, 1257.

59. JSU, Tätigkeitsbericht der Vorstandschaft der Jüdischen Studentenverbandes, Sommer-Semester 1947, 1. Oktober, 1947, YIVO reel 85, 1191.

60. M.S., "Der Begriff 'Produktivität,'" *Wiedergeburt/The New Life* vol. 1: 4–5 (April–May, 1947), 16.

61. Ibid.

62. Rafael Nenner from Nenner/Eislander interview.

63. Tanay, 191–192.

64. Tanay is a gifted chronicler of his own experience and its larger historical context, but there are reasons to question the accuracy of his memory of this episode. He dates the meeting to the fall of 1946, more than half a year before the crisis in the students' aid in the spring of 1947. Moreover, the Joint and Auerbach (whose first name he mistakenly records as "Otto") were very supportive of the students, though it is conceivable that, pressured by others, they might on such an occasion admonish the students.

65. Sabina Zimering interview.

66. Balaban interview.

67. Aliyah Bet refers to the largely illegal migrations to Palestine in defiance of restrictions imposed by Great Britain while Palestine was under the terms of the British Mandate. It started in 1934 and enjoyed a second life in the years 1945–1948.

68. Patt, 252.

69. The following outline of the substance of that crisis is drawn from Patt, 201–225.

70. Patt, 226.

71. Wetzel, 211.

72. Rafael Nenner in Nenner/Eislander interview. The details and precise sequence of the protest are now somewhat fuzzy. My account is based on a composite of Union documents, alumni recollections some fifty years after the fact, and Julianne Wetzel's rendition, based on contemporary sources, in Wetzel, 209–210.

73. Tanay, 192.

74. Ibid.

75. Ohrenstein interview.

76. Rafael Nenner from Nenner/Eislander interview.

77. JSU, To the Presidium of the CK of the Liberated Jews in Germany, 27. May 1947 (original in Yiddish), YIVO reel 89, 1251.

78. Ibid.

79. Official communiqué of the Central Committee, quoted in Wetzel, 310.

80. Wetzel, 310.

81. JSU, To the Central Committee, 6 June 1947 (original in Yiddish), YIVO reel 89, 1251. The letter references the CK's statement, as well as the Union's insistence that the CK formalize its promises.

82. JSU, Bekanntmachung, 9. Juni 1947, YIVO reel 87, 1241.

83. The agreement and the apology are recorded in JSU, Bekanntmachung, 18. Juni 1947, YIVO reel 87, 1241.

84. Ibid.

85. JSU, Protokoll der Vorstandschafts-Sitzung vom 12. Juni 1947, YIVO reel 87, 1234.

86. JSU, Tätigkeitsbericht der Vorstandschaft der Jüdischen Studentenverbandes, Sommer-Semester 1947, 1. Oktober, 1947, YIVO reel 85, 1191.

87. Piekarczyk, Condensed report for the period: January 1st–August 31st, 1947, YIVO reel 87, 1230. The specific arrangements varied greatly by city, based on the institutional landscape and the availability of resources from multiple quarters.

88. Roman A. Ohrenstein, "My Life, My Times, and My Research: An Autobiographical Sketch," *American Journal of Economics and Sociology*, 66: 4 (October, 2007), 653.

89. Wetzel, 311.

90. Rafael Nenner from Nenner/Eislander interview.

91. JSU, Letter to Albert Einstein, n.d., YIVO reel 85, 1197.

92. JSU, To Mr. Trygve Lie, Secretary-General of the United Nations, April 29. 1947, YIVO reel 85, 1198.

93. JSU, Rundschreiben, 30. April 1947, YIVO reel 85, 1194.

94. JSU, An alle Lokal-Vereinigung—politische Betätigung der Studentschaft, 2 November 1947, YIVO reel 85, 1194.

95. "Academy/Ceremony for the Establishment of the 'Gdud-Awoda,'" *Unzer Welt*, November 1947. Original in Yiddish. Article donated to author.

96. The following description and all quotes are drawn from L. K[nob]ler, *Jidisze Cajtung* 97 (165), 1947. Original in Yiddish. Article donated to author.

97. JSU, Protokoll der Zonenrats-Sitzung vom 14. Dezember 1947, YIVO reel 85, 1191.

98. JSU, Rundschreiben, 8. Januar 1948, YIVO reel 85, 1194.

99. M. M. Ovadyahu, "In Memoriam—The Milieu from Which He Came."

100. Eugene Miller, Survey.

101. Ziona Oberman, Survey—The Jewish Students of Postwar Germany, 3/14/2000.

102. Mark Fintel interview.

103. Michael Okunieff, Survey—Jewish Students of Postwar Germany, 1/7/2000. Video from USC Shoah Foundation Institute Interview, 3/27/1996, available at www.youtube.com/watch?v=Fk5FXeiL5Z8

104. Patt details the presence and influence of youth movement members on the *Exodus* on 228–234.

105. Robert Nenner interview. All material and quotes that follow are from this interview.

106. I have no way to corroborate Nenner's account of his activities but also have no reason to doubt its veracity. He in fact claimed in our interview that he had openly spoken only once before about his involvement with the Irgun, when by chance, at a Shabbat dinner in Great Neck, New York, he met other former clandestine operatives, who pieced together their places in the same broad network. Hearing the conversation, his American wife, who knew little of his past, "freaked out." He further testified that his work was never officially acknowledged by the Israeli state. American military officials, however, recognized his efforts, dramatically advancing his pay grade when he joined the US Air Force after immigrating to the United States.

107. Metzger interview.

108. JSU, Protokoll der Allgemeinen Versammlung, der Jüdisher Studenten, in München v.12.10.47, YIVO reel 87, 1234.

109. Ibid.

110. My description of the *giyus* is drawn from Patt, 236–258, and Myers Feinstein, 289–293. Patt reports that the Haganah had been active in Europe since early

1946, greatly expanding its operations in late 1947. He dates the advent of formal conscription efforts among DPs to "at least as early as mid-February 1948," when draft protocols where first codified. The students' own experiences, and documents in their archive, suggest that a broad call for volunteers had been issued somewhat earlier.

111. The various reasons for resisting the draft and the sanctions are discussed in Myers Feinstein, 251–253.

112. Myers Feinstein, 292.

113. JSU, Protokoll der Zonenrats-Sitzung vom 12. Januar 1948, YIVO reel 85, 1191.

114. JSU, Rundschreiben, Muenchen, 25.5.1948, YIVO reel 85, 1194.

115. One such list of registrants is JSU, Liste fun student welche hobn sich gemolden cum GIJUS, n.d., YIVO reel 85, 1192. A list of those appealing for exemptions is JSU, An die Jewish Agency: Folgende Studenten bitten um Befrieung vom Gius, 10 Juli 1948, YIVO reel 87, 1235.

116. JSU, Tätigkeitsbericht der Vorstandschaft für die Zeit vom 13. Okt. 47 bis zum 25. März 1948, YIVO reel 87, 1237.

117. Evidence suggests, however, that even those who went to Palestine as volunteers hoped to study in Israel, presumably when finished with military service. In January 1948 the Union wrote to the rector of Hebrew University recommending that one of the three students who accompanied Knobler in leaving for Israel, Tadeus Grynhaus (Tavya Greenhauser), be admitted. The Union described Grynhaus, who studied veterinary medicine, as "one of the best and most active students in our Union." JSU, An Seine Magnifizenz, Herr Rektor der Universität, Jerusalem, 23. Januar 48. YIVO, Reel 89, 1254.

118. JSU, Tätigkeitsbericht der Vorstandschaft des jüdischen Studentenverbandes, im Winter-Semester 1947/48, Muenchen, den 28. März 1948, YIVO reel 85, 1191.

119. Ruben Abromowicz, "Three Aspects" from "Free Tribune," 6–7.

120. Jews in Palestine, Europe, and elsewhere commonly viewed the Zionist struggle, especially in its military aspect, in heroic terms, as is common within nationalist perspectives. Of course the creation of the state of Israel and its military victory in 1948 were viewed by many Arabs at the time as a political and moral disaster, and has since inspired the resistance of Arabs and others. It is far beyond the intent of this study to pass judgment on the controversy surrounding Israel's founding and the Arab-Israeli conflict in the decades thereafter.

121. JSU, Bestätigung, 17. März 1949. Copy of document given to author by Knobler.

122. The figures that follow are from Myers Feinstein, 293–294. Somewhat different figures are provided by the Holocaust Memorial Museum at www.ushmm.org/wlc/en/article.php?ModuleId=10005462.

123. Patt, 212.

124. Ibid., 240–242, 250–253.

125. This is the argument, notably, of the Israeli scholar Yosef Grodzinsky in *In the Shadow of the Holocaust* (Monroe, Maine: Common Courage Press, 2004).

126. The figures are from Alexander Piekarczyk, "Condensed report for the period: January 1st–August 31st, 1947," YIVO reel 87, 1230.

127. Balaban interview.

128. See "Hillel Foreign Student Service, A Tribute," a booklet published on the occasion of a reunion of alumni of the program in 1992 in Washington, D.C. The booklet indicates that 124 students came to the United States between 1938 and 1950. Sixty-four had already arrived by 1940, when the program was suspended until after the war. I therefore assume that the remaining 80 were recruited between 1945 and 1950. The booklet gives no precise indication about how many of these were DPs in occupied Germany. Among the 108 alumni the publication lists, I identified five Jewish Students' Union members through comparison with its own rosters, though there may have been more. The most famous among the postwar alumni is Tom Lantos, a Hungarian Jew recruited for the Hillel scholarship at the University of Budapest in 1946. He received a PhD in economics and for many years worked as a professor. In 1980 he was elected to the US House of Representatives, where he served, as the only Holocaust survivor in Congress, until his death in 2008. Others profiled in the booklet include accomplished businessmen, university faculty and scholars, artists, and architects.

129. JSU, Tätigkeitsbericht der Vorstandschaft des Jüd. Studentenverbandes in der amerikanischen Zone, 24. Marz 1947, YIVO reel 85, 1198.

130. JSU, Tätigkeitsbericht der Vorstandschaft für die Zeit vom 13. Okt. 47 bis zum 25. März 1948, YIVO reel 87, 1237.

131. The trip is recorded in JSU, Tätigkeitsbericht der Vorstandschaft der Jüdischen Sudenetenverbandes in der Amerikanischen Zone Deutschlands für die Zeit vom Mai 1949 bis zum 16 April 1950, YIVO reel 85, 1204.

132. Siebald interview.

133. JSU, Protokoll der Allgemeinen Versammlung, der Jüdisher Studenten, in München v.12.10.47, YIVO reel 87, 1234.

134. Tanay, 199. The quote is verbatim from the letter, which his friend had saved and later gave to him.

135. Ibid., 203.

136. Ibid., 206.

137. This composite of what is sometimes called "post-Zionist" historiography is drawn primarily from Grodzinsky, and from Idith Zertal, *From Catastrophe to Power: Holocaust Survivors and the Emergence of Israel* (Berkeley: University of California Press, 1998), and *Israel's Holocaust and the Politics of Nationhood* (Cambridge: Cambridge University Press, 2005).

138. Grossman addresses scholarly debates over the issue of casualties in the 1948 war on 250–251, citing the relevant historiography on page 352, n 51. Grodzinsky, it should be noted, rejects the "cannon fodder" thesis.

139. JSU, Rundschrieben, 22. Juli 1948, YIVO reel 85, 1194.

140. JSU, Protokoll den 14.8.1948, YIVO reel 87, 1235 or 1235.

141. Ibid.

142. JSU, Protokoll von einer Sondersitzung der Vorstandschaft am 6.11.48, YIVO Reel 87, 1234.

143. Ibid.

144. JSU, Jüd. Studententvarbandes Sitzung, 28 November 1948, YIVO reel 85, 1195.

145. Ibid.

CONCLUSION

1. Grossmann, 252.

2. Ibid., 260.

3. Ibid., 267.

4. Ibid., 256.

5. JDC, Judah J. Shapiro to Mr. S. Tarahanksy, August 18, 1948, JDC-NY, 334.

6. Grossman, 252.

7. JSU, Roman Ohrenstein-Feifkopf, general-secretary to AJDC, February 18, 1949, YIVO reel 85, 1203.

8. JDC, Samuel L. Haber, to Mr. Judah J. Shapiro, AJDC Paris, 2nd March, 1949, JDC-NY, 334.

9. This dilemma is discussed in JDC, Judah J. Shapiro (Paris) to Mrs. Henrietta K. Buchman (New York), April 1, 1949, JDC-NY, 334.

10. JSU, to A.J.D.C. Centrale, New York, Paris, August 22, 1949, JDC-NY, 334.

11. JDC, Samuel L. Haber to A.J.D.C., Jewish Students' Union, September 15, 1949, JDC-NY, 334.

12. JDC, Samuel L. Haber to Reta L. Stern, Re: Jewish Students' Union, September 16, 1949, JDC-NY, 334.

13. Schochet interview.

14. JDC, Theodore D. Feder to Mr. M. Jacob Jaslow, AJDC New York, March 9, 1949, JDC-NY, 334.

15. JSU, Tätigkeitsberich der Vorstandschatf für die Zeit vom 20. Nov. 49–24. Apr. 50, YIVO reel 87, 1237.

16. Auxilium Academicum Judaicum, founding statute, n.d., YIVO reel 87, 1237. See also JSU, Tätigkeitsbericht der Vorstandschaft des Jüdischen Studentenverbandes in der Amerikanischen Zone Deutschlands für die Ziet vom 22 Mai 1949 bis zum 16 April 1950, YIVO reel 85, 1204.

17. JSU, Protokoll—Autoverkauf, 13. Sept. 1949, YIVO reel 87, 1236.

18. From the very partial paper trail in Union documents, I am unable to fully reconstruct, let alone judge, the accusations, so I merely refer to them here.

19. JSU, Bericht der Vorstandschaft der Jud. Studentenvereinigung, 17. Nov. 1949, YIVO reel 87, 1236.

20. Alexander Piekarczyk to the Juedischer Studentenverband in der Amerikanischen Zone Deutschlands, 10.10.1948, YIVO, no folder recorded.

21. JSU, Protokoll: Der Liquidierungs-Kommission für Verifikationsangelegenheiten 28. November, 1949, YIVO reel 87, 1236.

22. Ibid.

23. JSU, J. Klein to A.J.D.C.-Centrale, New York, Paris, August 22, 1949. JDC-NY, 334; JSU, Mitglieder der einzelnes Lokal-Vereinigungen, München, 10.

Februar, 1949, YIVO reel 87, 1229. A Joint document from January 1947 gives a figure of 729 students in the American Zone and 68 in Berlin, just before registration for the upcoming term closed. JDC, Alexander Piekarczyk to Mr. G. Muntz, 26.1.1947, YIVO reel 87, 1230.

24. JSU, Statistik der jüd Studenten der amer. Zone im Somersemester 1950, reel 87, 1229.

25. Ohrenstein, "My Life, My Times, and My Research," 650.

26. Ibid., 654.

27. Mark Hupert interview.

28. Cessia Hupert and Mark Hupert interviews.

29. These figures are from Myers Feinstein, 273–274. My percentages are based on adding several thousand additional immigrants she identifies to the numerical total she gives for the United States.

30. Global List of Jewish Alumni of German Universities, 1945–1955, 11/29/99. Donated to author by Mark Fintel. The total of 282 alumni addresses is clearly lower than the 700 or so Jewish university students, as some were deceased and others could not be located. The main ambiguity in the roster is that it lists couples as a single entry. In some cases both husband and wife were students, as I know from my research, but in others cases not. Thus the raw totals of alumni living in various locales are greater than the given figures, but by an indeterminate amount. My assumption is that alumni couples were more or less equally common in all countries where the students settled, keeping the proportions intact. In addition, the lists do not indicate if the alumni had resettled from their original destination. I assume also, based anecdotally from the alumni, that resettling from Israel to the United States was more common than the reverse, skewing the proportion toward America. However, the number who relocated is likely very small, so the percentages derived from the roster are not far off.

31. Marion Glaser, Survey—The Jewish Students of Postwar Germany, 3/26/2000.

32. Majewski interview.

33. Boldo Pinchas—Survey, The Jewish Students of Postwar Germany, 3/16/2000.

34. Anatol Chari, Survey—The Jewish Students of Postwar Germany, 12/30/99.

35. John Saunders, Survey.

36. Max Grieffez, Survey—The Jewish Students of Postwar Germany, 6/12/2000.

37. Eugene Miller, Survey.

38. Fred Reiter, Autobiographical Sketch.

39. Joseph Heimberg, Survey.

40. Alex White, Survey—The Jewish Students of Postwar Germany, 1/19/2000.

41. Isaac Minzberg, Survey—The Jewish Students of Postwar Germany, 12/27/1999.

42. Arnold Kerr, Survey—The Jewish Students of Postwar Germany, 2/1/2000.

43. Siebald interview.

44. Ohrenstein, "My Life, My Times, and My Research," 657.

45. Ohrenstein interview.

46. Cessia Hupert interview.

47. Brian Bergman, Panel Remarks at "Der Jüdische Studentenverband im nachkriegs München," at Gesellchaft zur Förderung jüdischer Kultur und Tradition, Munich, June 23, 2005.

48. As of the 1999/2000 survey, about two-thirds of the respondents had publicly shared their experiences, whether in memoirs or in testimonies archived at Steven Spielberg's Shoah Foundation, the United States Holocaust Memorial Museum, the Fortunoff Video Archive for Holocaust Testimony at Yale University, Yad Vashem, or some combination of these. In the years since, others have doubtless done so as well.

49. A handful of alumni indicate that they went into related fields; Arnold Kerr, for example, studied civil engineering in Munich but later specialized in aeronautics.

50. JSU, Certificate, Munich 22, November, 1949; Kliinik für Zahn-, Mund-und Kieferkrankenheiten, 24th July, 1949; LMU, Bestätigung, 25. Nov. 49, donated by Fred Reiter to author.

51. Alexander Bialywlos White, Autobiographical Sketch, written for the Jewish Alumni of German Universities, likely 1998 or 1999, donated by Mark Fintel to author.

52. Michael Okunieff, Survey.

53. Joseph Taler, Survey—The Jewish Students of Postwar Germany, 1/20/2000.

54. Ziona Oberman, Survey—The Jewish Students of Postwar Germany, 3/14/2000.

55. Zwi Markus, Survey—The Jewish Students of Postwar Germany, 3/20/2000.

56. See, inter alia, Henry Krystal, *Integration and Self-Healing: Affect—Trauma—Alexithymia* (New York: Routledge, 1998). Emanuel Tanay, profiled throughout this study, also deals with severe trauma in his practice.

57. Schochet interview.

58. Elias Epstein Survey. A professional dossier he gave me includes numerous commendations within the jewelry and diamond industries and from his company, Kaspar and Esh.

59. Laura G. Rubin, Secretary, National Committee for Resettlement of Foreign Physicians, to Mr. E. Epstein, November 7, 1949, donated to author by Elias Epstein.

60. Fred Reiter, Autobiographical Sketch.

61. Epstein's achievements are documented in a professional dossier he gave me.

62. Michael Okunieff, Video from USC Shoah Foundation Institute Interview, 3/27/1996, available at www.youtube.com/watch?v=Fk5FXe1L5Z8.

63. As was true for many others, Alexander White, Fred Reiter, and Robert Nenner all had short-term careers in the US military, in each case related to their medical training.

64. Interview with Joseph Zaphir; Zaphir curriculum vitae, donated to author.

65. The sketch of organizing efforts is drawn from a dossier of materials related to alumni events, such as event programs and promotional literature, donated to me by Fred Reiter. Especially helpful was a brief summary of the history of such efforts from 1971 to 1997, which had been compiled by the alumni association. The association itself went by various names, including the Munich Alumni Group, which

nonetheless organized alumni who had studied in other cities. Bella Brodzki and I attended international reunions in Boca Raton, Florida, in 2000 and 2005, as well several regional gatherings, including one at Kutsher's Country Club in New York's "Borscht Belt" in 2003.

66. One such issue was donated to me by the alumni association, "Reunion: Holocaust Survivors Who Studied in Munich and Other German Universities," vol. 4: 2 (Summer 1999).

67. Korn interview.

68. "Reunion: Holocaust Survivors Who Studied in Munich and Other German Universities," 1.

69. Siebald interview.

70. "A Statement to Our Parents. From the Second Generation of the University of Munich Jewish Alumni, January 2000," donated to author by Jeannie Zucker.

71. Simon Schochet, Letter to the Jewish Alumni of German Universities, May 4, 1998, donated by Schochet to author.

72. Korn interview.

73. Kanner interview.

74. Alumni Alexander White, Arnold Kerr, and Brian Bergman made the trip, along with one or possibly two more former students. Alexander White's son, as well as the son of an alumnus not in attendance, made the trip as well.

75. Reunion of Munich University Alumni, June 20–23, 2005, Program.

76. Brian Bergman, Panel Remarks at "Der Jüdische Studentenverband im nachkriegs München" at Gesellchaft zur Förderung jüdischer Kultur und Tradition, Munich, June 23, 2005.

Bibliography

INTERVIEWS

All interviews in 2004 were conducted in Israel; all others in the United States.

Philip Balaban, 6/29/2000
Lydia Eichenholz, 7/9/2001
Rochelle Eisenberg, 1/15/2002
Karl Eislander (with Rafael Nenner), 7/13/2000
Lucy Fink, 7/7/2001
Paul Fink, 7/7/2001
Mark Fintel, 1/12/2002
Nat Fintel, 1/13/2002
Eva Frenkel, 1/8/2004
Henry Frist, 1/7/2004
Alice Genis, 1/14/2002
Helen Gewitzman, 1/13/2002
Marion Glaser, 1/9/2004
Cessia Hupert, 11/2/2001
Mark Hupert, 10/26/2000
Guti Kanner, 1/8/2004
Frida Karp, 1/14/2002
Arnold Kerr, 6/2003
Yehuda Knobler, 1/10/2004
Felix Korn, 11/17/2001
Lea Langer (with Mark Langer) 1/9/2004
Mark Langer (with Lea Langer) 1/9/2004
Esther Lederman, 1/2001
Imek Metzger, 6/24/2003
Antonina Miller (with Henry Miller), 1/12/2002
Henry Miller (with Antonina Miller), 1/12/2002
Isaac Minzberg, 1/13/2002
Rafael Nenner (with Karl Eislander), 7/13/2000
Robert Nenner, 1/14/2002
Roman Ohrenstein, 1/18/2001; 12/1/2008
Frederick Reiter, 7/27/2001

Simon Schochet, 7/12/2000; 11/17/2008
Sophie Schorr-Reiner, 7/9/2001
Eva Siebald, 1/13/2004
Dov Steinfeld, 1/15/2004
Rubin Zimering, 7/8/2001
Sabina Zimering, 7/8/2001

ARCHIVES

The American Joint Distribution Committee Archives, New York City
Collection of the New York City Office, 1945–1954
United Nations Archive–United Nations Relief and Rehabilitation Administration, New York City
YIVO, Institute for Jewish Research, New York City
Record of the Displaced Persons Camps in Germany (294.2)

BOOKS, ARTICLES, AND CHAPTERS

Abramsky, Chimen, Maciej Jachimczyk, and Antony Polonsky, eds. *The Jews in Poland.* Oxford: Basil Blackwell, Ltd., 1986.

Abromowicz, Ruben. "Three Aspects" from "Free Tribune." *Wiedergeburt/The New Life* (January–February 1948).

Aleksiun, Natalia. "Ammunition in the Struggle for National Rights: Jewish Historians in Poland Between the Two World Wars." PhD dissertation, New York University, 2010.

Bacon, Gershon C. "Agudat Israel in Interwar Poland." In *The Jews of Poland Between Two World Wars,* edited by Yisrael Gutman, Ezra Mendelsohn, Jehuda Reinharz, and Chone Shmeruk. Hanover, N.H.: Brandeis University Press, 1989.

Bauer, Yehuda. *Flight and Rescue: Brichah.* New York: Random House, 1970.

———. *Out of the Ashes: The Impact of American Jews on Post-Holocaust European Jewry.* Oxford: Pergamon, 1989.

———. "The DP Legacy." In *Life Reborn: Jewish Displaced Persons, 1945–51: Conference Proceedings, Washington, D.C., January 14–17, 2000,* edited by Menachem Z. Rosensaft. Washington, D.C.: U.S. Holocaust Memorial Museum, 2001.

Berkowitz, Michael. *The Crime of My Very Existence: Nazism and the Myth of Jewish Criminality.* Berkeley: University of California Press, 2007.

Berkowitz, Michael, and Suzanne Brown-Fleming. "Perceptions of Jewish Displaced Persons as Criminals in Early Postwar Germany." In *"We Are Here": New Approaches to Displaced Persons in Postwar Germany,* edited by Avinoam Patt and Michael Berkowitz. Detroit: Wayne State University Press, 2009.

Bittner, David. "Schooling Survivors: Alumni of German University Recall Post-war Situation." *L'Chaim,* January 14, 1997.

Brenner, Michael. *After the Holocaust: Rebuilding Jewish Lives in Postwar Germany.* Translated by Barbara Harshav. Princeton, N.J.: Princeton University Press, 1997.

Brodzki, Bella. *Can These Bones Live? Translation, Survival, and Cultural Memory.* Palo Alto, Calif.: Stanford University Press, 2007.

Bronsztejn, Szyja. "Polish-Jewish Relations as Reflected in Memoirs of the Interwar Period." In *Jews in Independent Poland 1918–1939,* edited by Antony Polonsky, Ezra Mendelsohn, and Jerzy Tomaszewski. London: Littman Library of Jewish Civilization, 1994.

Camus, Albert. *The Rebel: An Essay on Man in Revolt.* Translated by Anthony Bower. New York: Bantam, 1955.

Cohen, Beth B. "Face to Face: American Jews and Holocaust Survivors." In *"We Are Here": New Approaches to Displaced Persons in Postwar Germany,* edited by Avinoam Patt and Michael Berkowitz, 136–166. Detroit: Wayne State University Press, 2009.

Cohen, Boaz. "Representing the Experience of Children in the Holocaust." In *"We Are Here": New Approaches to Displaced Persons in Postwar Germany,* edited by Avinoam Patt and Michael Berkowitz, 74–97. Detroit: Wayne State University Press, 2009.

Cohen, G. Daniel. "Between Relief and Politics: Refugee Humanitarianism in Postwar Europe." *Journal of Contemporary History* 43: 3 (July 2008), 437–449.

———. "The 'Human Rights Revolution' at Work: Refugees and Displaced Persons in Postwar Europe." In *Human Rights in the Twentieth Century,* edited by Stefan-Ludwig Hoffmann, 45–61. Cambridge: Cambridge University Press, 2011.

———. *In War's Wake: Europe's Displaced Persons in the Postwar Order.* Oxford: Oxford University Press, 2012.

Dabrowska, J. "The Situation of the Jewish Students in Germany." *Wiedergeburt/The New Life* 1: 6 (1947).

Davies, Norman. "Introduction." In *Jews in Eastern Poland and the USSR, 1939–46,* edited by Norman Davies and Antony Polonsky. London: Macmillan, 1991.

———. "Ethnic Diversity in Twentieth-Century Poland." In *From* Shtetl *to Socialism,* edited by Antony Polonsky. London: Littman Library of Jewish Civilization, 1993.

Davies, Norman, and Antony Polonsky, eds. *Jews in Eastern Poland and the USSR, 1939–46.* London: Macmillan, 1991.

Diner, Hasia R. *We Remember with Reverence and Love: American Jews and the Myth of Silence after the Holocaust, 1945–1962.* New York: New York University Press, 2009.

Dinnerstein, Leonard. *America and Survivors of the Holocaust.* New York: Columbia University Press, 1982.

Dobkin, Tony Blum. "The Landsberg Carnival: Purim in a Displaced Persons' Center." In *Purim: The Face and the Mask,* ed. Shifra Epstein. New York: Yeshiva University Museum, 1979.

Dobroszycki, Lucjan, and Jeffrey S. Gurock. *The Holocaust in the Soviet Union: The Destruction of the Jews in the Nazi-Occupied Territories of the USSR, 1941–1945.* New York: M. E. Sharpe, 1993.

Dwork, Deborah. *Children with a Star: Jewish Youth in Nazi Europe.* New Haven, Conn.: Yale University Press, 1991.

Eder, Angelika. *Fluechtige Heimat: Juedische displaced Persons in Landsbergam Lech 1945 bis 1950.* Munich: Kommissionsverlag UNI-Druck, 1998.

Eley, Geoff, ed. *The "Goldhagen Effect."* Ann Arbor: University of Michigan Press, 2000.

Flanzbaum, Hilene, ed. *The Americanization of the Holocaust.* Baltimore, Md.: Johns Hopkins University Press, 1999.

Frost, Shimon. *Schooling as Socio-Political Expression: Jewish Education in Interwar Poland.* Jerusalem: Magnes Press/Hebrew University, 1998.

Fürnrohr, Walter, and Felix Muschialik , eds. *Überleben und Neubeginn: DP-Hospital Gauting ab 1945.* Munich: P Krichheim Verlag, 2005.

Garncarska-Kadary, Bina. "Some Aspects of the Life of the Jewish Proletariat in Poland during the Interwar Period." In *Jews in Independent Poland 1918–1939*, edited by Antony Polonsky, Ezra Mendelsohn, and Jerzy Tomaszewski. London: Littman Library of Jewish Civilization, 1994.

Gay, Ruth. *Safe Among the Germans: Liberated Jews after World War II.* New Haven, Conn.: Yale University Press, 2002.

Geller, Jay Howard. *Jews in Post-Holocaust Germany, 1945–1952.* New York: Cambridge University Press, 2005.

Goldberg, Amos. "Forum: On Saul Friedländer's *The Years of Extermination*, (2) The Victim's Voice and Melodramatic Aesthetics in History." *History and Theory* 48: 3 (October 2009), 220–237.

Goldhagen, Daniel. *Hitler's Willing Executioners: Ordinary Germans and the Holocaust.* New York: Vintage, 1997.

Grammes, Philipp. "Sports in the DP Camps, 1945–48." In *Emancipation through Muscles: Jews and Sports in Europe*, edited by Michael Brenner and Gideon Reuveni, 187–212. Lincoln: University of Nebraska Press, 2006.

Greenspan, Henry. *On Listening to Holocaust Survivors: Recounting and Life History.* Westport, Conn.: Praeger, 1998.

———. "Imagining Survivors: Testimony and the Rise of Holocaust Consciousness." In *The Americanization of the Holocaust*, edited by Hilene Flanzbaum, 45–67. Baltimore, Md.: Johns Hopkins University Press, 1999.

Grodzinsky, Yosef. "Historic Commissions in DP Camps: The Resilience of Jewish Identity." In *Birth of a Refugee Nation: Displaced Persons in Postwar Europe, 1945–1951*, 7. Workshop Draft Papers. New York: Remarque Institute at New York University, April 20–21, 2001.

———. *In the Shadow of the Holocaust.* Monroe, Maine: Common Courage Press, 2004.

Gross, Jan T. *Fear: Anti-Semitism in Poland after Auschwitz: An Essay in Historical Interpretation.* New York: Random House, 2006.

Grossmann, Atina. *Jews, Germans, and Allies: Close Encounters in Occupied Germany.* Princeton, N.J.: Princeton University Press, 2007.

———. "Entangled Histories and Lost Memories: Jewish Survivors in Occupied Germany, 1945–49." In *"We Are Here": New Approaches to Displaced Persons in Postwar Germany*, edited by Avinoam Patt and Michael Berkowitz, 14–30. Detroit: Wayne State University Press, 2009.

Gutman, Yisrael. "Polish Antisemitism Between the Wars: An Overview." In *The Jews of Poland Between Two World Wars*, edited by Yisrael Gutman, Ezra Mendelsohn, Jehuda Reinharz, and Chone Shmeruk. Hanover, N.H.: Brandeis University Press, 1989.

Gutman, Yisrael, Ezra Mendelsohn, Jehuda Reinharz, and Chone Shmeruk, eds. *The Jews of Poland Between Two World Wars*. Hanover, N.H.: Brandeis University Press, 1989.

Hitchcock, William. *The Bitter Road to Freedom: A New History of the Liberation in Europe*. New York: Free Press, 2008.

Hoffmann, Stefan-Ludwig, ed., *Human Rights in the Twentieth Century*. Cambridge: Cambridge University Press, 2011.

Holian, Anna. "Between National Socialism and Soviet Communism: The Politics of Self-Representation among Displaced Persons in Munich, 1945–1951." PhD dissertation, University of Chicago, 2005.

———. "Displacement and the Postwar Reconstruction of Education: Displaced Persons at the UNRRA University of Munich, 1945–1948." *Contemporary European History* 17: 2 (2008).

———. *Between National Socialism and Soviet Communism: Displaced Persons in Postwar Germany*. Ann Arbor: University of Michigan Press, 2011.

Jacobmeyer, Wolfgang. *Vom Zwangsarbeiter zum Heimatlosen Ausländer: Die Displaced Persons in Westdeutschland, 1945–1951*. Göttingen: Vandenhoek and Ruprecht, 1985.

Jaroszynska-Kirchmann, Anna D. "Patriotic Responsibility: Polish Schools in German DP Camps." In *Birth of a Refugee Nation: Displaced Persons in Postwar Europe, 1945–1951*. Workshop Draft Papers. New York: Remarque Institute at New York University, April 20–21, 2001.

Knobler, Yehuda. "We Create." *Der Jüdische Student* (October/November 1946).

Jockusch, Laura. "A Folk Monument to Our Destruction and Heroism: Jewish Historical Commissions in the Displaced Persons Camps of Germany, Austria, and Italy." In *"We Are Here": New Approaches to Displaced Persons in Postwar Germany*, edited by Avinoam Patt and Michael Berkowitz, 31–73. Detroit: Wayne State University Press, 2009.

Jockusch, Laura, and Tamar Lewinsky. "Paradise Lost? Postwar Memory of Polish Jewish Survival in the Soviet Union." *Holocaust and Genocide Studies* 24: 3 (August 2010), 373–399.

Kaganovitch, Albert. "Jewish Refugees and Soviet Authorities during World War II." *Yad Vashem Studies* 38: 2 (2010).

Kauders, Anthony D. *Democratization and the Jews, 1945–1965*. Lincoln: University of Nebraska Press, 2004.

Kautz, Fred. *The German Historians: Hitler's Willing Executioners and Daniel Goldhagen*. New York: Black Rose Books, 2002.

Kessner, Carole S. *Marie Syrkin: Values Beyond the Self*. Waltham, Mass.: Brandeis University Press, 2008.

Knobler, Yehuda. "A Few Words for Joseph." In *On the Road: Notes on the Lives of Survivors*, edited by Yehuda Knobler and Yirmiyahu Rabina. Tel Aviv, 1952.

Knobler, Yehuda, and Yirmiyahu Rabina, eds. *On the Road: Notes on the Lives of Survivors.* Tel Aviv, 1952.

Koenigseder, Angelika, and Juliane Wetzel. *Lebensmut im Wartesaal: Die juedischen DPs (Displaced Persons) im Nachkriegsdeutschland.* Frankfurt am Main: Fischer, 1994.

Kraft, Richard N. *Memory Perceived: Recalling the Holocaust.* Psychological Dimensions to War and Peace. Westport, Conn.: Praeger, 2002.

Krystal, Henry. *Integration and Self-Healing: Affect—Trauma—Alexithymia.* New York: Routledge, 1998.

Langer, Lawrence L. *Holocaust Testimonies: The Ruins of Memory.* New Haven, Conn.: Yale University Press, 1993.

Lavsky, Hagit. *New Beginnings: Holocaust Survivors in Bergen-Belsen and the British Zone in Germany, 1945–1950.* Detroit: Wayne State University Press, 2002.

Levene, Mark. "Britain, a British Jew, and Jewish Relations in the New Poland: The Making of the Polish Minorities Treaty of 1919." In *Jews in Independent Poland 1918–1939*, edited by Antony Polonsky, Ezra Mendelsohn, and Jerzy Tomaszewski. London: Littman Library of Jewish Civilization, 1994.

Levin, Dov. *The Lesser of Two Evils: Eastern European Jewry under Soviet Rule, 1939–1941.* Translated by Naftali Greenwood. Philadelphia: Jewish Publication Society, [1989] 1995.

Lewinsky, Tamar. *Displaced Poets: Jiddische Schriftsteller im Nachkriegsdeutschland, 1945–51.* Göttingen: Vandenhoeck & Ruprecht, 2008.

Lichten, James. "Jewish Assimilation in Poland, 1863–1943." In *The Jews in Poland*, edited by Chimen Abramsky, Maciej Jachimczyk, and Antony Polonsky. Oxford: Basil Blackwell, Ltd., 1986.

Majewski, Georg D. *Only a Dead Soul Is Forgotten.* Translated by Gordon Shifman. Israel: Meida Techni, 1990.

Mankowitz, Zeev W. *Life Between Memory and Hope: The Survivors of the Holocaust in Occupied Germany.* Cambridge: Cambridge University Press, 2002.

Manley, Rebecca. *To the Tashkent Station: Evacuation and Survival in the Soviet Union at War.* Ithaca, N.Y.: Cornell University Press, 2009.

Marcus, Joseph. *Social and Political History of the Jews in Poland, 1919–1939.* Berlin: Mouton Publishers, 1983.

Melzer, Emanuel. "Antisemitism in the Last Years of the Second Polish Republic." In *The Jews of Poland Between Two World Wars*, edited by Yisrael Gutman, Ezra Mendelsohn, Jehuda Reinharz, and Chone Shmeruk. Hanover, N.H.: Brandeis University Press, 1989.

Mendelsohn, Ezra. "Jewish Historiography on Polish Jewry in the Interwar Period." In *The Jews of Poland Between Two World Wars*, edited by Yisrael Gutman, Ezra Mendelsohn, Jehuda Reinharz, and Chone Shmeruk. Hanover, N.H.: Brandeis University Press, 1989.

Mittler, Dietrich. "Wir waren alle Waisen: Wahlverwandtschaften dem Holocaust— Jüdische Studenten in München." *Suddeutsche Zeitung* (April 20/21, 1996).

Myers Feinstein, Margarete. "Domestic Life in Transit: Jewish DPs." In *Birth of a Refugee Nation: Displaced Persons in Postwar Europe, 1945–1951.* Workshop Draft

Papers. New York: Remarque Institute at New York University, April 20–21, 2001.

———. "Jewish Observance in Amelek's Shadow: Mourning, Marriage, and Birth Rituals among Displaced Persons in Germany." In *"We Are Here": New Approaches to Displaced Persons in Postwar Germany*, edited by Avinoam Patt and Michael Berkowitz. Detroit: Wayne State University Press, 2009.

———. *Holocaust Survivors in Postwar Germany, 1945–57*. New York: Cambridge University Press, 2010.

Novick, Peter. *The Holocaust in American Life*. New York: Houghton Mifflin, 2009.

Nussbaum, Klemens. "Jews in the Kosciusko Division and the First Polish Army." In *Jews in Eastern Poland and the USSR, 1939–46*, edited by Norman Davies and Antony Polonsky. London: Macmillan, 1991.

Ohrenstein, Roman A. "My Life, My Times, and My Research: An Autobiographical Sketch." *American Journal of Economics and Sociology* 66: 4 (October 2007).

Ohrnstein, Aron. "Das Rabbinat der Israel Kultusgemeinde für den 'Mifal-Hahaucach' in München." *Wiedergeburt/The New Life* 1: 6 (1947),

Orla-Bukowska, Annamaria. "Shtetl Communities: Another Image." In *Jews in Independent Poland 1918–1939*, edited by Antony Polonsky, Ezra Mendelsohn, and Jerzy Tomaszewski. London: Littman Library of Jewish Civilization, 1994.

Ovadyahu, M. "The Milieu from Which He Came." In *On the Road: Notes on the Lives of Survivors*, edited by Yehuda Knobler and Yirmiyahu Rabina. Tel Aviv, 1952.

Paczowski, Andrej. "The Jewish Press in the Political Life of the Second Republic." In *Jews in Independent Poland 1918–1939*, edited by Antony Polonsky, Ezra Mendelsohn, and Jerzy Tomaszewski. London: Littman Library of Jewish Civilization, 1994.

Patt, Avinoam J. *Finding Home and Homeland: Jewish Youth and Zionism in the Aftermath of the Holocaust*. Detroit: Wayne State University Press, 2009.

Patt, Avinoam, and Michael Berkowitz, eds. *"We Are Here": New Approaches to Displaced Persons in Postwar Germany*. Detroit: Wayne State University Press, 2009.

Peck, Abraham J. "A Continent in Chaos: Europe and the Displaced Persons." In *Liberation 1945*. Washington, D.C.: United States Holocaust Memorial Museum, 1995.

Pettiss, Susan T., with Lynne Taylor. *After the Shooting Stopped: The Story of an UNRRA Welfare Officer in Germany, 1945–1947*. Victoria, B.C.: Trafford Press, 2004.

Pinchuk, Ben-Cion. "Sovietisation and the Jewish Response to Nazi Policies of Mass Murder." In *Jews in Eastern Poland and the USSR, 1939–46*, edited by Norman Davies and Antony Polonsky, 137. London: Macmillan, 1991.

Pinson, Koppel S. "Jewish Life in Liberated Germany." *Jewish Social Studies* 9: 2 (April 1947), 101–126.

Polonsky, Antony, ed. *From Shtetl to Socialism*. London: Littman Library of Jewish Civilization, 1993.

Polonsky, Antony, Ezra Mendelsohn, and Jerzy Tomaszewski, eds. *Jews in Independent Poland 1918–1939*. London: Littman Library of Jewish Civilization, 1994.

Proudfoot, Malcolm J. *European Refugees: 1939–52: A Study in Forced Population Movement*. London: Faber and Faber Ltd., 1957.

Rapaport, Lynn. *Jews in Germany after the Holocaust: Memory, Identity, and Jewish-German Relations*. New York: Cambridge University Press, 1997.

Remy, Steven P. *The Heidelberg Myth: The Nazification and Denazification of a German University*. Cambridge, Mass.: Harvard University Press, 2003.

Rosenfeld, Gavriel. *Munich and Memory*. Berkeley: University of California Press, 2000.

Rosensaft, Menachem Z., ed. *Life Reborn: Jewish Displaced Persons, 1945–51: Conference Proceedings, Washington, D.C., January 14–17, 2000*. Washington, D.C.: U.S. Holocaust Memorial Museum, 2001.

Rudnicki, Szymon. "From 'Numerus Clausus' to 'Numerus Nullus.'" In *From Shtetl to Socialism*, edited by Antony Polonsky, 332–358. London: Littman Library of Jewish Civilization, 1993.

Schochet, Simon. *Feldafing*. Vancouver: November House, 1983.

———. "Polish Jewish Officers Who Were Killed in Katyn: An Ongoing Investigation in Light of Documents Recently Released by the USSR." In *The Holocaust in the Soviet Union: The Destruction of the Jews in the Nazi-Occupied Territories of the USSR, 1941–1945*, edited by Lucjan Dobroszycki and Jeffrey S. Gurock. New York: M. E. Sharpe, 1993.

Shmeruk, Chone. "Hebrew-Yiddish-Polish: A Trilingual Jewish Culture." In *The Jews of Poland Between Two World Wars*, edited by Yisrael Gutman, Ezra Mendelsohn, Jehuda Reinharz, and Chone Shmeruk. Hanover, N.H.: Brandeis University Press, 1989.

Siekierski, Maciej. "The Jews in Soviet-Occupied Eastern Poland at the End of 1939: Numbers and Distribution." In *Jews in Eastern Poland and the USSR, 1939–46*, edited by Norman Davies and Antony Polonsky. London: Macmillan, 1991.

Snopkowski, Simon. *Zuversicht trotz allem*. Munich: Olzog Verlag, 2000.

Snyder, Timothy. *Bloodlands: Europe Between Hitler and Stalin*. New York: Basic Books, 2010.

Steinert, Johannes-Dieter, and Inge Weber-Newth, eds. *Beyond Camps and Forced Labor: Current International Research on Survivors of Nazi Persecution*. Osnabrück: Secolo Publishing, 2005.

Stern, Frank. "The Historic Triangle: Occupiers, Germans, and Jews in Postwar Germany." *Tel Aviver Jahrbuch fuer deutsche Geschichte* 19 (1990).

———. *The Whitewashing of the Yellow Badge: Antisemitism and Philosemitism in Postwar Germany*. Oxford: Pergamon Press, 1992.

Syrkin, Marie. *The State of the Jews*. Washington, D.C.: New Republic Books, 1980.

Tanay, Emanuel. "Holocaust Survivors Who Studied at German Universities, 1945–1951." In *Life Reborn: Jewish Displaced Persons, 1945–51: Conference Proceedings, Washington, D.C., January 14–17, 2000*, edited by Menachem Z. Rosensaft. Washington, D.C.: U.S. Holocaust Memorial Museum, 2001.

———. *Passport to Life: Autobiographical Reflections on the Holocaust*. Ann Arbor, Mich.: Forensic Press, 2004.

Terlecki, Ryszard. "The Jewish Issue in the Polish Army in the USSR and the Near East, 1941–1944." In *Jews in Eastern Poland and the USSR, 1939–46*, edited by Norman Davies and Antony Polonsky, 161–171. London: Macmillan, 1991.

Tomaszewski, Jerzy. "The Role of Jews in Polish Commerce, 1918–39." In *The Jews of Poland Between Two World Wars*, edited by Yisrael Gutman, Ezra Mendelsohn, Jehuda Reinharz, and Chone Shmeruk. Hanover, N.H.: Brandeis University Press, 1989.

———. "The Civil Rights of Jews in Poland, 1918–1939." In *Jews in Independent Poland 1918–1939*, edited by Antony Polonsky, Ezra Mendelsohn, and Jerzy Tomaszewski. London: Littman Library of Jewish Civilization, 1994.

Wells, Leon W. *The Death Brigade (The Janowska Road)*. New York: Holocaust Library, 1978.

Wetzel, Juliane. *Jüdisches Leben in München, 1945–1951: Durchgangsstation oder Wiederaufbau?* Munich: Kommissionsverlag Uni-Druck, 1987.

White, Alexander B. *Be a Mensch: A Legacy of the Holocaust*. Scottsdale, Ariz.: Self-published, 2004.

Wilslicki, Alfred. "The Jewish Campaign against Nazi Germany and Its Culmination in the Halbersztadt Trial." In *Jews in Independent Poland 1918–1939*, edited by Antony Polonsky, Ezra Mendelsohn, and Jerzy Tomaszewski. London: Littman Library of Jewish Civilization, 1994.

Woodbridge, George. *UNRRA: The History of the United Nations Relief and Rehabilitation Administration*, vol. 2. New York: Columbia University Press, 1950.

Wyman, Mark. *DPs: Europe's Displaced Persons, 1945–1951*. Ithaca, N.Y.: Cornell University Press, [1989] 1998.

Zertal, Idith. *From Catastrophe to Power: Holocaust Survivors and the Emergence of Israel*. Berkeley: University of California Press, 1998.

———. *Israel's Holocaust and the Politics of Nationhood*. Cambridge: Cambridge University Press, 2005.

Zimering, Sabina. *Hiding in the Open: A Holocaust Memoir*. St. Paul, Minn.: St. Cloud Press, 2001.

Index

Note: Italic locators reference illustrations in the text.